"This volume is a superb theological examination of a key biblical theme that is all too often neglected in academic circles. Ranging widely across Old Testament and New Testament texts, with careful attention to the history of Christian interpretation on this issue, Middleton presents a very thoughtful treatment that deserves wide attention."

—**Terence E. Fretheim**, Luther Seminary

"Rooted in Scripture, chock-full of insight, clearly and fetchingly written, *A New Heaven and a New Earth* winsomely presents the biblical story of holistic salvation. Over against the all-too-common eschatology of heavenly rapture and earthly destruction, Richard Middleton's new book reclaims the scriptural vision of cosmic renewal. In a time when the Bible is often used to justify ecological degradation, since (it is argued) the earth will in the eschaton be burned up to nothing, *A New Heaven and a New Earth* could not be more timely. Simply put, this sorely needed volume is the best book of its kind. May it find a great multitude of readers."

—**Steven Bouma-Prediger**, Hope College;
author of *For the Beauty of the Earth*

"Richard Middleton is talking about a revolution! Why should Christians settle for the anemic goal of eternity spent in heaven when the Bible's robust vision is one of a resurrected humanity on the new earth? Set your imagination free from the chains of other-worldly dualism and enter into the brilliant and fascinating world of the biblical story, where the vision of all things redeemed breathes new life into our discipleship."

—**Sylvia Keesmaat**, Trinity College, University of Toronto

"*A New Heaven and a New Earth* is a very fine—I'm inclined to say magnificent—example of sound biblical scholarship based on decades of intense and careful scholarship and sustained by an integral theological vision which honors biblical authority. It delivers a strong blow to the long and powerful influence of an otherworldly Platonism on the Christian eschatological imagination and celebrates God's commitment to an integral and comprehensive restoration of the creation, including all its earthly and cultural dimensions."

—**Al Wolters**, Redeemer University College, Ancaster, Ontario

"Martin Buber once reconceived the exclusionary distinction between the holy and the unholy as the potentially inclusionary distinction between the holy and the not-yet-holy. In a similar vein, Richard Middleton, on solid biblical grounds, reenvisions this present world, in all its ambiguity, as the not-yet-new-heaven-and-new-earth of God's redemptive purpose. The upshot is a radical reorientation of human hope and an exhilarating call to participate in God's 'work for the redemptive transformation of this world.' I wish I had read this book sixty years ago; it would have made a world of difference in my life. Yet even at this date, it enables me to reread my past, and live toward my future, in a new light."

—**J. Gerald Janzen**, Christian Theological Seminary,
Indianapolis, Indiana

A New Heaven and a New Earth

Reclaiming Biblical Eschatology

J. Richard Middleton

B
Baker Academic
a division of Baker Publishing Group
Grand Rapids, Michigan

Published by Baker Academic
a division of Baker Publishing Group
P.O. Box 6287, Grand Rapids, MI 49516-6287
www.bakeracademic.com

Printed in the United States of America

Library of Congress Cataloging-in-Publication Data
Middleton, J. Richard, 1955–
   A new heaven and a new earth : reclaiming biblical eschatology / J. Richard Middleton.
     pages cm
   Includes bibliographical references and index.
   ISBN 978-0-8010-4868-5 (pbk.)
     1. Eschatology. 2. Earth (Planet)—Forecasting. 3. Heaven—Christianity. I. Title.
BT821.3.M53 2014
236′.9—dc23   2014029824

14 15 16 17 18 19 20   7 6 5 4 3 2 1

To Marcia,
my faithful friend and partner in the journey of life

Contents

List of Illustrations   9

Preface: How I Came to Write This Book   11

1. Introduction: The Problem of Otherworldly Hope   21

Part 1   From Creation to Eschaton

2. Why Are We Here? Being Human as Sacred Calling   37

3. The Plot of the Biblical Story   57

Part 2   Holistic Salvation in the Old Testament

4. The Exodus as Paradigm of Salvation   77

5. Earthly Flourishing in Law, Wisdom, and Prophecy   95

6. The Coming of God in Judgment and Salvation   109

Part 3   The New Testament's Vision of Cosmic Renewal

7. Resurrection and the Restoration of Rule   131

8. The Redemption of All Things   155

Part 4   Problem Texts for Holistic Eschatology

9. Cosmic Destruction at Christ's Return?   179

10. The Role of Heaven in Biblical Eschatology   211

Part 5 The Ethics of the Kingdom

11. The Good News at Nazareth   241

12. The Challenge of the Kingdom   263

Appendix: Whatever Happened to the New
Earth?   283

Subject Index   313

Scripture Index   321

Illustrations

Figures

2.1. Kings Mediating Divine Power and Presence   45

2.2. Humans Mediating God's Power and Presence   46

3.1. Categories for Plot Analysis   59

3.2. The Plot Structure of the Biblical Story   60

Tables

8.1. The Comprehensive Scope of Salvation   163

10.1. Preparation in Heaven (Present) for Revelation on Earth (Future)   214

11.1. Comparison of Isaiah 61:1–2 with Luke 4:18–19   253

12.1. The Nazareth Manifesto and Luke 7:22 Compared   270

12.2. The Dangers of Combining Two Types of Dualism   274

Preface

How I Came to Write This Book

I moved from Jamaica to Canada at the age of twenty-two, after completing an undergraduate degree in theology at the Jamaica Theological Seminary. During graduate studies in Canada (while pursuing an MA in philosophy at the University of Guelph) I coauthored a book with my friend Brian Walsh on developing a Christian worldview, titled *The Transforming Vision*.[1] This book was one of the first works in the relatively recent genre of Christian worldview studies that proposed a holistic vision of salvation, with an emphasis on the need to live out full-orbed Christian discipleship in the contemporary world. The book not only advocated a holistic worldview, without a sacred/secular split, but also explicitly grounded this worldview in the biblical teaching of the redemption of creation, including both the physical cosmos and human culture and society.

When Brian Walsh and I wrote *The Transforming Vision*, this holistic emphasis was not an entirely new insight for either of us. We had been students together some years before at the Institute for Christian Studies in Toronto, an interdisciplinary graduate school that grounded its integrative vision of faith and learning in the biblical teaching of the redemption of the cosmos.[2] But even before my time in Toronto I had already become convinced that

1. Brian J. Walsh and J. Richard Middleton, *The Transforming Vision: Shaping a Christian World View* (Downers Grove, IL: IVP Academic, 1984).
2. For a historical introduction to the Institute for Christian Studies (ICS), see Robert E. VanderVennen, *A University for the People: A History of the Institute for Christian Studies* (Sioux Center, IA: Dordt College Press, 2008). On the legacy of Abraham Kuyper, which grounds the vision of the ICS, see Peter S. Heslam, *Creating a Christian Worldview: Abraham Kuyper's*

11

the Bible taught the new heaven and new earth depicted in Revelation 21–22 as the final destiny of redeemed human beings, rather than an otherworldly life in heaven hereafter. I had become convinced of this holistic approach to eschatology (the doctrine of the end times) as part of a general shift in my worldview during my theological studies in Jamaica.[3]

Tracking a Worldview Shift

What led to this worldview shift? First of all, there was the basic logic of the Christian faith. It just made sense that the God of love whom I had come to know in Jesus Christ would want to rescue and redeem the world he made—a world deeply affected by human sin and corruption—rather than trashing it in favor of some other, immaterial realm or place. After all, God's plan was to redeem humanity; why then would God give up on the earthly environment in which he originally placed us?

I remember once, on a climbing trip to Blue Mountain Peak, the highest point on the island, watching a breathtaking sunrise at 7,500 feet above sea level. After some minutes of silence, my friend Junior commented wistfully, "This is so beautiful; it's such a shame that it will all be destroyed some day." I still remember the dawning awareness: *I don't think it will be.* It did not make sense to me that the beauty and wonder of earthly life, which I was coming to embrace joyfully as part of my growing Christian faith, could be disconnected from God's ultimate purposes of salvation.

This basic intuition or theological insight was confirmed by my study of Scripture during my undergraduate studies in Jamaica. Most contemporary Christians tend to live with an unresolved tension between a belief in the resurrection of the body and an immaterial heaven as final destiny. Many also have in the back of their minds the idea of the new heaven and new earth (from the book of Revelation), though they are not quite sure what to do with it. I too started my theological studies with this very confusion. But as I took courses in both Old and New Testaments and tried to understand the nature of God's salvation as portrayed in the various biblical writings, it became increasingly clear that the God who created the world "very good" (Gen.

Lectures on Calvinism (Grand Rapids: Eerdmans, 1998); Richard J. Mouw, *Abraham Kuyper: A Short and Personal Introduction* (Grand Rapids: Eerdmans, 2011).

3. Roger Ringenberg has written an informative study, "A History of Jamaica Theological Seminary, 1960–1992" (DMiss diss., Trinity Evangelical Divinity School, 1992). For a volume of essays sponsored by the Jamaica Theological Seminary, see Garnett Roper and J. Richard Middleton, eds., *A Kairos Moment for Caribbean Theology: Ecumenical Voices in Dialogue* (Eugene, OR: Pickwick, 2013).

1:31), and who became incarnate in Jesus Christ as a real human being, had affirmed by these very acts the value of the material universe and the validity of ordinary, earthly life. More than that, I came to realize that the Scriptures explicitly teach that God is committed to reclaiming creation (human and nonhuman) in order to bring it to its authentic and glorious destiny, a destiny that human sin had blocked.

During my third year of undergraduate studies I had begun to read the early works of Francis Schaeffer, which had a profound impact on my developing worldview.[4] One of the things that drew me to Schaeffer was that he grounded many of his early writings on contemporary culture in a view of holistic salvation. Schaeffer was not an academic theologian, but he attempted to work out the implications of salvation for the whole person as a social and cultural being, living in an earthly creation destined for redemption. And while I later came to see serious flaws in Schaeffer's analyses of contemporary culture, he nevertheless helped me catch a vision of life woven of one fabric, in which everything could be integrally related to the creator, who was also the redeemer.[5]

But it was the writings of New Testament scholar George Eldon Ladd that most helpfully clarified for me the interconnectedness of what the Bible taught on the redemption of creation, and he explicitly contrasted this teaching with the unbiblical idea of being taken out of this world to heaven.[6] Ladd's work on biblical theology prompted me to do my own investigation of the biblical theme of God's kingdom in relation to what we euphemistically call the "afterlife," to see what role there is for heaven and/or earth in God's ultimate purposes.

4. Works by Schaeffer that I read included *The God Who Is There* (Downers Grove, IL: InterVarsity, 1968); *He Is There and He Is Not Silent* (Wheaton: Tyndale House, 1972); *Escape from Reason* (Downers Grove, IL: InterVarsity, 1968); *Art and the Bible: Two Essays* (Downers Grove, IL: InterVarsity, 1973); *True Spirituality* (Wheaton: Tyndale House, 1971); *Pollution and the Death of Man* (Wheaton: Tyndale House, 1970). While the first three books involved a critical appraisal of Western culture in light of the lordship of Christ over all culture, the last three books were particularly helpful in showing the implications of a holistic vision for art, spirituality, and care for the earth.

5. There was a significant shift in Schaeffer's approach to culture beginning with *How Should We Then Live? The Rise and Decline of Western Thought and Culture* (Old Tappan, NJ: Revell, 1976). In this book (and its movie adaptation) Schaeffer began to embrace a decidedly unbiblical vision of America as a Christian nation. In *How Should We Then Live?* he seemed to be hankering after a purportedly lost ideal past, while in his writings after this point he began to propose an aggressive cultural takeover of America by Christians who shared his ideals; see especially *A Christian Manifesto* (Wheaton: Crossway, 1981; rev. ed., 1982).

6. Among the many works by Ladd, especially important for me were *The Pattern of New Testament Truth* (Grand Rapids: Eerdmans, 1968) and *The Presence of the Future: The Eschatology of Biblical Realism* (Grand Rapids: Eerdmans, 1974), both of which stand as worthwhile statements even today. The latter book is the revised edition of Ladd's *Jesus and the Kingdom* (New York: Harper & Row, 1964).

As a result of this investigation, while still an undergraduate student, I came to the startling realization that the Bible nowhere claims that "heaven" is the final home of the redeemed. Although there are many New Testament texts that Christians often read as if they teach a heavenly destiny, the texts do not actually say this. Rather, the Bible consistently anticipates the redemption of the entire created order, a motif that fits very well with the Christian hope of the resurrection, which Paul calls "the redemption of our bodies" (Rom. 8:23).

It was after this startling realization that I first challenged an adult Sunday school class that I was teaching at Grace Missionary Church (my home church in Jamaica) to find even one passage in the New Testament that clearly said Christians would live in heaven forever or that heaven was the final home of the righteous. I even offered a monetary reward if anyone could find such a text. I have been making this offer now for my entire adult life to church and campus ministry study groups and in many of the courses I have taught (in Canada, the United States, and Jamaica); I am happy to report that I still have all my money. No one has ever produced such a text, because there simply are none in the Bible.

After writing *The Transforming Vision* together, Brian Walsh and I teamed up some ten years later to address the implications of this same holistic vision for postmodern culture in *Truth Is Stranger Than It Used to Be*; like the former book, it combined biblical studies with cultural analysis.[7] Since that time the focus of my research has shifted more and more toward biblical studies, particularly Old Testament, the primary academic field in which I teach and write. In all my teaching and writing, the consistent background assumption has been the same basic vision of holistic salvation that I have been working with since my undergraduate days in Jamaica, though in recent years I have been able to flesh this out in much more detail.[8]

Why This Book?

Having had to explain this background assumption of the redemption of creation in many different settings and to different audiences, I finally decided to write an article that would marshal the central biblical evidence (as I understood it) for a holistic understanding of salvation, with a focus on eschatology.

7. J. Richard Middleton and Brian J. Walsh, *Truth Is Stranger Than It Used to Be: Biblical Faith in a Postmodern Age* (Downers Grove, IL: IVP Academic, 1995).

8. Looking back, I realize that I have gravitated toward writing on creation texts and themes as a way of addressing the grounding of holistic salvation in God's intent from the beginning. See, for example, J. Richard Middleton, *The Liberating Image: The* Imago Dei *in Genesis 1* (Grand Rapids: Brazos, 2005).

The article, titled "A New Heaven and a New Earth," was published in 2006.[9] Soon after its publication Rodney Clapp, then senior editor at Brazos Press/ Baker Academic, suggested that I turn the article into a book. "The time is ripe," he said, over a spicy dinner of Thai food, "for an accessible and clear book-length statement of holistic eschatology." This book is my attempt to respond to Rodney's eschatological-sounding challenge. Since then Rodney has moved on to another publishing company, and I am grateful for Jim Kinney's shepherding of this book to publication. I am also grateful for his patience as the book's completion—like the eschaton—was delayed.

Whereas earlier centuries have tried to clarify theological topics such as the incarnation, the Trinity, or justification by faith, the twentieth century has seen more intense focus on eschatology than ever before. Yet much of this eschatological reflection has been confused and inchoate, conflating an unbiblical impetus to transcend earthly life with the biblical affirmation of earthly life. This is true among both professional theologians and church members, and also among Christians of differing theological traditions.

The time is ripe, therefore, for a clearly articulated Christian eschatology that is rooted in responsible exegesis of Scripture and also attuned to the theological claims and ethical implications of the Bible's vision of salvation. This eschatology will also need to be serviceable for the church, pointing the way toward faithful living in the here and now.

This book is one small contribution toward such an eschatology. Its primary purpose is to clarify how New Testament eschatology, rather than being a speculative add-on to the Bible, actually coheres with, and is the logical outworking of, the consistently holistic theology of the entirety of Scripture. As Donald Fairbairn puts it, "Eschatology's significance lies in the way it testifies to the unity of Scripture, the unity of God's purposes, and ultimately the unity and goodness of the God we worship."[10]

The primary purpose of this book is to sketch the coherent biblical theology (beginning in the Old Testament) that culminates in the New Testament's explicit eschatological vision of the redemption of creation. But this book has two subsidiary purposes, both flowing from its primary orientation. First, I explore some of the ethical implications of a biblically grounded holistic

9. J. Richard Middleton, "A New Heaven and a New Earth: The Case for a Holistic Reading of the Biblical Story of Redemption," *Journal for Christian Theological Research* 11 (2006): 73–97, http://www.luthersem.edu/ctrf/JCTR/Vol11/Middleton_vol11.pdf.

10. Donald Fairbairn, "Contemporary Millennial/Tribulational Debates: Whose Side Was the Early Church On?," in *A Case for Historic Premillennialism: An Alternative to the Left Behind Eschatology*, ed. Craig L. Blomberg and Sung Wook Chung (Grand Rapids: Baker Academic, 2009), 130.

eschatology for our present life in God's world. And second, I investigate, at least in a preliminary way, what happened to the biblical vision of the redemption of the earth in the history of Christian eschatology.

Given my desire to make the Bible's vision of the redemption of creation available to a wide audience, I have endeavored to write a book that is accessible to those who do not specialize in biblical studies, yet without dumbing anything down. Over the years I have found that Christian laypeople can be theologically astute and that teachers need to respect the ability of their students to think through difficult concepts.

In light of this, this book does not shy away from addressing the interpretation of passages throughout the Bible (both Old and New Testaments) whose meaning is often disputed and, indeed, affected by the assumptions that we bring to the text. I have tried to uncover some of these assumptions and to lead the reader on a tour of Scripture understood (as far as possible) in terms of its own (ancient) worldview. In doing this, I have tried to avoid overly technical discussions of the matters at hand, and I have sought to explain complex issues in clear prose. I have also used a variety of charts and diagrams to clarify some of my analyses, especially to illustrate patterns that can be discerned throughout different biblical texts.

Although I have carefully considered many alternative points of view, including arguments against my own position, I have often omitted reference to them from my exposition if I judged that including them would sidetrack the reader from the issue at hand. Nevertheless, for those interested in following up such matters, I have provided numerous footnotes, some of which address alternative points of view, further grounding for my argument, or resources for further study.

The Plan of This Book

The book contains twelve chapters and an appendix. Chapter 1, "Introduction: The Problem of Otherworldly Hope," sets up the basic problem that the book addresses, first by explaining what is wrong with the traditional Christian view of heaven as final destiny, and then by sketching the historical origins of this otherworldly idea in the innovative teachings of the Greek philosopher Plato (427–347 BC). This historical analysis is continued in the appendix, "Whatever Happened to the New Earth?," which examines the broad sweep of church history in order to understand how the biblical expectation of the redemption of the cosmos came to be compromised by a Platonic otherworldly vision. The introduction and the appendix thus function as bookends for the main content of the study.

The in-between chapters focus on biblical theology, first by attempting to clarify how the Bible's consistent teaching about holistic salvation grounds its explicit eschatology, and then by exploring some of the ethical implications of this eschatology. This means that we need to delay our look at the New Testament's expectation of the "end times" (what most Christians think of as eschatology) in order to examine how this expectation is deeply rooted in the overall vision of the Bible. New Testament eschatology is not some sort of ad hoc jigsaw puzzle of crazy ideas appended to the rest of Scripture. Rather, New Testament eschatology is simply the logical and appropriate culmination of the consistent biblical vision of redemption, and it is vitally important for Christian living.

From Creation to Eschaton

Our foray into biblical theology begins in chapters 2 and 3 with the overarching story that the Bible tells. Chapter 2, "Why Are We Here?," focuses on the beginning of the biblical story: God's original intent for humans in the context of the created world and how that intent was impeded by sin. Contrary to the popular notion that we are made to worship God, the Bible suggests a more mundane purpose for humans made in God's image, involving the development of culture and care for our earthly environment. But human sin (understood as rebellion and violence) has blocked God's original intent for the flourishing of earthly life.

Chapter 3, "The Plot of the Biblical Story," is an overview chapter, sketching the panoramic sweep of the biblical story of redemption. Our primary interest here is to discern the basic plot structure of the biblical metanarrative from creation to eschaton, which clarifies God's unswerving purpose to redeem earthly creation (rather than take us out of earth to heaven).

Holistic Salvation in the Old Testament

With this overview in mind, chapters 4 through 6 address holistic salvation in the Old Testament and uncover some of the ways in which this ancient text portrays God's ongoing commitment to the flourishing of earthly life. Chapter 4, "The Exodus as Paradigm of Salvation," foregrounds the biblical story of God's deliverance of his people from bondage in Egypt and their concrete restoration to new life; the chapter suggests how this paradigmatic event functions as a pattern for understanding salvation in both Old and New Testaments.

Chapter 5, "Earthly Flourishing in Law, Wisdom, and Prophecy," then examines how Israel's laws and wisdom traditions, together with prophetic oracles of judgment and anticipations of restoration beyond exile, testify to a consistent, holistic vision of God's desire to bring shalom and blessing to ordinary human life on earth.

Yet the Old Testament is brutally honest about the presence of sin and corruption in God's world. Chapter 6, "The Coming of God in Judgment and Salvation," therefore addresses those texts that portray God's coming as a vivid theophany, accompanied by a shaking or melting of the world, as a prelude to salvation. These texts make the point that judgment is an inescapable reality for those who resist God's will. Nevertheless, God's ultimate purpose beyond judgment is to accomplish his original intent for the flourishing of humanity and the nonhuman world. This Old Testament vision thus functions as the essential theological background to the New Testament understanding of salvation.

Chapters 7 through 12 then turn to the holistic vision of the New Testament. First, chapters 7 through 10 focus on the New Testament's theology of cosmic redemption (including possible objections based on texts that do not seem to fit). Chapters 11 and 12 then address some of the ethical implications of this theology.

The New Testament's Vision of Cosmic Renewal

Chapter 7, "Resurrection and the Restoration of Rule," explores the inner logic of the hope of resurrection and its connection to the restoration of human rule of the earth, beginning with late Old Testament texts and on into the New Testament. The connection of resurrection and rule in the New Testament (first in the case of Jesus, the second Adam, and then for all those who follow him) is central to the biblical vision of God's coming in victory to conquer death and the corrupt powers of this age.

Chapter 8, "The Redemption of All Things," in order to illumine a cosmic vision of redemption, brings together various strands of the New Testament expectation that sin and evil will be reversed. It becomes clear from the New Testament that salvation includes not just moral transformation and the renewal of community (important as they are), but also the renewal of all things, including our bodies and the earth itself.

Problem Texts for Holistic Eschatology

However, since there are some New Testament texts that are typically misread as if they teach the annihilation of the cosmos and an otherworldly destiny in "heaven," we will need to take a look at this misreading. This is the burden of chapter 9, "Cosmic Destruction at Christ's Return?," and chapter 10, "The Role of Heaven in Biblical Eschatology"; it turns out that careful examination of these "problem" texts actually provides further support for the redemption of creation.

The Ethics of the Kingdom

Whereas chapters 7 through 10 address the New Testament's theology of cosmic redemption, along with clarifying the meaning of problem texts, chapters 11 and 12 take a look at some ethical implications of the kingdom of God in the teaching of Jesus, especially by attending to his programmatic sermon in the Nazareth synagogue, recorded in Luke 4.

Chapter 11, "The Good News at Nazareth," focuses on the holistic, this-worldly character of Jesus's announcement of good news at Nazareth, unpacking the implications of his message for the renewal of the entire person and the social order itself. But since the good news of his message was in danger of being misunderstood, Jesus added a critical caveat concerning the opening of the kingdom to outsiders, which led to an attempt on his life. This requires us to go beyond the good news of the kingdom to address the ethical challenge of the kingdom that Jesus brings, both in his day and ours; this is the task of chapter 12, "The Challenge of the Kingdom." Together these chapters begin to work through some of the implications of biblical eschatology for ethics, especially the call for the church to live boldly yet humanely as an alternative community in a broken world—a world in which the kingdom of God has been inaugurated but has not yet reached its fulfillment.

With our exploration of the consistent biblical teaching of holistic salvation in Old and New Testaments completed, the appendix of this book, "Whatever Happened to the New Earth?," looks at how the idea of a heavenly destiny came to dominate popular Christian eschatology by tracing the eclipse of the biblical vision of the renewal of the earth over the course of church history. The appendix concludes by noting hopeful recent signs of the recovery of a more holistic vision.

It is my hope that this book, in clarifying the biblical basis for holistic eschatology, will help readers see more clearly the profound effects of evil both around and within ourselves, while also impelling us forward to live lives of obedience and compassion in anticipation of the new heaven and new earth, which God has promised.

I believe that the time is ripe; could it be that a holistic eschatology is at hand?

1

Introduction

The Problem of Otherworldly Hope

In one of the courses I teach, I regularly set my students an interview assignment. They are asked to interview a pastor, church leader, or missionary whom they know, using a set of guided, though open-ended, questions. The questions ask how the interviewee understands a number of overlapping matters, including the nature of salvation or redemption, what it means to be a Christian in the world, the nature of one's calling as a Christian, what God requires of the faithful, and the nature of true worship, ministry, and discipleship. All the questions circle around one main goal: to uncover the worldview of the interviewees, in particular how they understand the relationship of so-called spiritual or religious matters to ordinary mundane matters of life in the world, and how they therefore should act in the world.[1]

---

1. Here I am using the term "worldview" not in the sense of a conceptual system or framework of ideas (as one tradition of Christian discourse understands the term), but rather to refer to how a pretheoretical, even precognitive, vision of life functions to orient people in the world and guide their life toward some goal or end. This usage of "worldview" derives from the tradition of Kuyperian Neocalvinism and underlies the analysis in Brian J. Walsh and J. Richard Middleton, *The Transforming Vision: Shaping a Christian World View* (Downers Grove, IL: IVP Academic, 1984); and James H. Olthuis, "On Worldviews," *Christian Scholar's Review* 14 (1985): 153–64, reprinted in *Stained Glass: Worldviews and Social Science*, ed. Paul A. Marshall, Sander Griffioen, and Richard J. Mouw (Christian Studies Today; Lanham, MD: University Press

The Elephant in the Room

It is common for interviewees to claim that the Christian faith should not be separated from life but ought to connect to this world. This is a relatively recent shift in attitudes, from a more otherworldly interpretation of faith to a desire for a more holistic and integrated vision. Along those lines, more and more people tend to recognize that our calling or ministry should not be divided into sacred and secular, but rather should relate to everything we do.

What is fascinating, however, is what interviewees actually mention as examples of "everything" and what they leave out. Some laudably list the need to care for "creation," since God made and loves the world. Some mention the terrible state that the world is in and declare that Christians ought to be involved in making things better. Many emphasize ethical matters such as valuing honesty and sexual purity and being against abortion (and sometimes war); they often say that faith should affect one's work (usually without specifying how, other than that one should model Christian behavior and be committed to excellence). And they particularly stress the importance of "relationships." Most interviewees, however, tend to reduce this to personal, intimate, or familial-type relationships.

Yet "relationships" is a large umbrella term that covers just about everything. I am *in relationship* not just to other persons, but also to social and political institutions, to traditions, to the environment, to animals, to food, to time and space, to birth and death, to history, to science and art. I am *related to* technology, to entertainment, to economic systems, to ideas and ideologies, to depression, illness, and suffering, to consumerism, to globalization, to violence, and so on. How then does one's salvation or faith relate to the entire spectrum of life on this planet?

It is telling that very few interviewees even attempt to address the range of everyday relationships that people have with broad swaths of mundane reality. While those who claim that faith is related to all of life do make some connections, there are nevertheless huge omissions. Even those who stress the need to care for creation tend to reduce "creation" to nature or the environment, with little reflection on the fact that human beings, and all the cultural and social formations that they have developed over history, are also part of the created order.

---

of America, 1989), 26–40. For a more recent work in the Neocalvinian tradition that helpfully relates this affective/precognitive understanding of "worldview" to the Augustinian tradition of desire and Charles Taylor's recent notion of the "social imaginary," see James K. A. Smith, *Desiring the Kingdom: Worship, Worldview, and Cultural Formation* (Cultural Liturgies 1; Grand Rapids: Baker Academic, 2009), esp. 65–71.

What becomes clear from reading these interviews over the years is that "culture" (for want of a better term) is the elephant in the room that nobody notices. While we are, in fact, at every moment in relationship with a complex web or network of cultural and social meanings, artifacts, and institutions, there tends to be a significant blind spot in the vision of many contemporary Christians (including pastors and church leaders) concerning such matters. The full range of human culture simply does not enter into the equation of faith.[2]

One of the questions my students put to the interviewees has to do with eschatology, the end-state vision of God's intent for humanity and the world. In particular, the interviewees are asked how they understand the final state of the righteous. Here the answers tend to be quite traditional, centering on judgment and going to heaven when you die. "Heaven" tends to be conceived in two main ways. First, heaven is understood as a transcendent realm beyond time and space. Second, heaven is characterized primarily by fellowship with and worship of God. The final destiny of the faithful is conceived as an unending worship service of perpetual praise in God's immediate presence in another world. While the traditional doctrine of the resurrection of the body is usually affirmed, this typically stands in some tension with the idea of an atemporal, immaterial realm. And there is certainly no conscious reflection on the redemption of human culture.

More and more, however, some respondents understand that an ethereal "heaven" is more traditional than biblical, and instead they articulate the vision of "a new heaven and a new earth" from the book of Revelation. However, even their articulation of this more cosmic vision tends to have no explicit place for the concreteness of human culture. The elephant is unnoticed in both ethics and eschatology.[3] Indeed, it is my conclusion, not only from the interviews but also from my experience in the church and my study of theology and Scripture, that eschatology is inevitably connected to ethics. I am not referring here to one's explicit statement of eschatology because some interviewees explicitly affirm a biblical vision of cosmic restoration; but it is clear that this is a bare confession and does not function as the sort of substantive vision that could guide significant action in the world. The point is that what we desire and anticipate as the culmination of salvation is what truly affects how we attempt to

2. One work that foregrounds the relationship of culture to faith is Andy Crouch, *Culture Making: Recovering Our Creative Calling* (Downers Grove, IL: IVP Academic, 2008). The book contains a wise analysis of culture (part 1), followed by a superb retelling of the biblical story in terms of culture (part 2), plus helpful reflection on norms for cultural engagement (part 3).

3. The omission of conscious reflection on the redemption of culture suggests that it has no significant place in the underlying (precognitive) worldview of the interviewee.

live in the present. Ethics is lived eschatology. It is, as New Testament scholar George Eldon Ladd put it, "the presence of the future."[4]

The Bible's Best-Kept Secret

Central to the way the New Testament conceives the final destiny of the world is Jesus's proclamation in Matthew 19:28 of a "regeneration" (KJV, NASB) that is coming; Matthew here uses the Greek word *palingenesia*, which both NIV and NRSV translate as "the renewal of all things," correctly getting at the sense of cosmic expectation in Jesus's prediction. Likewise, we have Peter's explicit proclamation of the "restoration [*apokatastasis*] of all things" (Acts 3:21), which does in fact contain the Greek for "all things" (*panta*). When we turn to the Epistles, we find God's intent to reconcile "all things" to himself through Christ articulated in Colossians 1:20, while Ephesians 1:10 speaks of God's desire to unify or bring together "all things" in Christ. In these two Pauline texts the phrase "all things" (*ta panta*) is immediately specified as things in heaven and things on earth. Since "the heavens and the earth" is precisely how Genesis 1:1 describes the world that God created, this New Testament language designates a vision of cosmic redemption. Such cosmic vision underlies the phrase "a new heaven/s and a new earth" found in both Revelation 21:1 and 2 Peter 3:13. The specific origin of the phrase, however, is the prophetic oracle of Isaiah 65:17 (and 66:22), which envisions a healed world with a redeemed community in rebuilt Jerusalem, where life is restored to flourishing and shalom after the devastation of the Babylonian exile. The this-worldly prophetic expectation in Isaiah is universalized to the entire cosmos and human society generally in late Second Temple Judaism and in the New Testament.

This holistic vision of God's intent to renew or redeem creation is perhaps the Bible's best-kept secret, typically unknown to most church members and even to many clergy, no matter what their theological stripe. While this introductory chapter is not the place for a full exposition of the biblical teaching about the redemption of the cosmos, some clarification is in order. It is particularly helpful to trace the Old Testament roots of the New Testament vision, in order to understand the inner logic of the idea.

A good starting point is that the Old Testament does not place any substantial hope in the afterlife; the dead do not have access to God in the grave or Sheol. Rather, God's purposes for blessing and shalom are expected for the

4. George Eldon Ladd, *The Presence of the Future: The Eschatology of Biblical Realism* (Grand Rapids: Eerdmans, 1974).

faithful in this life, in the midst of history. This perspective is theologically grounded in the biblical teaching about the goodness of creation, including earthly existence. God pronounced all creation (including materiality) good—indeed "very good" (Gen. 1:31)—and gave humanity the task to rule and develop this world as stewards made in the divine image (Gen. 1:26–28; 2:15; Ps. 8:5–8).

The affirmation of earthly life is further articulated in the central and paradigmatic act of God's salvation in the Old Testament: the exodus from Egyptian bondage. Not only does Israel's memory of this event testify to a God who intervenes in history in response to injustice and suffering, but the exodus is manifestly a case of sociopolitical deliverance whose fulfillment is attained when the redeemed are settled in a bountiful land and are restored to wholeness and flourishing as a community living according to God's Torah.

Indeed, the entire Old Testament reveals an interest in mundane matters such as the development of languages and cultures, the fertility of land and crops, the birth of children and stable family life, justice among neighbors, and peace in international relations. The Old Testament does not spiritualize salvation, but rather understands it as God's deliverance of people and land from all that destroys life and the consequent restoration of people and land to flourishing. And while God's salvific purpose narrows for a while to one elect nation in its own land, this "initially exclusive move" is, as Old Testament scholar Terence Fretheim puts it, in the service of "a maximally inclusive end," the redemption of all nations and ultimately the entire created order.[5]

Although the Old Testament initially did not envision any sort of positive afterlife, things begin to shift in some late texts.[6] Thus in Ezekiel's famous vision of the valley of dry bones (Ezek. 37), the restoration of Israel is portrayed by using the metaphor of resurrection, after the "death" that they suffered in Babylonian exile. But this is arguably still a metaphor, not an expectation of what we would call resurrection. Then a protoapocalyptic text, Isaiah 25:6–8, envisions the literal conquest of death itself at the messianic banquet on Mount Zion (where God will serve the redeemed the best meat and the most aged wines); this text anticipates the day when YHWH[7] will "swallow

5. Terence E. Fretheim, *God and World in the Old Testament: A Relational Theology of Creation* (Nashville: Abingdon, 2005), 29; also 103.

6. The rise of resurrection hope in the Old Testament will be addressed in more depth in chap. 7 below.

7. Throughout this book I am using "YHWH" to represent the ancient name of God in the Old Testament, which is rendered "the LORD" (small capitals) in most English translations. This name is also known as the Tetragrammaton, referring to the four Hebrew consonants transliterated as "YHWH." Most biblical scholars think that this name was originally pronounced *Yahweh*, although there is evidence that at the Jewish settlement in Elephantine (Egypt) it was

up death forever" (cited in 1 Cor. 15:54; cf. 15:26) and "wipe away all tears" (echoed in Rev. 21:4). But the most explicit Old Testament text on the topic of resurrection is the apocalyptic vision in Daniel 12:2–3, which promises that faithful martyrs will awaken from the dust of the earth (to which we all return at death, according to Gen. 3:19) to attain "eternal life."

It is important to note that this developing vision of the afterlife has nothing to do with "heaven hereafter"; the expectation is manifestly this-worldly, meant to guarantee for the faithful the earthly promises of shalom that death has cut short. Here, the third chapter of Wisdom of Solomon is particularly helpful. This text (which is in the Septuagint, though not in the Protestant canon) specifically associates "immortality" with reigning on earth (Wis. 3:1–9, esp. vv. 7–8); that is, resurrection is a reversal of the earthly situation of oppression (wicked people dominating and killing righteous martyrs). Resurrection thus fulfills the original human dignity and status in Genesis 1:26–28 and Psalm 8:4–8, where humans are granted rule of the earth.

These ancient Jewish expectations provide a coherent theological background for Jesus's proclamation of the kingdom of God, which he construes as "good news" for the poor and release for captives (Luke 4:18), and which he embodies in healings, exorcisms, and the forgiveness of sins (all ways in which the distortion of life was being reversed). These expectations also make sense of Jesus's teaching in the Sermon on the Mount that the meek will "inherit the earth" (Matt. 5:5), and later in Matthew that "at the renewal of all things" the disciples will reign and judge with him on thrones (Matt. 19:27–30).

Paul's description of Jesus's own resurrection from the dead as the "first fruits" of those who have fallen asleep (1 Cor. 15:20) signifies that the harvest of new creation has begun, the expected reversal of sin and death is inaugurated. This reversal is to be consummated when Christ returns in glory climactically to defeat evil and all that opposes God's intent for life and shalom on earth (1 Cor. 15:24–28). Then the words of the book of Revelation will be fulfilled:

---

pronounced *Yahu* (the Hebrew letter represented by *w* can function either as a consonant or as a silent marker for an *o* or *u* vowel). Sometime in the Second Temple period (perhaps by the third century BC), some Jews began to treat "YHWH" as too holy to pronounce and began orally to substitute "Lord" (Hebrew *'ădōnāy*; later, Greek *kyrios*) whenever they read the divine name in the Scriptures (the derivation of *'ădōnāy* is actually quite complicated, since it technically means "my lords," possibly a plural of majesty). Later, this tradition was codified in the Masoretic Text of the Hebrew Bible, which typically inserts the vowels from *'ădōnāy* into the consonants for "YHWH." The Dead Sea Scrolls (dating from the two centuries before Jesus) at some points use an archaic Hebrew script to write the Tetragrammaton, to distinguish it from the rest of the text. To this day, pious Jews will not say the divine name but will instead substitute "the Lord," "Adonai," "the Most High," "the Eternal," or "Ha-Shem" (literally, "the name"). My purpose in writing the divine name as "YHWH" is to allow readers to pronounce it as they wish.

"the kingdom of the world has become the kingdom of our Lord and of his Messiah" (11:15). At that time, explains Paul, creation itself, which has been groaning in its bondage to decay, will be liberated from this bondage into the same glory that God's children will experience (Rom. 8:19–22).

The inner logic of this vision of holistic salvation is that the creator has not given up on creation and is working to salvage and restore the world (human and nonhuman) to the fullness of shalom and flourishing intended from the beginning. And redeemed human beings, renewed in God's image, are to work toward and embody this vision in their daily lives.

Singing Lies in Church

Such a holistic vision of salvation is found only rarely in popular Christian piety or even in the liturgy of the church. Indeed, it is blatantly contradicted by many traditional hymns (and contemporary praise songs) sung in the context of communal worship. This is an important point because it is from what they sing that those in the pew (or auditorium) typically learn their theology, especially their eschatology.

From the classic Charles Wesley hymn "Love Divine, All Loves Excelling," which anticipates being "Changed from glory into glory, / Till in heaven we take our place,"[8] to "Away in a Manger," which prays, "And fit us for Heaven, to live with Thee there,"[9] congregations are exposed to, and assimilate, an otherworldly eschatology. Some hymns, such as "When the Roll Is Called Up Yonder," inconsistently combine the idea of resurrection with the hope of heaven:

> On that bright and cloudless morning when the dead in Christ shall
>   rise,
> And the glory of His resurrection share;
> When His chosen ones shall gather to their home beyond the skies,
> And the roll is called up yonder, I'll be there.[10]

Some hymns even interpret resurrection without reference to the body at all, such as "Must Jesus Bear the Cross Alone?," which in one stanza regards

8. Stanza 4 of "Love Divine, All Loves Excelling," written by Charles Wesley in 1747; this is published as hymn #92 in *The Hymnal for Worship & Celebration*, ed. Tom Fettke et al. (Irving, TX: Word Music, 1986).

9. Stanza 3 from "Away in a Manger," written by John Thomas McFarland sometime between 1904 and 1908 (the author of the hymn's first two stanzas is unknown); hymn #157/#158 in Fettke et al., *The Hymnal for Worship & Celebration*.

10. Stanza 2 from "When the Roll Is Called Up Yonder," written by James M. Black in 1893; hymn #543 in Fettke et al., *The Hymnal for Worship & Celebration*.

death as liberation ("Till death shall set me free") and in another asserts, "O resurrection day! / When Christ the Lord from Heav'n comes down / And bears my soul away."[11]

A hymn such as "When We All Get to Heaven" may be too obvious,[12] but notice that "The Old Rugged Cross" ends with the words "Then He'll call me some day to my home far away / Where his glory forever I'll share."[13] And "Just a Closer Walk with Thee" climaxes with these lines:

> When my feeble life is o'er,
> Time for me will be no more;
> Guide me gently, safely o'er
> To Thy kingdom's shore, to Thy shore.[14]

Likewise, "Come, Christians, Join to Sing" affirms, "On heaven's blissful shore, / His goodness we'll adore, / Singing forevermore, / 'Alleluia! Amen!'"[15]

This notion of a perpetual worship service in an otherworldly afterlife is a central motif in many hymns, such as "My Jesus, I Love Thee," which declares, "In mansions of glory and endless delight, / I'll ever adore Thee in heaven so bright."[16] In a similar vein, "As with Gladness Men of Old" asks in one stanza that "when earthly things are past, / Bring our ransomed souls at last / Where they need no star to guide," and in another stanza expresses the desire that "In the heavenly country bright / . . . There forever may we sing / Alleluias to our King!"[17]

Thankfully, most hymnals no longer have the sixth verse of "Amazing Grace," which predicts,

> The earth shall soon dissolve like snow,
> The sun forbear to shine;

---

11. Stanzas 2 and 4 from "Must Jesus Bear the Cross Alone?" Stanza 2 was written by Thomas Shepherd (published 1693) and stanza 4 by Henry Ward Beecher (published 1855); hymn #449 in Fettke et al., *The Hymnal for Worship & Celebration*. Stanza 4 originally read: "Ye angels from the stars come down / And bear my soul away."

12. Hymn #542 in Fettke et al., *The Hymnal for Worship & Celebration*.

13. Stanza 4 from "The Old Rugged Cross," written by George Bennard in 1913; hymn #186 in Fettke et al., *The Hymnal for Worship & Celebration*.

14. Stanza 3 from "Just a Closer Walk with Thee," author unknown (this American folk hymn became widely known during the 1930s); hymn #380 in Fettke et al., *The Hymnal for Worship & Celebration*.

15. Stanza 3 from "Come, Christians, Join to Sing," written by Christian H. Bateman in 1843; hymn #108 in Fettke et al., *The Hymnal for Worship & Celebration*.

16. Stanza 4 from "My Jesus, I Love Thee," written by William R. Featherston in 1864; hymn #364 in Fettke et al., *The Hymnal for Worship & Celebration*.

17. Stanzas 4 and 5 from "As with Gladness Men of Old," written by William C. Dix circa 1858; hymn #163 in Fettke et al., *The Hymnal for Worship & Celebration*.

But God, who called me here below,
Will be forever mine.[18]

Yet Chris Tomlin's contemporary revision of this classic hymn, known as "Amazing Grace (My Chains Are Gone)," reintroduces this very verse as the song's new climax, ready to shape the otherworldly mind-set of a fresh generation of young worshipers unacquainted with hymnals.[19]

And this just begins to scratch the surface of worship lyrics that portray the final destiny of the righteous as transferal from an earthly, historical existence to a transcendent, immaterial realm. As the popular theologian and preacher A. W. Tozer is reputed to have said, "Christians don't tell lies; they just go to church and sing them."[20] Perhaps that is too harsh; nevertheless, I can testify to the steady diet of such songs that I was exposed to growing up in the church in Kingston, Jamaica, which certainly reinforced the idea of heaven as otherworldly final destiny.

I am, however, perpetually grateful that along with such exposure I came to know, through sheer proximity, the this-worldly theology of Rastafarianism, especially as mediated through the music of Bob Marley and the Wailers. Being a committed Christian, I cannot affirm everything found in Rasta theology, but nevertheless I discern a deeply rooted biblical consciousness in the lyrics of many Wailers' songs.[21] For example, the song "We an' Dem" claims that "in the beginning Jah created everything / and he gave man dominion over

18. Stanza 6 from "Amazing Grace," written by John Newton, originally titled "Faith's Review and Expectation," in connection with a sermon he preached on New Year's Day 1773 on 1 Chron. 17:16–17; many hymnals contain the first four of the six stanzas that Newton wrote (first published in 1779), along with a fifth stanza, beginning with "When we've been here ten thousand years," which is sometimes attributed incorrectly to John P. Rees (Rees was born in 1828, and this stanza appears in print in 1790 as part of a hymn titled "Jerusalem, My Happy Home" and was first linked to two of the stanzas of Newton's hymn by Harriet Beecher Stowe in *Uncle Tom's Cabin*); stanza 6 is missing from "Amazing Grace," hymn #202 in Fettke et al., *The Hymnal for Worship & Celebration*.

19. Chris Tomlin, "Amazing Grace (My Chains Are Gone)," released on the album *See the Morning* (Six Steps Records, 2006).

20. This quote is found all over the Internet without an explicit citation to Tozer's works. Noted Tozer scholar James L. Snyder admits that while it may not be found in a specific published work, the quote accurately echoes what Tozer has said in some of his sermons (available in audio recordings); "it is Tozer and it expresses his feelings on the subject" (personal communication, December 20, 2010).

21. I have explored the theology of a number of songs by Bob Marley, Peter Tosh, and Bunny Wailer in "Identity and Subversion in Babylon: Strategies for 'Resisting against the System' in the Music of Bob Marley and the Wailers," in *Religion, Culture and Tradition in the Caribbean*, ed. Hemchand Gossai and N. Samuel Murrell (New York: St. Martin's Press, 2000), 181–204. For an excellent in-depth study of how Bob Marley's lyrics draw on biblical texts and themes, see Dean MacNeil, *The Bible and Bob Marley: Half the Story Has Never Been Told* (Eugene, OR: Cascade, 2013).

all things," and "Pass It On" proclaims, "In the kingdom of Jah / Man shall reign."[22] These lyrics express (in androcentric language, admittedly) the biblical vision of this-worldly dignity granted humans at creation, a dignity that will be restored in the kingdom of God.[23]

And Peter Tosh's version of "Get Up, Stand Up" (a song he coauthored with Marley) understands well the implications of eschatology for ethics when it contrasts the doctrine of the rapture with a desire for justice on earth:

> You know, most people think
> A great God will come from the skies,
> And take away every little thing
> And lef' everybody dry.
> But if you know what life is worth,
> You would look for yours
> Right here on earth.

The song goes on to critique the "preacher man" for taking the focus off earthly life and affirms that the singer is "sick and tired of this game of theology, / die and go to heaven in Jesus' name."[24] This is the very theology that leads Marley, in the song "Talkin' Blues," to admit, "I feel like bombing a church, / now that you know that the preacher is lying."[25] But if Tozer is right, it is not just the preacher who is lying, but also the worshipers who blithely sing hymns of escape to an ethereal heaven, when in fact the Bible teaches no such thing.

Where, then, did the idea of "going to heaven" come from? And how did this otherworldly destiny displace the biblical teaching of the renewal of the earth and end up dominating popular Christian eschatology?

---

22. "We an' Dem," by Bob Marley, released on the *Uprising* album by Bob Marley and the Wailers (Island Records, 1980); "Pass It On," by Bob Marley, released on the *Burnin'* album by The Wailers (Island Records, 1973). "Jah" is the shortened form of the divine name "YHWH" ("Yahweh/Jehovah") found in expressions such as "hallelujah" (which literally means "praise YHWH"). Rastafarians love to quote Ps. 68:4 in the King James Version of the Bible: "Sing unto God, / sing praises to his name: / extol him that rideth upon the heavens by his name JAH, / and rejoice before him."

23. Since these lyrics are not published in any fixed format and often vary (sometimes significantly) from one recording to the next, I have provided my own transcription of song lyrics, along with which version of the song I am citing. This complex state of affairs has led one Bob Marley biographer to comment that compiling an accurate discography of any Jamaican reggae group "would try the patience of anyone but Jah Rastafari himself" (Timothy White, *Catch a Fire: The Life of Bob Marley*, rev. ed. [New York: Henry Holt, 1996], 393).

24. "Get Up, Stand Up," by Bob Marley and Peter Tosh, released on the *Equal Rights* album by Peter Tosh (Columbia Records, 1977); originally recorded (with slightly different lyrics) on the *Burnin'* album by The Wailers (Island Records, 1973).

25. "Talkin' Blues," by Bob Marley, released on the *Natty Dread* album by The Wailers (Island Records, 1974).

The Origin of the Idea of a Heavenly Destiny

The idea of a transcendent nonearthly realm as the goal of salvation can be traced back to the innovative teaching of Plato in the late fifth and early fourth centuries (428–348) BC. Prior to Plato, the dominant view of the afterlife in Greek culture was basically that articulated by Homer in works such as *The Iliad* and *The Odyssey*. This present life was where glory and honor could be found, and death was tragedy; all that the dead could expect was a shadowy existence in Hades, not unlike how the Old Testament conceived Sheol. It was not at all a positive expectation, but rather a view that merely the shade of one's former vitality persisted in the realm of the underworld.[26]

Plato, however, influenced by Orphic myths of the soul's preexistence among the stars and subsequent entombment on earth, posited a view of the person as composed of immortal soul or mind (the true self) and transitory, corruptible body. Likewise, the cosmos was binary, composed of a transcendent, suprasensory, timeless realm of ideas (the Forms) and the sensory realm of changeability and flux. There certainly are different versions of Plato's dualism articulated in the different dialogues that he wrote. Thus we find the radical dualism of the *Phaedo*, where the rational soul is diametrically opposed to the corruptible body, which leads the former astray and drags it down; and philosophy is practice for death, since even in this life the philosopher (by pure, abstract thought) can separate his soul (mind) from his body.[27] Contrasted with that is the more relaxed dualism of the *Timaeus*, where time is a "moving image of eternity," and this world is a flawed but beautiful reflection of the ideal realm.[28] Nevertheless, the worldview that held together both versions of Plato's dualism, and that he bequeathed to later ages, involved the radically new assumption of an immortal, immaterial soul and the aspiration to transcend this present world of matter, sensation, and change in order to attain to a higher, divine reality. The only way out of the endless cycle of rebirth (or transmigration of souls) was purification of the inner person from all contamination with bodily influences.

26. See, for example, *Iliad* 23.99–107, where Achilles has a dream visitation from the dead Patroclus; and *Odyssey* 11, where Odysseus recounts his journeys into the underworld (especially his encounter with his dead mother, Anticleia, in 11.208–222, and with the dead Achilles in 11.475–491). For a lucid discussion of the nature of Hades in these Homeric texts, see N. T. Wright, *The Resurrection of the Son of God* (Christian Origins and the Question of God 3; Minneapolis: Fortress, 2003), 39–45; and on the Old Testament concept of Sheol, see ibid., 87–99.

27. See Plato, *Phaedo* 64a–68b. The language is intentionally androcentric.

28. For Plato's phrase a "moving image of eternity," see *Timaeus* 37d; for a description of the beauty of the cosmos, see *Timaeus* 29e–31b.

A slightly different version of Plato's philosophy was promulgated by his most famous student, Aristotle (384–322 BC). Although Aristotle came to understand the soul as the form or unity of the body, and not an immaterial substance separable from the body, he accepted Plato's fundamental conceptual distinction between form and matter or immaterial ideas and corruptible physical reality.[29] More important, he accepted Plato's *value* distinction, such that the immaterial and rational were superior to the bodily and the material. Over time, this shared dualistic vision of reality became more and more popular in hellenized cultures.[30]

Plato's idea of a positive afterlife, however, did not immediately replace the traditional concept of Hades. Indeed, Plato himself never actually taught that "heaven" was the realm the soul returned to at death, despite the "likely story" or myth that he has Timaeus recount about the astral origin (and possible destiny) of the human soul in *Timaeus* 41d–e. It is open to debate whether Plato actually believed in personal immortality (the survival of individual identity), but he did not think that the soul literally came from or returned to the supralunary incorruptible astral realm, populated by ethereal, subtle bodies (such as planets, stars, angels, and gods), which is how heaven was popularly conceived in ancient times. Rather, the abstract and strictly immaterial realm of the Forms that Plato posited was his attempt to "demythologize" this popular notion of the astral realm.

Plato's influence (esp. *Timaeus* 41d–e) led initially to scattered belief (throughout the ancient world) in the possibility of becoming a star (or like a star) in the astral realm after death.[31] Later, in the Christian era, it led to the idea of dwelling with God (in a resurrected body) in the heavens (located above and beyond the earth). It was not, however, until much later that the

29. Aristotle's view of the relationship of soul and body is articulated most clearly in *De anima*. "Form" is a technical term in the philosophy of Plato and Aristotle for universal concepts or "ideas," understood as the unifying factor in material things. Whereas Plato thought that these forms existed independently of the physical world (but were embodied in this world), Aristotle thought that they had no independent existence.

30. The term "dualism" is used in different ways in the literature of religion and philosophy. Historically, it has been used for the idea that there are two metaphysical principles of separate origin. More recently the term has come to be used to designate just about any duality or twoness (often referred to as binary oppositions). My usage is different from both of these. I am employing the term "dualism" to name any bifurcation in which one side of the distinction is given a *priority in value* over the other (that is, it is viewed as better, higher, more important, etc.) and the other side is correspondingly *devalued* (as lower, unimportant, or even downright evil). "Dualism" therefore refers not simply to a conceptual duality, but rather to a value distinction at the worldview/precognitive/affective level superimposed on what may (or may not) be a valid conceptual distinction. For further discussion of value or worldview dualism, see Walsh and Middleton, *Transforming Vision*, chaps. 6–7.

31. See, for example, Cicero, *De republica* 6.13–16.

Christian tradition came to embrace the more metaphysical notion that Plato actually held, concerning an immaterial, nonspatial eternal state.[32]

The Platonic worldview, and especially Plato's more abstract notion of the afterlife, were given extra impetus in the third century AD by the Greek philosopher Plotinus (204–270), who renovated Plato's conceptual framework (combined with Aristotelian and Stoic ideas) to promulgate a vision of reality that deeply influenced Christian theologians from Augustine to Pseudo-Dionysius and beyond. Known today as Neoplatonism, Plotinus's vision was regarded for centuries simply as an articulation of Plato's own views (until modern times, with the rise of historical criticism).[33]

Whereas at least some Christian theologians may have balked at Plato's notion that the rational soul or mind was immortal and the highest part of the person (which verged on the deification of reason), Plotinus made room for something beyond, and higher than, reason. He proposed that above (and in a certain sense, deeper within) the rational mind or soul (on both the personal and cosmic levels) could be found the intuitive, suprarational mind or Nous (later identified by some Christian theologians with Spirit or the Logos), and above (and within) that was the One, the unitary fullness and depth of being from which all reality flowed (some Christians identified this with the Father or the mystery of the Godhead). Plotinus thus explicitly identified the ascent to the divine with the turn inward, thereby initiating a Western form of mysticism that has reverberated throughout the church in the Middle Ages and even into the modern period.

Although it was specifically Plotinus's form of Platonism that influenced Augustine in the fourth and fifth centuries AD, it was the earlier form known as Middle Platonism that formed the dominant intellectual milieu for many of the church fathers of the second and third centuries. I believe that we must not be too hard on these Christian forebears who found Platonic ideas useful for articulating and communicating their theology in the context of Greco-Roman culture. After all, the Jewish conceptualities of New Testament theology needed to be brought to bear on the new cultural context in which the Christian faith found itself. That the church fathers drew on the best of the intellectual heritage of their times is natural. They were simply attempting to

---

32. The impact of Platonism can also be seen in differing views of the final destiny of the righteous in Second Temple Jewish apocalyptic literature; some texts expect the redeemed to dwell in a renewed cosmos, while others suggest transfer to an otherworldly heaven.

33. Note that in *Confessions* 7.9 and 7.20 Augustine refers to what are in fact *The Enneads* of Plotinus simply as the books of "the Platonists." Plotinus wrote dense philosophical treatises that were collected by his disciple Porphyry in *The Enneads* ("the nines": six groups of nine treatises each).

relate the gospel to their own culture, something that Christians of all ages have done, often unaware of the attendant dangers of assimilating practices and ideas that are antithetical to our faith.

Although I am sympathetic to the church fathers, I believe that we need to be aware of the negative consequences of their synthesis of Christian faith with Greek philosophy. Those consequences include (but are certainly not limited to) a transformation of Christian eschatology beyond anything that the writers of the New Testament would have envisioned. I will address the history of this transformation in more detail in the appendix of this book. For the present it will suffice to quote Richard Bauckham and Trevor Hart's summary of the pervasive legacy for Christian eschatology bequeathed by Plato (and intensified by Neoplatonism): "The Christian hope has constantly been understood as hope for human fulfillment in *another world* ('heaven') rather than as hope for the eternal future *of this world* in which we live."[34] In the chapters that follow, it will become clear how far we have departed from the biblical teaching of the redemption of creation.

34. Richard Bauckham and Trevor Hart, *Hope against Hope: Christian Eschatology in Contemporary Context* (Trinity and Truth; London: Darton, Longman & Todd, 1999), 129, emphasis added.

Part 1

From Creation to Eschaton

2

Why Are We Here?

Being Human as Sacred Calling

The best place to start is at the beginning.

In the movie *The Princess Bride*, after Fezzik the giant finds Inigo the Spaniard in the Thieves Forest, Inigo explains that Vizzini, the leader of the trio, always went back to the beginning whenever the job went wrong. "Well, this is where we got the job, so it's the beginning. And I am staying till Vizzini come."

We live in the midst of a fallen world, a broken reality, where the "job" has clearly gone badly wrong, To understand how we got here, and what our next steps should be, we need to go back to the beginning, to God's creational intentions for the world. Soon, in chapter 3, we will explore the full sweep of the biblical story from creation to eschaton, looking specifically at how an understanding of the plot brings coherence to God's work of creation and salvation. But first, in the present chapter, we will examine the beginning of the amazing story of God with the world, which clarifies the meaning and purpose of our life as human beings; and we will also look at how things went wrong—how we "lost the plot," to use a most appropriate British idiom. We have lost the plot not only in the existential sense of having lost our way, thus departing from God's original purposes, but also in the conceptual sense that we often do not understand the inner logic of the biblical story.

Reading the Bible as a Story

Although there are many components of a good story, plot is one of the most basic. The notion of plot is actually quite simple: it is a matter of something going wrong and being fixed. As far back as Aristotle, we find reflection on the nature of plot in terms of the two movements of "tying" (or "entanglement") and "loosing."[1] We often call this "narrative tension/complication" and "narrative resolution." It thus is easy to see that the Bible's story of sin and redemption constitutes the rudiments of a plot.

The plot of the biblical story may be summarized as *creation-fall-redemption* (sometimes with the addition of *consummation*). This indicates a movement from God's original intentions for the world, through a fundamental problem that prevents God's intentions from being realized, to a repairing or fixing of the problem (with the result that God's intentions finally come to fruition).[2] While many Christians would give lip service to this basic framework, it does not always function as a guide for actually reading the Bible. Not only is it easy to get lost, even overwhelmed, in the mass of details within Scripture, but also the movement of repair (which we call "redemption" or "salvation") tends to be the focus of our interest as Bible readers. And this redemptive movement certainly takes up most of the Bible's pages. The result is that many readers of Scripture tend to overlook the overall structure of the biblical plot (specifically its grounding in creation). But unless we have an understanding of the initial state (creation) and the nature of the problem (fall), we will systematically misread the nature of this repair (redemption)—and thus the nature of the final fulfillment of God's purposes. Indeed, it will be difficult to see it as repair at all, as in fixing something that has gone wrong.[3]

1. Aristotle, *Poetica* 18.1–3 (Aristotle was talking about drama and did not explicitly use the word "plot").

2. The creation-fall-redemption framework guides the biblical exposition in part 2 ("The Biblical World View") of Brian J. Walsh and J. Richard Middleton, *The Transforming Vision: Shaping a Christian World View* (Downers Grove, IL: IVP Academic, 1984); and in part 2 ("The Resources of Scripture") of J. Richard Middleton and Brian J. Walsh, *Truth Is Stranger Than It Used to Be: Biblical Faith in a Postmodern Age* (Downers Grove, IL: IVP Academic, 1995).

3. I understand the motivation of those who would summarize the plot of the biblical story as creation-fall-redemption-*consummation*, since this indicates that the climax of the story does not simply return to the primitive state of the beginning (that is, there is a certain discontinuity between creation and eschaton). I fully agree with this point (as will become clear in this chapter and the chapters that follow). However, it is important to emphasize that the final eschatological

This chapter therefore is devoted to clarifying the initial movement of the story (creation) in order to better understand God's original intent for humanity (why we are here) and the entire created order. This will make sense of the Bible's own portrayal of what went wrong.[4] Without a clear grasp of the purpose and goal of earthly life (including how that purpose went off track), we will be at the mercy of unbiblical notions of salvation and eschatology. But with a firm grasp on the original human purpose (and its distortion by sin), we will be in a solid position in the chapters that follow to sketch the main redemptive moves of the biblical plot, intended to restore human beings to fulfilling their earthly purpose.

Created to Worship God?

So what is that purpose? Why are we here? When we turn to the beginning of the Bible, it is clear that God creates the human race with an earthly vocation. In Genesis 1:26–28 the divinely commissioned human task is portrayed as ruling animals and subduing the earth, while in Genesis 2:15 the human task is described as working and protecting the garden. And Psalm 8:5–8 (although not at the start of the Bible) tells us that God made humans to rule over the works of his hands and has put "all things" under their feet, with various forms of animal life listed as examples. In all these creation texts, the movement is what we might call "missional"—from God via humans outward to the earth. The fundamental human task is conceived in rather mundane terms as the responsible exercise of power on God's behalf over our earthly environment.

In popular Christian lore, however, it is almost axiomatic that humans were created to worship God. How many times have churchgoers heard this common idea from the pulpit (or sung it from the pew)? It is sometimes shocking, therefore, for readers of the Bible to realize that the initial purpose and raison d'être of humanity is never explicitly portrayed in Scripture as the worship of God (or anything that would conform to our notion of the "spiritual," with

---

state does not transcend creation. While it transcends the initial state of creation, it is actually the fulfillment of God's creational intent (after the fracture of sin has been repaired).

4. This chapter draws on my previous work on creation theology, including the article "Image of God," in *Dictionary of Scripture and Ethics*, ed. Joel Green et al. (Grand Rapids: Baker Academic, 2011), 394–97; and especially my book *The Liberating Image: The Imago Dei in Genesis 1* (Grand Rapids: Brazos, 2005), which synthesizes much of my previous writing on the subject (including *Transforming Vision*, chap. 3, and *Truth Is Stranger*, chap. 6). At various points in the present chapter the footnotes will indicate sections of *The Liberating Image* that interested readers might consult for more extensive discussion of the topic at hand.

its dualistic categories). This, of course, does not mean that we should not worship God. Rather, what we need is a redefinition of "worship."

First of all, we should not reduce human worship of God to verbal, emotionally charged expressions of praise (which is what we usually mean by the term). Rather, our worship consists in all that we do.[5] This is well illustrated in Romans 12:1–2, where Paul borrows language of sacrifice and liturgy from Israel's temple cult in order to describe full-orbed bodily obedience (which, he says, is our true worship).[6] Second, worship, when rightly understood, is not specific to humans. Rather, all creatures in heaven and on earth are called to worship God.

This cosmic worship is the theme of Psalm 148. "Praise YHWH from the heavens," we read in verse 1. And then follows a catalog of heavenly creatures (vv. 1–4) that are all called to worship God, including the angelic host, all the heavenly bodies (sun, moon, stars), and the very highest heavens, including the waters above the heavens. But not only heavenly creatures are called to worship God. "Praise YHWH from the earth," we read in verse 7. And then follows a catalog of earthly creatures (vv. 7–12), including sea monsters, deep oceans, and meteorological phenomena (lightning, hail, snow, wind), followed by mountains, trees, animals and birds, and (finally) humans (vv. 11–12).[7] It is significant that humans are just one of many sets of creatures called to worship God. In fact, humans are mentioned in only two of the eleven verses (vv. 1–4, 6–12) that call on God's heavenly and earthly creatures to worship him.

If we look at the biblical texts that explicitly address the creation and purpose of human beings—such as Genesis 1–2, or Psalm 8, or even Psalm 104— not one of them says that we are created to "worship" God. Frankly, that would not be unique or distinctive to humans. We think that worship is unique

---

5. Reducing worship to emotionally charged expressions of praise is like reducing the love in a marriage to romance. As marriage partners know only too well, while Valentine's Day cards and bouquets of flowers are wonderful expressions of devotion, love needs to be expressed also in doing the dishes, cooking the meals, cleaning the house, planning the finances, feeding the baby at three in the morning, advocating for the autistic child at school, and so on.

6. Although in English we distinguish between "worship" and "service," the Bible does not typically use clearly distinct words for these ideas. Rather, the same word can apply both to priestly service in the temple and ordinary work or labor; both are forms of service or worship rendered to God.

7. According to Ps. 148:8, the wind obeys God. Other biblical texts that describe the obedience of nonhuman creatures to their creator include Jer. 8:7; Pss. 33:6, 9; 147:7–9; 148:5–6. Indeed, this motif is given fullest expression in Gen. 1, which pictures God creating by his word, simply commanding or instructing ("Let there be . . .") creatures to exist and function according to the divine will. Psalm 96 combines the rhetoric of divine fiats ("Let there be . . .") from Gen. 1 with the motif of worship when the psalm exhorts the nonhuman world to praise God: "Let the heavens be glad, / and let the earth rejoice; / let the sea roar, and all that fills it; / let the field exult, and everything in it" (vv. 11–12a).

to humans only because we have internalized an anthropocentric—human-centered—worldview. In the biblical worldview mountains and stars worship God just as much as humans do. This may seem an outrageous proposal to contemporary ears, but it is a clear implication of Psalm 148 (and other biblical texts too).[8]

But how do mountains and stars worship God? Certainly not verbally or with emotions. Rather, mountains worship God simply by being mountains, covered with lush vegetation or with steep crags or glaciers, depending on their elevation. And stars worship God by being stars, burning with nuclear energy according to their sizes and their life cycles, ranging from those like our own sun to red giants, white dwarfs, pulsars, and black holes.

If mountains worship God by being mountains and stars worship God by being stars, how do humans worship God? By being human, in the full glory of what that means. Humans, the Bible tells us, are cultural beings, defined not by our worship, for worship is what defines creation (all creatures are called to worship). But the human creature is made to worship God in a distinctive way: by interacting with the earth, using our God-given power to transform our earthly environment into a complex world (a sociocultural world) that glorifies our creator.

The Human Cultural Calling as *Imago Dei*

As anthropologists know, the basis for all culture is *agri*culture. We could not develop the sort of complex cultures that we have today—with cities, governments, technology, art, science, and academic institutions—if we did not first find a way to produce enough food for people to eat. Hunter-gatherers can develop only a rudimentary culture. In order to develop any form of complex social order, people must be able to settle down somewhere and have a dependable food supply. This makes sense of the garden of Eden as the original human environment in Genesis 2. God's encouragement to the first humans to eat freely from the trees of the garden (Gen. 2:16) clearly indicates that the garden is meant to provide food for human needs.

Paradoxically, however, the garden itself needs humans. Genesis 2 explains that God delayed planting the garden until there was a source of water (vv. 5a, 6), which is logical because plants need water to be able to grow; however, God also delayed the garden until there was a human to work it (vv. 5b, 7–8). This

---

8. See the amazing list of passages from the book of Psalms alone that portray creation's praise of God, in Terence E. Fretheim, *God and World in the Old Testament: A Relational Theology of Creation* (Nashville: Abingdon, 2005), 267–68; Fretheim's analysis of this theme is in chap. 8.

suggests that the garden in Genesis 2 is not simply a "natural" phenomenon, but rather a cultural project in which humans are to participate. Not only are humans made *from* the ground (v. 7), but also they are made *for* the ground, with a specific task or vocation in mind.[9] Envisioning something beyond a primitive hunter-gatherer society, Genesis 2:15 portrays the original human purpose as tilling (working/developing) and keeping (protecting/caring for) the garden. Genesis 2 thus represents agriculture (a cultivated garden) as the first communal, cultural project of humanity. Indeed, since it is the creator who first planted the garden, it could be said that God initiated the first cultural project, thus setting a pattern for humans—created in the divine image—to follow.[10]

Like Genesis 2, Psalm 104 also views agriculture as definitive for humans. There are few references to humans in this beautiful creation psalm (only 5 or so verses out of 35 verses total). But of the psalm's two main references to humans, one simply mentions human work or labor as a positive thing (v. 23), stated alongside the hunting for food done by lions (vv. 21–22). Lions do their defining thing (hunting); we do ours (work). The other main reference to humans in Psalm 104 describes God's gift of plants for humanity, listed along with his gift of grass for cattle. But whereas cattle (as biological organisms) simply eat the grass that God gives them, humans (as cultural beings) become farmers and bring forth produce from the earth, turning grapes, olives, and wheat into wine, oil, and bread, for their own sustenance and enjoyment (vv. 14–15).[11]

Whereas Psalm 104 and Genesis 2 focus on agriculture, Psalm 8 foregrounds animal husbandry as the basic human task in God's world. Humans are crowned with royal dignity and granted authority or dominion over various realms of animal life—land, air, and water (vv. 5–8 [6–9 MT]).[12] The domes-

9. There is a primal resonance between humans and the earth/ground that is communicated by the Hebrew wordplay between the words for "human" (*'ādām*) and "ground" (*'ādāmâ*) in Gen. 2:7 (note that in Gen. 2–3 *'ādām* is not yet the proper name "Adam," as it is in Gen. 4:1; rather, the Hebrew says "the human" (*hā'ādām*). An English equivalent of this pun might be that God created the "human" from the "humus." On this wordplay and its theological significance, see the close reading of Gen. 2–3 by Phyllis Trible in "A Love Story Gone Awry," in *God and the Rhetoric of Sexuality* (Overtures to Biblical Theology; Philadelphia: Fortress, 1984), 72–143.

10. For the insight that God was the first gardener/culture-maker, I am indebted to Andy Crouch, *Culture Making: Recovering Our Creative Calling* (Downers Grove, IL: IVP Academic, 2008), 108.

11. Another important reference to humans in Ps. 104 is the concluding verse (v. 35a), where the psalmist asks God to remove sinners from the earth; presumably their misuse of power impedes the proper functioning of earthly life (this perspective is important, as we will see in later chapters, for interpreting eschatological texts of judgment such as Matt. 24:37–41).

12. The Hebrew verse numbering for Ps. 8 is slightly different from the English, so that verses 6–9 in the Masoretic Text (MT) correspond to verses 5–8 in English translations.

a complex, well-constructed, peaceable world. Not only is each stage of this creative process judged by God to be "good" (vv. 4, 10, 12, 18, 21, 25), but also the whole created order is declared "very good" (v. 31). By these statements scattered throughout Genesis 1, the creator affirms not only his evident pleasure in the world he is making, but also the validity and goodness of creaturely existence itself. Thus the human use of power, if it is to truly image the biblical God, will be nonviolent and developmental, enhancing and celebrating the goodness of creation. Power is for the blessing of others.

God's care for creation in Genesis 1 is evident also from the way the text dissents from ancient Near Eastern religious practice, in which sacrifices were understood as providing food for the gods and were thought necessary to guarantee fertility of crops and flocks on earth. In contrast to this, the God of Genesis freely blesses animals and humans with perpetual fertility (1:22, 28) and grants food to both for their sustenance (1:29–30). Even more explicitly (and in more detail) than Genesis 1, Psalm 104 describes God's lavish care for creatures, especially the provision of food and water for plants, animals, and humans (vv. 10–30; see also the summary in Ps. 147:7–9). God's own generous exercise of power for the benefit of creatures thus provides a model for the human exercise of power in the world.

Perhaps most significant of all is that the biblical God does not hoard power as sovereign ruler of the cosmos; instead, he gladly assigns humanity a share in ruling the earth as his representatives (Gen. 1:26–28). God does not micromanage the world, but instead fully expects human beings, made in the divine image, to contribute to the developing beauty and complexity of earthly life. Evidence of this sharing of power is seen in God's somewhat limited involvement in naming in Genesis 1. The creator names day and night, as well as sky, land, and seas, on the first three days of creation (vv. 5, 8, 10), but he refrains from naming anything on days four through six, leaving this royal privilege for humans, made in the divine image, to take up. And in Genesis 2 the first human names the animals (vv. 19–20), an act that combines discernment with power but still leaves vast arenas of creation for future generations to name (perhaps our complex scientific taxonomies could be regarded in this light).[30]

This sharing of power is radically different from the ancient Near Eastern worldview, in which only some elite person (typically the king) was regarded as the image of God. Indeed, the entire social order in the ancient world was predicated on the concentration of power in the hands of a few who controlled

---

30. The level of responsibility (and freedom) God grants humanity in naming the animals is amazing. According to Gen. 2:19, whatever the first human called each animal, that became its name. God did not interfere to suggest alternatives, but simply allowed each name to stand. On this point, see Fretheim, *God and World*, 58.

access to blessing from the gods, thus reducing the majority of the populace to a lower, dependent social status.[31] Human imaging of God's power on earth will therefore need to take into account the fact that in the biblical account no human being is granted dominion over another at creation; all equally participate in the image of God. The process of cultural development is meant to flow from a cooperative sharing in dominion, modeled on God's own sharing of power with human beings.

The Genesis creation account provides a normative basis to critique interhuman injustice or the misuse of power over others, whether in individual cases or in systemic social formations. Specifically, since both male and female are made in God's image with a joint mandate to rule (Gen. 1:27–28), this calls into question the inequities of power between men and women that have arisen in patriarchal social systems and various forms of sexism throughout history. And since the *imago Dei* is prior to any ethnic, racial, or national divisions (see Gen. 10), this provides an alternative to ethnocentrism, racism, or any form of national superiority; beneath the legitimate diversity of cultures that have developed in the world, people constitute one human family.

God's intent from the beginning is thus for a cooperative world of shalom, generosity, and blessing, evident most fundamentally in his own mode of exercising power at creation. In the New Testament, Jesus even grounds love for enemies in the *imago Dei*, suggesting that this sort of radical generosity toward others reflects the creator's own "perfect" love toward all people, shown in his causing sun and rain to benefit both the righteous and the wicked (Matt. 5:43–48; cf. Luke 6:27–35). In the end, nothing less than God's own exercise of creative activity ought to function as the ethical paradigm or model for our development of culture, with attendant care of the earth and just and loving interhuman action. By our wise exercise of cultural power we truly function as *imago Dei*, mediating the creator's presence in the full range of earthly activities, thus fulfilling the initial narrative sequence of the biblical story.

The Problem of Human Violence

In the biblical account, however, the incursion of sin tragically compromises the human calling to image God. In Genesis 3 this sin is portrayed initially as transgression or violation of a boundary that God has prescribed (the tree of the knowledge of good and evil), rooted in lack of trust in the creator's word; this primal transgression vis-à-vis God has significant consequences

31. For an analysis of how creation myths grounded the social order in ancient Mesopotamia, see Middleton, *Liberating Image*, chap. 4, esp. 147–73.

for *interhuman* boundary transgression (violence) in the rest of the Primeval History (Gen. 1–11).[32]

According to Genesis, when humans rebel against their God-given limits by transgressing the single prohibition that God gave in the garden (2:17; 3:6) this results in "curses" on the serpent and the ground (3:14, 17; 5:29). These curses stand in tension with the primordial "blessings" that God granted creatures at creation (1:22, 28; 2:3). As a result of the initial transgression, humans are exiled from the garden and prevented access to the tree of life (3:23–24). More specific consequences are that work now becomes painful toil (3:17–19) and childbirth will henceforth yield excessive pain (3:16a).[33] We also find the origin of male power over women (3:16b), something that was not part of God's original intent (in either Gen. 1 or Gen. 2). As a consequence of human sin, death has begun to invade and destroy God's design for the flourishing of earthly life.[34]

It is crucial to recognize that humans do not, by their sin, cease being cultural creatures. What we find in Genesis 4 are examples of positive cultural innovation intertwined with innovations in the misuse of power, which impede God's purposes for the flourishing of earthly life and prevent God's presence from fully permeating creation.[35] Besides the first city (v. 17) and the first examples of livestock herding, musical instruments, and metal tools (vv. 20–22), we find also the first murder (v. 8), which leads explicitly to further "curse," this time on a human being (v. 11). Human violence then escalates in Genesis 4 with the account of Lamech. Not only is Lamech the first bigamist (v. 19)—that is, he initiates this particular form of violence against women—but also he engages in the first revenge killing (of a youth who injured him) and boasts about it to his two wives (vv. 23–24).

32. This is what Christian theology has traditionally referred to as the "fall." Although I have no problem using the term in a nontechnical sense to describe the first sin and its ensuing consequences for humanity and the earth, I agree with those biblical scholars who suggest that we should not allow this metaphor to control our reading of Gen. 3. While "fall" might be an appropriate metaphor to describe the Orphic myth of the soul's descent from heaven and entombment in a body, Gen. 3 portrays the primal sin more in terms of "transgression" or "fracture."

33. The "pain" in childbirth and "toil" in working the ground (Gen. 3:16–17) translate the very same Hebrew word (*'iṣṣābôn*). The King James Version is more democratic in translating both as "sorrow."

34. This suggests that the "death" God promised as the consequence of eating of the tree (Gen. 2:17) was neither immediate literal death (the original human couple did not immediately "die" in this sense) nor even the introduction of mortality (a limited time span) into what had been an originally immortal human life. Rather, the fullness of life began to be compromised, as death (the antithesis of life) invaded and corrupted the original flourishing of creation.

35. For further analysis of the misuse of power in the Primeval History, see Middleton, *Liberating Image*, 219–21.

Genesis shows, however, that the incursion of sin into God's good creation does not obliterate the *imago Dei*. God's creation of both male and female in his "likeness" is reiterated (5:1–2), and this image/likeness is passed on to future generations (5:3). Nevertheless, human violence (which is fundamentally the misuse of the power of *imago Dei*) spirals out of control in Genesis 6. In accordance with God's blessing of fertility in 1:28, humans indeed multiply and fill the earth (see the genealogy in 5:3–32), but they end up filling the earth with violence or bloodshed (6:11, 13) rather than contributing to the flourishing of God's world or extending the divine presence on earth. According to Genesis 6, human violence so corrupts or ruins the earth (vv. 5, 11–12) that God is grieved (v. 6) and engages in a restorative operation via the great flood, meant to cleanse the earth of this pollution.[36] Despite the massive destruction that the flood involved, Noah, his family, and a remnant of animal life are preserved to allow a fresh start (8:18–19), and God enters into a covenant with the earth (9:13) and all living things (9:11–12, 15–17), pledging to support the regularity of the seasons and the temporal cycle of day and night (8:22), without which earthly life cannot flourish.

After the flood God restates the blessing of fertility on the human race and the mandate to fill the earth (9:1, 7) and even reaffirms the creation of humans as *imago Dei* (9:6). Yet the human heart is not fundamentally changed (8:21; cf. 6:5). Furthermore, the reaffirmation of the image is now used explicitly to ground the sanctity of human life because murder remains a real possibility (9:6). Indeed, corruption soon permeates human life once again. Noah is depicted as planting the first vineyard (9:20), but this notable achievement is intertwined with his subsequent drunkenness (9:21), followed by a breakdown in father-son relationships, including his "curse" on later generations (9:22–27).

The Primeval History (Gen. 1–11) culminates with the account of the building project of Babel (11:1–9). It is important to note that this account comes after the diversification and spreading out of the human race over the earth (10:5, 18, 32), including the development of multiple cultures and languages (10:5, 20, 31), which has been taking place in response to the cultural mandate of Genesis 1:26–28. Babel thus represents a regressive human attempt to guarantee security by settling in one place and constructing a monolithic empire, with a single language, thus resisting God's original intent for humanity. The project of Babel ends with God confusing the single language of the builders

36. The verb for God being "grieved" in Gen. 6:6 derives from the same Hebrew root as the "pain" or "toil" that comes to humans as a result of their sin (3:16–17). In other words, we do not simply wound ourselves and affect other humans and the earth by our violent misuse of power; our violence wounds even God. The creator's pain echoes our pain, so intimately is God bound up with the world he made.

and scattering the people over the earth, thus diffusing human power and restarting the diversified human cultural project.[37]

Nevertheless, just as the flood did not change anything fundamental in human life, so the dispersion of Babel cannot be regarded as anything more than a temporary respite. Neither constitutes a permanent solution to the problem of human violence. The rest of Scripture, the history of the world, and our own experience testify to the fact that the human heart is still corrupt; we have not yet been cured of our violence. Indeed, we live in a world that glorifies violence and makes an ideal of conquest and military supremacy. Whereas God wants the cloud of his Glory-presence to fill and cover the earth (as it did the tabernacle), we, by our violent misuse of the power entrusted to us, have covered the earth with a cloud of pollution, both physical and moral, thus shutting earth off from God's full presence.[38]

The initial narrative sequence of Scripture expects humanity to work together, exercising power vis-à-vis their earthly environment, in order to transform the initially primitive earthly state into complex cultures that bring glory to God. But humans rebel against God and increasingly use their power against each other, resulting in the world of violence, brutality, and abuse that we know only too well—indeed, resulting in our subjection of the earth to corruption or futility. In Scripture, the narrative question that arises at this point is this: What will God do next to address this fundamental impediment to his creational purposes?

---

37. For a fuller exposition of the significance of Babel, see Middleton, *Liberating Image*, 221–28.

38. That the earth is shut off from God's presence, and from the rest of the "heavens" (the universe), is the basic idea behind C. S. Lewis's reference to Earth as the "silent planet" in the first volume of his space trilogy, *Out of the Silent Planet* (London: Bodley Head, 1938).

3

The Plot of the Biblical Story

I n the preceding chapter we examined God's creational intent for human beings, especially our cultural calling to image God on earth, and how that calling was distorted through sin. But what happens next? How does God get the story back on track?

My approach in this chapter is to sketch the broad outlines of the plot structure of Scripture, from Old Testament to New Testament. This sketch of the Bible's plot by no means covers all the twists and turns of the narrative. There is much that I simply summarize or even leave out. My focus is on the inner logic of the biblical story, especially how the main redemptive moves of the biblical plot relate to the opening scenes of the story, resulting in one coherent (though complex) macronarrative.[1] The value of remaining at the skeletal level of plot is that this allows the narrative thrust of the biblical story to be seen most clearly.[2]

1. This sketch of the biblical plot is developed from my essay "A New Heaven and a New Earth: The Case for a Holistic Reading of the Biblical Story of Redemption," *Journal for Christian Theological Research* 11 (2006): 73–97.

2. Various dimensions of the biblical narrative will be fleshed out more fully in the chapters that follow. Chapters 4 through 6 will explore the theme of holistic salvation in the Old Testament, while chaps. 7–10 address the notion of cosmic redemption in the New Testament, including texts that do not seem to fit that vision.

This sketch of the biblical plot serves to reinforce the holistic and this-worldly character of God's purposes. By attending to the basic thrust and movement of the plot, we will discover that eschatological redemption consists in the renewal of human cultural life on earth rather than our removal from earth to heaven. Close attention to the unfolding biblical story reveals that there is simply no role for heaven as the final destiny of the righteous.

Categories for Narrative Analysis

The preceding chapter summarized the Bible's plot in terms of sin (plot complication) and redemption (plot resolution): something goes wrong and gets fixed. But now I want to introduce a bit more complexity into the analysis. Here I turn to categories that I have adapted from Vladimir Propp and A. J. Greimas, mediated through the work of New Testament scholar N. T. Wright.[3] These categories focus on the sending of agents to accomplish tasks and are thus eminently applicable to the biblical macronarrative, which contains many examples of people called or elected by God for a particular mission.[4] But before applying these categories to the plot of the biblical story (and instead of just explaining them in an abstract manner), I think that it will be helpful to see how they work by applying them to a simple example: the story of Little Red Riding Hood (see fig. 3.1).[5]

The story begins when Little Red Riding Hood is sent by her mother to deliver a basket of goodies to her grandmother. Here we have an excellent illustration of an initial narrative sequence: sender, agent, task, receiver. Although the story begins with a mission or task, there is as yet no plot. The

3. Although N. T. Wright came to use these categories in *The New Testament and the People of God* (Christian Origins and the Question of God 1; Minneapolis: Fortress, 1992), I was stimulated to develop the rudiments of my own analysis while listening to Wright's five-part lecture series on the Gospel of Mark given at the Institute for Christian Studies (ICS) in Toronto, July 7–8, 1988, followed by his three-part series at the ICS titled "The Quest for the Historical Kingdom," January 31–February 1, 1989. For nuanced discussions of the applicability of Propp's and Greimas's categories for "actantal analysis" to biblical scholarship, see Pamela J. Milne, *Vladimir Propp and the Study of Structure in Biblical Hebrew Narrative* (Bible and Literature; Sheffield: Sheffield Academic Press, 1988); Daniel Patte, *The Religious Dimensions of Biblical Texts: Greimas's Structural Semiotics and Biblical Exegesis* (Semeia Studies; Atlanta: Scholars Press, 1990).

4. The specific terminology ("sender," "agent," "task," "receiver," "impediment," and "helper") is my own, and the model is considerably adapted (I have omitted much from the work of Propp and Greimas and simplified Wright's schema). It is intended only as a heuristic, nontechnical model for narrative analysis of the large-scale plot of Scripture. Indeed, this model is used, without flagging it as such, to sketch the plot of the biblical story in J. Richard Middleton and Brian J. Walsh, *Truth Is Stranger Than It Used to Be: Biblical Faith in a Postmodern Age* (Downers Grove, IL: IVP Academic, 1995), chap. 6.

5. I am indebted to N. T. Wright's 1988 lectures for this helpful example.

Figure 3.1. Categories for Plot Analysis

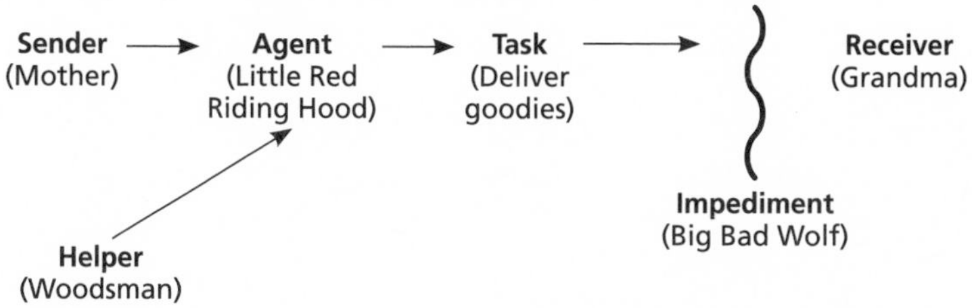

plot proper begins with the introduction of an impediment or complication, which prevents the initial narrative sequence from being completed. Enter the Big Bad Wolf. The initial agent now needs help in carrying out her mission. So we have a helper (really a second agent), whose task is to bring aid to the first agent by removing the impediment. In our story, the woodsman comes to the aid of Little Red Riding Hood by killing the Big Bad Wolf, who has swallowed the grandmother. But the removal of the impediment is not yet the end of the story. The story reaches its fruition—that is, narrative resolution occurs—only when the initial narrative sequence is finally completed. Since the story began with Little Red Riding Hood trying to deliver the basket of goodies to her grandmother, the story properly ends only when Little Red Riding Hood and her grandmother, and now also the woodsman, have a picnic together.[6]

With these categories for narrative analysis in hand, let us now sketch the plot structure of the biblical story that is represented in abbreviated form by the creation-fall-redemption paradigm (see fig. 3.2). In this plot structure there are three distinct narrative levels, and the story moves through them in the following order: 1, 2, 3, then back to 2, and then back to 1 (a chiastic or ring structure).[7]

Plot Level 1: Creation and the Human Calling

The initial narrative sequence of the Bible (level 1 of the plot) is quite clear: God creates the human race to rule the earth. This is the biblical version of the sequence: sender, agent, task, receiver. This narrative sequence is found in every primary statement of human creation in the Bible. Here we can recap the exposition of the preceding chapter. The original human task in Genesis 2:15 is to work and protect the garden, while in Psalm 8:5–8 humanity is entrusted with rule over animal life on land, in air, and in water. Genesis 1:26–28

---

6. The presence of the woodsman at the picnic is a new element, not envisioned in the initial narrative sequence. Likewise, the Lamb (who does not appear in the initial narrative sequence of the biblical story) is present in the new Jerusalem (Rev. 21:22–23; 22:3).

7. This is, however, a conceptual, not a literary, chiasm.

Figure 3.2. The Plot Structure of the Biblical Story

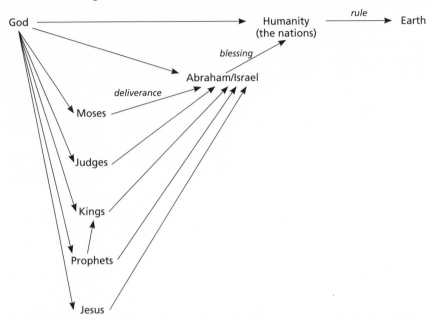

combines both agriculture and animal husbandry in its vision of humans as God's image on earth, commissioned to rule animals and subdue the earth.

In all cases the human vocation is missional and earth oriented, involving the responsible exercise of human power on God's behalf over the nonhuman world. While this vocation refers initially just to farming (tending animals and land), farming is the historical basis of all complex human social organization and cultural development. Ultimately the human vocation is a cultural mandate, grounded in agriculture, but including all forms of technological, societal, artistic, and intellectual production. Thus the initial narrative sequence can be understood as our development of the originally pristine earth into a complex and beautiful human civilization worthy of God's glory.

By our communal exercise of cultural power, the human race is meant to fulfill its calling to be God's royal priesthood, thus mediating the presence of the creator from heaven, where he is enthroned, to the earthly realm, until the world (God's temple) is filled with God's glory. This is the meaning of the *imago Dei*, which imparts a sacred and ultimate significance to the complexities of mundane human history.[8]

8. For a fuller exposition of this interpretation of the Bible's opening narrative sequence, see the preceding chapter.

But a complication or impediment arises to prevent completion of the initial narrative sequence. Humans misuse the power that God has given them, rebelling against their creator and turning against each other. This misuse of the power of *imago Dei* is manifest first of all in disobedience toward the creator (Gen. 3), which then blossoms into a pattern of violence and fractured relationships among people (Gen. 4–11). These consequences of the original transgression escalate in each generation that follows, until violence, which is fundamentally interhuman violation, fills the earth. Indeed, human violence or bloodshed, which has corrupted the earth, is named in Genesis 6 as the reason for the flood (vv. 11–13). Yet Genesis 8 understands the flood as an ultimately failed attempt at narrative resolution, since the human heart has not been changed (v. 21). When the Primeval History ends with the tower-of-Babel episode (Gen. 11:1–9), we are left wondering what God's next move will be to get the story back on track, so that his initial purposes might be fulfilled.

Plot Level 2: Abraham/Israel

At the start of Genesis 12, God initiates a secondary narrative sequence—a subplot in the biblical story—that will frame the rest of the Old Testament and most of the New Testament. In the context of a failed human project (since sin with attendant violence has impeded and distorted the human calling to be *imago Dei* on earth) God intervenes in history to set things right. The initial move in this redemptive project is the calling of Abraham and his descendants (Israel) out from the now-diversified human race (which has become the nations or the families of the earth [Gen. 10]).[9] The purpose of this calling or election is that they might be new agents or helpers, precisely to impact the human race, the original agents, in the fulfillment of their original calling.

God first promises to protect Abraham and to bless him with a large family—indeed a nation—and with its own land (Gen. 12:1–3). The parallel with the original human purpose, to fill the earth, suggests that this new human family will be a small-scale version (a microcosm) of the flourishing that God intended for all humanity. Yet the flourishing of Abraham's family is not the ultimate purpose for which he has been called. In five texts in Genesis (starting with 12:3), God tells Abraham, Isaac, and Jacob that the long-term purpose of their election (including that of their descendants) is that through them all the nations or families of the earth will find blessing.[10] Although there is

---

9. Originally named "Abram," his name is changed to "Abraham" in Gen. 17:5.
10. This ultimate purpose is stated in connection with Abraham (Gen. 12:1–3; 18:17–18; 22:17–18), Isaac (Gen. 26:4–5), and Jacob (Gen. 28:14).

some debate about the exact meaning of this blessing, it points to a broader purpose for Abraham's family beyond their own flourishing (although their flourishing certainly is included). This purpose of mediating blessing to the human race suggests that this new family will function as God's priests in the world (which becomes explicit in Exod. 19:3–6).

The task entrusted to Abraham and his descendants is, narratively speaking, to aid in reconciling humanity to God and thus restoring humanity to its original purpose, by helping to remove or overcome the impediment of sin/violence.[11] A famous Jewish midrash on Genesis 2:7 gets it exactly right. According to *Genesis Rabbah* 14.6, God thought, "I will create Adam first, so that if he sins, Abraham may come and set things right."[12]

There is thus a significant parallel between the human calling to image God, mediating the creator's presence on earth, and the redemptive calling of Abraham/Israel to bring blessing to the nations. Both involve the responsible exercise of agency, and both are missional. Human power or agency was originally to be used for cultural development of our earthly environment (plot level 1); in a postfall world, it is also to be used redemptively, for addressing the problem of human evil and brokenness (plot levels 2 and 3).

Plot Level 3: Moses to Jesus

But a new impediment arises to block God's purposes for the covenant people. Because of a famine, Israel is forced to leave the land of promise, and they settle in Egypt through the influence of Joseph (Abraham's great-grandson), who has risen high in Pharaoh's court. However, a later Egyptian king "who did not know Joseph" is threatened by Israel's fruitfulness (they are indeed being blessed by God), with the result that Abraham's descendants end up in bondage to the Egyptian Empire (Exod. 1:8–14). Although they are increasing in number, they are not in their own land, and the situation of bondage impedes both their own flourishing and their ability to bring blessing to the nations.

---

11. Although how this is to be done is not explicitly stated at Abraham's call, Gen. 18:19 suggests that Abraham is to "charge his children and his household after him to keep the way of the Lord by doing righteousness and justice," which would enable God's promises to Abraham to be fulfilled.

12. Translation from H. Freedman and Maurice Simon, eds., *Midrash Rabbah: Genesis* (10 vols.; London: Soncino, 1939), 1:114. This quotation is meant to answer the question of why God did not start with Abraham, given his preeminent stature in Judaism (indeed, the text says that he was worthy of being created before Adam). For a more recent though somewhat clumsy translation, see Jacob Neusner, *Genesis Rabbah: The Judaic Commentary to the Book of Genesis—A New American Translation*, vol. 1, *Parashiyyot One through Thirty-Three on Genesis 1:1–8:14* (Brown Judaic Studies 104; Atlanta: Scholars Press, 1985), 154.

MOSES

God then calls a new narrative agent to help the covenant people. This agent is Moses, whose call is narrated in Exodus 3:1–4:18 (and 6:1–13), and whose story (a sub-subplot of the biblical macronarrative) takes up four books of the Pentateuch (Exodus through Deuteronomy).[13] This begins level 3 in the plot structure of the Bible.

Initially, Moses is called to deliver Israel from Egyptian bondage, but that is only the beginning of his complex narrative task. Following on this deliverance (Exod. 1–18), Moses is to mediate the Torah (Exod. 19–24; Leviticus; Num. 1–10; Deuteronomy) as instruction for Israel's communal life, since the people need to be conformed to God's righteous and holy standards for living.[14] Through the work of Moses (including his intercession on their behalf when they break the second commandment [Exod. 32–34]), God's presence will dwell among the people via the tabernacle (Exod. 25–31; 35–40); and Moses's task concludes with his guidance of the newly liberated people back to the land initially promised to Abraham (they set out on the return journey in Num. 10:11–13). Moses is thus the primary agent, narratively speaking, who enables God's promises to Abraham to be fulfilled—promises centering on peoplehood and land, but including also communal righteousness and access to God's presence. Together these are necessary components of Israel's flourishing, without which they could not contribute to God's larger purpose of bringing blessing to the nations.

Given the shape of the unfolding Old Testament narrative, the enslavement of Israel in Egypt and their comprehensive deliverance through the mediation/agency of Moses (level 3) must therefore be understood at two overlapping levels: God's intent for Israel (level 2) and God's intent for the world (level 1). On the one hand, Egyptian bondage is an impediment to God's desire for the flourishing of the covenant people (level 2), and the exodus is the beginning of the process in which God will restore Israel to the blessing promised to the ancestors. On the other hand, Israel's bondage is an impediment not only to their own flourishing but also to God's purposes for the flourishing of all humanity (level 1), and Israel's deliverance is in the service of this larger purpose.

It thus makes sense that we find a rearticulation of the Abrahamic calling applied to the entire nation in Exodus 19, right after the exodus, when the

---

13. That it is a sub-subplot is clear from the chart in figure 3.2.
14. Bondage could be thought of as resulting in a deformation of the people, so Torah has a significant reformational purpose: to reshape this people into the sort of community that God desires.

people have arrived at Mount Sinai. Between the deliverance from Egypt and the covenant that God enters into with the newly freed people, we find this crucial statement delivered by YHWH through Moses:

> You have seen what I did to the Egyptians, and how I bore you on eagles' wings and brought you to myself. Now therefore, if you obey my voice and keep my covenant, you shall be my treasured possession out of all the peoples. Indeed, the whole earth is mine, but you shall be for me a priestly kingdom and a holy nation. (Exod. 19:4–6)

That Israel is to be God's "priestly kingdom" among the nations is another way of describing the election of Abraham's family to mediate blessing to the world.[15]

As an agent sent to help Israel, Moses is fundamentally successful in his task/mission. Although he himself is not allowed to enter the promised land (due to his disobedience), by the end of the book of Joshua we find the tribes of Israel settling in Canaan, each with its own allotted portion of the land. In terms of the plot, we would expect that Israel would now get on with the task of bringing blessing to the nations.[16]

JUDGES, KINGS, AND PROPHETS

But new impediments arise that hinder the fulfillment of this task. The beginning of the book of Judges portrays cycles of oppression and deliverance,

15. My reading of Exod. 19:6 as missional or vocational depends on interpreting God's pronouncement in the context of the unfolding plot. By itself, this text is cryptic enough to be read in multiple ways if framed by different understandings of the biblical story. Thus the notion of Israel as a priestly kingdom has been taken as a claim that Israel simply is the realm/kingdom over which God rules, or as an assertion of a governing/royal priesthood within the nation, or as a reference to Israel's privileged status as the only nation allowed to serve God with access to the heavenly temple. On the latter interpretation, see John A. Davies, *A Royal Priesthood: Literary and Intertextual Perspectives on an Image of Israel in Exodus 9:6* (Library of Hebrew Bible/Old Testament Studies 395; London: T&T Clark, 2004).

16. The conquest of Canaan, including the *ḥerem*, or "ban," by which Israel is to eradicate all the nations inhabiting the land of promise, is in significant tension with the overall plot of the biblical story, which assumes God's purposes for blessing to the nations. However we interpret the conquest of Canaan, it is clear that this episode cannot be taken as ethically normative for God's people, given the overall thrust of the biblical macronarrative. For a discussion of Christian interpretations of the conquest of Canaan, see C. S. Cowles et al., *Show Them No Mercy: Four Views on God and Canaanite Genocide* (Counterpoints; Grand Rapids: Zondervan, 2003). One of the best is Gordon H. Matties's commentary on *Joshua* (Believers Church Bible Commentary; Harrisonburg, VA: Herald Press, 2012), which grapples with the conquest from a Mennonite/pacifist perspective. For Matties's initial reflections on Joshua, see his "Reading Rahab's Story: Beyond the Moral of the Story (Joshua 2)," *Direction* 24 (1995): 57–70, http://www.directionjournal.org/article/?872.

as the Israelites fall into idolatry and moral corruption, are attacked by their Canaanite neighbors, cry out to God for help, and are delivered from their enemies by various military leaders called "judges" (Judg. 2:16). They then enjoy a temporary period of peace, only to fall back into idolatry and moral corruption. Then the cycle begins again. It is significant that in these cycles in the book of Judges the people do not typically cry out for forgiveness or deliverance from their sin.[17] That is, though the impediments to the people's flourishing are both internal (their own sin) and external (the oppression by enemy nations), they seek redress only for the external problem.

Nevertheless, God responds to their cries for help. A prime example is God's call of Gideon (Judg. 6:11–23) to deliver Israel from oppression by their enemies. And although God raises up other judges too, over and over again, all these plot resolutions are temporary. Indeed, the institution of judge degenerates in the person of Samson, whose larger-than-life story is told in great detail (Judg. 13–16). Samson is in some ways the anti-judge, the opposite of what a leader should be; he certainly provides no moral example for Israel, although in death he destroys many Philistines.

After Samson, the book of Judges portrays the nation devolving into bloody intertribal violence (chaps. 17–21), when everyone did what was right in their own eyes (17:6; 21:25). In sum, life has again regressed to the preflood situation, when violence filled the earth. The text, however, teases the reader with the repeated comment that "in those days there was no king in Israel" (18:1; 19:1; 21:25). Does this mean that a king would solve their problems?

When the people ask Samuel (the last judge, who is also a priest and prophet) for a king "like the other nations" (1 Sam. 8:4–5, 20), this request is prefaced by their dissatisfaction with the moral leadership of Samuel's sons. Yet the people's stated intent that the king would "govern" (literally, "judge") them (1 Sam. 8:5, 6, 20) and "go out before us and fight our battles" (8:20) suggests a continuity with the book of Judges and a role for the monarchy that is limited to (or focused on) the external problem of enemy attack. This is supported by 1 Samuel 9:15–16, where God interprets his choice of Saul as a response to the people's need for a military deliverer. Although Samuel initially resists the people's request for a king (1 Sam. 8:6), this request is granted through God's concession (8:7, 22a), accompanied by Samuel's stern warning about the oppressive dangers of the institution of monarchy (8:9–18).

17. The only time in the entire book that Israel admits to sin in their cries of distress comes in Judg. 10:10 (repeated in 10:15). YHWH, however, doesn't believe they are sincere and so refuses to rescue them (10:11–14), though he later does out of mercy (10:16).

After Saul, Israel's first king, is replaced by David,[18] the new king turns out to be an adulterer and murderer (2 Sam. 11–12), whose ineptitude in parenting his own family results in rape (of sister by brother), revenge killing (of brother by brother), and an attempted coup (of son against father).[19] Under the next king, Solomon, who takes the throne by political machinations rather than by God's design (1 Kings 1–2), we have the institution of corvée (forced labor) in Israel (1 Kings 5:13–18)[20] and the king's explicit idolatry (11:3–8), followed by exorbitant taxation by his son Rehoboam (12:1–20), resulting in civil war and the fracturing of the kingdom into north (Israel/Ephraim) and south (Judah).[21]

As the sordid history of the southern kingdom shows, the kings of the Davidic dynasty (with a few exceptions) do not match the ideal of the righteous ruler envisioned in Psalm 72, nor do they study and obey the Torah, which Deuteronomy 17:18–20 says is the prime responsibility of the Israelite king. Needless to say, these Davidic kings do not restore the nation to its priestly vocation. And what shall we say of the multiple dynasties of the northern kingdom, which follow one upon the heel of the other as successive kings are assassinated in a series of political coups?[22]

In the midst of a complex narrative of mostly failed kings (1 Sam. 9–2 Kings 25:30), who typically abuse their power and manifestly fail to help in restoring Israel to its mission of bringing blessing to the world, God begins sending prophets, initially to challenge the corruption of the kings (much as Moses was sent to Pharaoh); thus we have the prominent narratives of Elijah and Elisha (1 Kings 17:1–2 Kings 8:15) as the literary centerpiece of 1–2 Kings, signifying that the institution of prophet begins to overshadow that of the king in Israel's story. But the kings ignore the prophets, who then more and more address the people directly with a message calling for repentance. Nevertheless, the people also (with few exceptions) ignore the prophetic message to return

18. For an analysis of the factors that led to the rejection of Saul, see J. Richard Middleton, "Samuel *Agonistes*: A Conflicted Prophet's Resistance to God and Contribution to the Failure of Israel's First King," in *Prophets, Prophecy, and Ancient Israelite Historiography*, ed. Mark J. Boda and Lissa M. Wray Beal (Winona Lake, IN: Eisenbrauns, 2013), 69–91.

19. The fact that God establishes an unconditional covenant with David (2 Sam. 7) means that God does not necessarily approve of David's life but chooses to work through David and his descendants (despite their flaws) for the salvation of Israel.

20. It may be that Solomon did not institute the corvée but simply continued what his father David had started (see 2 Sam. 20:24; 1 Kings 5:14).

21. For a fascinating study of the moral and religious ambiguity of Solomon's life, see J. Daniel Hays, "Has the Narrator Come to Praise Solomon or to Bury Him? Narrative Subtlety in 1 Kings 1–11," *Journal for the Study of the Old Testament* 28 (2003): 149–74.

22. There are nine dynasties in the northern kingdom spanning two hundred years, most of which end after one or two kings. The exceptions are the dynasty of Omri (four kings over about forty-five years) and the dynasty of Jehu (five kings over about ninety years).

to YHWH, resulting in the Assyrian destruction of the northern kingdom in the eighth century and then the Babylonian invasion of Judah in the sixth century, followed by exile. And so the story seems to have hit a dead end once again. Even after the return from Babylonian exile, Israel is still mired in its own moral corruption and the continuing oppression of foreign nations (with only a brief respite after the Maccabean revolt). Together, these internal and external problems constitute what seems like an insurmountable impediment to God's purposes for the flourishing of the covenant people (level 2 of the plot) and therefore also for humanity and the created order (level 1 of the plot).

JESUS

In the midst of this dire situation of brokenness, after a long and complex history of redemption, God's saving action culminates in the coming of Jesus the Messiah/Christ, who is described in the New Testament as God's Son (Matt. 16:15–16), the incarnate Word (John 1:14), the paradigm *imago Dei* (2 Cor. 4:4–6; Col. 1:15; Heb. 1:3)—the one who completely manifested God's character and presence in the full range of his earthly, human life (John 1:18; 14:9). As the second Adam, Jesus fulfilled, through his obedience (even unto death [Phil. 2:6–8]), what the first Adam compromised by disobedience (Rom. 5:12–19). Through the life, teaching, death, and resurrection of Jesus, God has done battle with, and vanquished, the powers of evil and death that have held humanity and the world in bondage, thus bringing atonement for sin, deliverance from its multifaceted power, and the restoration of our relationships with God, one another, and the created order. Jesus is thus the ultimate helper, the one sent from God to accomplish the comprehensive healing of humanity and the entire creation.

However, it is important to note that in terms of the plot structure of the Bible, Jesus came initially not to save the world from sin, but rather to restore Israel to righteousness and blessing. This is not just an irrelevant technicality of history; it is crucial for our understanding of the role of Jesus as the turning point in the macronarrative of Scripture. As the Bible understands it, God sent Jesus as a helper or agent to restore Israel to its purpose and task, and through Israel ultimately to impact the human race. Indeed, Jesus fulfilled the Abrahamic task of bringing blessing—first to his own people, as Peter makes clear in an early sermon in Acts.

You are the descendants of the prophets and of the covenant that God gave to your ancestors, saying to Abraham, "And in your descendants all the families of the earth shall be blessed." When God raised up his servant, he sent him first to you, to bless you by turning each of you from your wicked ways. (Acts 3:25–26)

So before Jesus is the savior of the world, he is the savior of Israel, restoring them to their status and role as God's elect people.

This is confirmed by looking at Jesus's actual ministry and message in the Gospels. Although the cross and resurrection form the central turning point in the biblical story, Jesus first taught in Galilee and Judea for three years, gathering a community of the faithful—a community constituted initially by members of his own Israelite people. Thus we have Jesus's comment to a Canaanite woman that his mission is to the "lost sheep of the house of Israel" (Matt. 15:24). But he makes a similar comment in one other important place, toward the beginning of his public ministry (Matt. 10:6). After seeing the readiness of the fields for harvest and the scarcity of workers (Matt. 9:37), he commissions the twelve disciples (symbolizing the core of a restored Jewish remnant of the twelve tribes) to aid him in his mission to Israel (Matt. 10:1–16). In this first mention of disciples as apostles (Matt. 10:2)—that is, as "sent ones"—Jesus explicitly enjoins them,

> Go nowhere among the Gentiles, and enter no town of the Samaritans, but go rather to *the lost sheep of the house of Israel*. As you go, proclaim the good news, "The kingdom of heaven has come near." Cure the sick, raise the dead, cleanse the lepers, cast out demons. (Matt. 10:5–8a)

The disciples/apostles are called to continue Jesus's own ministry (Matt. 9:35) of proclaiming the kingdom and embodying this kingdom in acts of restoration, initially among the covenant people, until the twelve have grown into a much larger group of disciples following Jesus.

Plot Level 2: The Gentile Mission

Of course, by the end of the Gospel of Matthew, after Jesus's death and resurrection and when a sufficiently large body of Jewish disciples has been gathered, we find the so-called Great Commission. At that point, the risen Jesus commissions the eleven remaining apostles (representing the larger group of Jesus followers) to go to the gentiles with the message of the gospel:

> All authority in heaven and on earth has been given to me. Go therefore and make disciples of all nations, baptizing them in the name of the Father and of the Son and of the Holy Spirit, and teaching them to obey everything that I have commanded you. And remember, I am with you always, to the end of the age. (Matt. 28:18–20)

In the context of the overall biblical story, the Great Commission is best understood as a rearticulation of the Abrahamic calling, the vocation of the people of God to mediate blessing to all the nations of the world. In the New Testament, this vocation is understood as including the proclamation of the gospel, communicating the teachings of Jesus about the nature of the kingdom, and especially what God has done in the life, death, and resurrection of the Messiah. The result of this proclamation/teaching is that the band of originally Jewish disciples becomes greatly expanded as gentiles are added to their number.

The story of the gentile mission (level 2 of the story) then takes up much of the book of Acts and is the background to the Pauline and General Epistles, as various churches throughout Asia Minor are addressed with implications of Christian discipleship.

Plot Level 1: The Human Calling Restored

Indeed, the gentile mission is so successful that the New Testament portrays the risen Jesus as the head of the church (Col. 1:18), a multiethnic community of Jew and gentile reconciled to each other and to God and indwelt by God's Spirit (Eph. 2:11–22). Whereas the disciples may be understood as the restored remnant of Israel, the "olive tree" into which gentile believers are grafted (Rom. 11:17–24), the church has become the "new humanity" (Eph. 2:15 [a much better translation of *kainon anthrōpon* than "new self"]), which is being renewed in the image of God (Eph. 4:22–24; see also Col. 3:9–10; 2 Cor. 3:18).[23] Thus the church is called to live up to the stature of Christ, whose perfect imaging becomes the model for the life of the redeemed (Phil. 2:5–11; Eph. 4:13).[24] Indeed, the church will one day be conformed to the full likeness of Christ (1 John 3:2), which will include the resurrection of the body (1 Cor. 15:49) and reigning with Christ on earth (2 Tim. 2:12; Rev. 22:5)—that is, the restoration of their full humanity.

It may be helpful to conclude this sketch of the biblical plot by comparing two New Testament texts that describe the calling of the people of God. Both texts are clearly dependent on the articulation of Israel's calling at Mount Sinai (Exod. 19:5–6), and they illustrate how the biblical plot structure moves from level 3 back to level 2 and then back to level 1 again.

The first New Testament text, which comes after the successful plot resolution effected by Jesus (level 3), uses language taken from the Exodus 19 description of

23. It is interesting that *kainon anthrōpon* in Eph. 2:15 is typically translated as "new humanity" or "new man" or "new people," yet later in Eph. 4:24 it tends to be rendered "new self." Both Eph. 4:22–24 and Col. 3:9–10 contrast the old humanity (*palaion anthrōpon* [Eph. 4:22; Col. 3:9]) with the new humanity (though with different words for "new": *kainon* in Eph. 4:24, *neon* in Col. 3:10).

24. See also Eph. 4:7–16, 22–24; 5:1; Col. 3:5–17.

God's election of Israel to articulate the mission of the church, now composed of both Jews and gentiles (due to the continuing success of the gentile mission).

> But you are a chosen race, a royal priesthood, a holy nation, God's own people, in order that you may proclaim the mighty acts of him who called you out of darkness into his marvelous light. (1 Pet. 2:9)

Although the language is different from that found in the Great Commission (Matt. 28:18–20), the task here is fundamentally the same. The priestly vocation of God's redeemed people is to mediate blessing to the world by proclaiming the story of God's redemptive acts, a story of which they have themselves become a part. The church's mission is thus a continuation of the Abrahamic calling. We are back to level 2 in the plot structure.

However, we find a very different use of this Exodus 19 language in Revelation 5. There, in John's eschatological vision of worshipers around God's heavenly throne, we discover a group of heavenly creatures singing praise to the Lamb, who was slain and who is "standing" in resurrection victory (Rev. 5:6). The gentile mission that was inaugurated with the call of Abraham/Israel is here portrayed as complete; the nations have received the blessing of salvation. Therefore, the worshipers sing to the Lamb,

> You are worthy to take the scroll and to open its seals, for you were slaughtered and by your blood you ransomed for God saints from every tribe and language and people and nation; you have made them to be a kingdom and priests serving our God, and they will reign on earth. (Rev. 5:9–10)

Notice the shift from proclaiming the gospel (level 2) to ruling the earth (level 1) as the content of what it means to be God's royal priesthood.

The point is that once the subplot of the sending of Israel has been successful and the nations have received the blessing of salvation, the redeemed human race will once again utilize their God-given power and agency to rule the earth as God intended—a renewal of the human cultural task, but this time without sin. The initial narrative sequence of the biblical story will finally be fulfilled.[25] Far from being the end or cessation of history, this is history's true beginning, free from the constraints of human violation vis-à-vis God or other humans or the earth itself. The climax of the biblical story, which many have called the "eternal state," is fundamentally this-worldly. When God brings his original purposes to fruition, we find not escape from creation, but rather new (or renewed) creation.

---

25. Little Red Riding Hood and her grandmother finally have their picnic.

The Bible thus tells one comprehensive and ultimately coherent story of God's purposes for the flourishing of earthly life. Although the world has been in the grip of terrible evil, which has blocked God's purposes from coming to fruition, God has been at work throughout history—through a series of redemptive agents and ultimately through Jesus—to overcome all that impedes his purposes from being fulfilled.

The Already and the Not Yet

Unlike the plot of a discrete stand-alone story like Little Red Riding Hood, where the initial narrative sequence (level 1) is not accomplished until the very end of the story, the Bible envisions the beginning of the end in the midst of the story (this is what theologians call "inaugurated eschatology"). We do not have to wait for the final denouement before we begin living out the initial (or ultimate) narrative sequence. This is because in the biblical macrostory the agent bringing blessing (plot resolution) at level 2 (Israel/the church) is not fundamentally different from the original agent exercising cultural power on earth at level 1 (the human race). Unlike the woodsman in the fairy tale, who is simply a different agent from Little Red Riding Hood, God's redeemed people are elect from (and thus members of) the original agent in the biblical story (humanity), and their original cultural task is not held in abeyance until redemption is fully accomplished. Another way of putting it is that God's elect cannot be expected to delay being human until the eschaton. Besides their interim mission to mediate blessing to the nations, the people of God are also meant to be a paradigm example of restored humanity in the nitty-gritty of current history.

The Role of Heaven in the Biblical Plot

Note, however, that the difference between redeemed living in the present and in the eschatological future that God has in store has nothing to do with living on earth versus living in heaven (as it is often portrayed in popular Christian piety). When we attend to the basic thrust and movement of the biblical plot, it becomes abundantly clear that eschatological redemption consists in nothing other than the renewal of human cultural life on earth. The important point here is that the idea of "heaven" as the eternal hope of the righteous has no structural place in the story. It is simply irrelevant and extraneous to the plot. Heaven was never part of God's purposes for humanity in the beginning of the story and has no intrinsic role as the final destiny of human salvation.

Indeed, there is not one single reference in the entire biblical canon (Old and New Testaments) to heaven as the eternal destiny of the believer. Although this idea has a vastly important role in popular Christian imagination (and even in some theologies), not once does Scripture itself actually say that the righteous will live forever in heaven.

My point here is not to deny the reality of heaven. There is, indeed, an important role for heaven in the biblical worldview. In Scripture the term "heaven" (or the "heavens") represents, first of all, part of the created universe: "In the beginning God created the heavens and the earth" (Gen. 1:1).[26] In this context "heaven" certainly refers to that aspect of creation understood to be more transcendent (the realm beyond ordinary human access). This is why Scripture portrays heaven as the throne of God (with earth as God's footstool [Isa. 66:1–2])—an image, paradoxically, not only of God's transcendence but also of God's immanence, since the creator has chosen to dwell within the created order.[27] Yet transcendence is certainly implied, as when Psalm 115:16 asserts, "The heavens are the LORD's heavens, / but the earth he has given to human beings."

Since this transcendent part of the created order is pictured as the location of God's throne room and the source of his reign over the cosmos, heaven is also viewed as the realm, in contradistinction to earth, where God's will is perfectly accomplished prior to the eschaton.[28] This is the assumption behind the prayer that Jesus taught his disciples: "Your kingdom come. Your will be done, on earth as it is in heaven" (Matt. 6:10). It is the biblical eschatological hope that one day God's salvation (which is being prepared in heaven) will be manifest fully on earth. This is why the meek will "inherit the earth" (Matt. 5:5).

26. The word for "heaven" or "sky" in Hebrew (*šāmayim*) is always plural (technically, dual), thus "heavens." The New Testament uses both singular (*ouranos*) and plural (*ouranoi*), the latter occurring especially in Matthew's Gospel. For a discussion of the differences between the singular and plural in Matthew, see Jonathan T. Pennington, *Heaven and Earth in the Gospel of Matthew* (Supplements to Novum Testamentum 126; Leiden: Brill, 2007; reprint, Grand Rapids: Baker Academic, 2009), chap. 6.

27. Terence Fretheim has convincingly argued that because in the biblical worldview heaven is part of the created order, the location of God's throne in heaven is actually an image of the immanence of God within creation (*The Suffering of God: An Old Testament Perspective* [Overtures to Biblical Theology 14; Philadelphia: Fortress, 1984], 37; *God and World in the Old Testament: A Relational Theology of Creation* [Nashville: Abingdon, 2005], 26).

28. It should be acknowledged that this picture is complicated by other biblical texts that depict rebellion in the heavenly realm (as will be discussed in chaps. 6 and 9 of this book). For the motif of the ambiguity of "heaven" in the Bible, see Calvin R. Schoonhoven, *The Wrath of Heaven* (Grand Rapids: Eerdmans, 1966).

While it is therefore biblical to expect that at Christ's return earth will be fully conformed to heaven, the term "heaven" simply does not describe the Christian eschatological hope. Not only is "heaven" never used in Scripture for the eternal destiny of the redeemed, but continued use of "heaven" to name the Christian hope may well divert our attention from the legitimate biblical expectation for the transformation of our earthly life so that it conforms to God's purposes—a transformation that has already begun in Christ and that the church is called to live out in the present world.

By permission of John L. Hart FLP and Creators Syndicate, Inc.

Part 2

Holistic Salvation in the Old Testament

4

The Exodus as Paradigm of Salvation

As a teenager, I was given an easy-to-read New Testament in modern English (the Weymouth translation), which I read from cover to cover and brought to many Bible studies.[1] This New Testament proved very useful in introducing me to the basic teachings of Jesus, the nature of the atonement, and the contours of what Christian discipleship requires. At that time I had read hardly any of the Old Testament, having been put off by the "thee" and "thou" language of the King James Version; truth be told, I did not even own a copy of a full Bible.

Then I began my undergraduate education and took a seven-semester sequence of courses that covered both Old and New Testaments.[2] During this time I came to the realization that it was impossible to gain a genuine understanding of the New Testament without a solid grounding in the Old.

This does not mean that someone who reads the New Testament without the Old cannot understand anything worthwhile. I had come to a basic understanding of the Christian faith from my Weymouth New Testament,

1. Richard Francis Weymouth, *The New Testament in Modern Speech*, rev. James Alexander Robertson (5th ed.; London: James Clarke, 1934). Weymouth's translation was first published in 1903, based on his own eclectic Greek text, known as *The Resultant Greek Testament*; the fifth edition (revised by Robertson) was originally published in 1929.

2. I thank my professors at the Jamaica Theological Seminary for this rigorous, in-depth introduction to the Bible.

77

in tandem with church attendance and regular participation in Bible studies. But I soon found out how much I was missing. I am not talking about being able to pinpoint obscure "messianic" prophecies about Jesus or reading Jesus typologically into all sorts of Old Testament passages. That sort of artificial proof-texting never appealed to me.

Rather, what I came to realize is that we are prone to miss the amazing scope of God's redemption, and especially its full-bodied, this-worldly character, if we do not read the New Testament with the worldview of the Old Testament as our basis and guide. And I found that the more I understood the Old Testament (which was the Scripture for Jesus and the early church), the more depth and complexity I saw in the New Testament, and the more meaningful it became.

It was because I realized how much I had been missing, even misreading, in the New Testament that I decided to do formal graduate studies in Old Testament, which turned out to be a wise vocational path. Today the Old Testament is my primary area of research, and it grounds my teaching of the New Testament, both in academic settings and in the church.

Salvation as Earthly Flourishing in the Old Testament

The preceding two chapters of this book contained a healthy dose of the Old Testament. Chapter 2 addressed God's intent for human flourishing, grounded in creation, and how that intent has been thwarted by sin. Chapter 3 followed this with an overview of the plot structure of the entire biblical story of redemption, culminating in the vision of a redeemed people living on a renewed earth.

We are now in a position to look more closely at how the Old Testament affirms this overall biblical vision through its portrayal of earthly flourishing as the very purpose of salvation. To that end, the present chapter focuses on the story of the exodus, especially its function as a model or paradigm for salvation in the rest of the Old Testament (and in the New Testament too). The following chapter will address the goal of earthly flourishing in Old Testament law and wisdom, and the prophetic expectation for this-worldly restoration.[3] This examination of a sampling of Old Testament materials (and here I emphasize it will only be a sampling) will reinforce the overall biblical vision of salvation as holistic—affecting persons, the social order, and the natural world itself.

---

3. These two chapters draw on research for an article that I coauthored with Michael J. Gorman titled "Salvation," in the *New Interpreter's Dictionary of the Bible*, ed. Katharine Doob Sakenfeld (Nashville: Abingdon, 2009), 5:45–61.

But what do we mean by "salvation"? Some clarity here will be important.[4] For many contemporary Christians, "salvation" either refers to going to heaven when you die, which is simply not what the Bible means by this term, or is a synonym for what theological tradition has called "justification," being made right with God through the forgiveness of sins. This latter use of "salvation" is not wrong, but it leaves out a great deal. It focuses on the beginning of a right relationship with God through deliverance from the penalty of sin (anticipating that we will stand with confidence before God in the final judgment). Although this certainly is an important part of salvation, it is limited by both its individual focus and its fixation on the notion of deliverance. Salvation is much wider than that; it cannot be limited to forgiveness of sins or escaping judgment. In the Bible, salvation is a comprehensive reality, both future and present, and affects every aspect of existence.

The most fundamental meaning of salvation in Scripture is twofold: it is God's *deliverance* of those in a situation of need from that which impedes their well-being, resulting in their *restoration* to wholeness. Wholeness or well-being is God's original intent for creation, and that which impedes wholeness—sin, evil, and death in all their forms—is fundamentally anti-creational. Both the deliverance of the needy and their full restoration to well-being (in relationship with God, others, and the world) are crucial to salvation, and the term may be used for either or for both together.

The Exodus Pattern

We could search the Old Testament for various Hebrew nouns for "salvation" and Hebrew verbs that mean "to save," but this would not be particularly helpful. The meaning of salvation simply cannot be contained in such limited lexical use. Beneath the Old Testament's use of explicit salvation language lies a coherent worldview in which the exodus from Egyptian bondage, followed by entry into the promised land, forms the most important paradigm or model.

In the Old Testament the exodus is God's central saving act, which generates the very existence of Israel as a people; this saving act centers on God's rescue of Israel from Egyptian bondage (including both the plagues on Egypt and the Red Sea crossing) and culminates with their safe arrival in the land of promise. While verbs for "save," "deliver," and "redeem" are indeed used to describe God's action in freeing the Israelites from bondage (Exod. 3:8; 6:6;

---

4. For a helpful survey of ways of understanding salvation, see Terence E. Fretheim, "Salvation in the Bible vs. Salvation in the Church," *Word and World* 13 (1993): 363–72.

14:30; 15:13), with the result that YHWH becomes Israel's "salvation" (Exod. 15:2), it is the entire exodus story that functions paradigmatically. The complex of events of the exodus was so central in Israel's experience and memory that it decisively shaped much of the Old Testament, becoming the lens through which salvation is understood.

The first thing we should notice about the exodus is that it constitutes the sociopolitical deliverance of a historical community from a real, concrete situation of oppression. The exodus thus resists any "spiritualizing" of salvation, keeping it firmly rooted in life in this world. But beyond its concrete sociopolitical character, there are specific components of the exodus pattern that are paradigmatic for salvation throughout the entire Old Testament (and in the New Testament too).

Impediment to Flourishing and Well-Being

The exodus pattern begins, logically enough, with the need for salvation: a problem arises that impedes God's purposes for life and blessing. At the start of the book of Exodus, we find Israel initially fulfilling the creational mandate to multiply and fill the earth (1:7; cf. Gen. 1:28). Pharaoh, however, is intent on impeding God's purposes for the flourishing of Israel by enslaving and oppressing them (Exod. 1:10–11). When the Israelites nevertheless continue to multiply (1:12), the Egyptians increase the oppression (1:13–14), and Pharaoh tries to have newly born Israelite males murdered (1:16, 22), thus impeding God's desire for Israel's well-being (1:20).

But prior to the exodus it becomes clear that humanity (and even the earth) has been corrupted by sin and its consequences; death in all its manifestations has invaded and corrupted life. This constitutes a massive impediment to God's purposes for creational flourishing and requires an intervention if the fullness of life is to be restored. In every case the need for salvation results from some impediment that blocks God's purposes for blessing and well-being.

Cry for Help from Those in Need

The next factor in the exodus pattern is the cry for help from those in need. Thus the Israelites "groan" in their bondage and cry out to God. The book of Exodus twice recounts this cry for help in the narrative (2:23, 24), and it is twice mentioned in God's explanation to Moses of why he has come to intervene (3:7–10; 6:5–6). It is because of the centrality of this cry that Walter

Brueggemann poignantly describes the exodus as "the primal scream that permits the beginning of [redemptive] history."[5]

Later, we find Israel's cry of distress from the exodus repeated in the period of the judges, as the fledgling nation is oppressed by various enemies. The people's groaning (which echoes the exodus cry) is explicitly mentioned as what motivates God to intervene (Judg. 2:18). So paradigmatic is this exodus cry for help that Israel's most typical form of prayer is modeled on it. The most common genre of psalm in the Old Testament is the lament or complaint (basically a form of petition or supplication), in which the psalmist protests a concrete problem and appeals to God for help (classic lament prayers include Pss. 22; 39; 88).[6] Jesus himself tells two parables to teach his disciples about prayer (the friend at midnight in Luke 11:5–13; the importunate widow in Luke 18:1–8), each of which seems to be modeled on the lament psalms. Both parables highlight a person taking a need directly to God with persistent, even abrasive, determination. And in a profound appeal to the exodus story, Paul portrays the entire created order as groaning in its bondage to futility while awaiting God's final redemption (Rom. 8:19–23).

YHWH Comes from His Heavenly Throne into the Concrete, Historical Situation of Need

According to the exodus pattern, God responds to the cry of those in need. We are told that Israel's cry "rose up to God" (Exod. 2:23), and God tells Moses, "I have come down to deliver them from the Egyptians" (3:8). The vertical language ("up" and "down") reflects the background picture (found in many Old Testament texts) of God's throne in heaven (see Pss. 2:4; 11:4; 104:1–3; Isa. 40:22; 63:15; 66:1–2; Amos 9:6), from which God rules creation (heaven and earth) and from which God comes into human historical experience to remove all that impedes flourishing.

This background picture makes an important theological claim about God's transcendence. Precisely because YHWH rules from heaven, outside

5. Walter Brueggemann, *The Prophetic Imagination* (2nd ed.; Minneapolis: Fortress, 2001), 11. I have intentionally inserted the word "redemptive" in the quotation. Since in the biblical narrative it is creation that actually permits the beginning of history, it would be more accurate to say that the exodus restarts redemptive history, after the impediment of Egyptian bondage. For my dispute with Brueggemann on the function of creation in the Bible, see J. Richard Middleton, "Is Creation Theology Inherently Conservative? A Dialogue with Walter Brueggemann," *Harvard Theological Review* 87 (1994): 257–77; in the same issue is Brueggemann's "Response to J. Richard Middleton," 279–89.

6. For a comprehensive list of laments in the Psalter, see appendix B in Berhnard W. Anderson with Steven Bishop, *Out of the Depths: The Psalms Speak for Us Today* (3rd ed.; Louisville: Westminster John Knox, 2000).

the oppressive system of human evil (including Egyptian bondage), this God can be appealed to in a situation of injustice and can realistically be expected to care about human suffering (whereas appeals to Pharaoh, who is implicated in the oppressive system, are ineffectual [see Exod. 5:15–16]).[7] Further, as ruler and creator of all, God actually has the power to transform this situation of oppression. In the Bible, therefore, God's transcendence is not in contrast to God's involvement (or immanence), as it sometimes is in our theological systems; rather, God's transcendence is precisely the condition of his involvement.[8]

This pattern of God's action in response to human need is found in the cycles of oppression and salvation in the book of Judges as God sends a series of deliverers to rescue Israel. In the New Testament, many of Jesus's healings and exorcisms are in direct response to someone's articulated need. A classic example is the story of the blind man who hears that Jesus is passing by and begins crying out for help: "Jesus, Son of David, have mercy on me!" When bystanders try to quiet him, he cries out more insistently. When Jesus asks the blind man what he wants, he asks to be healed. Jesus immediately responds, removing the impediment of blindness and restoring his sight (Mark 10:46–52; Luke 18:35–43).[9]

The basic principle at work here is summarized in an Old Testament prophetic text addressing a time of national distress; according to Joel 2:32, "Everyone who calls on the name of the LORD shall be saved." This prophetic affirmation is then applied to the salvation found in Jesus, both in Peter's sermon on the day of Pentecost (Acts 2:21) and by Paul (Rom. 10:13). Thus, in both Testaments, God responds with salvation to those who cry out for help in their time of need.

The Divine King Fights for Those in Need, Removing the Impediment to Flourishing

The Song of the Sea celebrates YHWH as a warrior (Exod. 15:3), while the narrative of the sea crossing portrays YHWH as fighting on behalf of his

---

7. Brueggemann (*Prophetic Imagination*, 23, 25, 29, 32), drawing on the work of George Mendenhall, is particularly insightful on this point.

8. For a profound analysis both of the power of lament and the importance of being able to appeal to a transcendent God, see Cynthia L. Rigby, "Someone to Blame, Someone to Trust: Divine Power and the Self-Recovery of the Oppressed," in *Power, Powerlessness, and the Divine: New Inquiries in Bible and Theology*, ed. Cynthia L. Rigby (Studies in Theological Education; Atlanta: Scholars Press, 1997), 79–102.

9. In Mark's account he is identified as Bartimaeus, a blind beggar; in Luke he is simply described as a blind man.

people (14:14), overthrowing the forces of evil (in this case, Pharaoh's army).[10] Drawing on the standard Hebrew metaphor of heat for anger, the song vividly portrays YHWH's wrath burning up his adversaries like stubble (15:7) and blasting a path through the sea with the breath of his nostrils (15:8).[11] Like the sea crossing, the plagues (in Exod. 7–11) are portrayed as YHWH's mighty works, the signs and wonders that he brought upon Egypt to force Pharaoh to let the Israelites go (6:1; 7:3–4; 8:19; 9:3).

Because YHWH has intervened with power to confront the mighty Egyptian Empire and deliver Israel in its time of need, he is celebrated in the Song of the Sea as incomparable among the gods: there is no one like YHWH (15:11). And the song ends with the affirmation that YHWH (not Pharaoh) "will reign forever and ever" (15:18).[12]

The "coming" of YHWH as king of creation to judge evil is an important motif also in enthronement psalms and results in celebration among the nations and the nonhuman creation (see Pss. 96; 98). YHWH's coming as judge and savior also becomes a central theme of the Old Testament prophetic tradition. To take but one example, Micah 1:3–4 is a vivid vision (a theophany) of YHWH coming in judgment from his heavenly dwelling, and his arrival causes the mountains to disintegrate with earthquakes and landslides.

In the New Testament, Jesus, the incarnate Word, has entered history to do battle with the powers of evil, especially on the cross and in his resurrection.[13] Thus the apostle Paul describes the victory that Christ won as his conquest of every power that opposes God, culminating in the defeat of death itself (1 Cor. 15:24–28). The relevance for God's people is clear: "He has rescued us from the power of darkness and transferred us into the kingdom of his beloved Son" (Col. 1:13). But more than that, as a result of Christ's victory, "the creation itself will be set free from its bondage to decay and will obtain the freedom of the glory of the children of God" (Rom. 8:21).

10. It is significant that while the exodus is a case of sociopolitical or even military deliverance, in no case does Moses or Israel fight directly against Egypt; that is solely God's job. This anticipates the theme, found throughout the Bible, that salvation is accomplished only by God; it is never achieved by human "works."

11. This metaphor underlies the expression "slow to anger" in the Old Testament, which is used to describe God's patience (as in Exod. 34:6). "Slow to anger" translates a phrase that means literally "long of nose." The idea of the metaphor is that the heat of God's anger takes a long time to build up before it is released as an angry blast from his nostrils (as in Exod. 15:8). A contemporary equivalent (using a somewhat different metaphor) would be to say that YHWH does not have a short fuse.

12. For an insightful account of YHWH's kingship in the Old Testament, see Tryggve N. D. Mettinger, *In Search of God: The Meaning and Message of the Everlasting Names*, trans. Frederick H. Cryer (Minneapolis: Fortress, 1988), chap. 6, "The Lord as 'King': The Battling Deity."

13. This is sometimes called the "Christus Victor" theme.

God Often Uses Creaturely Agents to Assist in Bringing Salvation

One of the paradoxes of the exodus account is the interplay of divine and creaturely freedom in bringing salvation. Moses tells the people that they are to stand by and watch the salvation that God will work at the sea (Exod. 14:13). Yet God tells Moses to actively participate in the deliverance by stretching out his hand with the staff, thus dividing the waters (Exod. 14:16); in this participation Moses replicates God's primordial action of separating the waters on the second and third days of creation (Gen. 1:6–10). Even more strikingly, we find that YHWH calls Moses to "bring my people, Israel, out of Egypt" (Exod. 3:10), whereas he had just told Moses that he (YHWH) would "bring them up" (Exod. 3:8). This correspondence of human and divine action is rooted in our creation in God's image (Gen. 1:26–28), which allows us to adequately represent God on earth. That God is the ultimate agent of salvation, therefore, does not conflict with the fact that human agents are often used in the process of bringing salvation. And yet, while Moses directly confronts Pharaoh with the demand to let the Israelites go and even stretches out his hand over the sea, it is significant that neither he nor Israel has any direct role in fighting against the Egyptians; this is YHWH's victory.[14]

Beyond Moses's limited role in the exodus, various forces of the nonhuman creation participate in the plagues against Egypt (Exod. 7–11), thus convincing Pharaoh to let the Israelites go. Perhaps most significant, the waters of the Red Sea are God's instrument in overthrowing the Egyptian army. In an interesting twist, the waters are viewed not as God's enemy (as in some ancient Near Eastern creation accounts) but as an extension of YHWH's own

14. The fact that only YHWH fights against Egypt may help explain why the Song of the Sea (Exod. 15:1–18) is attributed to Moses rather than Miriam, against typical expectations. The fact that she and the women of Israel are relegated to repeating only the first few lines of the song (Exod. 15:20–21) has often been taken as evidence of male bias, since it is primarily women who sing victory songs (accompanied by tambourines and dancing) in the Bible; usually the men do not sing since they are the returning warriors (see Judg. 11:34; 1 Sam. 18:6–7). However, as Victor P. Hamilton (*Exodus: An Exegetical Commentary* [Grand Rapids: Baker Academic, 2011], 235–36) suggests, in this case Moses leads the Israelite men in the victory song, since neither he nor any Israelite male was an actual combatant in the battle; the victory at the sea belonged to YHWH. We should also take into account J. Gerald Janzen's argument that close attention to the Hebrew suggests that Moses and Israel sing this song *because* (*kî*) Miriam and her sisters lead them to do so. The *kî* following the song (15:1) is analeptic (functiong as a flashback), explaining why it is that the foregoing song was sung. Note that Moses says (literally), "I will sing to YHWH" (15:1), which may be a response to Miriam's exhortation, "Sing to YHWH!" (15:21). See Janzen, "Song of Moses, Song of Miriam: Who Is Seconding Whom?" *Catholic Biblical Quarterly* 54 (1982): 211–20. Reprinted in Athalya Brenner, ed., *A Feminist Companion to Exodus to Deuteronomy* (The Feminist Companion to the Bible 6; Sheffield: Sheffield Academic Press, 1994), 187–99.

power.[15] Thus the waters that drowned the Egyptian army can be described by the adjective "majestic" (*'addîr*) in Exodus 15:10.[16] Not only is a verbal form of this word (a participle from *'ādar*) used of God a few verses earlier, where YHWH (or YHWH's right hand) is said to be "majestic" in power (15:6),[17] but the assertion of YHWH's incomparability in the very next verse uses this same participle: "Who is like you, O LORD, among the gods? / Who is like you, majestic in holiness?" (15:11).[18] The implicit answer the song gives is that the gods of Egypt cannot be compared to YHWH, but the waters are like him. There is a sense, then, in which the waters (and not just humans) image God, acting appropriately on his behalf.[19]

After the exodus, God uses a series of human agents, such as judges, kings, and prophets, to effect salvation for the chosen people. In order to bring Israel back from Babylonian exile, God will even use a Persian king, Cyrus, who is called YHWH's "shepherd" and "anointed" or "messiah" (Isa. 44:28; 45:1; cf. 45:13). And the purpose of Israel's salvation is precisely that they, as God's servant people, might bring salvation to the nations of the world (42:1–7). In this tradition we find the mysterious figure of the Suffering Servant (52:13–53:12), whose humiliation (and even death) will accomplish salvation for others (see esp. 53:4–6, 10–12).[20] That God uses creaturely agents in bringing salvation underlies the development of messianic hope in Second Temple Judaism, culminating in the coming of Jesus of Nazareth, the one through whom God has decisively brought salvation. And after Jesus, God has given his people "the ministry of reconciliation," as Paul puts it (2 Cor. 5:18).

15. For the function of water in biblical creation accounts, see J. Richard Middleton, *The Liberating Image: The* Imago Dei *in Genesis 1* (Grand Rapids: Brazos, 2005), chap. 6, "Created in the Image of a Violent God?"

16. While many translations of Exod. 15:10 have "mighty waters," both the Jewish Publication Society Tanakh and Everett Fox (*The Five Books of Moses* [Schocken Bible; New York: Schocken Books, 1995], 337) correctly render the phrase "majestic waters."

17. The problem is whether the participle "majestic" qualifies YHWH or his hand (there are grammatical arguments for both). See the discussion in Hamilton, *Exodus*, 223–24.

18. The same adjective from Exod. 15:10 also appears in Ps. 8 to describe YHWH's name, which is "majestic" in all the earth (vv. 1, 9).

19. Similarly, in the creation account of Gen. 1, not only does God fill the earth and the seas with living creatures (vv. 20–21, 24–25), but also the earth (in response to God's word) brings forth vegetation, in a parallel act of filling (vv. 11–12). And although God separates the light from the dark on day one of creation (v. 4), he appoints the sun and moon to do the very same thing on day four (v. 18). For an analysis of ways in which the nonhuman creatures in Gen. 1 share (at least partially) in the *imago Dei*, see Middleton, *Liberating Image*, chap. 7, "Imaging God's Primal Generosity."

20. Although the Suffering Servant may have originally referred to Israel's mission (or possibly to that of an exilic prophet), the New Testament came to see its ultimate fulfillment in Jesus. For explicit quotations, see Matt. 8:17; Luke 22:37; John 12:38; Acts 8:32–34; 1 Pet. 2:22–25; allusions to this Isaiah text are woven throughout the New Testament.

God Restores the Needy to a Good Land, with Breathing Room to Live

As a consequence of removing the impediment that blocks flourishing, the situation of the needy is transformed as they are restored to the fullness of life. Deliverance is thus never solely a matter of being released from whatever impedes flourishing; it is goal oriented, moving the delivered ones toward the restoration of well-being. Central to this well-being in the exodus story is the promise of a good land where the Israelites can live in safety. Thus YHWH explains to Moses, "I have come down . . . to bring them up out of that land [Egypt] to a good and broad land, a land flowing with milk and honey" (Exod. 3:8). The exodus cannot, therefore, be reduced to freedom from bondage. The goal of this deliverance is that the people of Israel might flourish in their own land; without this flourishing the exodus would be incomplete.

This logic explains why the Song of the Sea does not end with YHWH overcoming the Egyptian army (Exod. 15:1–12), but instead goes on to speak of God leading the redeemed people to the promised land, where they can dwell securely (Exod. 15:13–17). The song thus anticipates the narrative arc from Exodus to Joshua. Indeed, in every retelling of Israel's founding story in the Bible, including the major storytelling psalms (e.g., Pss. 78; 105; 106; 136), the two linchpins are always the deliverance from bondage and the gift of land. Even with all the variation in the way the story is told, whether in prayers or other liturgical or prophetic restatements (Deut. 6:20–25; 26:5–10; Josh. 24:1–14; Jer. 2:6–7; 32:17–23; Neh. 9:6–31), these two poles of the exodus pattern are always present.[21]

This second pole (restoration to the land) is rooted in God's creation of humanity in the context of their concrete earthly environment. Genesis 1 thus lists the creation of human beings along with other land creatures on day six (vv. 24–28), and both humans and animals are dependent on the plants and trees of the land for nourishment (vv. 29–30). In Genesis 2 the link between humans and the land is emphasized by the Hebrew assonance between the words for human ('ādām) and ground ('ădamâ), roughly equivalent to "human" and "humus" in English. And in both cases the human purpose is earth oriented: to rule the earth and its animals (1:26–28), and to work and protect the garden (2:15). Thus when God redeems his people from Egyptian

---

21. For further reflection on the diverse ways Israel's founding story is recounted in the Old Testament, see J. Richard Middleton and Brian J. Walsh, *Truth Is Stranger Than It Used to Be: Biblical Faith in a Postmodern Age* (Downers Grove, IL: IVP Academic, 1995), chap. 5, "The Biblical Metanarrative."

bondage or Babylonian exile, this requires their return to a safe and fruitful land, where they can flourish. Ultimately this leads to the New Testament's vision of a new heaven and new earth as the eternal home of the redeemed (2 Pet. 3:13; Rev. 21:1).

A Life of Obedience to YHWH Is Necessary to Complete Salvation

Following upon the exodus from Egypt, on their way to the promised land, Israel arrives at Mount Sinai and receives the Torah—God's commandments and ordinances for right living. According to the book of Exodus, the Torah initially consists of the Ten Commandments or Decalogue (20:1–17) and an assortment of other laws (21:1–23:19), the "book of the covenant" (24:7) that YHWH is making with Israel at Sinai.

It is important to note that these laws and commandments do not come to Israel out of the blue; they are fundamentally grounded in Israel's deliverance from bondage. In the Old Testament as well as the New Testament, grace comes before law; the gift of deliverance precedes the obligation or duty of obedience. Indeed, obedience is an expression of gratitude for the gracious deliverance YHWH worked on behalf of his people.

God's first words to the people at Sinai explicitly connect deliverance with obedience: "You have seen what I did to the Egyptians, and how I bore you on eagles' wings and brought you to myself. Now therefore, if you obey my voice and keep my covenant . . ." (Exod. 19:4–5). The integral connection between deliverance and Torah obedience is also signaled at the start of the Decalogue, which identifies the divine lawgiver as the God of the exodus: "I am the LORD your God, who brought you out of the land of Egypt, out of the house of slavery" (Exod. 20:2). The exodus thus functions as the historical ground for Israel's allegiance to YHWH and for the expression of that allegiance in obedience to YHWH's Torah. This grounding of Israel's ethics in the exodus illustrates well Alasdair MacIntyre's famous claim: "I can only answer the question 'What am I to do?' if I can answer the prior question 'Of what story or stories do I find myself a part?'"[22] Biblical ethics is narratively shaped.

But obedience to the Torah is not simply the appropriate response to God's prior deliverance; in a fundamental sense, obedience completes the salvation begun in the exodus. The exodus was only the beginning of the process of Israel's salvation. Deliverance from bondage must now be matched by conformity

---

22. Alasdair MacIntyre, *After Virtue: A Study in Moral Theory* (2nd ed.; Notre Dame, IN: University of Notre Dame Press, 1984), 216.

to the creator's will, which will require substantial changes in the way of life of God's people. Salvation thus cannot be limited to deliverance from external circumstances; it must include what we might call "sanctification." The Torah given at Sinai constitutes God's instructions for holy living, meant to direct the life of the redeemed community toward justice and righteousness, that they might be restored to flourishing.

But there is a more focused way in which the exodus grounds obedience. Among the many injunctions and exhortations in the books of Exodus, Leviticus, and Deuteronomy, some pertain especially to the treatment of the needy or marginalized, and these are linked explicitly either to Israel's experience of suffering in Egypt or to God's compassion to liberate the oppressed from bondage. With explicit appeals to this twofold motivation, the Torah prohibits Israel from wronging and abusing aliens, widows, or orphans (Exod. 22:21–24; 23:9; Lev. 19:33–34; Deut. 24:17–18) or from taking advantage of anyone in need (Exod. 22:25–27; Lev. 25:35–38, 39–43). Indeed, God's people are enjoined to release all debt slaves in the Jubilee year (Lev. 25:54–55) and even to "love the alien as yourself" (Lev. 19:34; cf. Deut. 10:17–19). And all of this is explicitly grounded in the exodus.

The point is that by remembering their own bondage and by modeling their actions on their holy and gracious deliverer God (who was attentive to them in their need), Israel will enact righteousness toward the vulnerable in their midst. The exodus thus functions as a lens for understanding the requirements for societal flourishing in a broken world by generating a special concern among the covenant people for the needy or marginalized. The experience of the exodus grounds Israel's insight that human society cannot function properly—salvation is incomplete—unless the most vulnerable members are protected, provided for, and nourished.

The fact that obedience is a crucial aspect of salvation underlies Paul's encouragement to the New Testament church to "work out your own salvation" (Phil. 2:12)—this from the theologian of grace par excellence. Likewise, when the tax collector Zacchaeus pledged fourfold restitution for defrauding others (Luke 19:8), thus fulfilling the requirements of the Torah (Exod. 22:1), Jesus announced, "Today salvation has come to this house" (Luke 19:9). It is certainly possible (and traditional) to read Jesus's comments in terms of a truncated view of salvation as some internal "spiritual" transformation to which Zacchaeus's visible actions testify. However, the text reflects the biblical perspective that obedience (especially when it concerns the reestablishment of justice) is itself a crucial component of salvation, in the sense of the restoration of communal well-being.

God Comes to Dwell with the Redeemed
in a Concrete Historical Context

Interwoven with all other elements of the flourishing of the redeemed is God's presence among them. Thus, in the Song of the Sea, the land toward which Israel is journeying is described as God's "holy abode" (Exod. 15:13), and references in the song to God's "sanctuary" and to "the mountain of his possession" (15:17) might allude to the Jerusalem temple on Mount Zion, although it may be that the entire land of Israel is conceived of as the place of God's dwelling.[23] Indeed, that God will dwell with the Israelites is explicitly stated as the purpose of the exodus (29:45–46).

This emphasis on God's presence among the redeemed people makes sense of that significant section of the book of Exodus that describes the tabernacle (chaps. 25–40), the mobile tent whose function is to make God's presence available to the people as they journey toward the land of promise. The narrative of the golden calf (Exod. 32–34), which occurs in this section of the book, thus describes an unauthorized attempt to secure God's presence. Yet the paradox is that idolatry (constructing an image to mediate God's presence) is precisely what puts God's presence at risk. This is why, after Moses successfully convinces God to forgive the people's sin (32:11–14), we find him pleading for God not to renege on the promise of his presence (33:14–16).

In both Old and New Testaments, the tabernacle/temple motif of God dwelling with his people is associated with a specific promise of relationship: "I will be their God, and they shall be my people" (Lev. 26:11–12; Ezek. 34:30; 37:27; 2 Cor. 6:16). This promise is found in Jeremiah's famous oracle of a new covenant (Jer. 31:33), which is quoted in Hebrews 8:10 as being fulfilled in Jesus. Whereas much postbiblical Christian interpretation of God's dwelling with his people tends to decontextualize the "relationship" (as if the community merely sits around a campfire, holding hands and singing "Kumbayah"), the Old Testament portrays God's presence with the redeemed squarely in the context of their concrete earthly life, first on the wilderness journey, then in the land.

It is noteworthy that the promise "I will be their God, and they shall be my people" first shows up in connection with God's promise of land to Abraham (Gen. 17:7–8). When YHWH later rearticulates this same promise of "relationship" to Moses in Exodus (6:7), it is sandwiched between the announcement of

---

23. Carol Meyers (*Exodus* [New Cambridge Bible Commentary; Cambridge: Cambridge University Press, 2005], 121) suggests, however, that the language used here is not typically applied to the temple, Mount Zion, or the land of Israel and might be taken as a reference to Mount Sinai, the original site of YHWH's dwelling.

deliverance from bondage (6:6) and the gift of land (6:8). It thus makes sense that prophetic restatements of this ancient promise are explicitly linked with God's dwelling with the redeemed people in a safe and bountiful land after the return from exile, since this is what is required for human flourishing (Jer. 32:37–41; Ezek. 34:25–31; 37:24–28; Zech. 8:7–8).

This trajectory of God's presence among his people culminates in the New Testament's vision of a redeemed creation, with the new Jerusalem coming down out of heaven to earth, and at its center is God's throne (Rev. 21:1–22:5). Then the ancient promise will be finally fulfilled: "See, the home of God is with mortals. He will dwell with them as their God; they will be his peoples, and God himself will be with them" (Rev. 21:3).

Excursus: The Salvation of an Individual in Psalm 18

Not every component of the exodus pattern is found in every instance of salvation in the Bible (or even in the Old Testament), but it is instructive to consider how crucial elements of the pattern frame the testimony of God's deliverance of an individual in Psalm 18.[24] This is a long, complex psalm, comprising various literary genres, but we are concerned specifically with the section of the poem usually classified as a song of thanksgiving, which recounts a narrative of God's deliverance (vv. 1–19 [vv. 2–20 MT]).

This narrative begins by describing the impediment to the psalmist's flourishing, which is portrayed as death, perdition, and Sheol (vv. 4–5)—that which is antithetical to life and well-being. This generates the psalmist's cry of distress to God; and "from his temple he heard my voice" (v. 6). Then follows a description of God's intervention in the form of a vivid theophany, a vision of YHWH's descent from his heavenly throne in anger directed against the psalmist's enemies. In poetic language, YHWH is portrayed as riding on a cherub (described as the "wings of the wind") and shooting arrows of fire, accompanied by meteorological phenomena like smoke, hail, lightning, and dark clouds (vv. 7–14). Then in a clear parallel to God's breath that parted the sea (Exod. 15:8), the psalm describes "the channels of the sea" and the "foundations of the world" as uncovered by the blast of God's nostrils (v. 15).

The result of YHWH's coming down is twofold. The first result is deliverance from powerful enemies, also portrayed as "mighty waters" (vv. 16–18)—that is, the removal of that which impedes the psalmist's well-being. The second result is the restoration of the psalmist to a situation of safety and

24. A slightly different version of this psalm appears in 2 Sam. 22.

flourishing. Indeed, the statement that YHWH "brought me out into a broad place" (v. 19) echoes God's promise to Moses to bring Israel out of Egypt "to a good and broad land" (Exod. 3:8). Not only does the same Hebrew root underlie "broad" in both statements, but also the purpose of deliverance in both cases is a restoration of well-being.

The psalmist concludes the story of God's deliverance by explaining the basis of this deliverance in a prior relationship to God: YHWH delivered the psalmist "because he delighted in me" (v. 19). This prior relationship constitutes the final paradigmatic component of salvation in the exodus.

Salvation Is Grounded in God's Prior Relationship with Those in Need

Even before YHWH tells Moses of his plans to deliver the Israelites, and even before he mentions that he has heard their cry, YHWH identifies himself as "the God of your ancestor, the God of Abraham, the God of Isaac, and the God of Jacob" (Exod. 3:6). This identification places the exodus from Egypt firmly in the narrative context of the book of Genesis, recalling God's prior covenant with Israel's ancestors. In other words, God's deliverance of Israel is grounded in a prior relationship with the covenant people. But not only is Israel's salvation at the exodus rooted in a prior relationship with God; all of God's actions on behalf of human flourishing are rooted ultimately in the relationship of humans to their creator.

The Global Context of Israel's Salvation

This prior relationship of God with the world, a relationship not abrogated by the roadblock of sin, grounds God's election of Israel. Humans had become corrupted in their rebellion against God and had filled the earth with violence. As we saw in the preceding chapter, the creator then set in motion a plan of salvation, beginning with the call of Abraham, that would ultimately benefit all nations.

In the book of Exodus, this broader context of Israel's salvation is alluded to in numerous statements during the plague cycle and the sea crossing: not just Israel (6:7; 7:17; 10:2) but also Pharaoh and all Egypt (7:5; 8:10, 22; 9:14, 29; 10:7; 14:4, 18) would come to know who YHWH is through these miraculous events. The cosmic scope of the exodus is plainly stated in connection with the seventh plague, when YHWH affirms that his name will be proclaimed in all the earth (9:14). Indeed, at this point cosmic statements accumulate: Pharaoh will come to know that there is no one like YHWH in all the earth (9:16) and that the earth belongs to YHWH (9:29). The exodus clearly is not just for Israel's sake.

This global perspective on Israel's calling is also evident in Exodus when the newly freed people arrive at Mount Sinai after the deliverance at the sea. Although "the whole earth is mine" (19:5), says YHWH, Israel is to be "a priestly kingdom and a holy nation" (19:6), implying a vocation of mediating divine blessing and presence in a world that belongs to God.

This universal purpose of Israel's election then comes to particular clarity during the Babylonian exile, when Israel was no longer a nation with its own land. In that context of marginality, we find the so-called Servant Songs in the book of Isaiah, where God's servant (Israel) is described as God's "covenant" or pledge to the peoples of the world and is called to be a light to the nations (42:6; 49:6), facilitating their release from bondage (42:7).[25]

God's Saving Activity beyond Israel

Indeed, despite the distinctive role of Israel as God's elect, the creator is at work beyond the covenant people, bringing blessing and enhancing earthly flourishing for all humanity. Thus God is involved in the liberating of nations other than Israel from their bondage. The prophet Amos declares that the Philistines and the Arameans have had their exoduses (Amos 9:7), although such nations do not thereby become God's elect, with a specific vocation to the world.

And God's providential care for earthly life is evident prior to the existence of Israel, or even Abraham. Thus in the Primeval History in Genesis the original human couple bring forth life (4:1–2a, 25) in response to the divine command to be fruitful and multiply (1:28), and their offspring also have children (4:17–22, 26). Despite the primal human transgression and lack of access to the tree of life, the genealogies in Genesis (4:17–5:32; 10; 11:10–32)

25. John H. Stek's definition of covenant in the Bible makes sense of the idea of Israel as God's covenant to the nations (which initially might seem strange to us). According to Stek ("Covenant Overload in Reformed Theology," *Calvin Theological Journal* 29 [1994]: 12–24), a biblical covenant is a binding oath or pledge to be faithful to a relationship after it has been threatened. Thus the Noahic covenant is God's pledge to uphold his relationship with the earth after the flood, the Abrahamic covenant is God's pledge to fulfill his promises to Abraham after he and Sarah fail to have children, and the Sinai covenant is God's pledge to be Israel's God after Egyptian slavery. It is thus a brilliant rhetorical move to regard the very existence of Israel as God's "covenant" or pledge to redeem the nations of the world.

testify to the continuation, indeed the proliferation, of the human family, and the genealogy in Genesis 5 specifically portrays the transmission of the *imago Dei* (5:1–5) as part of this blessing from generation to generation; the *imago Dei* endures even after the flood (9:6).

Although they are outside the garden, Cain and Abel (still in God's image) continue the human vocation by fulfilling the divine injunction to subdue the earth and rule the animals (Gen. 4:2b; cf. 1:28). After Cain's murder of Abel, God ameliorates the ensuing curse that comes upon the murderer and shows compassion by placing a mark of protection on him (4:15). And in the midst of the violence that begins to fill the earth, Enoch (5:24) and Noah (6:9) walk with God, and Noah is explicitly described as a righteous man, who, at God's command, is instrumental in the salvation of both humans and animals (6:18–7:5).

Genesis records that after the flood, God promises the continuation of the seasons (8:22), rearticulates the primal blessing of fertility for Noah and his family (9:1, 7), and inaugurates a law to limit murder (9:6). God even enters into a covenant with Noah and his family, with all living creatures, and with the earth itself (9:9–17), pledging to sustain and protect the created order for their benefit.

In the context of this divine commitment to earthly flourishing, the human race proliferates and diversifies—linguistically, culturally, ethnically, geographically. People spread out over the face of the entire earth (Gen. 10), until the regressive move of Babel (Gen. 11:1–9), which God counters with a rescattering and a diversification of languages, for the benefit of the human race.

In all these diverse ways the biblical text not only portrays God's primal relationship with creation, but also testifies to God's intent for the flourishing of earthly life. Hence the psalmist's claim is justified: "You save human and animal alike, O LORD" (Ps. 36:6).[26]

---

26. The NIV translates this verse as "You, LORD, preserve both people and animals." While this is not wrong, since the Hebrew verb *yāša'* can include this meaning, we should not shy away from using the term "save" (as the NRSV and the ESV do); not only is this the usual meaning of the verb, but also it is appropriate because salvation encompasses all aspects of earthly flourishing.

5

Earthly Flourishing in Law, Wisdom, and Prophecy

The exodus of the Israelites from Egypt is the foundational saving event in the Old Testament. This paradigmatic work of YHWH on behalf of Israel establishes a movement toward this-worldly flourishing as the goal of salvation. The exodus pattern begins when God's original intent for his people's well-being and blessing has been disrupted, and its epicenter is God's intervention to deliver those in need and to restore them to a life of shalom in their concrete earthly environment.

But the exodus represents only one strand of the Old Testament's concern with earthly flourishing. We could, in principle, survey the entire Old Testament for this pervasive theme; however, that is not feasible given the scope of this book. Instead, as a follow-up to our focus on the exodus, it will be most fruitful to examine two primary dimensions of the Old Testament that clarify the holistic nature of salvation: the law and the prophets. Even then, we need to be selective.

First, it is important to understand how the Torah or law, in connection with the Old Testament idea of wisdom, contributes to a vision of the creator's intent for earthly flourishing; this vision of flourishing also undergirds the critique of injustice that pervades the prophetic literature. But along with prophetic critique is the expectation of restoration found in many Old Testament prophetic oracles, promising hope for Israel beyond the exile. Together, law/wisdom and prophecy emphasize the inescapable connection between the moral and cosmic orders and elucidate a profound and comprehensive vision of earthly flourishing.

A Parallel between Wisdom and Torah?

We might initially think that the Torah or laws of the Old Testament (articulated first in the book of Exodus, and then in Leviticus and Deuteronomy) address radically different realities from those of the wisdom literature (especially the book of Proverbs, but also Job and Ecclesiastes). But a closer look shows some remarkable similarities. Students of the Bible tend to think that whereas the Torah represents the specific revelation of God to Israel, the wisdom literature of the Old Testament shows international influences (reflecting traditions found in Egypt and Mesopotamia)[1] and teaches that anyone who fears YHWH can discern what it is to live wisely.[2]

These perceptions are not wrong. Torah and wisdom are not exactly the same in the Old Testament. Yet the convergence between the two is uncanny. Both Torah and wisdom describe, in strikingly parallel ways, God's norms for life and blessing (that is, the way of salvation or flourishing), and both are contrasted with paths that lead to death.

Torah as the Way of Life

Israel's Torah is grounded in a fundamental contrast between two opposing ways or paths, described most typically as life and death, and these are linked to the choice between obedience and disobedience to God's laws, commandments, statutes, decrees, or ordinances (all these terms refer to God's will for life). If God's people follow these laws, they will be blessed with the fullness of life; but if they turn away from divine instruction, they will experience the curses of the covenant.

Both Leviticus 26 and Deuteronomy 28 list a series of covenantal blessings and curses linked to obedience and disobedience. According to these texts,

---

1. Most introductions to Old Testament wisdom literature discuss the international character of wisdom, including Egyptian and Mesopotamian influences. Probably the most specific connection that scholars have discerned between the book of Proverbs and ancient Near Eastern wisdom literature is the remarkable similarity between many of the sayings in Prov. 22:17–24:22 (in a section attributed to "the words of the wise" [22:17]) and *The Instruction of Amenemope*, an Egyptian text likely dating to the eleventh or twelfth century BC. There are significant parallels between the two texts, both at conceptual and verbal levels.

2. Job is a non-Israelite, yet he is described as a blameless and upright man, who fears God and shuns evil (Job 1:1, 8; 2:3), which fits the definition of wisdom in Job 28:28.

obedience to God's law will lead to blessing across a broad spectrum of daily life (Lev. 26:3–13; Deut. 28:1–14). This blessing includes the birth of children and the fruitfulness of crops and herds, with regular rains to fertilize the land, and a life without fear of attack by wild animals or enemies. There will be blessing in the city, in the field, in the home—even "your basket and your kneading bowl" will be blessed (Deut. 28:5). Indeed, "Blessed shall you be when you come in, and blessed shall you be when you go out" (28:6).

On the other hand, disobedience will lead to being cursed (the opposite of life and flourishing) in equally comprehensive ways, some of which are the exact opposite of the blessings previously listed (Deut. 28:15–19). Both Leviticus 26 and Deuteronomy 28 conclude by portraying the consequences of disobedience in the most devastating and graphic terms, focusing on disease, disorientation, social disorder, robbery, violence, and enemy attack, resulting ultimately in exile—being ejected from the land of promise (Lev. 26:14–39; Deut. 28:20–68).

The list of covenantal blessings and curses clearly demonstrates the link between the moral and cosmic orders, so that when the human community is in harmony with God's design, their earthly life (including the nonhuman world) flourishes, but when they go against God's intent for flourishing, this affects also the earthly environment, to the extent that the land will vomit out its inhabitants (Lev. 18:24–28; 20:22).[3] Babylonian exile is the ultimate consequence for unfaithfulness to YHWH. It is no wonder, then, that obedience to God's Torah is vigorously commended ("choose life"), since this is what leads to shalom and flourishing in the land (Deut. 30:15–20).

But obedience is not viewed as merely external conformity to law; rather, true obedience is an expression of wholehearted allegiance or commitment to God. Thus the Shema ("Hear, O Israel" [Deut. 6:4]) enjoins God's people to love YHWH with all their heart, soul, and might (6:5).[4] The Decalogue (Ten Commandments) likewise begins by exhorting Israel to exclusive allegiance or commitment to the one true God ("I am the LORD your God, who brought you out of the land of Egypt, out of the house of slavery. You shall have no other gods before me" [Exod. 20:2–3]) and prohibits fashioning idols (20:4–6, 23), since idolatry means turning away from YHWH and rejecting the true source of life. This exclusive allegiance to the saving God of the exodus, articulated in

3. The linkage of cosmic and moral orders is grounded in Gen. 3, where human sin results in a curse on the ground (v. 17); likewise, exile from the land matches expulsion from the garden (v. 23).

4. We should not reduce this to a purely emotional attachment to God, since "love" is a term used in ancient Near Eastern political covenants for allegiance to a sovereign, the opposite of which is treason. See William L. Moran, "The Ancient Near Eastern Background of the Love of God in Deuteronomy," *Catholic Biblical Quarterly* 25 (1963): 77–87.

the first two commandments, is meant to ground the communal life of God's people as they seek to conform their lives to the character and purposes of YHWH, guided by the rest of the commandments in the Decalogue (20:7–17) and the Book of the Covenant (21:1–23:19).

Wisdom as the Way of Life

Parallel to the fundamental choice between obedience and disobedience in the Torah, the wisdom literature of the Old Testament presents wisdom and folly as the two ways set before each person (e.g., Prov. 2:20–22). Just as Deuteronomy encourages its readers to "choose life" (30:19), so wisdom is vigorously commended as God's way of righteousness (Prov. 2:1–8), which leads to life (3:13–18), while folly leads to death.

And although there is no specific list of blessings and curses in Proverbs comparable to Leviticus 26 and Deuteronomy 28, the concerns of wisdom are wide ranging, addressing matters of speech, sexuality, family, work, wealth, governance, and the use of power.

But wise living is never just a matter of perfunctory common sense: "The fear of the LORD is the beginning of wisdom" (Prov. 1:7); wisdom thus flows from the appropriate awe or reverence of God (Job 28:28; Ps. 111:10; Prov. 9:10; 14:27; 16:6; 19:23). The fear of YHWH, which grounds a life of wisdom, is functionally equivalent to love of YHWH in the Torah, which grounds obedience. Indeed, Deuteronomy 6 uses both terms synonymously ("fear" in v. 2; "love" in v. 5).

Especially significant is that both Torah and wisdom are portrayed as expressions of God's will from creation. This is the fundamental reason why living in accordance with God's law is equivalent to wisdom; it means living in harmony with God's original purposes for life. Obedience or wise living therefore naturally leads to blessing, flourishing, well-being. By contrast, disobedience to God's ordinances is utter folly because it means resisting the way things were meant to be. The intrinsic consequence is therefore death in all its forms—the corruption and destruction of life, whether personal or societal, with effects even on the natural environment.[5] Discerning wisdom and obeying the Torah are thus two equivalent ways in which the Scriptures speak of God's creational intent for flourishing.[6]

---

5. Compare the results of human disobedience in Gen. 3, which include the disruption of interhuman relationships and a "curse" on the ground itself.

6. For further discussion of the relation of Torah and wisdom to creation, see J. Richard Middleton, *The Liberating Image: The* Imago Dei *in Genesis 1* (Grand Rapids: Brazos, 2005), 65–88.

Wisdom and God's Creational Intent

That wisdom is grounded in creation is evident from the speech that Wisdom gives in Proverbs 8. In the book of Proverbs, both Wisdom and Folly (personified as women) call out to all who will hear (Wisdom in 1:20–33; 8:1–36; 9:1–12; Folly in 9:13–18; see also 7:1–27); each tries to convince listeners that she is the one who will enhance their lives.

Wisdom, however, advances a distinctive argument in Proverbs 8:22–31, explaining why it is better to follow her than Folly, who also beckons. Wisdom explains that her existence preceded the creation of the world; indeed, she was conceived or brought into being as the first of God's deeds and was appointed by God before he made the cosmos (vv. 22–26). Although there may be more nuances of meaning here, this suggests minimally that prior to creation, God came up with a wise plan for the cosmos, and Wisdom is that plan. But Wisdom was also there during (and after) the creative process, faithfully accompanying the creator (perhaps even his "master worker," though that translation is disputed),[7] rejoicing in the world—including the human race—that was coming into being (vv. 27–31). The implication is that Wisdom therefore takes precedence over Folly, and it is her guidance for living that should be followed (see Prov. 8:32–36).

In less dramatic form than Wisdom's speech in Proverbs 8, the short poem in Proverbs 3:19–20 simply asserts that God made the cosmos by wisdom, understanding, and knowledge, which is similar to Jeremiah's statement that God (in contrast to idols) is the one "who made the earth by his power, / who established the world by his wisdom, / and by his understanding stretched out the heavens" (Jer. 10:12). Likewise, Job 28:25–27 explains that in creating the world God appraised and tested wisdom, thus implying that he utilized it in the process of making everything. These texts suggest that wisdom is embedded into the very structure of reality; the logic of this claim yields the conclusion that living according to wisdom means going with the grain of the universe, while going against this grain is utmost folly—it destroys life and prevents flourishing.

7. The Hebrew word 'amôn in Prov. 8:30 is unusual, and it is typically translated in one of three ways: (1) some version of "master worker" (NRSV), "architect" (NLT), or "craftsman" (NIV 1984); (2) "child" (NCV); (3) some version of "faithfully" or "constantly" (NIV 2011). There are valid linguistic reasons for all three translation options, though the first has the support of the ancient versions (Greek Septuagint, Latin Vulgate, Syriac Peshitta), and the third option is found in the Greek of Theodotion and Symmachus. Some recent translations choose one option but footnote the other two (e.g., NIV 2011 and HCSB). For a recent argument in favor of the third option, see Stuart Weeks, "The Context and Meaning of Proverbs 8:30a," *Journal of Biblical Literature* 125 (2006): 433–42.

The expectation of earthly flourishing that results from living according to wisdom is what generates the books of Job and Ecclesiastes, which are often referred to as "protest wisdom." Both books address what happens when the creational/covenantal linkage between act and consequence does not seem to hold. In Job's case, his massive suffering does not match his own righteous actions; in the case of Ecclesiastes, life seems futile because no one can control the outcome or consequences of their own actions. The astute way the Bible addresses the problem of evil and suffering in Job (and also in the lament psalms) is a topic that deserves its own entire study; suffice it to say here that the very way the problem is raised assumes that God's will is for the holistic flourishing of earthly life.[8]

Torah and God's Creational Intent

Like wisdom, Torah is linked to God's intent at creation. Thus various psalms speak of creation by God's word, echoing (or anticipating) the fiats ("Let there be . . .") by which God ordered creation in Genesis 1. These psalms explicitly identify creation by the word as creation by God's command, statute, or decree, using these terms as rough equivalents (Pss. 33:6–9; 119:89–96; 148:5–6). This is the same range of terms used for the divinely revealed law that Israel is required to obey. Thus there is a fundamental unity between God's word in creation and God's Torah for Israel.

Torah therefore cannot be limited to the written law revealed at Sinai; it holds for the entire created order. This insight leads Psalm 148:8 to describe even the wind as obedient to the creator's word, while the poet in Psalm 119:91 says to YHWH, "All things are your servants." This sense that law is embedded in creation and grounds all proper creaturely functioning is also the basis for Jeremiah's contrast between birds and people. While the birds "observe" the time of their migration (thus doing the will of God), disobedient humans "do not know the ordinance of the LORD" (Jer. 8:7).[9]

The intimate connection between God's decrees for the entire creation and his statutes for his people is assumed in Psalm 19, which describes in parallel fashion God's revelation in the cosmic order (vv. 1–6) and God's word revealed in Israel's Torah (vv. 7–13). Psalm 147 links both even more explicitly,

8. For my preliminary reflections on the significance of biblical lament psalms and the book of Job for addressing the problem of evil, see J. Richard Middleton, "Why the 'Greater Good' Isn't a Defense: Classical Theodicy in Light of the Biblical Genre of Lament," *Koinonia* 9, nos. 1–2 (1997): 81–113. Further reflections will be forthcoming in a manuscript on Abraham and Job that I am working on.

9. The verb for "observe" (NRSV) in Jer. 8:7 is the same verb used for Israel's "keeping" (*šāmar*) the Torah.

first portraying God's providence in creation (the coming of winter and then spring) as effected by God's powerful word (vv. 15–18), and then explaining that this word was revealed to Israel in the Torah (vv. 19–20).

The assumption seems to be that before the revelation of the law at Sinai, God had already decreed a normative way for the world to be. Torah simply articulates relevant aspects of these primal decrees for Israel in their particular historical context, with their specific needs for moral and social restoration.[10]

The Convergence between Torah and Wisdom— Grounded in Creation

The evident parallel between Torah and wisdom in relation to creation leads to the clear conclusion that both describe a normative approach to life that is grounded in the order of the cosmos itself. This makes sense of two vignettes from the Old Testament that are, at least on the surface, something of a puzzle.

In Exodus 18 there is an episode in the life of Moses that, initially, makes no sense. This is the story of Moses adjudicating disputes from the people from morning until evening, which tires him out and results in advice from his father-in-law, Jethro, to appoint multiple judges who would hear minor cases, with Moses taking up only the really difficult ones (vv. 13–26). The puzzling part comes just before Jethro's advice. We are told that the people brought their cases to Moses, and he decided between one person and another and made known to them "the statutes and instructions of God" (vv. 15–16). Note that the word for "instructions" here is "torah" in the plural (*tôrōt*), and this episode comes *before* the giving of the law at Mount Sinai (the Israelites do not even get to Sinai until Exod. 19). But how can there be Torah before the giving of the Torah? What can this possibly mean?

In a similar vein, the book of Isaiah seems to confuse something that we might see as experiential learning with God's direct revelation. Wise farmers, Isaiah explains, know how to properly till the soil and thresh their grain for maximum benefit (28:24–25, 27–28). We would normally say that they learned these skills from trial and error, and from being apprenticed by other, more experienced farmers. Yet according to the prophet, their wisdom in farming

---

10. This helps to explain why there are revisions in the written Torah (evident when various biblical law codes are compared with each other), and why the newly formed church in the book of Acts had to struggle with which aspects of the written Torah were still applicable (see Acts 15). God's norms for creation are constant, but the articulation of these norms might need to change in order to address the actual historical situation that God's people find themselves to be in. For an important discussion of changes in the biblical Torah, see Bernard M. Levinson, *Legal Revision and Religious Renewal in Ancient Israel* (Cambridge: Cambridge University Press, 2008).

comes from nothing less than the counsel or instruction of YHWH of hosts (28:26, 29). If we did not understand the creational grounding of wisdom and Torah, these two texts would be obscure to us.

What this means is that in principle there is no difference between wisely discerning God's will structured into the created order and obeying God's revealed word. Most fundamentally, Torah or wisdom is that which discloses, and thus orients the community to, God's creational intent for flourishing. And when Israel lives according to God's wise instruction, their flourishing will attract the notice of other nations. As Deuteronomy puts it, "You must observe them [these laws] diligently, for this will show your wisdom and discernment to the peoples, who, when they hear all these statutes, will say, 'Surely this great nation is a wise and discerning people!'" (4:6).

The Range of Concerns Addressed by Torah and Wisdom

It is the connection to God's creational intent that grounds the broad range of everyday concerns addressed in the Old Testament legal and wisdom literature. As John Stek puts it, "Yahweh's will for Israel ranged across the whole spectrum of Israel's life: personal, familial, and national. All aspects of Israel's life came under his regulation: social, political, economic, educational, and cultic. No corner of life, no private domain, no human relationship lay outside the sphere of his royal authority; his rule was absolute. In all things Israel was to be 'holy,' consecrated *in toto* to the service of Yahweh."[11]

The range of concerns addressed in Israel's legal and wisdom literature includes matters of family, justice, work, debts, clothing, housing, food, disease, sex, war, speech, anger, worship, and leadership. There are laws for the protection of the disabled, the poor, widows, orphans, and aliens, and even laws that address the well-being of domestic and wild animals, birds, trees, and the land itself. There is no distinction between sacred and secular to be found here. The God of the Scriptures (unlike the deity imagined in some of our churches) is concerned for the entire range of earthly life and desires flourishing, well-being, and shalom—in short, salvation—for both humanity and the nonhuman creation. The way of wisdom, which is parallel to obedience to Torah, is meant to nurture holistic earthly flourishing, restoring the whole of life to what it was meant to be.

A similar understanding of Torah and holistic flourishing undergirds the message of the Old Testament prophets, both in their critique of Israel's

11. John H. Stek, "Salvation, Justice and Liberation in the Old Testament," *Calvin Theological Journal* 13 (1978): 150.

unfaithfulness to YHWH and in their offer of hope after judgment. In a fundamental sense, the prophets are grounded in Torah.

Injustice as Unfaithfulness to YHWH in the Prophets

Prophetic texts that call God's people to repentance often utilize an "if-then" structure that draws (explicitly or implicitly) on the covenant sanctions of the Torah—the consequences of blessing and curse. Repentance and new obedience (described especially as right treatment of the neighbor) will result in renewed blessing and shalom (Isa. 1:19; 58:6–14; Jer. 7:3, 5–7; Amos 5:14–15); persistence in disobedience will inevitably result in destruction and even exile from the land (Isa. 1:20; Jer. 7:8–9, 14–15; Amos 5:10–12, 16–17, 26–27).

But beyond this utilization of an act-consequence schema, the prophetic literature is patterned on the Torah in an even more profound way. Jesus himself links the prophets with the Torah in his famous answer to the question about which is the greatest commandment in the law. In his answer, Jesus connects wholehearted love of God (from Deut. 6:5) with love of neighbor (quoting Lev. 19:18), astutely observing, "On these two commandments hang all the law and the prophets" (Matt. 22:40).[12]

In this, Jesus is exactly right. Just as the Torah affirms that the love of God should lead to a life of obedience, the prophets emphasize that Israel's allegiance or submission to YHWH, the God of the exodus, ought to be manifest in a life that embodies righteousness and justice, since these are central to the interhuman flourishing that God desires. In the prophetic perspective, allegiance to the one true God inevitably flows into a life of obedience characterized especially by justice in human relations; by contrast, idolatry or false allegiance flows into a life of disobedience characterized by injustice. This is most fundamentally a matter of imaging God; the life of a person or community reflects the sort of god they are committed to. The two main targets of prophetic critique are thus idolatry and injustice, since false worship is inextricably linked to corrupt living.

12. Three versions of this exchange are recorded in the Gospels, all of which have Jesus include loving God with all one's mind, which is not mentioned in Deut. 6:5 (Matt. 22:37 has heart, soul, and mind; Mark 12:30 has heart, soul, mind, and strength; Luke 10:27 has heart, soul, strength, and mind). The addition of "mind" is likely meant for a Greek-speaking audience, which might have separated heart from mind (no ancient Israelite would have done so: the Hebrew word for "heart" designates the center of thought and decision making; the Hebrew word for "soul" designates a person's life energies and desires; the Hebrew word for "strength" is actually an adverb usually rendered "very," as when God saw all he had made and it was "very" good [Gen. 1:31]).

And yet the prophets are aware that a claim to serve YHWH that is not matched by a life in accord with that claim is a blatant contradiction. Thus one significant stream of prophetic critique casts correct "worship" activities as relatively unimportant vis-à-vis matters of justice.[13] Not only is Israel's injustice (the mistreatment of other human beings) subject to critique, but also their "worship" or cultic activities (such as sacrifices, assemblies, Sabbaths, festivals, and fasting) are anathema to YHWH when such "worship" is substituted for compassion and justice toward others (Isa. 1:10–20; 58:1–14; Jer. 7:1–15; Amos 5 [esp. vv. 4–7, 11–12, 14–15, 21–24]; Mic. 6:1–8 [esp. vv. 6–8]). Jesus himself (in the prophetic tradition) affirms that actions typically regarded as expressing devotion or worship (such as tithing) are not equivalent to allegiance to God and are of less importance than a life of justice, mercy, and faithfulness, which he calls "the weightier matters of the law" (Matt. 23:23).[14]

The logic of the prophetic critique is that although "worship" is an explicit claim of allegiance to YHWH, such a claim must be backed up with justice, which is a concrete demonstration of this allegiance. What God really wants is human flourishing, embodied in the healing of the social order, and those who want what God wants will manifest this in their lives. Indeed, the bond between allegiance to YHWH and practice of justice toward the neighbor is so strong that Jeremiah tells King Jehoiakim that doing justice (particularly caring for the marginal) is equivalent to knowing God (Jer. 22:15–16).

In the New Testament the equivalent of knowing God, or the fear or love of YHWH, is faith. Thus the famous passage in Ephesians 2 that celebrates faith as central to salvation ("by grace you have been saved through faith, . . . so that no one may boast" [vv. 8–9]) goes on to say that those saved by faith are "created in Christ Jesus for good works, which God prepared beforehand to be our way of life" (v. 10). Indeed, Paul clearly affirms that everyone will be judged by their actions: "For all of us must appear before the judgment seat of Christ, so that each may receive recompense for what has been done in the body, whether good or evil" (2 Cor. 5:10).

The book of James, though perhaps more radical than Paul in its rhetoric, is nevertheless on the same track when it declares that faith without works is

13. I have put "worship" in quotation marks to distinguish this more limited form of our response to God from the more comprehensive biblical sense of worship pertaining to all of life offered to God; see the discussion of this distinction in chap. 2 above.

14. On the insignificance of what we call "worship" for the life of the church in the New Testament, see I. Howard Marshall, "How Far Did the Early Christians *Worship* God?," *Churchman* 99 (1985): 216–29, http://www.churchsociety.org/churchman/documents/Cman_099_3_Marshall.pdf.

dead (2:14–26). This is why James says, "Religion that is pure and undefiled before God, the Father, is this: to care for orphans and widows in their distress, and to keep oneself unstained by the world" (1:27).

This is clearly shown in Jesus's contrast between the wise man who built his house on a rock, and the foolish man who built on the sand; what matters is not a verbal acknowledgment of Jesus as "Lord," but rather putting his teachings into action (Matt. 7:21–29). Likewise, in the parable of the sheep and the goats, Jesus explains that the nations are judged on the basis of their actions of compassion toward those in need (Matt. 25:31–46). In both Testaments allegiance to God must be shown in the pattern of one's life.

Prophetic Visions of Restoration beyond Exile

Thankfully, the prophets do not leave Israel in judgment. Beyond exile there is the hope of restoration. Many prophetic texts promise a renewal of people and land after their expulsion from the land. A sketch of the major components of this renewal sheds light on the Old Testament's vision of holistic salvation. In particular, there are seven promised components of renewal in prophetic texts that together testify to God's purpose for earthly flourishing.

1. Return to the land. First, the return from exile is promised, which involves a resettling of the promised land (Isa. 11:10–12, 16; 35:8–10; 55:12–13; 60:4; Jer. 32:37; Ezek. 34:27; 36:8–11; 37:11–14; Amos 9:15; Zeph. 3:19–20; Zech. 8:7–8). This is the sine qua non of all the prophetic promises of restoration. Since the judgment of exile was fundamentally characterized by landlessness and alienation, a return to the land is key to Israel's renewal. This return also fulfills the original purpose of humanity at creation, commissioned to subdue the earth (Gen. 1) or to work the ground from which they are taken (Gen. 2). The Old Testament simply cannot conceive of full salvation or flourishing without earthly, landed existence.

2. Restoration and healing of God's people in society. But the promise is not for a bare or marginal existence in the land. Rather, Israel is promised renewal and healing as a people, such that their communal and even urban life will be restored to flourishing, fruitfulness, and blessing (Isa. 35:5–6, 10; 60:1–2, 18–22; 61:1–4, 7, 9; 62:4–7, 12; 65:18–24; Jer. 31:4–6, 11–14; Ezek. 34:25–31; 36:33–36; 37:5–6, 12, 14; Amos 9:14; Zeph. 3:11–18; Zech. 8:1–5, 11–15). Instead of mourning over the corrupt city and bringing judgment on Zion, God will one day "rejoice in Jerusalem" and "delight" in the people (Isa. 65:19). This promise reverses Israel's corruption and the destitution and shame of exile, to which they have been subject.

3. *Flourishing of the natural world, including peace among animals.* Some prophetic visions of restoration depict the flourishing of nature as Israel returns home, both during the return journey from Babylon and when the people resettle the land (Isa. 35:1–2, 6–7; 55:12–13; Ezek. 34:26–29; 36:8–11, 34–35; 47:1–12; Joel 2:23–24; 3:18; Amos 9:13; Zech. 8:12; 14:8). Some texts portray a new harmony with the animal kingdom, such that people and animals will live in peace (Isa. 11:6–9; 65:25; Ezek. 34:25, 28), while Isaiah 65:17 even envisions a new cosmos ("new heavens and a new earth") as the context for societal renewal. The salvation of humanity thus has ramifications for the restoration of the nonhuman world.

4. *New relationship with the nations, centered in Zion.* But it is not only the people's relationship with the natural order and the animal kingdom that will flourish. Since Israel often has been oppressed by other nations (hence the Babylonian exile), the prophets promise a new relationship with the nations, in which enmity is transformed into service, and some texts envision the fulfillment of Israel's vocation of mediating God's blessings to the world as the nations stream to Zion to seek God and his ways (Isa. 2:2–4; 60:3; 61:5–6, 9, 11; Jer. 3:17; Mic. 4:1–4; Zech. 2:11; 8:20–23).[15] Isaiah 60 even has the best cultural contributions of the nations being brought to Jerusalem to be transformed and used for Israel's benefit and YHWH's glory (vv. 5–16; cf. Rev. 21:26), while Isaiah 19 predicts a future parity between Israel, Egypt, and Assyria, in which all of them will be YHWH's people (vv. 23–25).

5. *Forgiveness of sin and new heart, enabling God's people to keep Torah.* Some prophetic texts also promise inner renewal for the people in the form of a new covenant, through which God forgives sins, pours out his Spirit, or grants a new heart that will enable the people to conform to God's requirements (Isa. 30:20–21; 59:20–21; Jer. 31:31–34; 32:40; 50:20; Ezek. 11:19; 36:26; 37:23; Joel 2:28–29). Given the history of Israel's apostasy and disobedience, it becomes clear that a radical new act of God's grace is required to empower the people to live in righteousness and peace.

6. *Restoration of righteous leadership for Israel.* Some prophetic texts also promise new, trustworthy leaders for the nation, replacing the corrupt leadership of the past, that the people may be led into righteousness (Isa. 11:1–5; 32:1;

---

15. There are two general prophetic articulations of Israel's future relationship to the nations. The first envisions Israel's "abiding privilege," sometimes even a reversal or turning of the tables, so that the nations will submit to Israel, which will rule them with a rod of iron. The second stream of interpretation is more generous, envisioning Israel's "service to other nations," a process whereby they are restored to equity with Israel. For this distinction, see Christopher Zoccali, *Whom God Has Called: The Relationship of Church and Israel in Pauline Interpretation, 1920 to the Present* (Eugene, OR: Pickwick, 2010), 160–62.

Jer. 3:15; 23:5–6; 30:9; Ezek. 34:23–24; 37:22–25; Hosea 3:5; Amos 9:11–12; Mic. 5:2–4; Zech. 9:9–10). These promises are quite disparate, yet in the Second Temple period they become the basis of messianic hope, the anticipation that God will raise up someone (from either a royal or priestly line) who will truly lead the nation in fulfilling God's will, thus establishing God's kingdom on earth. Grounded in God's use of creaturely agents in bringing salvation (especially humanity created as *imago Dei*), this theme finds its fulfillment in the New Testament understanding of Jesus as the Christ, God's chosen one to restore Israel and, indeed, the world.

7. *God's presence among the people in the renewed land.* Tying the above themes together is the promise of God's permanent presence among the redeemed people in the context of the flourishing, bountiful land (Jer. 32:37–41; Ezek. 34:25–31; 37:24–28; Zech. 8:7–8). This is the fulfillment of the ancient and often reiterated claim that it is God's intent to dwell among the redeemed in the context of a divine-human relationship, where he would be their God and they would be his people (Exod. 29:45–46; Lev. 26:11–12). This intent is rooted, ultimately, in God's purpose from the beginning to manifest his presence on earth through the mediating role of humanity as the authorized image of God in the cosmic temple. Although Israel needed to function as the mediator of God's presence to the nations (because of their sin), the divine presence cannot ultimately be limited to Israel, to the temple, or to the promised land. Thus the book of Zechariah envisions God dwelling in the midst of Israel, along with the "many nations" that will have joined God's people (2:11), and speaks of the day when YHWH will become king over all the earth (14:9; cf. 10:9). Indeed, the prophets predict a day when the earth will finally be filled with the knowledge of God, or of his glory, "as the waters cover the sea" (Isa. 11:9; Hab. 2:14). In the end, the Old Testament anticipates that salvation will be as wide as creation.

6

The Coming of God in Judgment and Salvation

The preceding chapter ended with prophetic visions of God's renewal of people and land after the exile, including the promise of "new heavens and a new earth" (Isa. 65:17). These visions inspire us to expect a new world order in which the redeemed will live in peace and righteousness on the earth.

Yet the Old Testament also describes, often in calamitous apocalyptic language, the destruction of the world. As a prelude to the coming salvation, many prophetic oracles evoke a vivid theophany (an appearance or manifestation of God), accompanied by a shaking or melting of the cosmos as the divine judge approaches. These texts draw on visionary aspects of YHWH's coming to save in the Song of the Sea (Exod. 15:1–18) and especially his terrifying descent upon Mount Sinai (19:16–20). These theophanic visions can depict great destruction, as if the created order itself is coming radically undone.[1]

But the coming of the Holy One initiates the destruction not of creation as such, but of sin and evil. Ultimately, God's coming is good news. Thus the

1. Some of the language of Old Testament theophanies shows up in New Testament depictions of eschatological judgment, which many contemporary readers misinterpret as the annihilation of the cosmos (to be followed by "going to heaven"). This misreading of New Testament eschatology will be addressed in chap. 9 below, for which the present chapter lays an indispensable foundation.

enthronement psalms picture the nonhuman creation rejoicing at YHWH's coming to judge evil and restore justice on earth (Pss. 96:10–13; 98:7–9).

But before salvation there is judgment.

The Sinai Theophany

To understand the Old Testament imagery of cosmic destruction, we need to turn to the central and paradigmatic theophany in the Old Testament: YHWH's descent upon Mount Sinai in Exodus 19 in cloud, fire, thunder, and earthquake. The Sinai theophany draws on the terrifying experience of thunderstorms and also on classic storm images found in theophanies of ancient Near Eastern deities from Canaan and Mesopotamia. Perhaps more important for our purposes, the Sinai theophany becomes a model for many other Old Testament manifestations of the God of Israel, which tend to be depicted in poetic and prophetic visions.[2]

The book of Exodus records that prior to the theophany at Sinai, YHWH tells Moses, "I am going to come to you in a dense cloud" (19:9). He warns Moses to consecrate (or "make holy") both people (19:10) and priests (19:22) and says that any person or animal that touches the mountain will be put to death (19:12–13). Indeed, limits must be placed around the mountain to "keep it holy" (19:23), and those who "break through" these limits in an attempt to see God will perish (19:21): YHWH "will break out against them" (19:24). This dire warning evokes the ancient connotation of "holiness" as danger or threat; it communicates the powerful awareness that sinful humanity ordinarily cannot come into direct contact with the transcendent creator.

The Sinai theophany proper begins with the manifestation of YHWH in an awe-inspiring storm: There was "thunder and lightning, as well as a thick cloud on the mountain" and "a blast of a trumpet so loud that all the people who were in the camp trembled" (19:16). Just as the terrible holiness of God's presence is manifest in the imagery of a thunderstorm, so the trembling of the people is matched by the shaking of the mountain itself: "Mount Sinai was wrapped in smoke, because the LORD had descended upon it in fire; the smoke went up like the smoke of a kiln, while the whole mountain shook violently" (19:18).

Although the ultimate purpose of God's coming, at Sinai or elsewhere in the Old Testament, is the redemption or vindication of God's people, this coming typically includes judgment on evil. Thus the coming of the Holy One of Israel

---

2. For an important study of the Sinai theophany and its many echoes throughout the Old Testament, including similar imagery from Mesopotamian and Canaanite texts, see Jeffrey J. Niehaus, *God at Sinai: Covenant and Theophany in the Bible and Ancient Near East* (Studies in Old Testament Biblical Theology; Grand Rapids: Zondervan, 1995).

is often portrayed as having a visceral effect on those exposed to his presence and a tangible effect on the physical world. Both people and cosmos tremble or quake before the Lord. This is to be expected, since the biblical tradition consistently understands people as embodied earth creatures; YHWH's coming affects humanity at personal and bodily levels, and even shakes the earth, which is the inextricable context for human life.

Storm and Earthquake Accompany YHWH's Coming

Many examples of the use of storm imagery to portray YHWH's coming could be given, but one of the most vivid is Psalm 29. This psalm delights in envisioning a storm coming over the land of Israel as a manifestation of YHWH's power (he is "enthroned over the flood" [v. 10a]); the psalm even identifies thunder with the voice of God:

> The voice of the LORD is over the waters;
>   the God of glory thunders,
>   the LORD, over mighty waters.
> The voice of the LORD is powerful;
>   the voice of the LORD is full of majesty.
>   Psalm 29:3–4

Thunder is, naturally, accompanied by lightning: "The voice of the LORD flashes forth flames of fire" (v. 7). And although no explicit judgment appears in Psalm 29, this storm profoundly affects the physical world:

> The voice of the LORD breaks the cedars;
>   the LORD breaks the cedars of Lebanon.
> He makes Lebanon skip like a calf,
>   and Sirion like a young wild ox.
>   Psalm 29:5–6

> The voice of the LORD shakes the wilderness;
>   the LORD shakes the wilderness of Kadesh.
> The voice of the LORD causes the oaks to whirl,
>   and strips the forest bare;
>   and in his temple all say, "Glory!"
>   Psalm 29:8–9[3]

3. Although it is possible to see the "temple" in Ps. 29:9 as the sanctuary in Jerusalem, where God's people praise him for his power manifest in the storm (at some distance), it makes better

Consistent with the Sinai theophany, storm and earthquake imagery often appears throughout the Old Testament in descriptions of God's coming to judge and to save. Thus Judges 5 (often thought to be one of the oldest poetic texts in Scripture) declares,

> LORD, when you went out from Seir,
>> when you marched from the region of Edom,
> the earth trembled,
>> and the heavens poured,
>> the clouds indeed poured water.
> The mountains quaked before the LORD, the One of Sinai,
>> before the LORD, the God of Israel.
>
>> Judges 5:4–5

Likewise, God's coming in judgment is described in Isaiah 29 as a visitation:

> You will be visited by the LORD of hosts
>> with thunder and earthquake and great noise,
> with whirlwind and tempest,
>> and the flame of a devouring fire.[4]
>
>> Isaiah 29:6

In the very next chapter of Isaiah, God's judgment on the Assyrians uses similar imagery:

> And the LORD will cause his majestic voice to be heard
>> and the descending blow of his arm to be seen,
> in furious anger and a flame of devouring fire,
>> with a cloudburst and tempest and hailstones.
>
>> Isaiah 30:30

This last text reflects the standard metaphorical understanding of anger in the Old Testament as a sort of heat or fire (hence God's anger can "burn"). The result of this Hebrew metaphor is that fire in biblical theophanies can do double duty for the lightning of a storm and for God's wrath upon evil, visibly manifest as the brightness of his "glory."

---

sense of the context that the creatures in the wilderness and forest (part of the cosmic temple) respond to God's awe-inspiring presence in their midst.

4. The expectation of these typical manifestations of God's presence leads to Elijah's perplexity in 1 Kings 19:9–13. God told him to stand before the mountain of YHWH and that the divine presence would pass by. First there came a powerful windstorm causing landslides, then an earthquake, then a fire, but YHWH was not in any of them. Finally came the "sound of sheer silence" (traditionally, "a still small voice" [KJV]).

Fire as lightning explains why the blazing glory of God is often combined with the darkness of clouds in biblical theophanies; both lightning/fire and clouds/darkness are phenomena associated with thunderstorms, by which God's dangerous holiness is visibly and tangibly expressed. Thus God's presence accompanies Israel on the wilderness journey as a pillar of cloud by day and a pillar of fire by night (Exod. 13:21–22).

The combination of fire as lightning (in the midst of storm clouds) and as a means of judgment shows up in the vivid description of YHWH's descent from heaven to bring salvation in Psalm 18:

> He made darkness his covering around him,
>   his canopy thick clouds dark with water.
> Out of the brightness before him
>   there broke through his clouds
>   hailstones and coals of fire.
>
> The LORD also thundered in the heavens,
>   and the Most High uttered his voice.
> And he sent out his arrows, and scattered them;
>   he flashed forth lightnings, and routed them.
>
> Psalm 18:11–14

Psalm 97 likewise describes YHWH as reigning from the midst of the theophanic storm, with fire/lightning destroying his enemies:

> Clouds and thick darkness are all around him;
>   righteousness and justice are the foundation of his throne.
> Fire goes before him,
>   and consumes his adversaries on every side.
>
> His lightnings light up the world;
>   the earth sees and trembles.
> The mountains melt like wax before the LORD,
>   before the Lord of all the earth.
>
> Psalm 97:2–5

This particular psalm goes beyond the imagery of Sinai in envisioning the mountains as melting at YHWH's coming, which may well be an extrapolation from the Sinai earthquake and the red-hot fire of God's holy wrath.[5]

---

5. Earthquake imagery is common to many more texts of judgment in the Old Testament than can be cited here. Some examples are the splitting in two of the Mount of Olives (Zech. 14:3–5) and the shaking of the land of Israel, including all fish, birds, animals, and humans, resulting in the falling

The melting of the mountains when the Holy One comes from heaven to judge his people is also portrayed in the first chapter of Micah:

> The LORD is coming out of his place,
>   and will come down and tread
>   upon the high places of the earth.
> Then the mountains will melt under him
>   and the valleys will burst open,
>   like wax near the fire,
>   like waters poured down a steep place.[6]
>   Micah 1:3–4

This vivid language is meant as a poetic description of God's earthshaking judgment on Israel by the hand of Assyria.

Likewise, in Habakkuk 3, when God comes to deliver Israel from the Babylonians, the quaking of the earth is in parallel with the trembling of the peoples of the world:

> He stopped and shook the earth;
>   he looked and made the nations tremble.
> The eternal mountains were shattered;
>   along his ancient pathways the everlasting hills sank low.
>   Habakkuk 3:6

Although the effect of the storm theophany at Sinai was strictly limited to Israel and the mountain itself (both were shaken), we find much wider cosmic effects at God's coming in the last three texts cited (Ps. 97:2–5; Mic. 1:3–4; Hab. 3:6). There God's coming rocks the earth, causes the mountains to melt, and shakes the nations to the core.

The Heavens Are Affected by YHWH's Coming

But this is not the end of the cosmic effects of God's theophanic judgments. Beyond extending of the impact of God's coming from Israel and Mount

---

of all mountains, cliffs, and walls (Ezek. 38:19–20); in the Ezekiel text the earthquake is due to God's "blazing wrath" (v. 19a). Earthquake imagery is linked to God's anger also in Ps. 18:7; Nah. 1:5–6.

6. Other Old Testament texts can be cited that portray the melting of mountains or of the earth. Thus, according to Ps. 46:6, "The nations are in an uproar, / the kingdoms totter; / he utters his voice, / the earth melts." Likewise, Amos 9:5 speaks of YHWH thus: "The Lord, GOD of hosts, / he who touches the earth and it melts, / and all who live in it mourn, / and all of it rises like the Nile, / and sinks again, like the Nile of Egypt." In the course of praising YHWH, Ps. 104:33 comments that YHWH has only to look at the earth, and it trembles; and when he touches the mountains, they smoke (probably anticipating the judgment on the wicked, as in v. 35).

Sinai to the nations and the mountains (plural), and even to the earth itself, in other texts we find that God's coming affects even celestial phenomena. Thus YHWH states about the coming judgment, "I will make the heavens tremble, / and the earth will be shaken out of its place" (Isa. 13:13). In this vein, the prophet Jeremiah has a vision of God's judgment as a shaking of the cosmos (heaven and earth) until it returns to a precreation state as described in Genesis 1:2 (when the earth was "waste and void," prior to God declaring, "Let there be light" [1:3]):

> I looked on the earth, and lo, it was waste and void;
>> and to the heavens, and they had no light.
> I looked on the mountains, and lo, they were quaking,
>> and all the hills moved to and fro.
>> Jeremiah 4:23–24

A few verses later Jeremiah goes on to suggest that the lack of light in the heavens is caused by the grief of creation at God's judgment: "Because of this the earth shall mourn, / and the heavens above grow black" (4:28).

In Joel 3, the motif of the heavens giving no light as part of the shaking of creation is applied specifically to the heavenly bodies—sun, moon, and stars. This is how the text poetically portrays judgment on the nations after God brings his people back from exile:

> The sun and the moon are darkened,
>> and the stars withdraw their shining.
> The Lord roars from Zion,
>> and utters his voice from Jerusalem,
>> and the heavens and the earth shake.
>> Joel 3:15–16[7]

In other words, the return from exile is an earth-shattering (and heaven-shattering) event. And in this context the heavenly bodies are dimmed.

This dimming is also portrayed in the judgment oracle against Babylon in Isaiah 13:

> See, the day of the Lord comes,
>> cruel, with wrath and fierce anger,
> to make the earth a desolation,
>> and to destroy its sinners from it.

7. Joel 4:15–16 MT.

> For the stars of the heavens and their constellations
>   will not give their light;
> the sun will be dark at its rising,
>   and the moon will not shed its light.
>
> Isaiah 13:9–10

But why are the sun and moon dimmed? Some texts, like Joel 2, associate this darkening of the heavens and the heavenly bodies with smoke rising from earthly destruction:

> I will show portents in the heavens and on the earth,
>   blood and fire and columns of smoke.
> The sun shall be turned to darkness,
>   and the moon to blood,
>   before the great and terrible day of the Lord comes.
>
> Joel 2:30–31[8]

Alternatively, Ezekiel 32, which is addressed to an Egyptian Pharaoh, suggests that God will cover the sky with clouds, thus dimming the light of the heavenly bodies, possibly evoking the scene when God brought darkness over the land of Egypt at the exodus.

> When I blot you out, I will cover the heavens,
>   and make their stars dark;
> I will cover the sun with a cloud,
>   and the moon shall not give its light.
> All the shining lights of the heavens I will darken above you,
>   and put darkness on your land, says the Lord God.
>
> Ezekiel 32:7–8

However, in Habakkuk's vision of YHWH coming to deliver Israel from its enemies, God's effect on the cosmos is depicted by personification of the heavenly bodies; they seem surprised or transfixed by God's actions, possibly by the visible glory or brightness that accompanies God's judgment:

> The sun raised high its hands;
>   the moon stood still in its exalted place,
> at the light of your arrows speeding by,
>   at the gleam of your flashing spear.
>
> Habakkuk 3:10b–11

---

8. Joel 3:3–4 MT. This is part of a longer passage (Joel 2:28–32 [3:1–5 MT]) quoted in Acts 2:16–21 by the apostle Peter, which he claims has come to fulfillment on the day of Pentecost. The coming of the Spirit, resulting in the birth of the church, is an earth-shattering and heaven-shattering event.

Isaiah 24 goes further in this personification by portraying the darkening of the heavenly bodies as their shame in the glorious presence of YHWH.[9]

> Then the moon will be abashed,
>   and the sun ashamed;
> for the LORD of hosts will reign on Mount Zion and in Jerusalem,
>   and before his elders he will manifest his glory.
>
> Isaiah 24:23

Why are the sun and moon ashamed at God's presence? Perhaps they are ashamed because of the corruption of the earth (mentioned in Isa. 24:19–20), since heaven and earth are inextricably linked in the Old Testament. But the heavenly bodies might be ashamed because they share the sky with corrupt heavenly powers (false gods or angelic beings). Just two verses earlier the text had declared, "On that day the LORD will punish the host of heaven in heaven, / and on earth the kings of the earth" (Isa. 24:21). This punishment suggests that "the host of heaven" refers to more than just the stars, and that the sun and moon are ashamed by association with them (after all, both inhabit the same sphere).

Elsewhere in the Old Testament (as in the ancient Near East generally) it is quite clear that celestial bodies can stand for angelic or divine beings, which are either good or evil. In some texts they are YHWH's servants, as "when the morning stars sang together / and all the heavenly beings [lit. "sons of God"] shouted for joy" (Job 38:7) at creation. Presumably, the stars in Judges 5 represent heavenly forces coming to the aid of God's people: "The stars fought from heaven, / from their courses they fought against Sisera" (Judg. 5:20). This gives support to the idea that God's punishment of "the host of heaven" in Isaiah 24:21 (in parallel to kings on the earth) is a reference to judgment on false gods.

The same seems to be the case in Isaiah 34, which begins with judgment in heaven:

> All the host of heaven shall rot away,
>   and the skies roll up like a scroll.
> All their host shall wither like a leaf withering on a vine,
>   or fruit withering on a fig tree.
>
> Isaiah 34:4[10]

---

9. The darkening of the heavenly bodies is seen in other Old Testament texts, such as Ezek. 32:7 and Amos 8:9. Although not specifically mentioning heavenly bodies, both Amos 5:20 and Zeph. 1:15 describe the day of YHWH as a time of general darkness.

10. Note that both "heaven" and "skies" (NRSV) in verse 4 are translations of the same Hebrew word (*šāmayim*).

Then the text turns to judgment on earth, with a focus on one of the nations:

> When my sword has drunk its fill in the heavens,
>   lo, it will descend upon Edom,
> upon the people I have doomed to judgment.
>   Isaiah 34:5[11]

While Isaiah 34:4 uses the image of the heavens/sky being rolled up like a scroll, language about the heavens passing away (along with the earth) occurs in Isaiah 51, in an oracle of redemption for Israel and judgment against the nations. There YHWH exhorts his people,

> Lift up your eyes to the heavens,
>   and look at the earth beneath;
> for the heavens will vanish like smoke,
>   the earth will wear out like a garment,
> and those who live on it will die like gnats;
>   but my salvation will be forever,
> and my deliverance will never be ended.
>   Isaiah 51:6

Whereas in Isaiah 34:4 the NRSV can't quite make up its mind about how to translate *šāmayim*, rendering it as "heaven" in one line (perhaps thinking of "the host of heaven" as false gods or demonic forces) and as "skies" in the next line (taking the term more literally), here the tension is not between the meaning of the heavens as the literal sky or as fallen angelic powers. Instead, we have what seems to be the destruction of heaven and earth (and all the earth's inhabitants), followed by God's salvation. But what sort of salvation/deliverance is expected here if heaven and earth no longer exist? There certainly is no nonearthly salvation in the Old Testament; indeed, there would not even be a "heaven" to go to if it vanished like smoke, as this text indicates. And who is saved if all people on earth are destroyed?

In context, the salvation intended in Isaiah 51 is God's vindication of his people after oppression by their enemies, supremely by their return to the land after Babylonian exile. That salvation is central here is evident both from the preceding verse ("I will bring near my deliverance swiftly, / my salvation has gone out and my arms will rule the peoples" [v. 5]) and the end of verse 6 ("My salvation will be forever, / and my deliverance will never be ended"). Yet the

---

11. It is unclear why God singles out Edom here, since the oracle proclaims judgment on "all the nations" (Isa. 34:2).

text can use quite extreme language to refer to the judgment that precedes this salvation.

We find a similar dynamic at work in Psalm 102. Addressing God, the psalmist says,

> Long ago you laid the foundation of the earth,
>   and the heavens are the work of your hands.
> They will perish, but you endure;
>   they will all wear out like a garment.
> You change them like clothing, and they pass away;
>   but you are the same, and your years have no end.
>
> Psalm 102:25–27

Unlike the other Old Testament texts examined thus far, this is not a judgment oracle; it is a lament psalm in which the supplicant is desperate for God's help. The verses above (which contrast the transience of the created order with God's permanence) function as the "confession of trust" typical of laments, a confession that provides the basis for the psalmist's expectation that God will respond to the prayer for help. In this case, God is able to save because he is the eternal creator; he outlasts and is more dependable than any merely creaturely help.

This is made clear in Psalm 102 by the verses immediately preceding and following. In the preceding verse, the psalmist grounds his plea in the fact that God is everlasting: "'O my God,' I say, 'do not take me away at the mid-point of my life, / you whose years endure throughout all generations'" (v. 24). Then, after verses 25–27, which expand on God's everlastingness, the psalmist affirms to the Lord, "The children of your servants shall live secure; / their offspring shall be established in your presence" (v. 28).

The contrast between God and the cosmos thus serves as the basis for the psalmist's confidence that his prayer will be answered; because God is eternally faithful (and can even outlast the cosmos), salvation is assured. Psalm 102 is not predicting the ending of the world; rather, it is better taken as affirming that *even if* the world did come to an end, God would still be faithful. Indeed, the Hebrew verbs in verse 26 translated as future in the NRSV (along with most English versions) could just as well be taken as (modal) statements of possibility: "They may perish / but you would stand. / All of them could wear out like clothes; like a garment you could make them pass on."[12]

---

12. This is the translation by John Goldingay, *Psalms* (Baker Commentary on the Old Testament: Wisdom and Psalms; Grand Rapids: Baker Academic, 2008), 3:148. On the idea that the

Similar hypothetical statements of cosmic destruction are found in Psalm 46:2–3:

> Therefore we will not fear, though the earth should change,
>   though the mountains shake in the heart of the sea;
> though its waters roar and foam,
>   though the mountains tremble with its tumult.

and in Isaiah 54:10:

> For the mountains may depart and the hills be removed,
> but my steadfast love shall not depart from you,
>   and my covenant of peace shall not be removed,
> says the LORD, who has compassion on you.

Despite the fact that the contrast between God and the cosmos in Psalm 102:25–27 sounds absolute, few if any Old Testament scholars think that the salvation of verse 28 is envisioned in "heaven" (not least because both heaven and earth are said to wear out and pass away).[13] As we saw in the last two chapters, the Old Testament consistently expects earthly salvation.

This should warn us about forcing Old Testament imagery of cosmic destruction into a preconceived (literalistic) mold. Instead, we need to discern the theological claims undergirding this imagery by interpreting it with sensitivity to its context.

The Flexible Nature of Biblical Imagery

We also need to be attentive to the multivalent character of this imagery, especially since it occurs primarily in poetic texts. The fact that celestial phenomena can sometimes stand for false gods (or later, fallen angels) makes it very difficult for us to figure out the exact meaning of every Old Testament text about celestial destruction. Should we understand the image to refer to the physical sky above, or to God's judgment on the evil powers understood to dwell in the heavens, or to both?

---

cosmos will come to an end, Goldingay comments, "The OT does not elsewhere make such a statement" (ibid., 3:160).

13. Another possible interpretation of the metaphor of the cosmos as clothing that God will change focuses on the transformation of the world rather than its transience, but this reading does not arise until the New Testament. In chap. 9 I will address the allusions to Ps. 102 in the New Testament, as well as the function of the cosmos "passing away" as a part of the sequence of redemptive transformation.

This ambiguity brings to mind the multiple layers of meaning that light and fire may have in theophanies of judgment. Storm imagery suggests bolts of lightning, pictured as YHWH's arrows, but some texts also draw on the metaphor of anger as heat or burning, while others suggest the "glory" or brightness of God visibly manifest.

Likewise, the darkening of sun and moon is multivalent. This darkening can result from columns of smoke rising from the earth (Joel 2) or from God covering the sky with clouds (Ezek. 32); it might evoke a precreation state (prior to "Let there be light") or refer to the grief or mourning of creation over human sin (Jer. 4); the darkening of the heavenly bodies can even result from their shame in connection with God's judgment of heavenly beings and also in contrast to God's surpassing glory (Isa. 24).

Perhaps we need to allow the imagery of these biblical texts a certain poetic flexibility: they are describing momentous events and realities that cannot be adequately conveyed in ordinary descriptive prose.[14] The point of using the hyperbolic language of cosmic destruction in Old Testament theophanies to refer to ordinary historical events (like the rescue of Israel from oppression by the nations) is to forcefully and vividly convey both that God is the agent behind these events and that radical judgment is necessary to accomplish salvation. Indeed, this judgment is so radical as to destabilize the present order. But make no mistake, in each case salvation, and not simply judgment, is the intended outcome.

God's Judgment Is Ultimately Redemptive

We have seen that salvation is the outcome in the case of Isaiah 51 and Psalm 102, but perhaps a few more examples are appropriate. Take, for example, the vision in Isaiah 24, which speaks of the violent shaking of the earth (both people and environment [vv. 1–13, 17–20]) and the punishing of the host of heaven, along with the shaming of sun and moon (vv. 21–23a). This vision

14. Poets have often used vivid imagery to convey the significance of world-shaking events. Thus William Butler Yeats portrays the decline and corruption of early twentieth-century European society in his poem "The Second Coming" (first published in *The Dial*, November 1920): "Things fall apart; the centre cannot hold; / Mere anarchy is loosed upon the world, / The blood-dimmed tide is loosed." Yeats is not quite sure about a positive resolution of this crisis, so the poem ends ambiguously with this question: "And what rough beast, its hour come round at last, / Slouches towards Bethlehem to be born?" In a more positive (and personal) vein, Carole King sings of being in the presence of a special person, using imagery that resonates with Old Testament theophanies: "I feel the earth move under my feet, / I feel the sky tumbling down. / I feel my heart start to trembling / whenever you're around" (Carole King, "I Feel the Earth Move," on the 1971 album *Tapestry*).

of destruction is punctuated by the songs of praise of the redeemed from the ends of the earth (vv. 14–16a) and concludes with the glory of YHWH reigning on Mount Zion (v. 23b).

Likewise, Psalm 97, which portrays God's burning anger that causes the earth to tremble and the mountains to melt (vv. 2–5), is surrounded by a call for the earth to rejoice (v. 1) and a statement that all the peoples see God's glory (v. 6); indeed, the rest of the psalm speaks of Zion's joy and God's rescue of the righteous (vv. 8–12). These last two examples are from among the many texts that we have already examined.

One text that we have not yet looked at is Haggai 2. In the context of the postexilic rebuilding of the temple, YHWH promises, "Once again, in a little while, I will shake the heavens and the earth and the sea and the dry land; and I will shake all the nations" (vv. 6–7). This promise is repeated a few verses later, where it is made clear that this cosmic shakeup describes God's judgment on the oppressive military might of the nations: "I am about to shake the heavens and the earth, and to overthrow the throne of kingdoms; I am about to destroy the strength of the kingdoms of the nations, and overthrow the chariots and their riders; and the horses and their riders shall fall, every one by the sword of a comrade" (vv. 21–22). But this cosmic shaking is not ultimately about destruction; rather, it is for the benefit of the temple, with the result that "the treasure of all nations shall come, and I will fill this house with splendor, says the LORD of hosts" (v. 7).

Further examples are possible, but they would take us too far afield. Suffice it to say that if we were to investigate every case of theophanic judgment in the Old Testament, we would find not only that the language of extreme destruction typically describes some intrahistorical event, but also that it is always for the ultimate purpose of salvation.

Judgment as Refining by Fire

The relevant point is well expressed by the image of smelting or refining found in some prophetic texts. Thus Zechariah 13 makes clear that the fire of God is not simply destructive; or, to be precise, we might say that it is destructive of sin and not creation. The oracle begins with reference to "a fountain" by which God will cleanse his people from sin and impurity (v. 1). But the metaphor soon changes to fire, by which God will "refine them [the remnant that survives judgment] as one refines silver, / and test them as gold is tested" (v. 9a). The result is that they will once more call on YHWH, who will acknowledge them as his people, while they acknowledge him as their God (v. 9b). God's fiery judgment is thus ultimately for salvation.

The metaphor of fire as refining is even more prominent in Isaiah 1. Describing the injustice of Jerusalem as the tarnishing of silver ("Your silver has become dross" [v. 22]), the text goes on to describe the process of judgment by which repentant Zion will be restored:

> I will smelt away your dross as with lye
>   and remove all your alloy.
> And I will restore your judges as at the first,
>   and your counselors as at the beginning.
> Afterward you shall be called the city of righteousness,
>   the faithful city.
> Zion shall be redeemed by justice,
>   and those in her who repent, by righteousness.
>
> Isaiah 1:25–27

Interestingly, the metaphor of fire continues in Isaiah 1, but this time to describe the destruction of unrepentant evildoers and their deeds:

> The strong shall become like tinder,
>   and their work like a spark;
> they and their work shall burn together,
>   with no one to quench them.
>
> Isaiah 1:31

The image of the refining fire is perhaps most prominent in the book of Malachi. Chapter 3 begins by introducing the messenger of the covenant, whom YHWH is sending to Israel, especially to purify the Levitical priesthood.[15]

> But who can endure the day of his coming,
>   and who can stand when he appears?
> For he is like a refiner's fire and like fullers' soap;
>   he will sit as a refiner and purifier of silver,
> and he will purify the descendants of Levi
>   and refine them like gold and silver,
>   until they present offerings to the LORD in righteousness.
>
> Malachi 3:2–3

---

15. In Mal. 3:1 YHWH calls this figure "my messenger" (*mal'ākî*), from which the prophetic book derives its name.

But the fire does not just cleanse. As in Isaiah 1, here Malachi 4 goes on to describe the fiery destruction of those who continue to do evil:

> See, the day is coming, burning like an oven,
>> when all the arrogant and all evildoers will be stubble;
> the day that comes shall burn them up, says the LORD of hosts,
>> so that it will leave them neither root nor branch.
>>>> Malachi 4:1 (3:19 MT)

Yet for those who revere YHWH, "the sun of righteousness shall rise, with healing in its wings" (Mal. 4:2 [3:20 MT]).

What Are the Ships of Tarshish Doing Here?

An illuminating example of judgment that radically transforms without totally destroying what is judged is found in the vision of Isaiah 60, which describes a purified Jerusalem after the Babylonian exile—especially when this vision is contrasted with the oracle of judgment in Isaiah 2.[16] According to Isaiah 60, the nations that formerly oppressed Israel will now contribute to Zion's glory. In particular, we are told that the temple will be rebuilt with lumber from the trees of Lebanon (v. 13), and that the ships of Tarshish will bring the exiles home (v. 9).

Yet we should note that the prophetic oracle in Isaiah 2 voiced a radical critique of both the trees of Lebanon and the ships of Tarshish.

> For the LORD of hosts has a day against all that is proud and lofty,
>> against all that is lifted up and high;
> against all the cedars of Lebanon, lofty and lifted up;
>> and against all the oaks of Bashan;
> against all the high mountains,
>> and against all the lofty hills;
> against every high tower,
>> and against every fortified wall;
> against all the ships of Tarshish,
>> and against all the beautiful craft.
>>>> Isaiah 2:12–16

16. For an excellent analysis of Isa. 60, see Richard J. Mouw, *When the Kings Come Marching In: Isaiah and the New Jerusalem* (Grand Rapids: Eerdmans, 1983), especially the chapter "What Are the Ships of Tarshish Doing Here?"

The point is not that God is against tall trees, high mountains, or beautiful ships (indeed, Ps. 104:16 describes the cedars of Lebanon as "trees of YHWH," which he planted). Rather, what we have in Isaiah 2 is the critique of all that is used to oppose God, which have become symbols of human pride. In contrast to all that is lifted up against God, Isaiah 2 begins with a vision of the future exaltation of God's temple in Zion as the highest of all mountains, to which the nations will come to learn God's ways (vv. 1–4); this vision is expanded in Isaiah 60. The point is that precisely what has been judged by God (the lofty cedars of Lebanon and the mighty ships of Tarshish) finds a place (suitably transformed) in the purified city of God.

Isaiah 2 also condemns the ill-gotten wealth of Israel ("Their land is filled with silver and gold, and there is no end to their treasures" [v. 7]), observing that this wealth has been used for idolatrous purposes, hence the mention of "their idols of silver and their idols of gold" (v. 20). Yet Isaiah 60 envisions a renewed Jerusalem, where the wealth of nations is brought into the city (vv. 5, 11); silver and gold are specifically mentioned (vv. 6, 9, 17). How can the very items subject to God's judgment in Isaiah 2 reappear in the holy city? The principle at work here is that judgment is ultimately not for destruction, but rather for transformation. After all, Isaiah 2 is the origin of the famous statement "They shall beat their swords into plowshares, and their spears into pruning hooks" (v. 4).[17]

Judgment for the Healing of the World

Judgment for the sake of redemption is the consistent pattern of Scripture. Thus the scattering of Babel and confusion of languages allowed a fresh beginning for humanity, without imperial oppression. At the flood, the violence of the world was subjected to radical cleansing so that Noah and his family could start over. The Babylonian exile, likewise, served to dismantle Israel's idolatry and injustice in order to permit a new beginning for God's people, on different footing. The biblical pattern is that God smites and heals.

This suggests that language of apocalyptic destruction in the Old Testament intends not the annihilation of the cosmos, but rather a new world cleansed of evil. Judgment is real because sin is a serious matter; and extreme language is often used to emphasize the radical nature of the purging required for salvation. While judgment is an inescapable reality for those who resist God's will,

17. The oracle in Isa. 2:1–4 is repeated in Mic. 4:1–3.

God's ultimate purpose is to accomplish his original intent for the flourishing of humanity (Israel and the nations) and the nonhuman world.

The reality of judgment even intrudes into Psalm 104, a beautiful creation psalm that is permeated throughout by the vision of a harmonious, well-functioning creation.[18] Although the concluding stanza of the psalm opens with the prayer "May the glory of the LORD endure forever; / may the LORD rejoice in his works" (v. 31), the psalmist realizes that if YHWH is going to rejoice in the world he made (his works), evil will have to be dealt with. So the psalm ends just a few verses later with a wish that "sinners be consumed from the earth" and that "the wicked be no more" (v. 35). In anticipation of this concluding wish, the psalmist utilizes language from the judgment theophanies: when YHWH "looks at the earth, . . . it trembles," and when he "touches the mountains, . . . they smoke" (v. 32).

Yet Psalm 104 is clear that while God's judgment of evil (temporarily) destabilizes the cosmos, this is not God's normative relationship to the world he loves. Earlier in the psalm we are told that God "waters the mountains" and that "the earth is satisfied from the fruit of [God's] work" (v. 13). Indeed, at creation YHWH "set the earth on its foundations, / so that it shall never be shaken" (v. 5). The paradox is that God's initially unshakable world, now distorted by evil, will indeed be shaken when evil is removed, but that is precisely so that creation can once again stand secure.

That this cosmic shaking is for the sake of earthly flourishing is even clearer in Psalm 96, which like Psalm 104 affirms the unshakable nature of the cosmos God made. Psalm 96 proclaims to the nations, "The LORD is king! / The world is firmly established; / it shall never be moved," and adds, "He will judge the peoples with equity" (v. 10), since this is how God maintains or restores cosmic order. As in a typical theophany, Psalm 96 portrays the created order as moved or shaken at God's coming in judgment. However, the "movement" of creation in Psalm 96 is less like cosmic destabilization and more akin to a cosmic dance—an excited celebration of YHWH's coming.

> Let the heavens be glad,
>   and let the earth rejoice;
> let the sea roar,
>   and all that fills it;
> let the field exult,
>   and everything in it.

18. For an analysis of the understanding of evil in Ps. 104, see J. Richard Middleton, "The Role of Human Beings in the Cosmic Temple: The Intersection of Worldviews in Psalms 8 and 104," *Canadian Theological Review* 2 (2013): 44–58.

> Then shall all the trees of the forest sing for joy
>   before the LORD; for he is coming,
>   for he is coming to judge the earth.
> He will judge the world with righteousness,
>   and the peoples with his truth.
>
> Psalm 96:11–13[19]

This language evokes aspects of the vision in Psalm 29, which we examined near the start of this chapter. Although Psalm 29 uses imagery typical of cosmic theophanies, there is no specific reference to judgment, but rather a positive portrayal of God's awesome presence in the midst of a storm, which "makes Lebanon skip like a calf" (v. 6) and "causes the oaks to whirl" (v. 9).[20]

C. S. Lewis evokes similar images of the celebration of the nonhuman world in his novel *Prince Caspian*, where he pictures the dance of the trees as Aslan, the rightful Lord of Narnia, arrives.[21] Prior to Aslan's arrival, one of the characters in the novel, Trufflehunter, notices that the forests and streams of Narnia had been affected negatively by human evil; another character, Lucy, longs for the old days when the trees were awake.[22] Then when Aslan returns to put an end to the evil in Narnia, the trees of the forest awaken and begin to move in a joyous dance around their Lord, who has come to redeem the world.[23]

As in *Prince Caspian*, the more positive emphasis of Psalm 96 is due to the fact that the focus is not on the fearsomeness of the judgment required to remove evil (as in many of the theophanies that we have examined). Rather, Psalm 96, like *Prince Caspian*, portrays the rejoicing of creation at the result

19. Psalm 98, using almost identical language, lays out a similar vision of the rejoicing of the natural order at God's coming.

20. Interestingly, Frank Moore Cross has discerned a twofold mythic pattern in ancient Canaanite poetry that has its echoes also in biblical theophanies. On the one hand, when the Divine Warrior goes forth to battle against the forces of chaos, "nature convulses (writhes) and languishes when the Warrior manifests his wrath"; but when the Divine Warrior comes to take up kingship and is enthroned, "Nature again responds. The heavens fertilize the earth, animals writhe in giving birth, and men and mountains whirl in dancing and festive glee" (*Canaanite Myth and Hebrew Epic: Essays in the History of the Religion of Israel* [Cambridge, MA: Harvard University Press, 1973], 162–63).

21. C. S. Lewis, *Prince Caspian: The Return to Narnia* (New York: Macmillan, 1951).

22. Ibid., 76 (for Trufflehunter), 112 (for Lucy). Lucy's plaintive cry, "O trees, trees, trees" may well evoke Jeremiah's appeal, "O land, land, land" (Jer. 22:29).

23. Ibid., 132–35. For a fascinating analysis of trees responding to God (in science and Scripture), see Brian J. Walsh, Marianne B. Karsh, and Nik Ansell, "Trees, Forestry, and the Responsiveness of Creation," *Cross Currents* 44 (1994): 149–62, http://www.crosscurrents.org/trees.htm. For a dramatic account of the role of trees in the Bible, from the garden of Eden to the new Jerusalem, see Sylvia C. Keesmaat, "The Beautiful Creatures: Trees in the Biblical Story," http://theotherjournal.com/2009/07/16/the-beautiful-creatures-trees-in-the-biblical-story/.

of God's judgment: the liberation of the nonhuman world from the burden of human evil.

In the end, when YHWH comes to judge evil and restore justice on earth, the Old Testament anticipates a grand celebration. Then all the redeemed (human and nonhuman alike) will enjoy the flourishing and blessing that God intended; then God's salvation will indeed be as wide as creation itself.

Part 3

The New Testament's Vision of Cosmic Renewal

7

Resurrection and the Restoration of Rule

In the preceding three chapters we examined representative aspects of the Old Testament's concern with earthly flourishing. It is now time to turn to the New Testament (while still dipping into the Old Testament, as needed). The present chapter focuses on the biblical hope of resurrection and its connection to the restoration of human rule of the earth; in the next chapter we will explore the New Testament's consistent expectation of the redemption of all things, including its vision of a new heaven and a new earth.

But let us start with resurrection. One of the distinctive doctrines of the Christian faith is the resurrection of the body—both the raising of Jesus three days after his crucifixion and the expected resurrection of believers at the end of the age. Indeed, it was the centrality of the resurrection that served to distinguish orthodox Christian faith from gnostic interpretations in the first centuries of the early church. Whereas the variant ancient traditions that came to be called "gnosticism" are suspicious of materiality (thus denying God's direct creation of the cosmos, as well as the importance of the incarnation and the resurrection), orthodox faith wholeheartedly affirms that God loves this world he made, became flesh in the man Jesus, and is committed to redeeming the created order, with resurrection being central to that redemption.

The resurrection of Jesus is recounted as the climax of all four Gospels (Matt. 28; Mark 16; Luke 24; John 20–21), and it begins the book of Acts, which links the origins of the church to the story told in Luke (Acts 1:1–9). Beyond these narrative accounts, many other parts of the New Testament support the importance of the resurrection, especially 1 Corinthians 15. The first eleven verses of 1 Corinthians 15 focus on Jesus's resurrection as central to the gospel message, while the rest of the chapter contains a lengthy clarification of the nature of resurrection (in response to misunderstandings in the early church).[1] But for the most part, mention of Jesus's resurrection tends to be a subtheme interwoven into various theological statements and ethical injunctions throughout the New Testament, where it is treated as a nonnegotiable core of the gospel and often connected to the anticipated resurrection of those who follow Jesus.

Beyond the passages mentioned above, there are numerous other explicit references to the resurrection in the Gospels and Acts (Matt. 12:40; 16:21; 17:9, 22–23; 20:19; Mark 8:31; 9:9, 31; 10:34; 12:24–27; Luke 9:22; 14:14; 18:33; John 2:19–22; 10:17–18; Acts 1:3, 22; 2:24, 32; 3:15; 10:39–41), as well as in the Epistles and the book of Revelation (Rom. 1:2–4; 4:23–25; 6:4–5; 7:4; 8:11, 34; 10:9; 1 Cor. 6:14; 15:1–58; 2 Cor. 1:9; 4:14; 5:15; Gal. 1:1; Eph. 1:20; Phil. 3:10–11, 21; 1 Thess. 1:10; 4:14, 16; 2 Tim. 2:8, 11, 18; Heb. 6:2; 11:35; 13:20; 1 Pet. 1:3, 21; Rev. 5:6; 20:5–6). And this is not yet to mention the multitude of implicit references, some of which will be addressed in the discussion to follow. The New Testament clearly teaches not only that Christ was raised bodily from death, but also that all who share in Christ's death (by repentance and faith) will share in his resurrection and new life.[2]

Since the centrality of resurrection (both of Jesus and believers) in the New Testament is effectively beyond dispute, this chapter does not seek to demonstrate it. Rather, the goal here is to clarify the inner logic of resurrection. Why is resurrection important for biblical theology? How does it fit with the overall holistic vision of the Scriptures?

Sheol as the End of Earthly Life in the Old Testament

One of the contrasts between the Old Testament and the New Testament is their understanding of the afterlife. In contrast to the centrality of resurrection

---

1. For the questions that Paul was addressing, see 1 Cor. 15:12, 35; the practical upshot of the chapter is summarized in 15:58.

2. For an in-depth study of resurrection in the New Testament (with analysis of Old Testament, Second Temple, and pagan backgrounds), see N. T. Wright, *The Resurrection of the Son of God* (Christian Origins and the Question of God 3; Minneapolis: Fortress, 2003). Wright's work has been very helpful for honing my own thoughts about the significance of resurrection. Wright's book (chaps. 5–10) is particularly insightful in showing how the resurrection often functions as an implicit subtheme in the New Testament, shaping the discussion even when it is not explicitly named.

in the New Testament (and late Second Temple Judaism), the Old Testament does not typically place any significant hope in life after death.[3] The closest the Old Testament gets to the idea of an afterlife is in its references to Sheol as the place of the dead. As Psalm 89:48 puts it, "Who can live and never see death? / Who can escape the power of Sheol?" While the numerous Old Testament references to Sheol, the grave, or the pit present a somewhat inchoate picture of a shadowy or diminished existence in the underworld (similar to the Greek notion of Hades), one thing is clear: there is no access to God after death.[4]

Not only do the dead in Sheol have no memory of God or know of his faithfulness and salvation, but also they are unable to praise him (Pss. 6:5; 88:4–5, 10–12; 115:17); this final sentiment is echoed by King Hezekiah as he contemplates his own death (Isa. 38:18). Thus we find the psalmist's desperate plea with God for rescue or healing: "What profit is there in my death, / if I go down to the Pit? / Will the dust praise you? / Will it tell of your faithfulness?" (Ps. 30:9). The point is that if God wants the psalmist's praise, he must prevent the psalmist from dying.

Despite a vivid picture in Isaiah 14 of the shades of the dead receiving the king of Babylon into the underworld, accompanied by taunts about going down to the maggots and worms (vv. 9–11), the usual picture of Sheol is more passive: the dead do not do anything (and hence can be said to be "asleep").[5] This is why Job yearns for the grave; there he will finally be at rest from his intolerable sufferings (Job 3:13–15, 17–19). But Job's outburst in chapter 3 is unusual in longing for death. Even the author of Ecclesiastes thinks that a living dog is better off than a dead lion, since the dead know nothing and no longer have a share in life (9:4–6); indeed, "there is no work or thought or knowledge or wisdom in Sheol" (9:10).[6]

3. On the resurrection in Christianity and Judaism, see Kevin J. Madigan and Jon D. Levenson, *Resurrection: The Power of God for Christians and Jews* (New Haven: Yale University Press, 2008).

4. There is one text that, on the surface, seems to contradict this point. In Ps. 139 the writer asks, "Where can I go from your spirit? / Or where can I flee from your presence?," and answers, "If I ascend to heaven, you are there; / if I make my bed in Sheol, you are there" (vv. 7–8). But this is not a formal theological statement; it is a prayer affirming (in hyperbolic language) the psalmist's trust in God's providential care.

5. The metaphor of "sleep" (*koimaō*) is common in the New Testament as a way of speaking of death (Matt. 27:52; John 11:11; Acts 7:60; 1 Cor. 7:39; 11:30; 15:6, 18, 20, 51; 1 Thess. 4:13–15; 2 Pet. 3:4). The metaphor seems to be derived from Old Testament references to someone "lying down" (*šākab*) with their ancestors (Gen. 47:30; Deut. 31:16; 2 Sam. 7:12; 1 Kings 2:10; 2 Chron. 14:1); see also 2 Macc. 12:45, which indicates death by the same Greek verb for "sleep" (*koimaō*) found in the New Testament texts.

6. Does this mean that Sheol is simply a metaphor for being dead? Is the grave or the pit just a reference to being buried in the ground? Or is there something more? While there is clearly an

The negative picture of the afterlife is confirmed by the use of language associated with Sheol to describe a life that has been invaded by death, a life that does not manifest the flourishing and shalom that God intends.[7] Thus many psalms equate suffering or persecution with the pit, the grave, or death (e.g., Pss. 18:3–6; 69:14–15; 116:3, 8; 143:7). And when Jacob mourns Joseph, thinking him dead, we are told that "he refused to be comforted, and said, 'No, I shall go down to Sheol to my son, mourning'" (Gen. 37:35). Jacob was not planning suicide. Rather, the quality of his life had been compromised; life had become as death to him.

Likewise, the writer of Psalm 88, who clearly is not yet dead, compares his suffering to being in Sheol:

> For my soul is full of troubles,
>   and my life draws near to Sheol.
> I am counted among those who go down to the Pit;
>   I am like those who have no help,
> like those forsaken among the dead,
>   like the slain that lie in the grave,
> like those whom you remember no more,
>   for they are cut off from your hand.
> You have put me in the depths of the Pit,
>   in the regions dark and deep.
>
> Psalm 88:3–6

The point is that life has become death-like; the presence and blessing of God are not being experienced. Indeed, the presence of God is typically associated with life and God's absence with death; thus Psalm 104 states, "When you hide your face, they are dismayed; / when you take away their breath, they die and return to their dust" (v. 29).[8] So when another psalmist tells God, "You hid your face; I was dismayed" (Ps. 30:7b), he is saying that his life has become as death to him. Even before the cessation of one's physical existence, it is

---

association between literally being buried in a grave and going down to Sheol, they do not seem to be identical. Thus we find the statement "David slept with his ancestors, and was buried in the city of David" (1 Kings 2:10). Since none of David's ancestors were actually buried in Jerusalem (David was from Bethlehem, and Jerusalem was not an Israelite city before David captured it), "sleeping with ancestors" must refer to something more than simply being interred in a family burial plot. On this point, see Wright, *Resurrection*, 90.

7. Especially insightful on this point is Jon D. Levenson, *Resurrection and the Restoration of Israel: The Ultimate Victory of the God of Life* (New Haven: Yale University Press, 2006), 37–46.

8. The Old Testament uses the term "face" (*pānîm*, technically a plural) to refer to someone's presence; thus the "face of God" typically refers to God's presence.

possible to experience the antithesis of the shalom or fullness of life that God intends, and which he has promised the faithful.[9]

This negative view of the afterlife paradoxically serves a positive function in the Old Testament: it emphasizes that earthly life is what really matters. It is in present history and our concrete this-worldly context that we are called to serve God and experience the blessings that God has for us. The lack of interest in an otherworldly future focuses attention squarely on this world.

Looking beyond Death in the Old Testament

Yet Sheol poses a significant problem for the Old Testament's view of earthly flourishing, since it is clear that not all persons get to experience the fullness of life that they deserve (Job is a prime example). Indeed, while the righteous often suffer, the wicked (who should be experiencing the covenant curses for their disobedience) often flourish. Our actual experience of the world often contradicts the Torah and wisdom teaching about the two ways (see chap. 5 above).

It is precisely this situation that leads to a crisis of faith in the case of the author of Psalm 73; he almost lost his footing when he saw the prosperity of the wicked, their this-worldly success despite their arrogance toward God and neighbor (vv. 1–14). At first the psalmist is dismayed and can make no sense of this injustice (vv. 16, 21–22), but he comes to an understanding (while in the temple) that the wicked will ultimately receive what they deserve (vv. 17–20, 27). More positively, he affirms that the God he has known in this life will "afterward . . . take" him (vv. 23–24). Indeed, the psalmist concludes, "My flesh and my heart may fail, / but God is the strength of my heart and my portion forever" (v. 26). There is no clear picture here of what sort of future is anticipated, just a sense that the present cannot be all there is, since life

9. The fact that references to Sheol tend to be found in psalms and other first-person accounts of people who are suffering or who have just been rescued from suffering leads Jon Levenson to suggest that there is no universal expectation of Sheol in the Old Testament. Rather, he argues that this expectation is colored by the negative experiences of the sufferer; they project the negativity of the present into the postmortem future. Elsewhere in the Old Testament, he notes, we find more positive references to the death of the righteous (e.g., old and full of years; gathered to the ancestors). See Levenson, *Resurrection*, 46, and especially chap. 4. This is not the place to engage in a full discussion of this disputed issue; it is sufficient to notice that Levenson has opened up the question of whether the Old Testament distinguishes between a good death and a bad death (with only the latter associated with Sheol). However this issue is resolved, it is clear that the Old Testament does not normally expect a blessed postmortem existence for the righteous (except metaphorically, through one's descendants).

as the psalmist knows it is significantly out of alignment with the way it is supposed to be.[10]

One of the fascinating details about Psalm 73 is the use of the verb "take" (*lāqah*) in verse 24 (rendered by most translations as "receive"). That God will "take" the psalmist seems to be an echo of Genesis 5:24, which states, "Enoch walked with God; then he was no more, because God took him." This same verb is used in Psalm 49, which, like Psalm 73, suggests that death is not the final end for the righteous. The dominant note of this wisdom psalm is that no one (neither the wise nor the foolish) can escape death; certainly the wealthy cannot pay God a ransom to avoid Sheol (vv. 7–10). But whereas the wicked can expect Sheol to be their permanent home (vv. 11–14), the psalmist affirms that God will ransom his life from Sheol, "for he will receive [lit. "take"] me" (v. 15).

Resurrection Proper in the Old Testament

A few individuals in the Old Testament are brought back to life by miraculous acts associated with the prophets Elijah and Elisha (1 Kings 17:7–24; 2 Kings 4:32–37; 13:21), and a few texts such as Psalm 49 and Psalm 73 (along with Gen. 5:24) testify to a relatively undefined awareness of something positive beyond death, but it is not until we get to protoapocalyptic descriptions of the future that we find what seems to be a more generalized expectation of resurrection. This expectation is found in two passages in Isaiah 24–27, a section of the book sometimes referred to as the Little Isaianic Apocalypse and thought to be of postexilic origin.

Isaiah 25 announces a time when YHWH of hosts will vindicate Israel, with ramifications for the entire world. The text describes a banquet of the best meat and the most aged wines that God will prepare on Mount Zion "for all peoples" (v. 6). Significantly, this sumptuous feast (a symbol of earthly blessing) will be accompanied by YHWH putting an end to death and mourning.

> And he will destroy on this mountain
>   the shroud that is cast over all peoples,
>   the sheet that is spread over all nations;
>   he will swallow up death forever.
> Then the Lord GOD will wipe away the tears from all faces,
>   and the disgrace of his people he will take away from all the earth.
>   Isaiah 25:7–8

10. For a profound study of Ps. 73, see Martin Buber, "The Heart Determines: Psalm 73," in *Theodicy in the Old Testament*, ed. James L. Crenshaw (Issues in Religion and Theology 4; Philadelphia: Fortress, 1983), 109–18.

Beyond removing the funeral shroud that covers all the peoples of the earth, YHWH will turn the tables on death. Instead of death swallowing people into its wide mouth (a well-known image from Canaanite mythology), it is death that will be swallowed up.[11]

The permanent abolition of death implies resurrection, and Paul indeed cites Isaiah 25:8 in 1 Corinthians 15, noting that when the dead are raised, "then the saying that is written will be fulfilled: 'Death has been swallowed up in victory'" (1 Cor. 15:54b).[12] An echo of this picture of death's destruction is also found in Revelation 20, which describes "Death and Hades," after giving up the dead that are in them, being cast into the lake of fire (vv. 13–14).[13] And Revelation 21 continues to allude to Isaiah 25 when it says that in the new Jerusalem God "will wipe every tear from their eyes," and that "Death will be no more" (v. 4).

The abolition of death in Isaiah 25 is reiterated in Isaiah 26, in response to a lament of God's people (vv. 13–18); this lament combines despair and complaint with affirmations of trust in YHWH (which is typical of biblical laments). Here is the complaint:

> The dead do not live;
> ˙ shades do not rise—
> because you have punished and destroyed them,
> and wiped out all memory of them.
> Isaiah 26:14

> Like a woman with child,
> who writhes and cries out in her pangs
> when she is near her time,

11. This image is known elsewhere in the Old Testament: "Sheol has enlarged its appetite / and opened its mouth beyond measure" (Isa. 5:14); and Proverbs portrays the wicked saying, "Like Sheol let us swallow them alive and whole, / like those who go down to the Pit" (Prov. 1:12). References to the wide and insatiable mouth of Mot (Ugaritic for "Death"), the god of the underworld, are found in the Ugaritic Baal Cycle (1.4 VIII 17–12; 1.5 I 6–8, 14–16; 1.5 II 2–6, 21–24; 1.6 II 15–23). For an accessible English translation, see Michael David Coogan and Mark S. Smith, eds., *Stories from Ancient Canaan* (2nd ed.; Louisville: Westminster John Knox, 2012), 96–153.

12. Although the Hebrew word *nēṣaḥ* typically means "enduring" or "forever," Paul renders it by the Greek *nikos* ("victory"), which agrees with the Greek of two ancient versions (Aquila and Theodotion, but not the Septuagint) and may reflect the meaning of Aramaic *nēṣaḥ* ("surpass, overcome, prevail"). The NRSV translates *nēṣaḥ* as "successfully" in Prov. 21:28 (though many other English translations have "forever"), while most English translations of *nēṣaḥ* in 1 Chron. 29:11 have "victory," and the Septuagint renders it as *nikē*.

13. The conquest of death is indicated from the very first chapter of Revelation, when Jesus says, "I was dead, and see, I am alive forever and ever; and I have the keys of Death and of Hades" (1:18).

> so were we because of you, O LORD;
>   we were with child, we writhed,
>   but we gave birth only to wind.
> We have won no victories on earth,
>   and no one is born to inhabit the world.
>   Isaiah 26:17–18

In the next verse we find God's remarkable response to this despairing lament. Though the futility of death seems inevitable to Israel, YHWH announces a new thing:

> Your dead shall live,
>   their corpses shall rise.
> O dwellers in the dust, awake and sing for joy!
>   For your dew is a radiant dew,
>   and the earth will give birth to those long dead.
>   Isaiah 26:19

It is, of course, possible to argue that this text identifies death with the exile and that the new life signifies return to the land. There is a great deal of truth to this reading, as is clear from Ezekiel 37, where resurrection stands for return from exile. That famous prophecy of the revivification of Israel, their reconstitution as a people and return to the land, portrays this momentous event as equivalent to coming back from the dead. Even though later Judaism came to interpret Ezekiel 37 as literal resurrection, in its original context the text uses resurrection as a metaphor for the rebirth of Israel after the death of exile (a resurrection of the social body, the *polis* of Israel). As Jon Levenson has brilliantly elucidated, the raising of the dead in the Hebrew Scriptures is associated in multiple ways with the birth of children, and resurrection is an outgrowth of hope for the future of Israel as a community.[14] So perhaps we should not distinguish too sharply between the two realities of literal resurrection and the revivification of the people; after all, even Paul (likely drawing on Ezek. 37) compares the future salvation of Israel with "life from the dead" (Rom. 11:15). Nevertheless, Isaiah 26 seems to push beyond metaphor, in the direction of literal resurrection, with its talk of corpses rising and dwellers in the dust awakening (v. 19).

The most explicit mention of resurrection in the Old Testament occurs in the book of Daniel, the only full-fledged apocalypse in the Hebrew canon.

---

14. See Levenson, *Resurrection*, chap. 7; also Madigan and Levenson, *Resurrection*, chaps. 6–8.

According to Daniel 12, a time of future distress or trouble is coming; but beyond the distress there will be deliverance for Israel (v. 1). This deliverance is then described in explicit language of resurrection: "Many of those who sleep in the dust of the earth shall awake, some to everlasting life, and some to shame and everlasting contempt. Those who are wise shall shine like the brightness of the sky, and those who lead many to righteousness, like the stars forever and ever" (vv. 2–3).

Not only does this text echo language from Isaiah 26 about awakening from the dust, but also both texts allude to Genesis 3:19, which describes death as our returning to the dust from which we were made (also Ps. 104:29). This reversal of death, awakening to either eternal life or eternal shame, is not yet the hope of a universal resurrection; it merely says that "some" will awaken. The context suggests that the "some" are faithful martyrs (described here as the wise, who lead many to righteousness) and also those who oppressed and killed them—two opposite extremes among the peoples of the world.[15]

The Connection between Resurrection and Earthly Rule

Corresponding to these two groups in Daniel 12 is the contrast found in Daniel 7 between four beasts and a human being, which Daniel sees in a vision (vv. 2–27). Daniel's vision is explained as a contrast between two sorts of people: the kings of the nations, pictured as wild beasts (vv. 2–8, 17, 19–21, 23–26), and "one like a human being" (literally, "one like a son of man" [v. 13])—that is, someone who acts not as a beast, but humanely. This human one approaches the throne of God in heaven and receives an everlasting dominion and kingdom (vv. 13–14), whereas the beastly rulers have their dominion stripped from them (vv. 11–12, 26). The distinction between beast and human is equivalent to the earlier contrast between those destined for everlasting contempt and those raised to everlasting glory.

Although the "son of man" figure in Daniel 7 came to have messianic connotations in later Judaism (and Jesus's use of "Son of Man" language may

15. We have here the origin of the idea of a general resurrection of the righteous and the wicked, to stand before God's judgment, with two outcomes: "the resurrection of life" and "the resurrection of condemnation" (John 5:28–29; see also Acts 24:15; Rev. 20:5–6, 11–15). At this point terminology can become a bit confusing. The initial raising of righteous and wicked to stand before the judgment might better be called "resuscitation" (as are all the miracles of raising individuals in both Testaments), whereas the final state of the righteous (after judgment) is resurrection proper (applicable to Jesus's resurrection and to believers by Paul in 1 Cor. 15); the final state of the wicked can only be called "resurrection" by analogy, but it is actually the opposite of eternal life.

allude to this),[16] the original context suggests that the human one is equivalent to "the holy ones [or saints] of the Most High" (v. 22) or "the people of the holy ones of the Most High" (v. 27), who are also described as receiving dominion and an eternal kingdom.[17] The point is that whereas in the present the oppressive rulers of the world persecute the righteous, in the future there will be a great reversal: the oppressors will be judged, and the righteous will receive the kingdom that is rightfully theirs. This reversal of dominion for God's people is manifested in being raised to eternal life in Daniel 12. In the linkage between Daniel 7 and Daniel 12, we find an unmistakable connection between resurrection and the restoration of rule.

That a great reversal is coming is basic to the biblical picture of God's justice. As Mary sings in her song known as the Magnificat, God "has brought down the powerful from their thrones, / and lifted up the lowly" (Luke 1:52). But before the Magnificat, there was Hannah's victory song in 1 Samuel 2, on which Mary's song was modeled.

> The LORD makes poor and makes rich;
>   he brings low, he also exalts.
> He raises up the poor from the dust;
>   he lifts the needy from the ash heap,
> to make them sit with princes
>   and inherit a seat of honor.
> For the pillars of the earth are the LORD's,
>   and on them he has set the world.
> He will guard the feet of his faithful ones,
>   but the wicked shall be cut off in darkness;
>   for not by might does one prevail.
>   1 Samuel 2:7–9

This picture of being lifted up from the dust to rightful rule (sitting with princes) provides the theological grounding of resurrection.[18] This exaltation

16. Jesus even quotes Dan. 7:13 (Mark 13:26; 14:62). For a recent discussion of the significance of Jesus's use of "Son of Man," see the essays in *"Who Is This Son of Man?": The Latest Scholarship on a Puzzling Expression of the Historical Jesus*, ed. Larry W. Hurtado and Paul L. Owen (Library of New Testament Studies 390; London: T&T Clark, 2011).

17. Some interpreters take "the holy ones of the Most High" to refer to angels, as the term does in *1 Enoch*, where they are also known as the Watchers (for this view, see John J. Collins, "Apocalyptic Eschatology as the Transcendence of Death," *Catholic Biblical Quarterly* 36 [1974]: 21–43). Even if that were so, the phrase "people of the holy ones of the Most High" clearly refers to Israel. And what unifies the human one, the holy ones, and the people of the holy ones is that all of them receive eternal dominion from God.

18. As Jesus explains, "All who exalt themselves will be humbled, and those who humble themselves will be exalted" (Luke 14:11); and he adds, "You will be repaid at the resurrection of the righteous" (14:14).

is accomplished by none other than the God of creation, the one who set the world firmly on its foundations (1 Sam. 2:8) and who attends to the humble and lowly (Isa. 57:15; 66:1–2). Indeed, the creator restores them to their rightful status, for humanity was originally crowned with royal dignity (Ps. 8:4–8) to be God's vice-regent on earth (Gen. 1:26–28).

The raising of the humble coheres with the reference to the righteous shining like stars in Daniel 12. That this reference is an image of exaltation and glory can be see in Numbers 24:17, which compares a future ruler of Israel to a rising star. And Jesus tells the disciples that after the final judgment "the righteous will shine like the sun in the kingdom of their Father" (Matt. 13:43). In Philippians 2 Paul even uses astral imagery for the Christian life after he exhorts his readers to have the same mind that Christ had (v. 5) by willingly embracing servanthood and suffering (vv. 6–8), which leads to exaltation and cosmic rule (vv. 9–11). This *imitatio Christi* (which is the restoration of the *imago Dei*) results in Christians becoming "children of God without blemish in the midst of a crooked and perverse generation, in which you shine like stars in the world" (v. 15).[19]

We should be clear that the exaltation associated with resurrection in Daniel 12 has nothing to do with going to heaven or literally becoming a celestial being; it certainly does not describe the immortality of the soul.[20] Rather, this is a metaphor for the restoration of dignity to the faithful who had been subjected to an ignoble death at the hands of the wicked; it refers to their rising up from death to stand on solid ground once again, since humanity was created to live with dignity on earth. Thus "rising up" and "standing" (Hebrew *qûm*; Greek *anastasis*) become synonyms for resurrection in the Bible (note that Jesus raises Jairus's daughter with the Aramaic words *Talitha cum*, meaning "Little girl, arise" [Mark 5:41]). And since Daniel 12 draws on the Isaiah 26 image of awakening from the dust, we do well to note the this-worldly reference in Isaiah 26, especially in the final words of the lament to which resurrection is God's response: "We have won no victories on earth, / and no one is born to inhabit the world" (Isa. 26:18b).[21]

---

19. Note also the imagery in Prov. 4:18: "But the path of the righteous is like the light of dawn, / which shines brighter and brighter until full day."

20. A clear contrast between the biblical idea of bodily resurrection (in an earthly context) and the unbiblical notion of the immortality of the soul (in heaven) is found in Oscar Cullmann's classic study *Immortality of the Soul or Resurrection of the Dead? The Witness of the New Testament* (London: Epworth, 1958). Although some details of Cullmann's argument might be disputed, this is still a landmark work that can be very helpful for anyone confused about what the New Testament teaches on the subject.

21. Other possible translations are "We have not given salvation to the earth, / nor brought life into the world" (NLT) and "We have accomplished no deliverance in the earth, / and the

The expectation of Scripture, along with many extrabiblical writings in Second Temple Judaism, is that God will decisively rectify this situation by raising the righteous from the dead to a position of royal honor. This is well illustrated by a powerful chapter on martyrdom and resurrection in 2 Maccabees (in the Jewish Apocrypha, part of the Septuagint). There we have the account of seven Jewish brothers and their mother tortured and killed by Antiochus IV Epiphanes (arguably the horn of the fourth beast in Dan. 7). The vivid account in 2 Maccabees 7 of martyrdom for refusing to disobey the Torah contains multiple references to the hope of resurrection, grounded in God's compassion on the faithful (vv. 6, 9, 11, 14, 20, 23, 29, 36). According to the second son, "The King of the universe will raise us up to an everlasting renewal of life, because we have died for his laws" (v. 9). Or, as the mother tells the youngest son, "The Creator of the world, who shaped the beginning of humankind and devised the origin of all things, will in his mercy give life and breath back to you again" (v. 23); so she encourages him: "Accept death, so that in God's mercy I may get you back again along with your brothers" (v. 29). And the opposite of new life for the faithful is God's judgment on the oppressors, expressly articulated for the tyrant Antiochus (vv. 17, 19, 31, 34–35).

The earthly content of this future hope for the faithful can be seen in *1 Enoch*, a Jewish apocalyptic text known primarily from ancient Ethiopic manuscripts (*1 Enoch* 1:19 is quoted in Jude 14–15).[22] In the first section of *1 Enoch*, called the Book of the Watchers (chaps. 1–36), the elect (the righteous), having been granted forgiveness and wisdom by God, are to "inherit the earth" and live a full life in a sinless state of "rejoicing and eternal peace" (5:7–9).[23] And a later chapter in the Book of the Watchers portrays God's throne in paradise (Eden) on a high mountain, in the midst of which is the tree of life, with the elect given access to its fruit, resulting in "a long life on earth" with no more sorrow or calamity (25:1–6) because God "has prepared such things for people (who are) righteous" (25:7).[24]

Later in *1 Enoch*, in the Book of Parables (chaps. 37–71), there is a description of the messianic age, when "the Chosen One" sits on God's throne; at that time Sheol will give back what has been entrusted to it (that is, the dead), the mountains and hills will skip like lambs, and "the earth will rejoice / and

---

inhabitants of the world have not fallen" (ESV). Whether the reference is to new life coming (literally, "falling") to the earth or the fall of the wicked on earth (both are possible meanings), the reference is clearly this-worldly.

22. *1 Enoch* is perhaps the most important extrabiblical Jewish apocalypse; it is part of what has traditionally been called the Pseudepigrapha.

23. Quotations of *1 Enoch* are from George W. E. Nickelsburg and James C. VanderKam, *1 Enoch: A New Translation* (Minneapolis: Fortress, 2004).

24. Translators' parentheses.

the righteous will dwell on it" (51:1–5). This picture is expanded in a rather lengthy chapter that describes the Chosen One (identified as the "son of man" from Dan. 7) sitting on his throne, delivering the rulers of the earth over for judgment, but participating in a banquet with the righteous, who have risen from their graves and are clothed with eternal glory (62:1–16).

The association of resurrection and rule is also found in a fragmentary text from the Dead Sea Scrolls known as the *Messianic Apocalypse* (4Q521), which dates to the first century BC. There we are told that when the Messiah comes, not only will the Lord "perform marvellous acts such as have not existed," including healing the wounded and making the dead live, but also "he will honor the pious upon the throne of an eternal kingdom."[25] Resurrection and rule go hand in hand when God restores his people.[26]

The Wisdom of Solomon (another Jewish apocryphal writing) confirms the Jewish expectation for this-worldly hope, explicitly associating resurrection with reigning and executing judgment on earth. Wisdom 3 begins by assuming an intermediate state between death and resurrection, during which the righteous are with God (3:1). While fools may view the death of the righteous negatively, thinking that they are being punished, the text affirms that they are actually at peace (3:2–3). But such a state is only temporary, for "their hope is full of immortality" (3:4); this is in pointed contrast to the ungodly, whose "hope is vain" (3:11), like an ephemeral frost or smoke that quickly dissipates (5:14).

While "immortality" might sound like endorsement of a disembodied heavenly existence, the immortality in 3:4 is a hope, not a present possession, for "they will receive great good" (3:5)—a reference to what is yet to come. This future immortality is then unpacked in language from Daniel 12 (which depicts resurrection), followed by images of governance and judgment.

> In the time of their visitation they will shine forth,
>   and will run like sparks through the stubble.
> They will govern nations and rule over peoples,
>   and the Lord will reign over them for ever.
>   Wisdom 3:7–8

25. *Messianic Apocalypse* (4Q521), fragment 2, column 2, lines 11–12 and 7, respectively. Translation from Florentino García Martínez and Eibert J. C. Tigchelaar, *The Dead Sea Scrolls Study Edition* (Leiden: Brill; Grand Rapids: Eerdmans, 1999), 2:1045.

26. Many more examples from the Dead Sea Scrolls could be adduced on the issue of this-worldly eschatological expectation; my purpose in citing the *Messianic Apocalypse* is to be illustrative, not exhaustive. For more on this-worldly hope in the Scrolls, see Albert L. A. Hogeterp, *Expectations of the End: A Comparative Traditio-Historical Study of Eschatological, Apocalyptic and Messianic Ideas in the Dead Sea Scrolls and the New Testament* (Studies on Texts of the Desert of Judah 83; Leiden: Brill, 2009).

Not only will the righteous shine forth (the Dan. 12 allusion), but also this metaphor is mined to include both light and heat, as the righteous burn up the stubble of wickedness. And besides executing judgment, the righteous ones (now immortal) will exercise dominion over the nations—precisely the reversal envisioned in Daniel 7 and other Second Temple texts.

Two chapters later the resurrection of God's elect is linked even more explicitly to their royal status:

> But the righteous live forever,
>   and their reward is with the Lord;
>   the Most High takes care of them.
> Therefore they will receive a glorious crown
>   and a beautiful diadem from the hand of the Lord,
> because with his right hand he will cover them,
>   and with his arm he will shield them.
>   Wisdom 5:15–16

What we have here is the restoration of the faithful to their rightful human status, with echoes of Psalm 8 (crowned with glory and honor). The eschaton will bring to fruition God's original intent at creation. This interpretation is congruent with the emphasis in the Wisdom of Solomon on the goodness of creation:

> God did not make death,
>   and he does not delight in the death of the living.
> For he created all things so that they might exist;
>   the generative forces of the world are wholesome,
> and there is no destructive poison in them,
>   and the dominion of Hades is not on earth.
> For righteousness is immortal.
>   Wisdom 1:13–15

It becomes clear, then, that "immortality" (*athanasia*) in Wisdom 3:4 refers to a this-worldly reality, resurrection from the dead, just as it does in 1 Corinthians 15, where Paul uses the very same word to propound an embodied immortality.[27]

For the trumpet will sound, and the dead will be raised imperishable, and we will be changed. For this perishable body must put on imperishability, and this

27. The examples given above are not meant to claim that all Second Temple Jewish writers envision an earthly context for resurrection; some (under the influence of Platonism) indeed affirm ascent to heaven. But such expectation is discontinuous both with the basic tenor of the Old Testament and with the inner logic of resurrection: the restoration of God's creational intentions for humanity.

mortal body must put on immortality [*athanasia*]. When this perishable body puts on imperishability, and this mortal body puts on immortality [*athanasia*], then the saying that is written will be fulfilled: "Death has been swallowed up in victory." (1 Cor. 15:52–54)[28]

So, finally, we have arrived at the New Testament! But we needed to ground the New in the Old in order to show the fundamental continuity of earthly hope in both Testaments.

Reigning with Christ in the New Testament

Given the numerous references to resurrection in the New Testament (see the list at the start of this chapter), there is no need to establish its centrality. Instead, it will be more helpful to focus on the motif of eschatological rule for God's people—a motif interwoven into many New Testament texts, often in connection with resurrection, as if it were an obvious component of early Christian hope.

Take, for example, the reason Paul gives in 1 Corinthians 6:1–6 why Christians should not take each other to court (in the pagan legal system), but instead should settle their disagreements in the church. "Do you not know that the saints will judge the world?" he asks. "And if the world is to be judged by you, are you incompetent to try trivial cases? Do you not know that we are to judge angels—to say nothing of ordinary matters?" (vv. 2–3). If Paul were to ask most Christians these questions today, he would probably receive some uncomprehending stares. The saints will judge the world? They will judge angels?

But Paul is simply drawing on Second Temple Jewish expectation of the great reversal, with the accompanying restoration of rule for the elect. And judgment (which includes making wise decisions and even pronouncing sentence when evil needs to be rectified) is an integral aspect of exercising rule. In fact, wherever we find language in the New Testament of the saints ruling, reigning, judging, or otherwise exercising authority, including reference to thrones or crowns, we are moving in the conceptual field of the eschatological kingdom of God, which is the promised inheritance of God's people.

---

28. Paul's use of "victory" (*nikos*) in 1 Cor. 15:54 further suggests the this-worldly character of resurrection. As Matthew Forrest Lowe ("Death Dismantled: Reading Christological and Soteriological Language in 1 Corinthians 15 in Light of Roman Imperial Ideology" [PhD diss., McMaster Divinity College, 2011]) explains, *nikos/nikē* was part of the vocabulary of Roman imperial ideology, and since Paul understands Christ's resurrection as overcoming death in all its forms, including the Roman imperium, resurrection has this-worldly, sociopolitical implications.

Jesus himself appeals to the great reversal at the end of the age in response to Peter's question, on behalf of the disciples, about their reward for leaving everything and following him (Matt. 19:27). Jesus explains that his followers will receive a hundredfold for what they have lost and will "inherit eternal life," for "many who are first will be last, and the last will be first" (Matt. 19:29–30). But Jesus also connects this reversal to thrones and judgment: "Truly I tell you, at the renewal of all things, when the Son of Man is seated on the throne of his glory, you who have followed me will also sit on twelve thrones, judging the twelve tribes of Israel" (Matt. 19:28).

Jesus makes a similar statement about the future of his disciples in response to a dispute among them about which of them is the greatest (Luke 22:24). There he challenges them to model their authority not on the kings of the gentiles (who misuse power), but on his own life of service (Luke 22:25–27). He ends with these words: "You are those who have stood by me in my trials; and I confer on you, just as my Father has conferred on me, a kingdom, that you may eat and drink at my table in my kingdom, and you will sit on thrones judging the twelve tribes of Israel" (Luke 22:28–30).

Not only is it clear that Jesus was steeped in Second Temple expectation of the eschatological rule of the saints, but also he grounds this rule in his own life pattern: if his followers share in his suffering, they will share in his kingdom (Luke 22:28–29). This sharing or participation in Christ's life is fundamental to the way the Bible conceives the Christian hope. So Paul can say that believers are "heirs of God and joint heirs with Christ—if, in fact, we suffer with him so that we may also be glorified with him" (Rom. 8:17).

Elsewhere Paul affirms his own need to share in Christ's sufferings if he is to attain to the resurrection from the dead (Phil. 3:10–11), and he uses the sequence of Jesus's self-emptying unto death and consequent exaltation to cosmic lordship as the model for the church (Phil. 2:5–11).

Paul's focus is the humble use of power to serve one another, as Jesus served sinful humanity by his sacrificial death (Phil. 2:5–8); in a fallen world, service often leads to suffering. This clearly calls into question any superficial, triumphalistic understanding of the kingdom of God or the restoration of rule, especially to engage in "culture wars" on behalf of the Christian faith (a powerful temptation in some varieties of contemporary Christianity). We should heed N. T. Wright's helpful emphasis on the abasement and submission of Jesus (the incarnate Word) as crucial to God's mode of kingship—hence the title of Wright's profound study of the Gospels, *How God Became King*.[29] Likewise,

---

29. N. T. Wright, *How God Became King: The Forgotten Story of the Gospels* (New York: HarperOne, 2012); published with a different subtitle by SPCK in the United Kingdom.

Michael Gorman has insightfully described the Pauline understanding of the Christian life as "cruciform," conforming to the pattern of Christ's sacrifice.[30]

Yet Jesus was raised from death victorious; and the climax of the Christ hymn in Philippians 2 states the end point of the exaltation: "so that at the name of Jesus every knee should bend, in heaven and on earth and under the earth, and every tongue should confess that Jesus Christ is Lord, to the glory of God the Father" (Phil. 2:10–11).[31]

This cosmic and eschatological reign of God's Messiah, the Suffering Servant, is integral to the pattern in which Christians will share. The key point here is that the abuse of power that characterizes our world does not mean we should avoid the clear teaching of Scripture about eschatological rule. Power itself is not the problem; it is the misuse of power. Humans were commissioned at creation to rule the earth in the image of a loving God, and Jesus embodied this rule in his own life and death as the incarnate Word (John 1:14–18).[32] The very point of the coming reversal is that dominion is taken from those who abuse power and given to those who humble themselves to follow the Messiah, on the path of discipleship and service.[33]

Christ as Representative of Israel and Humanity

The paradigmatic character of Jesus's death/humiliation and resurrection/rule is grounded in the developing Second Temple expectation that a representative of Israel (who is also a representative of humanity) will bring about the vindication of the people as a whole. It is this representative sense of the "son of man" in Daniel 7 that allows the term to stand both for the people (in its original context) and (legitimately) for a messianic figure to come.

30. Michael J. Gorman, *Cruciformity: Paul's Narrative Spirituality of the Cross* (Grand Rapids: Eerdmans, 2001); idem, *Inhabiting the Cruciform God: Kenosis, Justification, and Theosis in Paul's Narrative Soteriology* (Grand Rapids: Eerdmans, 2009).

31. The integral connection between the humiliation and exaltation of God's servant is found in the famous poem of the Suffering Servant in Isa. 52:13–53:12. The servant's exaltation in 52:13 and 53:10–11 came to be interpreted in Second Temple Judaism explicitly as resurrection. And when Jesus speaks of being "lifted up" in the Gospel of John (3:14; 8:28; 12:32–34), the reference is to both his crucifixion and his glorification (resurrection and ascension); in fact, the verb for "lifted up" is *hypsoō*, which was used in the Septuagint of Isa. 52:13 for the servant's exaltation. See Raymond E. Brown, *The Gospel according to John: Introduction, Translation, and Notes* (Anchor Bible 29–29A; Garden City, NY: Doubleday, 1966–70), 1:146, 475–78.

32. For more on the ethics of the image of God, see J. Richard Middleton, "Image of God," in *Dictionary of Scripture and Ethics*, ed. Joel B. Green et al. (Grand Rapids: Baker Academic, 2011), 394–97.

33. As the master says to the faithful servant in Matt. 25:23, "You have been trustworthy in a few things, I will put you in charge of many things" (see also Luke 16:10).

This representative idea helps us understand the logic of Paul's sermon at the Areopagus in Athens, recorded in Acts 17. After informing his hearers about God's creation of the cosmos and their status as *imago Dei* (vv. 24–29), he calls them to repentance (v. 30), because God "has fixed a day on which he will have the world judged in righteousness by a man whom he has appointed, and of this he has given assurance to all by raising him from the dead" (v. 31). Since the resurrected one who exercises judgment is the representative of righteous humanity (Jesus perfectly manifests the *imago Dei*), his resurrection and rule become the pattern for those whom he represents.[34]

Hebrews 2 is extremely helpful in clarifying how the participation of God's people in Christ's exaltation and rule is grounded in creation and the original human calling. Having portrayed Christ as the perfect revelation of God, by which he is superior to angels (1:1–2:4), the writer declares, "Now God did not subject the coming world, about which we are speaking, to angels" (2:5). Coming on the heels of Hebrews 1, this could easily be mistaken as a reference to Christ's eschatological reign; but anyone steeped in Second Temple expectation will understand that God has entrusted the future world to humanity (specifically, righteous humanity). And the reference to human rule is enhanced when 2:6–8 goes on to quote the Septuagint of Psalm 8:4–6. In the Old Testament, Psalm 8 clearly refers to the original human status and role—created a little lower than God (*'ĕlōhîm*), crowned with glory and honor, granted rule of all God has made.

Since Hebrews 2 is sometimes misread as providing a straightforward messianic interpretation of Psalm 8, we must be careful to understand the actual argument that the author marshals.[35] The writer of Hebrews does not apply the psalm text to Jesus in any uncritical and simplistic way, as if it were directly referring to the Messiah. Rather, he starts with the original human calling, which has been compromised because of sin. Hebrews 2:5–9 is worth quoting in full:

> Now God did not subject the coming world, about which we are speaking, to angels. But someone has testified somewhere,
>
> > "What are human beings that you are mindful of them,
> >   or mortals, that you care for them?

---

34. According to John 5:27, God has given Jesus "authority to execute judgment, because he is the Son of Man," which wonderfully draws on both senses of "Son of Man"—Jesus as the representative of humanity (to whom rule was originally given) and as the chosen Messiah.

35. The assumption of a straightforward messianic reference for Ps. 8 underlies the interpretation in Wilber B. Wallis, "The Use of Psalms 8 and 110 in 1 Corinthians 15:25–27 and in Hebrews 1 and 2," *Journal of the Evangelical Theological Society* 15 (1972): 25–29.

> You have made them for a little while lower than the angels;
> you have crowned them with glory and honor,
> subjecting all things under their feet."

Now in subjecting all things to them, God left nothing outside their control. As it is, we do not yet see everything in subjection to them, but we do see Jesus, who for a little while was made lower than the angels, now crowned with glory and honor because of the suffering of death, so that by the grace of God he might taste death for everyone.[36]

The Septuagint, which Hebrews quotes here, has two divergences from the original Hebrew. The first narrows down the meaning of *'ĕlohîm* to "angels," which may well have been part of the meaning of the term (*'ĕlohîm* can refer to God, divine beings, angels).[37] But the second divergence actually makes the Hebrew more ambiguous; the Greek phrase *brachy ti par'* in connection with the verb *elattoō* ("make lower") in Hebrews 2:7 can mean made "a little lower than" (in conformity with the original Hebrew, followed by KJV and NIV) or "for a little while lower than" (NRSV and ESV). It is this latter, temporal meaning that the author mines for his interpretation.[38]

Humanity was created to rule the world (at creation and at the eschaton), but we do not see this at present; instead, it is death that rules, and the human race is "held in slavery by the fear of death" (Heb. 2:15). But we do see Jesus, who was temporarily subordinated to the angels, becoming "flesh and blood" in solidarity with the human family (described both as his brothers/sisters and as God's children [2:11–14, 17]). Because Jesus became fully human ("like his brothers and sisters in every respect" [2:17]), even to the point of death, he was able to conquer the devil, resulting in atonement for the human race and their liberation from the power of death (2:14–17). Now exalted in resurrection and ascension, Jesus fulfills the royal vision of Psalm 8 ("crowned with glory and honor" [Heb. 2:9]).

But this risen Jesus, to use Pauline language, is "the firstborn within a large family" (Rom. 8:29). The Gospel of John explains that the unique Son of God

---

36. Note that Heb. 2 and Ps. 8 (in both Hebrew and Greek) use singular pronouns ("he" and "him") to refer to the one ruling. This allows the Ps. 8 quotation to refer both to humanity and to Jesus. However, this may have contributed to the confusion of some interpreters, who in their hurry to get to Jesus too quickly jumped over the reference to humanity. The NRSV helpfully pluralizes the pronouns when they refer to humanity but keeps the singular when Jesus is intended, thus elucidating the actual argument of Heb. 2.

37. For further discussion of this point, see J. Richard Middleton, *The Liberating Image: The* Imago Dei *in Genesis 1* (Grand Rapids: Brazos, 2005), 55–60.

38. *Brachy* is used elsewhere in the New Testament to refer to a small quantity (John 6:7), a little distance (Acts 27:58), and a short time (Luke 22:58; Acts 5:34).

(1:14, 18) does not hoard the privilege of his royal status; rather, he gives "power to become children of God" to all who trust in him (1:12). This is fundamentally in line with Hebrews 2, which affirms that through the incarnation and death of Jesus, God is "bringing many children to glory" (v. 10). Just as Jesus has shared in the human condition (including the humiliation of death), so too all who follow him will share in his exaltation and rule, thus fulfilling God's purpose for humanity. And just to be clear, the writer of Hebrews states that Jesus "did not come to help angels, but the descendants of Abraham" (2:16).

In line with Hebrews 2, Paul affirms that Abraham's descendants were indeed given the promise that they would "inherit the world" (Rom. 4:13). Contrasting the consequences of Adam's sin and Christ's obedience, Paul explains that whereas "death exercised dominion" through the former, those who are the recipients of God's grace and righteousness will themselves "exercise dominion in life through the one man, Jesus Christ" (Rom. 5:17). Thus, Paul can speak of Jesus's resurrection as the "first fruits" of a harvest of resurrection that is to come (1 Cor. 15:20–23). Or as 2 Timothy 2 puts it, "The saying is sure: If we have died with him, we will also live with him; if we endure, we will also reign with him" (vv. 11–12a). New life in Christ is clearly associated with eschatological rule.[39]

A "Spiritual" Reign?

But is this necessarily a rule on earth? New Testament references to the reign of the saints have often been read as referring to a "spiritual" reign in heaven. And there is a grain of truth to this interpretation. Unlike the verb "rule," which often requires an object, "reign" (whether in English or in Greek *basileuō* and its derivatives) does not; this grammatical possibility of a decontextualized reign is often grounded by biblical interpreters in the motif of being seated in the "heavenly places" (literally, "heavenlies," *epouraniois*) found in the book of Ephesians.[40] That this is a royal image is clear from the Old Testament picture of God seated on his heavenly throne and from Christ's ascension in the New Testament, resulting in his being seated at the right hand of the Father; the royal character of these references is further borne out by their context in Ephesians, yet they do not seem to refer to an earthly reign.

39. That this new life is resurrection is evident not only from the overall pattern of New Testament theology, but also from the context in 2 Timothy; just three verses earlier we find this statement, which introduces the saying about sharing in Christ's life and reign: "Remember Jesus Christ, raised from the dead, a descendant of David—that is my gospel" (2 Tim. 2:8).

40. For a thorough study of this motif, see M. Jeff Brannon, *The Heavenlies in Ephesians: A Lexical, Exegetical, and Conceptual Analysis* (Library of New Testament Studies 447; London: T&T Clark, 2011).

The most important reference in Ephesians focuses on the resurrection and ascension of Christ, with resulting cosmic rule, described in the most extravagant terms: "God . . . raised him [Christ] from the dead and seated him at his right hand in the heavenly places, far above all rule and authority and power and dominion, and above every name that is named, not only in this age but also in the age to come. And he has put all things under his feet and has made him the head over all things for the church" (1:20–22).

Another Ephesians reference depicts the church as sharing in both Christ's resurrection life and his reign: "God, who is rich in mercy, . . . made us alive together with Christ . . . and raised us up with him and seated us with him in the heavenly places in Christ Jesus" (2:4–6). Since the participation of believers in Christ's resurrection and ascension begins in the present, and is conceived as happening in the heavenlies, this does not match the earthly rule envisioned in the great reversal. It certainly sounds as if the resurrection and rule of the church are here spiritualized (or at least are nonearthly). And this interpretation is supported by an earlier statement in Ephesians that believers have been "blessed . . . in Christ with every spiritual blessing in the heavenly places" (1:3).

The final two references to the heavenlies in Ephesians speak of a cosmic conflict between God and the forces of darkness, taking place in the heavenlies, in which the church has an important role. In Ephesians 3 we read of the "mystery" of God's plan to include the gentiles as coheirs in his purposes (vv. 5–9), a plan hidden in previous times but revealed in the church, "so that through the church the wisdom of God in its rich variety might now be made known to the rulers and authorities in the heavenly places" (v. 10). Amazingly, the reconciliation of Jew and gentile as the new humanity is a proclamation of God's victory over demonic heavenly powers. But the battle is not over. Ephesians 6:10–18 speaks of putting on the armor of God to stand firm in prayer against the devil and all the powers of evil; "for our struggle is not against enemies of blood and flesh, but against the rulers, against the authorities, against the cosmic powers of this present darkness, against the spiritual forces of evil in the heavenly places" (v. 12).

The partial truth of the interpretation that would spiritualize the reign of the saints is that we do not simply wait for the great reversal. As Ephesians reveals, this renewal has already begun in Christ; we may participate in his new life and victory in the present, even while we continue to struggle with evil and are subject to the suffering that often accompanies discipleship.[41] But

41. Indeed, reigning from heaven does not mean the earth is excluded, since even Caesar was thought to exercise divine rule from heaven in a manner that held the Roman Empire together. See J. R. Harrison, "Paul and the Imperial Gospel at Thessaloniki," *Journal for the Study of the New Testament* 25 (2002): 71–96.

the point is that what is presently hidden (in heaven) will be revealed on earth at the last day. This is the apocalyptic pattern of the New Testament (as we will see more clearly in chap. 10 below). This pattern is clarified by a text from Colossians that, on first reading, might actually seem to counsel otherworldly escape from earth.

> So if you have been raised with Christ, seek the things that are above, where Christ is, seated at the right hand of God. Set your minds on things that are above, not on things that are on earth, for you have died, and your life is hidden with Christ in God. When Christ who is your life is revealed, then you also will be revealed with him in glory. (Col. 3:1–4)

Far from being a counsel of escape, this is an honest recognition that present earthly life is compromised by evil, and so we need to pattern our behavior on a heavenly model (in practice, on Christ himself). But what is "hidden" (our resurrection life) will on the last day be "revealed"—with Christ in glory.

Reigning on Earth as the Final State

To gain a clearer picture of the eschatological unveiling of what is now hidden, we must turn, appropriately enough, to the book of Revelation, the only New Testament apocalypse; both the name of the book and its genre speak of an unveiling ("apocalypse" and "apocalyptic" are derived from a Greek word meaning "reveal"). In the book of Revelation we find clear confirmation of the picture of earthly rule we have been discerning from both Old and New Testaments.

To begin with, the letters to the seven churches (Rev. 2–3) encourage the faithful with mention of crowns, thrones, and rule over the nations as reward for conquering or overcoming—that is, faithful endurance under persecution (2:10, 26–28; 3:11, 21; also 21:7).[42]

While rule over the nations certainly suggests an earthly context, this is confirmed by the vision of celestial worshipers around the throne of God and the Lamb in Revelation 5; there, four living creatures and twenty-four elders praise the crucified one for his sacrifice, by which he redeemed people "from every tribe and language and people and nation" (v. 9). Through his sacrifice, the Lamb has constituted the redeemed as "a kingdom and priests to serve our God, and they will reign on the earth" (v. 10). A clearer statement of an earthly final state for God's people can hardly be found.

---

42. Notice the verbal link between "the one who conquers" (*ho nikōn*) in these texts and "Death has been swallowed up in victory [*nikos*]" in 1 Cor. 15:54.

This earthly reign is explicitly connected with resurrection in Revelation 20. There we find a vision of the millennium, where faithful martyrs ("those who had been beheaded for their testimony to Jesus and for the word of God") "came to life and reigned with Christ a thousand years" (v. 4). This seems to be the first stage in a two-stage future; hence it is designated "the first resurrection" (v. 5).[43] Then, in language reminiscent of Revelation 5, we are told that these risen ones "will be priests of God and of Christ, and they will reign with him a thousand years" (20:6). The context suggests an earthly reign, though a temporary one.

But almost identical language is found in the vision in Revelation 22, describing not a temporary millennium for martyrs, but the final state of all the righteous. Between the millennium and the final state comes a general resurrection of all people to face final judgment, at which time death itself is cast into the lake of fire (20:13–14). Then John sees a new heaven and earth, with a new Jerusalem coming down from heaven to earth (21:1–2), and this vision is accompanied by a variety of images to depict God's full presence to his people, including God's dwelling, face, throne, and light (21:3; 22:1–5). Not only will God's people (now risen to new life) worship and commune with him (22:3–4), but also, in accordance with Old Testament and Second Temple expectation, "they will reign forever and ever" (22:5). Thus, the final state of the righteous is unmistakably depicted in terms of resurrection and earthly rule.

The Logic of Resurrection and Rule

As we come to the end of this overview of resurrection themes in the New Testament, it becomes evident that resurrection is grounded in the reversal of injustice, intended to rectify a situation in which death has impeded God's purposes for earthly blessing and shalom. Especially in oppressive situations where those faithful to God's covenant are persecuted, it may look like death has the last word. But the biblical tradition came to the profound insight (to use language from the Song of Songs) that God's "love is as strong as death" (8:6); indeed, it is stronger than death. YHWH's love for his people and faithfulness to his promises led to the expectation of a return from exile

---

43. The (implied) second resurrection is either the general resurrection (resuscitation) of righteous and wicked to stand before God in judgment (Rev. 20:11–13) or the final state of all the righteous; that this latter might be thought of as a second resurrection (though the term is not used) is suggested by the term "second death" to describe the final outcome for the wicked (Rev. 20:6, 14–15). But the issue is by no means easily resolved.

and a gathering of the remnant from the nations (as we saw in chap. 5 above). But it also led to the passionate hope that death itself could not, in the end, thwart God's purposes.

The doctrine of resurrection is thus grounded in a vision of God's restorative justice. This leads N. T. Wright to claim that "resurrection was from the beginning a revolutionary doctrine."[44] It inspired martyrs to resist tyranny in the hope of a future beyond death. This may be why the Sadducees, who were among the ruling elites of Judaism and thus had a stake in maintaining the status quo, objected to resurrection (see Matt. 22:23–33; Mark 12:18–27; Acts 23:6–10); they were invested in the present world order. But resurrection means that the present order will not last forever. Resurrection turns the world upside down.

Hope of the resurrection is thus able to inspire believers to expect that God's original purposes for human life will ultimately come to fruition, despite what suffering we experience in the present. Paul's affirmation in Philippians 1:6 is apropos: "I am confident of this, that the one who began a good work among you will bring it to completion by the day of Jesus Christ." Resurrection is the ultimate completion of God's purposes.

It is in God's purposes from creation that the unbreakable linkage between resurrection and the restoration of rule is forged. From the beginning, God's intent for human life was centered on the royal status of humanity and our commission to image our creator in loving and wise stewardship of the earth, which has been entrusted to our care (Gen. 1:26–28; 2:15; Ps. 8:4–8). This is the cultural mandate, our sacred calling to develop earthly life in a manner that glorifies God and reflects his intentions for a world of shalom (as we saw in chap. 2 above). God's intent was for the holistic flourishing of embodied people in the entirety of their earthly, cultural existence. Since resurrection is God's restoration of human life to what it was meant to be, it naturally requires the fulfillment of the original human dignity and status, which have been compromised by sin. Resurrection, therefore, when biblically understood, cannot be separated from the fulfillment of the cultural mandate.

Indeed, hope of resurrection can be a significant spur to action in the present as the church seeks to manifest God's kingdom in daily life. Thus, Paul concludes his lengthy discourse on resurrection in 1 Corinthians 15 with this encouragement: "Therefore, my beloved, be steadfast, immovable, always excelling in the work of the Lord, because you know that in the Lord your labor is not in vain" (v. 58). By our present earthly life, as we live between the times, if we are faithful to our Lord, we anticipate and embody God's new world that is coming.

44. Wright, *Resurrection*, 138.

8

The Redemption of All Things

As we saw in the preceding chapter, resurrection is integrally connected to the restoration of earthly rule for the redeemed, and this rule is best understood as a fulfillment of the original human dignity of *imago Dei*. The earth is clearly the original context or environment for the exercise of the *imago Dei*, and this is also the implied context for the eschatological rule that accompanies the resurrection. But does this mean that the Bible actually intends us to understand that the earth itself will be redeemed?

We now confront the explicit issue with which this book began: a renewed earthly creation versus an immaterial heaven as the eternal dwelling of the righteous. This has become a hot topic in contemporary eschatology. However, it is not a new topic. As far back as his groundbreaking 1958 work on the theology of resurrection, Oscar Cullmann affirmed that Christians need to "place our resurrection within the framework of a cosmic redemption and of a new creation of the universe."[1] The resurrection of the body, he noted, "is only a part of the *whole new creation*,"[2] and he contrasted belief in the

1. Oscar Cullmann, *Immortality of the Soul or Resurrection of the Dead? The Witness of the New Testament* (London: Epworth, 1958), 9.
2. Ibid., 37 (emphasis in orginal).

immortality of the soul with belief in "a divine miracle of new creation which will embrace everything, every part of the world created by God."[3]

For anyone who has worked through the previous chapters of this book, Cullmann's perspective might seem obvious. The entire story of Scripture—indeed, the very logic of salvation in the Bible—leads us to expect the redemption of the created order (including the earth) as the context for redeemed human life.

But can this be justified by reference to what Scripture explicitly teaches? My strategy in the present chapter is to lay out the clearest evidence for cosmic redemption in the New Testament. Beginning with a few core passages that address the ultimate purpose of salvation in the most comprehensive terms possible, this chapter then moves on to sketch the climactic vision of God's intentions for the created order as portrayed in Revelation 21–22.[4]

There are, however, a number of biblical texts that are typically adduced as counterexamples to the holistic model of redemption proposed here, since they seem to suggest either that the earth will be destroyed or that the future of the redeemed is a supramundane destiny in heaven. I intend to take such texts seriously. To that end, the next two chapters will explicitly address texts that seem to stand in tension with the redemption of creation, focusing first on those that seem to expect the destruction of the cosmos, then on those that seem to affirm a heavenly destiny.

But the goal of the present chapter is first to clarify how the New Testament understands the future of God's good but fallen creation.

The Comprehensive Scope of Salvation in the New Testament

The best place to start is with specific statements made in various New Testament texts that describe the final, eschatological completion of salvation—what is expected to happen when God's redemptive purposes come to fruition. I will examine five such texts that are relatively clear. In each of these texts, I am interested in two interconnected questions: First, how is salvation, or the saving activity of God, described? And second, what is the object or recipient of God's saving activity? That is, who or what gets saved? When we ask these two questions of each text, we will see a definite pattern emerge (this pattern is displayed in table 8.1).

3. Ibid., 59. The preface to Cullmann's book recounts the hate mail that he received for affirming resurrection and new creation instead of disembodied immortality in heaven as the final destiny of believers.

4. I do not intend to address every aspect of contemporary eschatological interest, such as the millennium, the antichrist, and the tribulation, since they are not central to my purpose. Rather, I will focus resolutely on one crucial question: Does Scripture teach the redemption of creation?

Acts 3:19–21

The simplest, though seemingly most cryptic, of the five texts is in Acts 3. Here Peter is preaching the gospel in Jerusalem, at the entrance to the temple courts. As part of his message, Peter exhorts his hearers,

> Repent therefore, and turn to God so that your sins may be wiped out, so that times of refreshing may come from the presence of the Lord, and that he may send the Messiah appointed for you, that is, Jesus, who must remain in heaven until the time of *universal restoration* that God announced long ago through his holy prophets. (Acts 3:19–21)

When we put our two questions to Acts 3:21, concerning how God's eschatological saving activity is conceived and who or what is saved, the answers are clear, though not much detail is given.

First, the eschatological saving activity of God, which is to be accomplished when Christ returns, is described as "restoration" (*apokatastasis*). Second, it is applied as comprehensively as possible; note the word "universal" in the · NRSV or "everything" in the NIV (*panta*). Salvation, according to Peter, is essentially restorative (it repairs what sin has marred), and it is holistic in that it impacts all of created reality.[5] Peter evidently expects something quite radical and comprehensive at the eschaton, which he claims is in line with the Old Testament prophetic message. In this he is no different from much Second Temple Jewish expectation of the coming kingdom of God.

The somewhat brief statement of universal restoration in Acts 3:21 gains clarity when it is compared to other statements in various New Testament Epistles.

Ephesians 1:9–10

In Ephesians 1 we have a long Pauline sentence describing God's plan of salvation. The most important section for our purposes is verses 9–10, which state that God

> has made known to us the mystery of his will, according to his good pleasure that he set forth in Christ, as a plan for the fullness of time, *to gather up all things in him, things in heaven and things on earth*. (Eph. 1:9–10)

---

5. Contrary to how the church father Origen may have interpreted *apokatastasis*, the term in Acts 3:21 does not refer to the ultimate salvation of all people (there was debate in the patristic period about exactly what Origen's position was, a debate that continues today). The point is that full-fledged universalist soteriology (in this sense) needs to be clearly distinguished from cosmic redemption.

The verb translated "gather up" in the NRSV (*anakephalaiōsasthai*) has also been translated "unite" (ESV), "sum up" (NASB), "bring together" (NLT), or even "bring together under one head" (NIV), which places some importance on the presence of *kephalē* ("head") as part of the verb.[6] Here salvation (God's plan for the fullness of time) is understood as gathering up or unifying in Christ that which has been fragmented (or perhaps alienated) through sin. And this unifying action is applied comprehensively to "all things" in heaven and on earth (v. 10). Since "the heavens and the earth" is how the first verse of Genesis describes the cosmos that God created in the beginning, Ephesians 1 effectively proclaims that eschatological salvation will be as wide as creation.

Colossians 1:19–20

Our third text is from Colossians 1 and comes at the conclusion of an elevated theological statement (possibly a hymnic or poetic piece) describing the role of Christ as the agent of creation and redemption (vv. 15–20). Verses 19–20 constitute the climax of this statement; they articulate God's ultimate purpose in the incarnation.

> For in him [Christ] all the fullness of God was pleased to dwell, and through him God was pleased *to reconcile to himself all things, whether on earth or in heaven*, by making peace through the blood of his cross. (Col. 1:19–20)

Salvation is here conceived as reconciliation or making peace between those who are at enmity, presumably by removing the source of that enmity, namely, sin. Indeed, verse 20 contains the idea of atonement through the blood of Christ; this is how reconciliation is achieved. But in contrast to much Christian preaching, which emphasizes that the blood of Christ was shed for "me" (and we are told to put our name there), Colossians 1 does not myopically limit the efficacy of Christ's atonement to the individual or even to humanity. Without denying that the atonement suffices for individual people, the text applies the reconciliation effected by Christ's shed blood as comprehensively as possible, to "all things, whether on earth or in heaven."

This wording brings us back to verse 16 (just four verses earlier), which affirms that in Christ "all things in heaven and on earth were created." When verse 17 goes on to say that "in him all things hold together," we are warranted

---

6. For a discussion of the interplay of this "magnificent verb" with *kephalē* through the book of Ephesians (and then with a possible intertextual echo from Daniel), see J. Gerald Janzen, *When Prayer Takes Place: Forays into a Biblical World*, ed. Brent A. Strawn and Patrick D. Miller (Eugene, OR: Cascade, 2012), 368–69.

in thinking that the reconciliation spoken of in verse 20 continues and brings to completion Christ's unifying work as creator, which has been disrupted by sin. The point is that redemption is as wide as creation; it is literally cosmic in scope.

Romans 8:19–23

Our fourth text is Romans 8:19–23. Here Paul speaks of creation as groaning in pain. While some translations interpret Paul as alluding to childbirth (labor pains)—and this is entirely possible—he is more clearly drawing on the language of Exodus 2:23–24, which portrays the Israelites as groaning in their bondage under Pharaoh (a different sort of labor pains).[7] In Romans 8, Paul applies this image both to the human condition under sin and to the entire created order.

> For the creation waits with eager longing for the revealing of the children of God; for the creation was subjected to futility, not of its own will but by the will of the one who subjected it, in hope that *the creation itself will be set free from its bondage to decay and will obtain the freedom of the glory of the children of God*. We know that the whole creation has been groaning in labor pains until now; and not only the creation, but we ourselves, who have the first fruits of the Spirit, groan inwardly while we wait for adoption, *the redemption of our bodies*. (Rom. 8:19–23)

So how does this text answer our two questions, about the nature of salvation and who or what gets saved? We could fruitfully explore Paul's metaphor of the deliverance/delivery of childbirth (with its implicit picture of creation being born again), but his emphasis lies with the other image. Utilizing the exodus model of deliverance from Egyptian bondage, Paul portrays salvation in verse 21 as liberation or setting free from slavery, and the recipient of this salvation is both "creation itself" (v. 21) and "the children of God" (v. 23).[8]

The holistic thrust of this text is evident in two ways. First, human liberation, as Paul understands it, cannot be limited to the inner person (affecting only the "soul"); instead, "redemption" (a term characteristically used in connection with the exodus [see Exod. 6:6; 15:13]) is applied in verse 23 to our very bodies—an unusual (though entirely appropriate) reference to the resurrection from the dead.

---

7. For Paul's use of the exodus traditions (including a discussion of Rom. 8), see Sylvia C. Keesmaat, *Paul and His Story: (Re)Interpreting the Exodus Tradition* (Journal for the Study of the New Testament: Supplement Series 181; Sheffield: Sheffield Academic, 1999).

8. The exodus as a paradigm of salvation was discussed in chap. 4 above.

But the text is holistic also in its emphasis that "creation" (*ktisis*) itself will participate in God's salvation.[9] Indeed, both "the whole creation" (v. 22) and "we ourselves" (v. 23) long for redemption—a redemption that is cosmic in scope.

It is important here to understand the logic by which Paul includes the nonhuman creation in God's salvific plan. In Paul's picture the human race implicitly takes the place of Pharaoh; we have subjected creation to futility or frustration, much as the Egyptian king oppressed the Israelites. According to the first chapters of Genesis, humanity was granted stewardship over their earthly environment. But then came the fall, which distorted but did not abrogate our stewardship. Just as an abusive parent can destroy a family or a dictator can devastate a nation, so human corruption has affected that which has been entrusted to our care, with the result that the nonhuman realm is now "subjected to futility."[10] There are echoes here of the curse on the ground in Genesis 3:17, stemming from human disobedience, and the effect of rampant human violence in corrupting or ruining the earth at the time of the flood (Gen. 6:11).

The first step in the process of redemption, therefore, is that the oppressors (the human race) must be liberated from their own sin. Then the redemption of the nonhuman world can begin, when it will be set free from the bondage of sinful human rule. But this redemption is not simply a matter of being released from bondage; there is an implied positive goal or telos: the future redeemed exercise of human rule over the earth, which (as we saw in the preceding chapter) accompanies the biblical hope of resurrection. Thus, beyond teaching the redemption of creation, Romans 8 fits well into the background framework of Scripture that understands renewed cultural earthly activity as the eschatological purpose of redemption in Christ.

2 Peter 3:10–13

The fifth text is 2 Peter 3:10–13. These verses have often been misunderstood as being entirely negative about the future of this world, since they are

9. I am not engaging in the debate about what *ktisis* ("creation") refers to here. The term can be used in different ways in different contexts, which leads some to take its use in Rom. 8 as referring to gentiles, or to unbelievers, or to the human body. But understanding it as the nonhuman creation fits the Rom. 8 context best (especially the expressions "the creation itself" in v. 21 and "the whole creation" in v. 22).

10. Commentators have historically been divided as to the identity of the one who subjected creation to futility, positing variously God, the devil (a minority view), or humanity (Adam). Humanity is certainly the most likely candidate (or even if it is God, this is a divine response to human sin, mediating its cosmic consequences).

dominated by language of fiery judgment and destruction. Yet there are two positive statements of redemption nestled in the text (vv. 10, 13).

> But the day of the Lord will come like a thief, and then the heavens will pass away with a loud noise, and the elements will be dissolved with fire, and *the earth and everything that is done on it will be disclosed.* Since all these things are to be dissolved in this way, what sort of persons ought you to be in leading lives of holiness and godliness, waiting for and hastening the coming of the day of God, because of which the heavens will be set ablaze and dissolved, and the elements will melt with fire? But, in accordance with his promise, we wait for *new heavens and a new earth, where righteousness is at home.* (2 Pet. 3:10–13)

The first positive statement of God's saving activity is in verse 10, where the verb is "disclosed" with "the earth" (and all that is done on it—literally, "the works in it") designated as the object of this activity. Then at the end of verse 13, God's saving activity is pictured as renewal, implied by the twofold use of the word "new," and this is applied to the entire created universe ("new heavens and a new earth"), which will be characterized by righteousness. Like the other four texts that we have examined, salvation is here understood as comprehensive and holistic, bringing transformation and newness to the entire created order of heaven and earth.

Admittedly, the presence of the verb "disclosed" in verse 10 may come as something of a surprise. Given the predominance of images of destruction, the reader might initially be excused from thinking that a verb such as "destroyed," "wiped out," or "annihilated" might fit better, since the text seems to be describing the utter obliteration of the created order (including the earth). Along these lines, the King James Version (KJV) famously says that the earth will be "burned up," which certainly fits the dominant image of destruction in the text.

"Burned up" (*katakaēsetai*) is the reading in the Textus Receptus ("received text"), going back to Erasmus's edition of the Greek New Testament (1516), which he based on the Byzantine manuscript tradition.[11] "Burned up" was also used in other English translations besides the KJV prior to 1973 (e.g., RV, ASV, RSV, Douay-Rheims, Weymouth New Testament, Young's Literal Translation). But when the NIV New Testament was published in 1973, English translators for the first time bucked the trend by rendering the verb in 2 Peter 3:10 as "laid bare." This translation trend is followed by the NET

---

11. Various minority textual traditions have "disappear" or "be dissolved." The GNT (also known as TEV) seems to follow one of these minority traditions by its rendering "will vanish."

Bible ("laid bare"), NRSV, HCSB, Lexham English Bible ("disclosed"), the ESV, NCV, CEB ("exposed"), the NAB ("found out"), and the CEV ("seen for what they are").

As is well known to New Testament scholars, this is not a translation decision at all, but rather a matter of textual criticism. The NIV translators intentionally translated not the verb *katakaēsetai* from the Textus Receptus, but rather the verb *heurethēsetai* (future passive of *heuriskō*), which means, literally, "will be found."[12] This verb occurs in Codex Vaticanus and Codex Siniaticus, two of the oldest and most reliable of the ancient Greek manuscripts (both dating from the middle of the fourth century AD).

Already when Erasmus utilized the Byzantine manuscript tradition, he had known of the existence of Codex Vaticanus in the Vatican library; but it was not until the nineteenth century that scholars came to realize its value for establishing the text of the New Testament. Codex Siniaticus was only discovered in 1859 in the Orthodox monastery at Mount Sinai by the textual critic Constantin von Tischendorf. When von Tischendorf published his critical edition of the Greek New Testament in 1872, his text of 2 Peter 3:10 had *heurethēsetai*, as did the famous critical edition of Westcott and Hort published in 1881. And since the nineteenth century, biblical scholars have been aware that the more trustworthy manuscripts of the New Testament of 2 Peter 3:10 have *heurethēsetai*.

Despite this, many later English translators continued to utilize the inferior reading (even the latest edition of the NASB is based on the inferior reading). As Al Wolters has argued, this is a matter of worldview trumping the text.[13] It seems that, aided and abetted by a dualistic worldview, which devalued earthly life and assumed a supramundane destiny for the redeemed, translators allowed the tenor of judgment in 2 Peter 3 to overwhelm the text and determine their text-critical choices (going against the dictum that the more difficult reading is probably the better one). While the text undoubtedly speaks of judgment and destruction (using the image of a cosmic conflagration), it describes the destruction not of creation, but of sin, thus cleansing or purifying creation. We will return to this crucial point in the next chapter.

12. This is the verb that Archimedes used in the well-known story of his discovery of the principle of water displacement by a solid body (while he was taking a bath). He is said to have been so excited that he ran through the streets naked, shouting, "Eureka!" (*heurēka*, "I have found it"). This is the verb from which we get "heuristic" (an idea is heuristic if it leads to further discovery).

13. Al Wolters, "Worldview and Textual Criticism in 2 Peter 3:10," *Westminster Theological Journal* 49 (1987): 405–13. I am grateful to Professor Wolters for his incisive analysis on this and other issues relevant to the Bible's worldview, which I learned from him at the Institute for Christian Studies, Toronto, in the late 1970s.

Table 8.1. The Comprehensive Scope of Salvation

Scripture	Saving *Activity* of God	*Object* of God's Saving Activity
Acts 3:17–21 (esp. v. 21)	Restoration	All things
Eph. 1:7–10 (esp. v. 10)	Gathering up, bringing together, uniting	All things in heaven and on earth
Col. 1:16–20 (esp. v. 20)	Reconciliation (by removing the source of enmity, through the blood of the cross)	All things, whether on earth or in heaven
Rom. 8:19–23 (esp. vv. 21, 23)	Liberation, setting free from bondage	Creation itself
	Redemption	Our bodies
2 Pet. 3:10–13 (esp. vv. 10, 13)	Finding, disclosing, laying bare (having purified)	The earth and the works in it
	Renewal, making new, re-creation	Heaven and earth
Basic Characteristics of Salvation	*Restorative*—Salvation is God repairing what went wrong with creation (not taking us out of the world to "heaven")	*Comprehensive and holistic*—God intends to redeem or restore "all things" in heaven and on earth, including our bodies (salvation does not apply only to the human "soul")

When we pull together the unifying strands of these five texts, a clear pattern emerges (see table 8.1). First, salvation is conceived not as God doing something completely new, but rather as redoing something, fixing or repairing what went wrong; this point is expressed in the language of restoration, reconciliation, renewal, and redemption found in these texts. Second, this restorative work is applied as holistically and comprehensively as possible, to all things in heaven and on earth, where the phrase "heaven and earth" is how Scripture typically designates the entire created order (with earth understood as the distinctively human realm [Ps. 115:16]). The point is that the final salvific state envisioned in these five texts clearly contradicts an understanding of an immaterial, supramundane "heaven" as the ultimate dwelling place of the redeemed.

God's Intentions for the Cosmic Temple

Along with the five key texts explored so far, there is also John's vision of the new Jerusalem in the context of "a new heaven and new earth" (Rev. 21:1), a phrase that echoes 2 Peter 3:13.[14] John's extended vision of the final destiny

14. The only difference is that whereas Rev. 21:1 uses the singular "heaven," 2 Pet. 3:13 uses the plural "heavens."

of creation, encompassing Revelation 21–22, is worth lingering over not only because it reinforces the holistic or comprehensive understanding of salvation described in the five texts just examined, but also because it describes the culmination of a trajectory found throughout Scripture, which we have touched on numerous times in this book: the intended destiny of heaven and earth as the cosmic temple, a place for God's sacred dwelling.

Previously, in chapter 2, I sketched the biblical vision of the cosmos as God's temple, with heaven as the holy of holies, where God's throne is—an image both of transcendence (since heaven is not directly accessible to us) and of immanence (since God has elected to dwell within the cosmos he created).[15] As God's living image in the cosmic temple, human beings are meant to channel or mediate the divine presence into all the world by their faithful representation of the creator in their cultural endeavors, as they rule the earth (Gen. 1:26–28) or till and keep the garden (Gen. 2:15).

Many recent studies of the garden of Eden in Genesis suggest that this garden, in its relationship to the rest of the earth, functions as an analogue of the holy of holies in the tabernacle or the Jerusalem temple. The garden is the initial core location of God's presence on earth; this is where God's presence is first manifest, both in giving instructions to humanity (2:15–17) and in declaring judgment (3:8–19).[16] The garden is thus the link between earth and heaven, at least at the beginning of human history. The implication is that as the human race faithfully tended this garden or cultivated the earth, the garden would spread, until the entire earthly realm was transformed into a fit habitation for humanity. But it would thereby also become a fit habitation for God.[17]

---

15. Terence Fretheim makes the important point that because in the biblical worldview "heaven" is part of the created order, the location of God's throne in "heaven" is actually an image of the immanence of God within creation (*The Suffering of God: An Old Testament Perspective* [Overtures to Biblical Theology 14; Philadelphia: Fortress, 1984], 37).

16. It is traditional to interpret Gen. 3:8 (which introduces God's judgment) to mean that the first humans heard the sound of YHWH God walking in the garden in "the cool of the day" (literally, in the *ruaḥ* of the *yôm*), which makes some sense since *ruaḥ* can mean "wind," and a wind brings lower temperatures, while *yôm* normally means "day." This interpretation goes back to the Septuagint, which renders the phrase "in the evening" (*to deilinon*). However, there is a secondary (less common) meaning for *yôm* given in some lexicons (derived from an Akkadian word), "storm" (hence the expression might mean "the wind of the storm"). Thus, instead of describing God as taking a leisurely evening stroll in the garden, the "sound" the first humans heard might well be the trees whipping around in a tempest, which is the physical effect of God's coming in judgment. This would fit the pattern of theophanies in the Old Testament, which are often accompanied by a storm, with great noise (for a classic storm theophany in a forest, with trees splitting and crashing, see Ps. 29). On this interpretation of Gen. 3:8, see Jeffrey J. Niehaus, *God at Sinai: Covenant and Theophany in the Bible and Ancient Near East* (Studies in Old Testament Biblical Theology; Grand Rapids: Zondervan, 1995), 155–57.

17. Among the many works of recent biblical scholarship that develop this theme, see Gordon J. Wenham, "Sanctuary Symbolism in the Garden of Eden Story," in *I Studied Inscriptions*

When the human race was commissioned to "fill the earth" in order to rule it (Gen. 1:28), this biological imperative implied more than simple reproduction. Of course, in order to rule the earth, humanity had to multiply. But on analogy with the image or cult statue in a pagan temple, the human calling to be *imago Dei* in God's cosmic temple involved also filling the earth with the divine presence. The human purpose was to mediate God's holy presence from heaven to earth precisely through faithful cultural development of the earth, as the human race continued to multiply and increase.

But sin got in the way of that sacred calling. As Genesis tells it, through their deviation from God's purposes, humans filled the earth not just with their offspring, but also with their violence, thus corrupting the earth (Gen. 6:11). And so the developmental, historical process of the transformation of the world into a fit place for God's habitation has never been completed.

But the good news is that God has not given up on creation. The creator began a process of redemption to restore humanity and the cosmos to what it was meant to be. Thus, we have the relentlessly eschatological, forward-looking press of the biblical story, anticipating a future that God has prepared (see the discussion of the biblical plot in chap. 3).

God's Intentions Renewed through Israel

Since violence has impeded and distorted the human calling to be God's image on earth, God has intervened in history to set things right. As the Bible tells it, the creator began a new initiative in his redemptive work through the election of Abraham and his descendants as a "royal priesthood" (Exod. 19:6), that they might mediate blessing to all families and nations (Gen. 12:3; 18:18; 22:18; 26:4; 28:14). Israel's vocation vis-à-vis the nations is thus analogous to the human calling as *imago Dei* vis-à-vis the earth, which implies a vocation of bringing others into a redemptive relationship with the creator God, who had revealed himself to Abraham. The redemption of Israel thus constitutes the beginning of God's renewal of the image, a process that started with one family but that is intended to spread to the entire human race.

from Before the Flood: Ancient Near Eastern Literary and Linguistic Approaches to Genesis, ed. Richard S. Hess and David Toshio Tsumura (Sources for Biblical and Theological Study: Old Testament Series; Winona Lake, IN: Eisenbrauns, 1994), 399–404; Gregory K. Beale, *The Temple and the Church's Mission: A Biblical Theology of the Dwelling Place of God* (New Studies in Biblical Theology 17; Downers Grove, IL: IVP Academic, 2004); T. Desmond Alexander, *From Eden to the New Jerusalem: An Introduction to Biblical Theology* (Grand Rapids: Kregel, 2009); T. Desmond Alexander and Simon J. Gathercole, eds., *Heaven on Earth: The Temple in Biblical Theology* (Carlisle: Paternoster, 2004).

In a similar way, the tabernacle (Exod. 25–40) is God's initial postfall move to dwell on earth among a people who are being redeemed. When the building was completed, a cloud descended over the tent of meeting, and the tabernacle was filled with the glory of YHWH's presence (Exod. 40:34–35).[18] Then, whenever the cloud rose from the tabernacle and set out, the Israelites followed; thus God's presence was among the people during the journey in the wilderness as a cloud by day and as a fire by night (Exod. 40:36–38).

God's distinctive face-to-face presence with Israel is emphasized by Moses in Numbers 14:14, at a crucial point in Israel's history (when the people refuse to enter the promised land because they fear the inhabitants), and he specifically mentions the cloud and fire of Exodus 40:38 as integral to that presence. Having interceded with God on behalf of the people, as he did during the episode of the golden calf (Exod. 32–34), Moses gets God to agree to forgive their sin once again (Num. 14:20). Yet God swears that none of the current generation will enter the promised land (14:22–23). Indeed, God grounds this oath of judgment against the wilderness generation in a larger purpose: "Nevertheless—as I live, and as all the earth shall be filled with the glory of the LORD . . . " (14:21). The reason that YHWH's anger is here kindled against Israel is that they were to be the means by which the cosmic temple would be pervaded with the divine presence. And his oath commits God to this purpose despite the recalcitrance of the present generation.[19]

Image and Presence in Jesus and the Church

After a long and complex history of redemption, God's saving action culminates in the coming of Jesus, who is the paradigm *imago Dei* (2 Cor. 4:4–6; Col. 1:15; Heb. 1:3), the second Adam, who accomplished through his obedience (even unto death) what the first Adam compromised by disobedience (Rom. 5:12–19). Given the Old Testament background of humanity as God's image, this implies that Jesus succeeded, where the human race had failed, in manifesting the divine presence on earth. And this is exactly what the New Testament claims. At Jesus's birth, Matthew declares that Jesus fulfilled the *'immānû'ēl* ("God-with-us") prophecy of Isaiah 7:14 (Matt. 1:22–23), and Colossians 1:19 explains that "in him all the fullness of God was pleased to

18. According to 1 Kings 8:10–11 and 2 Chron. 7:1–3, God's glory also filled the Jerusalem temple when it was built.

19. Although some translations render the imperfect verb in Num. 14:21 as present tense ("is filled"), the NRSV's translation of the verb as future ("shall be filled") is the typical sense of the imperfect and makes much better sense of the context. In older Hebrew grammars the "imperfect" often was called the "future."

dwell." Indeed, Jesus so manifested God's character and presence in the full range of his earthly life that he can tell his disciples, "Whoever has seen me has seen the Father" (John 14:9).

Particularly significant is that the incarnation is described in language that alludes to the tabernacle and the divine presence: "And the Word became flesh and lived among us, and we have seen his glory, the glory as of a father's only son, full of grace and truth" (John 1:14). Not only is "glory" a term used for YHWH's presence among Israel and in the tabernacle but "lived" translates the Greek verb *skēnoō*, which in the Septuagint often translates Hebrew *šākan* ("dwell"), from which comes the noun *miškan* ("tabernacle") and the later rabbinic idea of the Shekinah, God's glorious presence in the world.[20]

We also have Jesus's famous words, "Where two or three are gathered in my name, I am there among them" (Matt. 18:20). This statement takes on greater depth when we compare it to the rabbinic saying, "If two sit together and words of the Law [are spoken] between them, the Divine Presence [Shekinah] rests between them."[21] In the words of N. T. Wright, Jesus spoke and acted "as if he were the Shekinah in person, the presence of YHWH tabernacling with his people."[22] And many New Testament scholars have explored ways in which the Gospels portray Jesus as the replacement temple, the one who claimed to be the definitive site of divine presence and means of connection to God, which the Jerusalem temple was supposed to have accomplished.[23]

Through his resurrection and ascension, Jesus has now become the head of the church, an international community of Jew and gentile reconciled to each other and to God, described in the New Testament as the "body of Christ"

20. Part of the Jewish background for the Word in John's prologue (John 1:1–18) is the portrayal in Sir. 24:1–12 of God's Wisdom coming down from heaven to dwell in the tabernacle. This Greek text uses the compound verb *kataskēnoō* when God tells Wisdom to "make your dwelling" in Israel and uses the related noun *skēnē* for the holy "tent" or tabernacle (24:8, 10). For a brief and lucid introduction to the Jewish background of John's prologue, see Daniel Boyarin, "Logos, A Jewish Word: John's Prologue as Midrash," in *The Jewish Annotated New Testament*, ed. Amy-Jill Levine and Marc Zvi Brettler (Oxford: Oxford University Press, 2011), 546–49. For a more extended study, see Daniel Boyarin, "The Gospel of the *Memra*: Jewish Binitarianism and the Prologue to John," *Harvard Theological Review* 94 (2001): 243–84.

21. Rabbi Hananiah ben Teradion, quoted in the Mishnah, 'Abot 3:2; translation from Benedict Thomas Viviano, *Study as Worship: Aboth and the New Testament* (Studies in Judaism in Late Antiquity 26; Leiden: Brill, 1978), 67. The first use of square brackets is Viviano's insertion; the second is mine.

22. N. T. Wright, *The Challenge of Jesus: Recovering Who Jesus Was and Is* (Downers Grove, IL: InterVarsity, 1999), 114.

23. This is a wonderfully rich theme that opens up a great deal of the Gospels. Among the many works on the subject, see Brant Pitre, "Jesus, the New Temple, and the New Priesthood," *Letter and Spirit* 4 (2008): 48–83; Nicholas Perrin, *Jesus the Temple* (Grand Rapids: Baker Academic, 2010).

(1 Cor. 12:12–27) and as the "new humanity," renewed in the image of God
(Eph. 4:24; Col. 3:9–10; cf. 2 Cor. 3:18).[24] But the church is also God's temple,
indwelt by the Holy Spirit (the divine Shekinah) as a foretaste of the promised
future (1 Cor. 3:16–17; 6:19; 2 Cor. 6:16). Indeed, Ephesians 2 first describes
the church as the "one new humanity" of Jew and gentile (v. 15), then goes on
to portray this new humanity as a "holy temple in the Lord" (v. 21), which is
being built into "a dwelling place for God" (v. 22). These three images—body
of Christ, new humanity, temple of God—are integrally connected, since they
refer to the reality and calling of the church as the continuation of Christ's
mission to bring God's salvific presence fully into earthly life, with the consequent healing that this would engender.

It is God's intent that the divine presence extend from heaven to earth, to
unify earth and heaven. That is why Jesus taught us to pray, "Your kingdom
come; your will be done on earth as it is in heaven" (Matt. 6:10); it is God's
will to conform earth to heaven. And so the prophets envision a day when
"the earth will be filled with the knowledge of the glory of the Lord as the
waters cover the sea" (Isa. 11:9; Hab. 2:14).

In a similar vein, Ephesians 4 tells us that the ascension of Christ from the
earth was only temporary. Its ultimate purpose is that he might "fill all things"
(v. 10). Or as Paul puts it in 1 Corinthians 15, after Christ has conquered death
(v. 26) on the last day and has handed the kingdom over to the Father, God will
be "all in all" (v. 28). I used to be uncomfortable with language about Christ
filling all things or of God being all in all because it sounded pantheistic to
me. My fears were laid to rest when I came to understand that this is temple
imagery describing God's glorious presence permeating the cosmic sanctuary.

The Destiny of the Cosmic Temple

In John's vision of the new Jerusalem in Revelation 21–22, we find a description
of what it will be like when God's purposes for creation are finally fulfilled.
Coming as they do within the New Testament's only full-fledged apocalypse,
these chapters are full of strange symbolism, so we need to be careful not to
be overly literalistic in our interpretation.[25] Nevertheless, even symbols are
meant to convey truths.

24. Although the expression *kainon anthrōpon* in Eph. 4:24 ("new man" in the KJV) is often
translated as "new self" in many contemporary versions (e.g., the NIV), the rendering "new
humanity" better gets at the communal meaning of a renewed human race in God's image,
meant to attain to their original purpose, which the fall impeded.
25. G. C. Berkouwer warns that when it comes to eschatological, especially apocalyptic,
imagery, we should distinguish the mode of expression from the intent of the imagery; while

For example, the disappearance of the sea in Revelation 21:1 ("and the sea was no more") is not making the point that no one goes swimming in the new creation. Rather, the sea is a traditional symbol in the ancient Near East for the forces of chaos and evil (thus in Rev. 13:1 one of the beasts comes from the sea).[26] The point is that the forces of evil and chaos will be eradicated. Beyond the traditional background of this image, the book of Revelation previously mentioned the exploitative sea trade of the Roman Empire, which will end when Rome, the great city (called, symbolically, "Babylon"), falls (18:11–18); that is why among those who mourn the passing of the city are "all shipmasters and seafarers, sailors and all whose trade is on the sea" (18:17–18). It is therefore good news that in the eschaton the sea (which facilitated the economic expansion of the Roman Empire) will be no more.[27]

Perhaps the most important point about the new Jerusalem is that through its descent from heaven, God's presence decisively shifts from heaven to earth. There are two aspects to this, one expected, one more surprising.

Given the trajectory of Scripture, it is perhaps to be expected that the voice from God's throne declares, "See, the home of God is among mortals. He will dwell with them as their God; they will be his peoples, and God himself will be with them" (Rev. 21:3). This is clearly a fulfillment of the ancient promise, articulated in the Pentateuch, that YHWH would "dwell" [šākan] among Israel as his people (Exod. 29:45–46) or set his "dwelling" [miškān] among them (Lev. 26:11–12). Indeed, the Greek word for "dwell" in Revelation 21:3 is skēnoō (which typically translates šākan), the same verb used of the incarnation of the Word in John 1:14. Similarly, "home" in Revelation 21:3 translates the related noun skēnē, which the Septuagint uses for the tabernacle (Hebrew miškan). So far, so good.[28]

---

the former may be confusing if taken literally, we can still understand what the passage is trying to communicate (*The Return of Christ*, trans. James Van Oosterom, ed. Marlin J. Van Elderen [Studies in Dogmatics; Grand Rapids: Eerdmans, 1972], 216–17).

26. For a discussion of this symbolism, see J. Richard Middleton, "Created in the Image of a Violent God? The Ethical Problem of the Conquest of Chaos in Biblical Creation Texts," *Interpretation* 58 (2004): 341–55.

27. For a discussion of the sea in the book of Revelation, see David J. Hawkin, "The Critique of Ideology in the Book of Revelation and Its Implications for Ecology," *Ecotheology* 8 (2003): 161–72. It is also possible that the disappearance of the sea in Rev. 21:1 refers to the removal of the "sea of glass" (4:6; 15:2), which J. Mealy Webb describes as "the age-old barrier between heaven and earth" (*After the Thousand Years: Resurrection and Judgment in Revelation 20* [JSOTSup 70; Sheffield: JSOT Press, 1992], 242).

28. It is sometimes thought that the Hebrew verb šākan, which underlies Greek skēnoō, refers only to temporary or impermanent presence (after all, the tabernacle was an impermanent structure). This interpretation goes back to an early article by Frank Moore Cross ("The Tabernacle: A Study from an Archeological and Historical Approach," *Biblical Archeologist* 10 [1947]: 45–68) and has found its way into much popular thinking on the subject. However,

There are, however, two distinctive verbs used in the Old Testament for God's presence. The verb *šākan* is often used for God's "dwelling" with Israel, especially in the tabernacle, and Ezekiel 43:7 promises God's permanent or eternal dwelling (also using *šākan*) in the eschatological temple; yet the verb *yāšab* is reserved for God "sitting" (on a throne, thus "ruling") in heaven.[29] Some Israelites may have thought that YHWH was domiciled in the Jerusalem temple, but Isaiah has a vision of "the Lord sitting [*yāšab*] on a throne, high and lofty; and [only] the hem of his robe filled the temple" (Isa. 6:1). The scale of the vision is staggering; YHWH simply cannot be contained in the Jerusalem temple (as Solomon recognizes in 1 Kings 8:27). Isaiah's vision thus implies that the ark of the covenant in the holy of holies is not God's throne (as might have been popularly thought), but only God's footstool; indeed, as YHWH proclaims later in Isaiah, "Heaven is my throne and the earth is my footstool" (Isa. 66:1).

Although God rules the earth from his heavenly throne in the Old Testament (Pss. 11:4; 14:2), when we get to Revelation 22:3, things have decisively changed. The text tells us that there is no longer any curse (or anything accursed) in the holy city (the curse on the earth from Gen. 3:17 is effectively reversed). This allows for a radically new thing: God's throne is now no longer in heaven but is in the midst of the city (Rev. 22:3; see also 21:3, 5; 22:1). The center of God's governance of the cosmos from now on will be permanently established on a renewed earth. Thus the destiny of the cosmic temple is complete. The definitive presence of God is now manifest in the earthly creation.

Given the presence of God in the new Jerusalem, it is significant that the city is described as a cube: "its length and width and height are equal" (Rev. 21:16). This is something that John learns from an angel with a measuring rod (drawn from a similar motif in Ezek. 40–44); the city turns out to be enormous: twelve hundred stadia, somewhat less than 1,500 miles (though it is unclear if this is the measurement of each side or of all the sides of the cube). When Robert Heinlein describes in ludicrous detail the city as tall as it is wide in his novel *Job: A Comedy of Justice*, this only reinforces why we should not take these symbols literally.[30] The point of the enormous size of the

---

not only does *šākan* occur in the Hebrew Bible with words that signify permanence, but also Ezek. 43:7 directly claims that YHWH will "dwell [*šākan*] forever" with God's people in the eschatological temple.

29. Eric Baker makes a persuasive argument for this distinction in a paper titled "The Enthronement of God in Heaven, the Dwelling of God on Earth: A New Look at the Hebrew Scriptures," presented at the Eastern Great Lakes Biblical Society annual meeting in Cambridge, OH, March 26–27, 2009. This is part of Baker's PhD dissertation research on "The Eschatological Role of the Jerusalem Temple in Second Temple Judaism."

30. Robert A. Heinlein, *Job: A Comedy of Justice* (New York: Ballantine, 1984).

city is that there is room for many people there ("There's a wideness in God's mercy" [Faber]), while the city is a cube because these are the proportions of the holy of holies in the Jerusalem temple (1 Kings 6:20; cf. Ezek. 41:4). In the context of the new creation, the new Jerusalem is a megasized analogue of the holy of holies in the tabernacle or temple; it is also directly parallel to the garden of Eden in the original creation.

The parallel between the new Jerusalem and the garden as the focused center of God's presence on earth explains why various elements of the garden from Genesis 2 are found integrated into the city in Revelation 21–22. Just as the garden was watered by a river, which then flowed outward into the world (Gen. 2:10), so there is a river (described as the "water of life") flowing from God's throne down the city's main street (Rev. 22:1; also 21:6), and this water of life is offered for free to any who are thirsty (22:17). This free offer to anyone who is thirsty picks up on the language of grace from Isaiah 55:1, while the river from God's throne echoes Ezekiel's vision of a river flowing from the threshold of the temple (47:1–12), the central locus of God's earthly presence.

Just as there was a tree of life in the garden (Gen. 2:9), so there is one in the new Jerusalem (Rev. 22:2). But whereas in Genesis 3:23–24 humanity is exiled from the garden and the way to this tree is guarded by cherubim and flaming sword, in Revelation 22:14 those who are cleansed from sin "will have the right to the tree of life and may enter the city by the gates," which are always open (21:25).[31]

The ending of Genesis 3, with the way to the tree of life barred, led to various Jewish traditions about the fate of the "garden" (Hebrew *gan*), which is consistently translated as "paradise" (Greek *paradeisos*) in the Septuagint of Genesis 2–3.[32] This paradise/garden was sometimes thought to have been taken up into heaven or removed to the top of a high mountain at the ends of the earth, making it inaccessible to humanity—until the last day, when God would once more grant the redeemed access to the tree of life. The association of garden and mountain occurs in Ezekiel 28:1–19, in an oracle of judgment against the king of Tyre, who is described as having been "in Eden, the garden of God" (v. 13), which is then identified as "the mountain of God" (v. 14).

The picture of renewed human access to paradise on a high mountain, resulting in earthly renewal and flourishing (which God has "prepared" for the righteous), is seen in *1 Enoch* 25:1–7 (a Jewish apocalyptic work that we touched on in chap. 7 above). It thus makes sense that John is taken to "a

---

31. Nevertheless, only the righteous may enter the city (Rev. 21:27; 22:14); the unrighteous have their "place" in the lake of fire, which is the second death (Rev. 21:8).

32. In Gen. 2:8, 9, 10, 15, 16; 3:1, 2, 3, 8, 10, 23, 24.

great, high mountain" to see the holy city descending out of heaven from
God (Rev. 21:10).

This means, however, that we should not identify "paradise" in the New
Testament with "heaven" (a point to which we will return in chap. 10); rather,
"paradise" more correctly refers to God's original intent for human earthly
flourishing (the garden of Gen. 2), which now comes to fruition in a garden-
city, on a renewed (even grander) Mount Zion, as the focused center of God's
presence in the new heaven and new earth.

Just as the water of life echoed Ezekiel's vision, so John notes that the tree
of life (singular) is on both sides of the river; this evokes Ezekiel 47:7, which
mentions multiple trees on both sides of the river.[33] John also notes that the
tree produces fruit each month and that "the leaves of the tree are for the
healing of the nations" (Rev. 22:2), a clear echo of Ezekiel 47:12: "Their fruit
will be for food, and their leaves for healing."

However, John's vision in Revelation has one significant difference from
Ezekiel's. He states (perhaps in perplexity), "I saw no temple in the city"
(21:22); as one steeped in Ezekiel's vision, he seems to have expected one. But
in the case of the new Jerusalem, "its temple is the Lord God the Almighty
and the Lamb" (21:22); the city itself is the central locus of God's presence
on earth, which is why John can describe it as having "the glory of God"
(21:11; cf. 21:23).

The Destiny of Redeemed Humanity—
The Cultural Mandate Renewed

Paradoxically, in Revelation the holy city is also described as the bride of the
Lamb (21:2); the new Jerusalem is thus equivalent to God's people. This complex image suggests the redemption of humanity in its sociocultural, even urban
character; God redeems not human abstractions, but rather people in their
inextricably communal and cultural realities.[34] And, given the human purpose
at the start of creation, the movement from garden to city is to be expected.

33. It is paradoxical for a single tree to be on both sides of a river, but we need to search for
the point of the symbol rather than take it literally.

34. The difficulty of interpreting the symbolism of these chapters is illustrated by Robert H.
Gundry's single-minded argument that the city is a symbol for God's people and is not at all
to be understood as a place (the center of the new earth), although he does not deny that the
people are to be found on the new earth (indeed, his interpretation of the text is actually quite
helpful) ("The New Jerusalem: People as Place, Not Place for People," *Novum Testamentum*
29 [1987]: 254–64). It is unclear to me why we need to choose between people and place as the
referent of the city, especially why we should exclude an emphasis on place, since the city is
clearly intended as the fulfillment of the garden of Eden.

For what happens when humans faithfully work the primitive landscape of a garden throughout history? The complexity of a city is a natural outcome. But this city, unlike all cities we have known, will be without sin.

Back in Genesis 2 the garden of Eden was portrayed as being rich in gold and semiprecious stones (vv. 11–12); although no details are given, they were presumably present in their natural state. By contrast, the new Jerusalem has gold and both precious and semiprecious stones worked into its very construction (Rev. 21:18–21). Indeed, both the city and its main street are made of "pure gold, clear/transparent as glass" (21:18, 21). Andy Crouch makes the intriguing observation that there is an ancient Japanese artistic tradition, known as *nihonga*, which works with pure minerals. As practiced by New York artist Makoto Fujiura, this sometimes involves beating out gold leaf until it is so thin as to become translucent, enabling the viewer to see objects behind it bathed in a golden sheen. Could the gold of the new Jerusalem, he wonders, be gold transformed from its natural state by the craft of a "master Artist"?[35] In other words, just as God originally planted a garden in Eden (Gen. 2:8), so God builds the eschatological city in Revelation 21–22.

But not all cultural production in the new Jerusalem is the direct work of God. Although the divine artist is indeed the one who has "prepared" and "adorned" the holy city for its descent from heaven to earth (Rev. 21:2), nevertheless kings and nations will bring their "glory" and "honor" into the city (21:24, 26), a reference to the best of human workmanship that has been developed throughout history.[36] This echoes the vision in Isaiah 60 of a renewed Jerusalem after the exile, where various elements of human culture from other nations (including flock and herds, lumber, ships, gold, silver, iron) find their way into the city, transformed into means of glorifying the God of Israel. "Your gates shall always be open; day and night they shall not be shut, so that nations shall bring you their wealth, with their kings led in procession" (60:11).[37] The human contribution to the new Jerusalem should not be downplayed.

The reference to kings and nations in the new creation is a telling signal that cultural and even national diversity is not abrogated by redemption. Salvation

---

35. Andy Crouch, *Culture Making: Recovering Our Creative Calling* (Downers Grove, IL: IVP Academic, 2008), 248–49.

36. Indeed, the synergy of divine and human action in the new Jerusalem is evident when the multitude in Rev. 19 cries out, "'The marriage of the Lamb has come, and his bride has made herself ready; to her it has been granted to be clothed with fine linen, bright and pure'—for the fine linen is the righteous deeds of the saints" (vv. 7–8). Both "prepared" in Rev. 21:2 and "made ready" in 19:7 represent the same Greek verb (*hetoimazō*). The paradox is that while God certainly prepares eschatological salvation, the human contribution is duly noted.

37. For an excellent study of Isa. 60, see Richard J. Mouw, *When the Kings Come Marching In: Isaiah and the New Jerusalem* (Grand Rapids: Eerdmans, 1983).

does not erase cultural differences; rather, the human race, still distinguished by nationality, now walks by the glory or light of the holy city, which is itself illuminated by the Lamb (Rev. 21:24).[38] The international character of God's people in the eschaton brings to fruition God's purposes from the beginning, where God is the creator of all people, and Israel's election was for the sake of the nations. Thus we find John's vision of a "great multitude that no one could count, from every nation, from all tribes and peoples and languages" (Rev. 7:9), ransomed for God to serve him on earth (5:9–10). Such an understanding of the international character of God's people should lead the church to actively seek to embody all that is good from the complex cultures of the world. Ethnocentrism is not an option in the new creation.

The international focus of the eschaton helps explain a telling detail in Revelation 21:3 that some translations obscure: God "will dwell with them [humanity] as their God; they will be his peoples." This shift from "people" in the singular—characteristic of the Old Testament promise that YHWH would be Israel's God and they would be his people (Gen. 17:7–8; Exod. 6:7)—to the plural "peoples" certainly manifests the general thrust of the biblical story, which expands the boundaries of the covenant people to include all humanity. But the plural also echoes Isaiah 25, where God has promised to prepare an eschatological feast on Mount Zion for "all peoples" (v. 6), at which time death would be defeated (v. 7) and all tears wiped away (v. 8). And indeed, both of these accompanying promises are mentioned as coming to fruition in the very next verse of John's vision (Rev. 21:4).

But what are redeemed people to do in the new creation? Just as we have to get rid of the unbiblical idea of "going to heaven" as our final destiny, so we need to drop pious ideas of a perpetual worship service as our ultimate purpose in the eschaton.[39]

Whereas in Genesis 1 God made humans in his image to represent his rule by developing the earth, in Genesis 2 the human purpose was to work the garden, thereby extending God's presence throughout this world. It thus comes as no surprise that Revelation 21–22 portrays the renewal of the fundamental human purpose in God's world.

The fact that the new Jerusalem does not encompass the entirety of the new creation, but instead represents the central locus of God's presence, might lead

---

38. There is a basis here for agreeing with the dispensationalist perspective that wants to affirm a role for national Israel in the eschaton, as long as we affirm a role also for Canada, Jamaica, Haiti, Ghana, Korea, and so on. I am indebted for this insight to Steven James, himself a "progressive dispensationalist" (for more on progressive dispensationalism, see the appendix to this book).

39. Not to mention the caricature of the redeemed sitting on clouds and playing harps.

one to wonder if the cultural development of the earth is a continuing human task. Such development can happen as the redeemed do their part in filling the earth with the healing presence of God, thereby extending the parameters of the city and participating in the eschatological destiny of the world.

Confirmation for this intuition is found in Revelation 22:5, which declares that on this newly redeemed earth, God's people will serve him and "reign forever and ever." Initially, this is paradoxical, since Revelation 11:15 has proclaimed that when the "kingdom of the world" becomes "the kingdom of our Lord and of his Messiah," then "he will reign forever and ever" (the text for the famous "Hallelujah Chorus" in Handel's *Messiah*). But there is no tension in the biblical worldview between God's sovereign rule (God's "throne" is mentioned throughout Rev. 21–22) and human rule; after all, we are made in God's image. Thus, Revelation 5:10 states that those ransomed by Christ from all tribes and nations will serve as priests of God and will "reign on the earth." And when Revelation 22:5 explains that their service to God involves an everlasting rule—"forever and ever"—this should disabuse us of thinking that the text refers to some temporary millennium, followed by a nonearthly eternal state. On the contrary, the figure of the new Jerusalem, in the context of a new heaven and new earth, represents nothing less than the renewal of human cultural life in all its fullness—this time without sin—in the context of a redeemed creation. That is the destiny of God's cosmic temple.

In the present, as the church lives between the times, those being renewed in the *imago Dei* are called to instantiate an embodied culture or social reality alternative to the violent and deathly formations and practices that dominate the world. By this conformity to Christ—the paradigm image of God—the church manifests God's rule and participates in God's mission to flood the world with the divine presence. In its concrete communal life the church as the body of Christ is called to witness to the promised future of a new heaven and a new earth, in which righteousness dwells (2 Pet. 3:13).

Part 4

Problem Texts
for Holistic Eschatology

9

Cosmic Destruction at Christ's Return?

The New Testament clearly teaches the redemption of *this* world. In the last chapter we examined key texts that emphasized God's plan for reconciling "all things" in heaven and on earth to himself, thus bringing the present creation to its intended destiny as a cosmic temple filled with the divine presence. Then all that has corrupted and deformed God's good world will be healed, and the created order (human and nonhuman) will be transformed into what God meant it to be.

There are, however, various New Testament texts that do not, on the surface, fit this model of holistic redemption, and such texts typically are adduced as counterexamples, since they seem to suggest an otherworldly destiny for the redeemed. In the many years I have been teaching the Bible, I have seen just about every possible counterexample raised by some student or church member. Some of the relevant texts seem to portray the destruction or annihilation of the world at Christ's return, while others suggest that heaven is the ultimate destiny for God's people.

It is important that such texts not be swept under the rug, but faced squarely. The present chapter examines the first set of "problem" texts: those that seem to describe the destruction of the world when Christ returns. My purpose is to try to understand what these texts are really saying and how they fit into the biblical vision of cosmic redemption. The following chapter will look at texts that seem to promise a heavenly destiny (and texts on the "rapture" fit well here, since this event is usually understood as equivalent to "going to heaven"); my purpose there will be to clarify what such texts really teach about the role of "heaven" in biblical eschatology. Indeed, when we examine these proposed counterexamples fully for what they actually say, we will find that they provide further support for a holistic view of redemption.

The Destruction of the Cosmos in the New Testament?

Let us begin with those New Testament texts that seem to expect the annihilation or destruction of the world. One important passage is found in Jesus's Olivet discourse in the Synoptic Gospels (the parallel texts are in Matt. 24; Mark 13; Luke 21).[1] Here Jesus speaks of the sun and moon being darkened, the stars falling from heaven, and the powers of heaven being shaken (Matt. 24:29; Mark 13:24–25; Luke 21:25–26). But these references are small potatoes in comparison with his later statement: "Heaven and earth will pass away, but my words will not pass away" (Matt. 24:35; Mark 13:31; Luke 21:33). Is Jesus teaching the annihilation of the universe?

Beyond the Olivet discourse, other New Testament texts seem to speak of the eschatological destruction of the world. In Hebrews 12:26–28 the author identifies God's promised shaking of heaven and earth as the removal of created things so that what is not created—the kingdom of God—may remain. This certainly suggests a picture of an acosmic, otherworldly future (though if this is a nonearthly future, it would also be a nonheavenly one).

Likewise, 2 Peter 3 describes what appears to be a cosmic conflagration in which the heavens will be dissolved and the elements will melt in the heat (vv. 10, 12), although, as we saw in the preceding chapter, there is nothing explicit in that text about the destruction of the earth (according to the best Greek manuscripts). Nevertheless, this is certainly a dire picture that needs to be addressed.

Certain passages in the book of Revelation are also relevant here. Revelation 6:12–14 gives a description of cosmic events initiated by the sixth seal; these events include the stars falling from heaven, heaven disappearing like a rolled-up scroll, along with an earthquake, with mountains and islands being moved out of their place. A possibly related text is Revelation 20:11, which says that the fearsome presence of God on his throne of judgment causes the

---

1. This is referred to as the Olivet discourse because it took place on the Mount of Olives (Matt. 24:3; Mark 13:3). The location may be significant in light of Zech. 14:4, which refers to the splitting of the Mount of Olives as part of the eschatological theophany when God comes in judgment.

earth and heavens (that is, the entire universe) to flee away, so that no place is found for them.

Finally, we might notice that, as a prelude to the new heaven and new earth in Revelation 21:1, "the first heaven and the first earth had passed away." While chapters 6 and 20 of Revelation could be taken to refer to the destruction of the cosmos in order to usher in an otherworldly final state, Revelation 21 seems to suggest the eradication of the present cosmos in order to replace it with a new one (which is not quite as extreme, but still seems to undervalue the present world).

The obvious problem with texts like these is that they seem to stand in significant tension with the central thrust of Scripture, which is that God loves and intends to redeem creation. Given this central biblical thrust, I do not think we can approach these problem texts as simple contradictions to what the Bible says elsewhere, unless we seriously think that Scripture is confused on this issue. On the surface these texts may seem contradictory, and certainly we should address the contradiction in each case. But rather than view these texts simply as an alternative to holistic eschatology, we need to ask how these texts (with their differing emphases) fit with the overall biblical vision of God's purposes for this world.

The Old Testament Background of Judgment Theophanies

We should start by noting that New Testament texts of cosmic destruction are dependent on a large fund of Old Testament imagery about God's coming as judge. In these Old Testament texts (many of which we examined in chap. 6), we find mention of nations, mountains, the earth, and even the heavens being shaken at God's presence. This idea is clearly behind Hebrews 12, which quotes Haggai 2:6 concerning the eschatological shaking of heaven and earth. In connection with this cosmic shaking, many Old Testament texts describe the darkening of sun and moon, which provides a ready background for Revelation 6 and Jesus's predictions in the Olivet discourse about celestial signs (although the precedent for stars falling from heaven is a bit more complex).

A few prophetic texts also mention the disappearance of the heavens at God's judgment. Although not specifically a prophetic text, Psalm 102:25–26 likely lies behind Jesus's statement about heaven and earth passing away (and this psalm might lie behind the passing away of the first heaven and earth in Rev. 21:1).

Given the significant repertoire of images of cosmic destruction that the New Testament authors had available to them to depict the coming day of the Lord, we need to read the New Testament imagery of cosmic destruction in light of the Old Testament background, while making necessary allowances for the transformation of imagery that might have taken place between the Testaments. This is an important alternative to simply reading our own contemporary biases and perceptions into Scripture. Since some of the same imagery and themes recur in different New Testament texts, my approach in this chapter is to separate out the themes or images and treat relevant texts together.

Celestial (and Earthly) Disruption in the Olivet Discourse and Revelation 6

Let us start with the image in the Olivet discourse of the sun and moon being darkened (Matt. 24:29; Mark 13:24; Luke 21:25). This motif occurs in a series of dire predictions that Jesus makes in response to a question from his disciples. First he tells the disciples about the coming destruction of the Jerusalem temple, which prompts them to ask him when this will be and what would be the sign of its accomplishment (Matt. 24:1–3; Mark 13:1–4; Luke 21:5–7).[2] In response, Jesus warns them of earthquakes and famines on the horizon, but he states that this is not the end, so they should not be led astray (Matt. 24:4–8; Mark 13:5–8; Luke 21:8–11).[3] He then explains that the disciples will be handed over for trial and persecution, but if they endure to the end, they will be saved (Matt. 24:9–14; Mark 13:9–13; Luke 21:12–19). At this point Jesus mentions a time of "great suffering" (traditionally, "great tribulation" [Matt. 24:21]) that will surpass all suffering, both past and future (Matt. 24:15–26; Mark 13:14–23; Luke 21:20–24).

Then come the words that seem to refer to cosmic destruction (or at least heavenly destabilization), followed by the coming of the Son of Man (Matt. 24:29–30; Mark 13:24–26; Luke 21:25–27). This is Mark's version:

> But in those days, after that suffering,
>   the sun will be darkened,
>   and the moon will not give its light,
>   and the stars will be falling from heaven,
>   and the powers in the heavens will be shaken.

2. Matthew expands their question, taking it as equivalent to asking about Jesus's coming and the end of the age (24:3), which certainly fits the rest of the Olivet discourse.

3. Luke adds plagues to earthquakes and famine and mentions portents and signs from heaven (21:11).

> Then they will see "the Son of Man coming in clouds" with great
> power and glory.
>
> Mark 13:24–26[4]

I do not intend to enter fully into the debate about whether this list of signs in the Olivet discourse refers to the events leading up to AD 70 (the Roman-Jewish war and the destruction of Jerusalem) or to events in the eschatological future when Christ returns in final judgment (both can be spoken of, in some sense, as Christ's "coming"). Many biblical commentators suggest that, up to a certain point in the text, Jesus refers to events on the historical horizon (which certainly seems justified in light of the disciples' initial question), and that after this point (exactly where is debated) his words refer to his coming in final judgment.[5]

Without denying any of this, I would also note that it is possible for the language of celestial signs and (seeming) cosmic destruction to have a double referent, pointing to both sets of events simultaneously, much as some Old Testament prophecies clearly refer to events in the prophet's own day and also have a later and more climactic fulfillment in New Testament times (for example, Isaiah's prediction in 7:14 of a royal birth in Ahaz's court, or possibly the prophet's own son, later applied to the birth of Jesus in Matt. 1:23). Indeed, as we saw in chapter 6, the Old Testament commonly uses language of cosmic destruction in multivalent, complex ways to refer to the judgment that precedes salvation. I therefore have no problem with thinking that Jesus's words about the destabilization of heavenly phenomena could well refer both to events on the historical horizon and to his final coming in universal judgment and salvation.

Language similar to Jesus's predictions in the Olivet discourse occurs in Revelation 6, though that chapter also includes references to the shaking of earth and the rolling back of the sky/heaven:

> When he [the angel] opened the sixth seal, I looked, and there came a great earthquake; the sun became black as sackcloth, the full moon became like blood, and the stars of the sky fell to the earth as the fig tree drops its winter fruit

---

4. All three Gospels refer to the same celestial events, but Luke inserts (just before the shaking of the heavenly powers) a reference to distress on the earth among the nations, who are "confused by the roaring of the sea and the waves" and who faint through fear at what is happening to the world (21:25–26).

5. It is possible to argue that all the signs of the Olivet discourse were fulfilled in AD 70 (the so-called preterist interpretation), but I am unconvinced by the consistent or full preterist point of view that all biblical prophecies of Christ's return are already fulfilled, and that we are now living in the new heaven and new earth.

when shaken by a gale. The sky vanished like a scroll rolling itself up, and every mountain and island was removed from its place. (Rev. 6:12–14)

We will come back to the idea of the disappearance of the sky/heaven, since this seems to occur in other texts as well. However, there is no reason, given the Old Testament background of judgment theophanies, for us to take the earthquake imagery of Revelation 6 or the language of heavenly destabilization either in that chapter or in the Olivet discourse as referring to the actual destruction of the universe.

None of the multiple Old Testament precedents for the shaking of the earth or the darkening of sun and moon imply the eradication of the cosmos; rather, these celestial signs indicate the momentous nature of the events they portend. This is also the case in the Olivet discourse and in Revelation 6. Indeed, in the latter text the sun turning to sackcloth suggests cosmic mourning (likely alluding to God clothing the heavens with sackcloth in Isa. 50:3), while the moon turning to blood seems to draw specifically on Joel 2:31, where the color of the moon reflects bloody destruction occurring on earth.[6] It thus makes perfect sense for the New Testament to use this celestial imagery for the world-shaking significance of the judgment that precedes eschatological salvation.

Stars Falling from Heaven in the Olivet Discourse and Revelation 6

Beyond the darkening of sun and moon, both the Olivet discourse and Revelation 6 mention the falling of stars from heaven, something for which there is no clear precedent in the Hebrew text of Old Testament theophanies. However, we have the interesting phenomenon of the Septuagint of Isaiah 34:4, which renders the Hebrew for "all their host shall wither" with the Greek for "all the stars shall fall." That the Septuagint of Isaiah 34 is in the background of Revelation 6 seems clear not only from the reference to stars falling, but also from the analogy of the fig tree in both texts (falling leaves in Isa. 34:4, falling fruit in Rev. 6:13) and from the mention of kings (*basileis*) and great ones (*megistanes*) being judged in Revelation 6:15 and Isaiah 34:12 (in each case Rev. 6 specifically matches the Septuagint of Isa. 34 rather than the Hebrew).

While it is typical to refer to the stars as the "host of heaven" in the Old Testament, the notion of stars falling in the Septuagint of Isaiah 34 requires

6. The fact that the Joel text was also applied to the day of Pentecost by the apostle Peter (Acts 2) suggests that the "last days" mentioned in Acts 2:17 mean the period from Pentecost to the consummation, when Christ returns to make all things new.

some explanation. This idea seems to have developed out of texts that depict the stars as corrupt heavenly beings, which are being judged at God's coming (Isa. 24:21 says that YHWH will "punish the host of heaven in heaven").[7]

One important place in the Old Testament where "star" imagery refers both to the heavens above and to sinful self-exaltation on earth is the prophetic oracle against the king of Babylon in Isaiah 14:2–21. In verses 4–11 the fallen king is mocked for having been taken down (as we might say) all the way to Sheol. Then we find these words:

> How you are fallen from heaven,
>   O Day Star, son of Dawn!
> How you are cut down to the ground,
>   you who laid the nations low!
> You said in your heart,
>   "I will ascend to heaven;
> I will raise my throne
>   above the stars of God;
> I will sit on the mount of assembly
>   on the heights of Zaphon;
> I will ascend to the tops of the clouds,
>   I will make myself like the Most High."
>   Isaiah 14:12–14

Here the interplay with literal and metaphorical "height" is evident, which is why "heaven" can be a symbol in the Bible for God's transcendence. In Isaiah 14 it symbolizes the exaltation and pride of the Babylonian monarch, and ancient Near Eastern kings did, in fact, understand themselves to have divine or quasi-divine qualities, which justified their earthly dominion.

Isaiah 14 is also the famous passage that later interpreters used to speak of the fall of Satan. The Vulgate translation of this text gives us the name "Lucifer" (Latin for "light-bearing"), an attempt to translate *hêlēl*, a word occurring only here in the Old Testament with this meaning (NRSV: "Day Star"). The fact that "Lucifer" became a name for the devil in later Christian speculation is connected to the notion that he fell from heaven in the distant past, an idea not explicitly taught anywhere in the Bible but made popular in patristic and especially medieval theology (which developed a complex system of angelology and demonology).

The first use of Isaiah 14 to refer to a fallen angel, however, may be *2 Enoch* 29, a Jewish text that tells of one of the archangels who thought to exalt himself

---

7. In chap. 6 we explored the motif of stars as heavenly powers, whether good or evil.

to be equal to God and was thrown down from heaven with his angels on the second day of creation.[8] The connection of Isaiah 14 with speculation in the Enoch literature about corrupt angels may well be the conceptual origin of the stars falling from heaven in the Septuagint of Isaiah 34 and in the New Testament, although this is envisioned in the eschatological future, not at the dawn of time.

Given this conceptual background, it makes sense that when the seventy disciples report to Jesus that the demons have submitted to them in his name (Luke 10:17), he responds, "I watched Satan fall from heaven like a flash of lightning" (Luke 10:18). Just one chapter later, on the occasion of Jesus himself casting out a demon (Luke 11:14), he explains, "If it is by the finger of God that I cast out the demons, then the kingdom of God has come to you" (Luke 11:20); and this is followed by the metaphor of the binding or overpowering of the "strong man" (Luke 11:21–22). Whereas the "fall" of Satan in Luke 10 (equivalent to his being overpowered in Luke 11) has reference to the advance of God's kingdom in the lifetime of Jesus, the book of Revelation speaks of the fall of the devil and his angels from heaven in the future, as God's kingdom moves toward completion.

That stars can stand for angels is evident from Revelation 9:1, which mentions the fall of a star from heaven to earth, who is then given the key to the bottomless pit (this star is identified as an angel in Rev. 20:1). Likewise, Revelation 12:4 notes that the tail of a "great red dragon" swept down a third of the stars from heaven to earth (here stars might also stand for angels).

Perhaps more explicit is the war in heaven, which results in the defeat of the dragon (also described as the ancient serpent, the devil, and Satan) along with his angels (Rev. 12:7–8), who are thrown down to the earth (12:9–10). That this casting of the devil out of heaven has nothing to do with some primeval "fall" of Satan is clear from the announcement, "*Now* have come the salvation and the power and the kingdom of our God and the authority of his Messiah, for the accuser of our comrades has been thrown down, who accuses them day and night before our God" (12:10).[9] Later the dragon (again identified with

8. Although it is likely that the extant Slavonic version of 2 *Enoch* is based on a Greek first-century BC Jewish text, a minority of scholars consider it a Christian text originating in the first century AD. For a discussion, see Harry Alan Hahne, *The Corruption and Redemption of Creation: Nature in Romans 8:19–22 and Jewish Apocalyptic Literature* (Library of Biblical Studies; London: Continuum, 2006), 83–86. However, the notion of fallen angels in 2 *Enoch* seems to be dependent on 1 *Enoch*, which is clearly a pre-Christian Jewish text. In 1 *Enoch* 6–9 these angels are called the "Watchers," a term taken from Dan. 4:13 and identified with the "sons of God" in Gen. 6:1–4.

9. The imagery of Revelation is notably difficult to interpret, but this casting down of the devil/dragon/serpent to earth seems to be correlated with the period after Jesus's birth, perhaps

the devil) is cast into the bottomless pit (20:1–3), and finally, after a thousand years of freedom, into the lake of fire and sulfur (20:10).[10]

It is thus likely that the image of stars falling from heaven in the New Testament refers to the eschatological judgment of corrupt heavenly powers, associated with the coming of God's kingdom, rather than to the literal annihilation of part of the cosmos. This would be true not only of the Septuagint of Isaiah 34:4, but also of the New Testament references in the Olivet discourse and Revelation 6.

A similar interpretation would hold for Jesus's prediction in the Olivet discourse that "the powers of heaven will be shaken" (Matt. 24:29; also Mark 13:24; Luke 21:25). Not only does this prediction fit the imagery of many Old Testament texts that portray the shaking of the heavens as a component of judgment, but also "powers" in the heavens makes best sense as an allusion to corrupt angelic beings. Although in the Olivet discourse the reference to powers in heaven comes just after the falling of stars, the order is reversed in the Septuagint of Isaiah 34:4, which renders the Hebrew for "the host of heaven shall rot away" with the Greek for "the powers of the heavens will melt."[11] This convergence of terms suggests that the Olivet discourse, like Revelation 6, has the Septuagint of Isaiah 34 in the background, which further supports taking the shaking of the powers in heaven as judgment on fallen angels.

---

referring to the tribulations of the Roman-Jewish war and beyond. When the devil is cast down to earth, "he knows that his time is short" (Rev. 12:12), and in wrath he pursues "the woman who had given birth to the male child" (12:13), where the woman seems to be Israel, who gave birth to the Messiah. This is followed by his waging war on "the rest of her children, those who keep the commandments of God and hold the testimony of Jesus" (12:17), a reference to the persecution of the church.

10. If we want to apply Isa. 14 to the fall of Satan, it makes more sense to see an analogy between the Babylonian king being taken down to Sheol and the devil cast into the lake of fire than to think that it refers to some primeval fall of Satan, since this is never taught in the Bible. The place of the devil in biblical revelation is a much-debated issue, not least because he is absent (as a full-fledged figure) from the Old Testament. There are only three (late) references to an "accuser" or "adversary" (śāṭān) in the Old Testament, where the term is not being used of an ordinary human being (1 Chron. 21:1; Job 1–2; Zech. 3:1–2). In all three places not only is the term śāṭān a description and not a name (*the* accuser/adversary in Zechariah and Job; *an* accuser/adversary in 1 Chronicles), but also a full-fledged doctrine of the devil does not develop until postbiblical Judaism, in the centuries immediately before the New Testament. For an intriguing proposal of how to understand the historical origin and development of the present reality of the devil and the demonic, see Nicholas Ansell, "The Call of Wisdom / The Voice of the Serpent: A Canonical Approach to the Tree of Knowledge," *Christian Scholar's Review* 31 (2001): 31–57. Whether or not Ansell's argument can be supported at all points, his ability to tackle an old problem from a new angle makes his proposal well worth pondering.

11. The line is found in Codex Vaticanus and the so-called Lucianic recension of the Septuagint; it is entirely missing from other Septuagint manuscripts.

The Disappearance of the Sky/Heaven in Revelation 6

Beyond the darkening of sun and moon and the stars falling in Revelation 6:12–13, we find this statement: "The sky vanished like a scroll rolling itself up, and every mountain and island was removed from its place" (6:14). While the removal of the earthly terrain is consonant with the general Old Testament picture of God shaking the earth (and may allude to Isa. 54:10: "the mountains may depart and the hills be removed"), the unusual imagery of the sky/heaven in Revelation 6:14 brings us back to Isaiah 34:4 ("and the skies roll up like a scroll").[12]

Here we should notice that the NRSV translation "vanished" (also ESV) for *apochōrizō* in Revelation 6:14 does not get at the basic meaning of "separated" (the NASB and NET are better with "split apart," while the NIV has "receded").[13] The point is not the literal annihilation of a part of the cosmos, but rather a vivid picture of God peeling back the sky (analogous with rolling up a scroll), so that after the corrupt heavenly powers have been judged, the earth is then exposed for judgment. This is particularly clear from the Isaiah 34 background text, where the sequence is first judgment in heaven (v. 4), then judgment on earth (v. 5).[14]

The rolling back of the sky like a scroll is similar to the picture assumed in Isaiah 64. There we find the prophet imploring YHWH,

> O that you would tear open the heavens and come down,
>   so that the mountains would quake at your presence—
> as when fire kindles brushwood
>   and the fire causes water to boil—
> to make your name known to your adversaries,
>   so that the nations might tremble at your presence!
> When you did awesome deeds that we did not expect,
>   you came down, the mountains quaked at your presence.
>   Isaiah 64:1–3[15]

Not only does this text speak of opening the sky/heavens so that YHWH might descend in judgment, as in ancient times, it also uses a rare verb for the quaking (*zālal*) of the mountains in verses 1 and 3, which alludes to the

---

12. Revelation 6:14 may also allude to Jer. 4:24, where the mountains and hills move to and fro.

13. This is a variant of the verb Jesus uses in his statement, "Therefore what God has joined together, let no one separate [*chōrizō*]" (Mark 10:9; Matt. 19:6).

14. See the analysis in chap. 6 above.

15. In English versions, Isa. 64:1 = 63:19b MT, so verse 2 NRSV = verse 3 MT, and so on.

judgment theophany in Judges 5:5, where the quaking of the mountains is expressed by what most scholars take to be the identical verb.[16]

An interesting parallel to this vivid picture is found in the account of Jesus's baptism, when the heavens were opened so the Spirit might descend, though this descent from heaven is meant as positive approval of God's chosen, and not for judgment. While Matthew 3:16 and Luke 3:21 have heaven "opening" (*anoigō*, the same verb used in the Septuagint of Isa. 64:1 [Septuagint 63:19b]), Mark 1:10 speaks of heaven being "torn" or "split" (*schizō*). This latter is the same verb used for the tearing of the temple curtain at Jesus's death (Matt. 27:51; Mark 15:38; Luke 23:45).

While the tearing of the temple curtain is a much-debated issue, with many possible meanings (including which of two possible curtains is being referred to), it symbolizes minimally the undoing of the barrier between heaven and earth, so that God's presence has now come near.[17] What is fascinating is that Matthew's account of the temple curtain adds a note about cosmic effects typical of a theophany: "At that moment the curtain of the temple was torn in two, from top to bottom. The earth shook, and the rocks were split" (Matt. 27:51). It thus makes sense to take the splitting of the heavens in Revelation 6:14 and Mark 1:10 as symbolic, presaging God's coming in judgment and salvation, rather than as a prediction of the annihilation of the sky.

The Destruction of the Heavens and the Elements in 2 Peter 3

The picture of opening or splitting of the sky/heaven so that earth may be judged is the dominant image in 2 Peter 3, though that may not be evident at first glance. This text is so crucial (and debated) in New Testament eschatology that we must spend a bit more time exploring it than some of the previous texts we have looked at. In the context of speaking of the second coming of Christ, Peter predicts certain destructive cosmic events:[18]

16. Although the pointing of the Hebrew of Judg. 5:5 MT suggests that the verb is *nāzal* ("to flow or trickle" [followed by the KJV]), this does not make sense of the context. The ancient versions (Septuagint, Peshitta, and Targum) take the verb to be *zālal* and render it accordingly. This is followed by modern translations of Judg. 5:5, where we find "quake" (NRSV, ESV, NASB), "tremble" (NIV, NET), or "shake" (NKJV).

17. See the discussion in Andy Johnson, "The 'New Creation,' the Crucified and Risen Christ, and the Temple: A Pauline Audience for Mark," *Journal of Theological Interpretation* 1 (2007): 171–91, which contains references to the scholarly discussion. Johnson notes the twofold use of *schizō* as an inclusio in Mark's Gospel, signifying the beginning of the heavens being opened in 1:10 (with the use of a participle) and the completion of the process in 15:38 (with the use of the aorist).

18. I am not making a judgment here as to whether the author of 2 Peter is the same as the author of 1 Peter. I am happy to call both "Peter" and leave the question of authorship to the reader.

But the day of the Lord will come like a thief, and then *the heavens will pass away* with a loud noise, and *the elements will be dissolved with fire*, and the earth and everything that is done on it will be disclosed. Since all these things are to be dissolved in this way, what sort of persons ought you to be in leading lives of holiness and godliness, waiting for and hastening the coming of the day of God, because of which *the heavens will be set ablaze and dissolved*, and *the elements will melt with fire*? (2 Pet. 3:10–12)

According to verse 10, "the day of the Lord" will involve two destructive events: the passing away of the heavens and the dissolution of the elements. Verse 12 restates the two destructive events that will occur on "the day of God" in slightly different language—the dissolution of the heavens and the melting of the elements. When we combine verses 10 and 12, we get this composite picture: the heavens will pass away (v. 10) and/or be dissolved (v. 12); the elements will be dissolved (v. 10) and/or will melt (v. 12).

Although many Christians throughout history have read 2 Peter 3 as if it describes the annihilation of the entire cosmos, this does not make sense of the fact that the earth is not destroyed in verse 10. As we saw in the preceding chapter, the earth is not "burned up" (as pre-NIV English translations had it). Rather, "the earth and everything that is done on it will be disclosed" (NRSV); or, to be more literal, "the earth and the works in it will be found." We will come back to the meaning of this intriguing line. For now, we should recognize that whatever "elements" (*stoicheia*) means, it does not seem to include the earth, since the elements melt and are dissolved, but the earth will be "found."

The fact that the same verb (the passive of *lyō*, thus, "be loosed, undone, dissolved") is applied both to the heavens and to the elements is significant. This clearly connects the heavens and the elements, and whatever is to happen to them takes place by a conflagration of some sort; burning is the dominant image in both verses. This means that when verse 11 says, "since all these things are to be dissolved in this way," a contextual reading of "all these things" refers specifically back to the heavens/elements, not the earth.

The Meaning of "Elements" in 2 Peter 3

Although the word "elements" (*stoicheia*; singular *stoicheion*) has a wide range of meanings in extrabiblical literature, often having to do with rudiments or constituent elements (sometimes in a series), three meanings typically are proposed for 2 Peter 3.[19] The first possibility is that the term refers to the

19. For an analysis of possible meanings, see Gerhard Delling, "στοιχέω, συστοιχέω, στοιχεῖον," *Theological Dictionary of the New Testament*, ed. Gerhard Kittel and Gerhard Friedrich, trans. Geoffrey W. Bromiley (Grand Rapids: Eerdmans, 1971), 7:666–87.

constituents of the physical universe. While modern readers following this line of thought might interpret "elements" by reference to the periodic/atomic table, this is obviously anachronistic. Instead, there is evidence that *stoicheia* was used in the ancient world for the four constituent elements of earth, air, fire, and water (especially in Platonic and Stoic thought). This is how Edward Adams understands the term, in his suggestion that Peter is drawing on the Stoic notion of *expyrōsis*, the cosmic conflagration that dissolves the cosmos back to (almost) nothing so that it may be reconstituted anew, rising like the phoenix from its ashes (though Adams is at pains to point out that Peter views this as a onetime, climactic event, not an endless cycle as in Stoicism).[20]

The image of a cosmic meltdown and rebirth is indeed a possible background to 2 Peter 3, echoing the image of smelting or refining in the Old Testament prophetic tradition (Isa. 1; Zech. 3; Mal. 3) that we examined in chapter 6. But taking *stoicheia* as the four elements of ancient cosmology would mean that the earth is included in the meltdown since it is part of the cosmos, whereas in 2 Peter 3 the earth is not said to be destroyed. Granted, we could still take *stoicheia* as the four elements of ancient cosmology if we understand the image of their dissolution or melting to refer to the cleansing or purification of the cosmos by the fire of judgment. Yet we would still need to answer the question of why Peter rhetorically exempts the earth from this dissolution (why is it only the earth that is "found"?). I will come back to Adam's notion of the cosmic meltdown after examining the other possibilities for the meaning of "elements."

The next two interpretations explicitly connect the term "elements" (*stoicheia*) to the heavens (thus fitting the context better than the idea of the four elements). One possibility is to take *stoicheia* as a reference to the heavenly bodies (sun, moon, and stars [as in the ESV and NET]);[21] the other is to take it as a reference to angelic powers in the heavens. As we saw from the Old Testament background of judgment theophanies, these are often associated with each other.[22]

20. Edward Adams, *The Stars Will Fall from Heaven: "Cosmic Catastrophe" in the New Testament and Its World* (Library of New Testament Studies 347; Edinburgh: T&T Clark, 2007), chap. 6, "'The Elements Will Melt with Fire': 2 Peter 3:5–13."

21. Although most contemporary commentators take *stoicheia* in 2 Pet. 3 as the heavenly bodies, the earliest evidence for this interpretation derives from the second century AD, especially among the church fathers. See Delling, "στοιχέω," 681–82.

22. In an important but overlooked study, Calvin R. Schoonhoven analyzes the pervasive biblical motif of the judment and purification of heaven (*The Wrath of Heaven* [Grand Rapids: Eerdmans, 1966]). His analysis serves to demonstrate that "heaven" in the Bible is part of the created cosmos (and not some otherworldly realm as it is often conceived in Christian theology) since, like the earth, it is in need of redemption.

Sodom and Gomorrah as Background to 2 Peter 3

In a recent study, Ryan Juza has persuasively argued that 2 Peter 3 draws on the motif of the judgment of Sodom and Gomorrah by fire from heaven (Gen. 19), which had become a standard image for judgment in Second Temple Jewish literature.[23] Indeed, this motif already shows up in some of the Old Testament judgment theophanies that we examined in chapter 6. Thus, the oracle in Isaiah 13:1–22, which portrays the day of YHWH (v. 6) against Babylon by the hand of the Medes (v. 17), accompanied by the darkening of sun, moon, and stars (v. 10) and the shaking of heaven and earth (v. 13), states that the outcome of this judgment is that "Babylon, the glory of kingdoms, / the splendor and pride of the Chaldeans, / will be like Sodom and Gomorrah when God overthrew them" (v. 19).

Likewise, the oracle in Isaiah 34:1–17, which begins with judgment on the "host of heaven" and the picture of the sky rolling up as a scroll (v. 4), and then focuses on the earth, specifically Edom (vv. 5–10), utilizes classic images of the destruction of Sodom and Gomorrah.[24] Not only does God's judgment descend from the heavens to the earth (v. 5), but also the result is that the land turns to "sulfur" and "burning pitch," characterized by perpetual burning (vv. 9–10). The reference to sulfur and burning is a clear reflection of Genesis 19:24, and the perpetual nature of Sodom's destruction became a standard trope in Second Temple Jewish literature.[25]

The picture that Juza discerns in 2 Peter 3:10 (consistent with the theophanic descent of YHWH in the Old Testament) is of God destroying the demonic forces in the heavens and stripping away the upper layer of the cosmos in order to expose the earth to divine judgment. This allows for the ambiguity of *stoicheia*, referring to both the heavenly bodies and the corrupt powers in the heavens. Not only does this ambiguity make sense of 2 Peter 3, but also the dual reference to the heavens and corrupt heavenly powers fits the Sodom and Gomorrah judgment tradition, since this tradition came to understand the sin of Sodom as involving the idolatrous worship of heavenly bodies and the evil spirits associated with them. This ambiguity is also consistent with the Septuagint translation of the first line of Isaiah 34:4, that "the powers of the

---

23. Ryan Juza, "Echoes of Sodom and Gomorrah on the Day of the Lord: Intertextuality and Tradition in 2 Peter 3:7–13," *Bulletin for Biblical Research* 24 (2014): 227–45. I had the privilege of being a respondent to Juza's paper at the Graduate Student Theological Seminar, September 29, 2012, held at the Free Methodist World Ministries Center, Indianapolis.

24. Edom seems to be representative of "all the nations," which are to be judged (Isa. 34:2).

25. This is not the place to go into all the details of Juza's argument for Sodom and Gomorrah as the background to the conflagration of 2 Pet. 3; suffice it to say that he gives multiple, overlapping lines of evidence, and his essay will reward the careful reader.

heavens will melt,"[26] since "the powers of the heavens" seem to refer to false gods, while "melt" is more appropriate to the physical cosmos. This ambiguity of *stoicheia* prevents us from being overly literalistic about the nature of this heavenly "destruction."

The Earth and Its Works Will Be "Found"

The choice of the verb "found" (*heuriskō*) for what happens to "the earth and the works in it" (2 Pet. 3:10) is significant for a number of reasons. First, this coheres with the Sodom and Gomorrah paradigm that Peter is drawing on, since the dialogue of Abraham with God in Genesis 18:22–33 is precisely over whether or not righteous people will be "found" in Sodom; the verb *heuriskō* occurs seven times in the Septuagint of Genesis 18:26–32.[27]

This verb also appears in the context of Jesus's teaching in the Olivet discourse about the coming of the Son of Man. Not only will the day of the Lord come "like a thief" in 2 Peter 3:10, which probably depends on Jesus's analogy of the thief in the night (Matt. 24:43; Luke 12:39), but the verb *heuriskō* occurs in Jesus's parable of the slave put in charge of his master's household: "Blessed is that slave whom his master will find [*heuriskō*] at work when he arrives" (Matt. 24:46; Luke 12:43).[28]

This sense of eschatological "finding" in connection with the coming of God in judgment makes perfect sense of Peter's exhortation to his readers right after the promise of a new heaven and earth: "Therefore, beloved, while you are waiting for these things, strive to be found [*heuriskō*] by him at peace, without spot or blemish" (2 Pet. 3:14). Peter thus challenges his readers to be ready, by their righteous behavior, for the day when the Lord comes to judge "the earth and the works in it." In a similar manner, the extrabiblical Christian text known as the *Epistle of Barnabas* encourages believers to "act in order that you may be found [*heuriskō*] in the day of judgment" (21.6).

While some interpretations of the earth being "found" (*heuriskō*) in 2 Peter 3:10 take it in the negative (or possibly neutral) sense of being exposed to

---

26. Codex Vaticanus and the Lucianic recension.

27. In his dialogue with God, Abraham seems to be motivated by a desire to save Lot and his family. And as Juza ("Echoes of Sodom and Gomorrah") argues, the statement in 2 Pet. 3:9 about the Lord's patience, not wanting any to perish, alludes to YHWH sending angels to rescue Lot and his family (Gen. 19:12–23). God's rescue of Lot, who is explicitly called "righteous," is mentioned in 2 Pet. 2:6–9. Likewise, the scoffers or mockers, who think that judgment is not really coming (3:3–4), correspond to Lot's sons-in-law, who thought that Lot was joking when he invited them to flee Sodom with the angels (Gen. 19:14).

28. Beyond this, Jesus clearly compares judgment on his own generation with the judgment on Sodom and Gomorrah (Matt. 10:15; Luke 10:12).

judgment, the positive uses of the verb in 2 Peter 3:14 and in the *Epistle of Barnabas* suggest an alternative meaning, more like withstanding judgment.

This more positive interpretation is suggested by Al Wolters in an important article on 2 Peter 3 that explores various lines of linguistic and intertextual evidence and proposes a metallurgical background for Peter's use of "found" in 2 Peter 3:10.[29] Whether or not *heuriskō* turns out to be a technical term in metallurgy, as Wolters proposes, he seems to be on the right track in suggesting that the image of judgment by fire in 2 Peter 3 is not purely destructive, but instead may be understood as a smelting process by which the dross of human sinfulness is burned off, so that "found" means something like "standing the test" or "showing one's mettle" (where "mettle" in that phrase was originally "metal").[30] The fire of judgment might then be compared to a "foundry," where metals are melted down and reshaped into useful products.[31]

Evidence for connecting a positive use of "found" (*heuriskō*) to fire and metals occurs in 1 Peter, where the author explains that the outcome of suffering is "that the genuineness of your faith—being more precious than gold that, though perishable, is tested by fire—may be found [*heuriskō*] to result in praise and glory and honor when Jesus Christ is revealed" (1:7).

Yet not only does Wolters posit a metallurgical background for 2 Peter 3; he also suggests that the text specifically draws on the vivid picture from Malachi 3–4 of God refining the Levitical priesthood on analogy with the smelting of precious metals.[32] As we saw in chapter 6, the day of God's coming in Malachi will both cleanse like a refiner's fire (3:2–3) and destroy "burning like an oven" (4:1 [3:19 MT]), depending on one's response.

In support of Wolters's suggestion, at least one ancient Christian text explicitly links the Malachi reference with 2 Peter 3. According to *2 Clement* 16.3, "You know that the day of judgment is already coming like a burning oven, and some of the heavens will melt, as will the whole earth, like lead

29. Al Wolters, "Worldview and Textual Criticism in 2 Peter 3:10," *Westminster Theological Journal* 49 (1987): 405–13.

30. Ibid., 412 (the comment about "metal" is my own, but it is implied by Wolters).

31. I am not claiming that the meaning of "foundry" can be traced directly to the idea of "finding" the pure metal under the dross; the term seems to come from the verb "to found," in the sense of "to cast metals." There is also another sense of "to found," as in "to establish or lay a foundation." But it could be argued that both of these meanings have ultimately to do with "finding" in the sense of getting back or down to basics (melting down the metal to its basics, in one case, and starting at the base of something, on the other). So, could we say that the "foundry" of God's judgment gets down to the foundations of creation in order to remake a purified world from the ground up?

32. For an extended analysis of Mal. 3 as the background to the theology of suffering in 1 Peter, see Dennis E. Johnson, "Fire in God's House: Imagery from Malachi 3 in Peter's Theology of Suffering (1 Peter 4:12–19)," *Journal of the Evangelical Theological Society* 29 (1986): 285–94.

melting due to its fire, and then the hidden and manifest works of men will appear."[33]

The Analogy of the Flood in 2 Peter 3

Further support of Wolters's claim that the fire spoken of in 2 Peter 3 is ultimately cleansing and not destructive is found in the analogy that Peter draws between the judgment at Christ's return and the flood, which was meant to cleanse the world of evil. Whereas the Sodom and Gomorrah background to 2 Peter 3 is only implicit and thus has to be inferred, this is not the case with the flood tradition.[34] In the midst of contrasting the earlier judgment by water with the coming judgment by fire, Peter clarifies what sort of cosmic destruction he envisages.[35]

Peter explains that "the world of that time was deluged with water and perished" (2 Pet. 3:6). But in what sense did the world of Noah's time "perish"? Certainly not in the sense that the cosmos (or even the earth) was obliterated. Rather, the evil deeds of corrupt humanity were judged and the earth was cleansed to allow for a new beginning by Noah and his family. The same is true of the judgment that is to come, since "the present heavens and earth have been reserved for fire, being kept until the day of judgment and destruction of the godless" (3:7).

Note that both the heavens and the earth have been "reserved for fire," yet it is not the earth, but rather the godless, that will be destroyed (on the contrary, the earth will be "found"). This suggests that the language about the destruction of the heavens by fire should not be taken as literal obliteration either. Hence, after "the present heavens and earth" pass through the Sodom-and-Gomorrah-like judgment on the day of the Lord, the "new heavens and a new earth" that Peter says we are waiting for (3:13) are not a replacement for a world that is annihilated; rather, this is a transformed cosmos, "where righteousness is at home."

This interpretation of 2 Peter 3 makes sense of Paul's picture of the judgment of the deeds of believers by fire in 1 Corinthians 3:10–15. There, Paul speaks of laying a foundation for the church in Corinth, like a skilled master builder

33. Though the melting of the earth does not happen in 2 Pet. 3.

34. Jesus himself compares the coming of the Son of Man to both Sodom and Gomorrah and to the flood (Luke 17:22–37).

35. One fascinating link between the accounts of the flood and Sodom in Genesis is that both texts use the verb for "rain" to describe the judgment; whereas the rain in the first case is water, in the second it is "sulfur and fire" (7:4; 19:24). For a series of other significant thematic and verbal parallels between the flood story and the destruction of Sodom, see Gordon Wenham, *Genesis 16–50* (Word Biblical Commentary 2; Waco: Word, 1994), 42–43.

(v. 10). On this foundation, which is Christ (v. 11), each person builds his or her life using materials of differing quality—"gold, silver, precious stones, wood, hay, straw" (v. 12). The work of each builder, Paul explains, will be disclosed on the day of judgment, "because it will be revealed with fire, and the fire will test what sort of work each has done" (v. 13). Some work will survive, with resulting reward (v. 14), while the work of others will be "burned up," with the result that "the builder will be saved, but only as through fire" (v. 15). Even here the fire of judgment is ultimately for salvation.[36]

Taking all the complex layers of meaning in 2 Peter 3 together, we find a picture of radical judgment on the last day, in which God destroys corrupt demonic powers, metaphorically strips back the sky, and then comes to judge the earth—a judgment intended to purge the world of evil so that it might be renewed and, ultimately, saved. This means that whatever vivid language of destruction Peter uses to portray the final judgment, there is no good reason to take any of it as referring to the literal obliteration of the cosmos.

Edward Adams on the Eschatological Remaking of the World

So far, I have endorsed Ryan Juza's insight about the Sodom and Gomorrah background of 2 Peter 3, while qualifying this with Al Wolters's discernment of the ultimately salvific nature of the judgment envisioned. But this does not mean that there is no value to Edward Adams's proposal of Stoic *expyrōsis*, the cosmic conflagration that destroys the world before it is remade, as a background to 2 Peter 3. But first we have to clarify what Adams actually proposes.

Here it is crucial to notice that Adams frames his overall argument as a disagreement with N. T. Wright on the nature of eschatological imagery of cosmic destruction and dissents specifically from Wolters's reading of 2 Peter 3.[37] Yet his interpretation of cosmic destruction in this text is remarkably consonant with both Wright and Wolters. This is often obscured by the absolute-sounding

36. The expression "saved through [*dia*] fire" is usually taken to mean being saved despite passing "through" the fire of judgment (the locative use of *dia*)—saved by the skin of one's teeth, we might say. However, Daniel Frayer-Griggs has marshaled impressive linguistic evidence to argue that Paul is using *dia* in this passage to mean saved "by" fire, in the sense that the fire of God's judgment is the refining instrument of salvation ("Neither Proof Text Nor Proverb: The Instrumental Sense of *dia* and the Soteriological Function of Fire in 1 Corinthians 3:15" [paper presented at the annual meeting of the Eastern Great Lakes Biblical Society, Erie, PA, April 5, 2013]). Frayer-Griggs even shows a number of fascinating parallels between terms used in 1 Cor. 3 and language from the Septuagint of Mal. 3. John Proctor also suggests that the refining fire in Mal. 3 lies behind the imagery of 1 Cor. 3 ("Fire in God's House: Influence of Malachi 3 in the New Testament," *Journal of the Evangelical Theological Society* 36 [1993]: 9–14).

37. For his initial articulation of his disagreement with N. T. Wright, see Adams, *Stars Will Fall*, 5–16, esp. 12–13; for his dissent from Wolters, see ibid., 225–28, esp. 228.

rhetoric that Adams uses throughout his book about the "end," "destruction," or "dissolution" of the cosmos.[38]

Adams's emphatic language of cosmic destruction is meant as a corrective to his take on N. T. Wright's general position (derived especially from the Olivet discourse) that New Testament images of cosmic destabilization are simply a picturesque way of speaking of intrahistorical events, supremely the fall of Jerusalem in AD 70. While Adams admits that much of the Old Testament use of this language can be read as vivid description of the fall of nations or cities, he takes the transformation of this language in some intertestamental Jewish apocalypses to refer to the unmaking or destruction of the cosmos prior to its radical remaking. And he thinks that this militates against taking the language of cosmic destruction in the New Testament as referring to simply local events (as Wright does).

Yet on the topic of whether the cosmos is literally annihilated, Adams actually agrees with Wright. Adams admits that neither the Jewish apocalyptic works that he considers nor the New Testament (not even 2 Pet. 3) thinks that "the existing world is dissolved into nothing and a completely new world, materially discontinuous with the old, takes its place."[39] Indeed, "up to and including New Testament times, belief in absolute cosmic dissolution, as far as we can tell, was not a genuine cosmological option."[40] And he explicitly agrees with Wright that 2 Peter 3 does not teach the annihilation of the world followed by a replacement cosmos.[41]

Then why does Adams protest so vigorously against Wright's position? As far as I can tell, Adams wants to make the point that New Testament eschatology goes beyond the local judgments found in the Old Testament in that it envisions a truly cosmic/universal judgment at Christ's return. Yet Wright does not object to the cosmic nature of eschatological judgment, but only to the notion that this requires the end of the space-time universe.[42]

---

38. Despite his preference for such terms, Adams does not envision the literal annihilation of the world, but rather the return of the world to something like precreation chaos prior to its redemptive remaking (ibid., 21, 238).

39. Ibid., 13.

40. Ibid., 21.

41. Ibid., 233 ("Wright is thus correct . . .").

42. This is why Adams is confused by Wright's position on Heb. 12:26–27 and 2 Pet. 3:5–13. He thinks that Wright is inconsistent to see these texts as referring to a genuinely "cosmic change," given his understanding of Wright's "general claim" about New Testament eschatology (ibid., 15–16). In reference to Heb. 12, Adams twice mentions the interpretation "we might have expected" Wright to have (ibid., 192–93). That this misunderstands Wright's overall position is evident from explicit comments that Wright has made to clarify his position (*The Challenge of Jesus: Rediscovering Who Jesus Was and Is* [Downers Grove, IL: InterVarsity, 1999], 117; for more on this, see the appendix of this book). This means that Wright's view

Adams's characterization of the images of destruction in 2 Peter 3 as analogous to a meltdown of the cosmos, prior to its glorious rebirth, is also in essential agreement with Wolters.[43] The difference is that whereas Adams posits a Stoic background for this meltdown (which is hypothetically possible), Wolters suggests the Old Testament image of the refining of metals (which is more plausible). That Adams does not see this basic agreement is strange, since he admits that Wolters only denies "the *absolute* destruction" of the universe, that is, its "disappearance from existence."[44] The main point for our purposes, however, is that even Adams affirms that 2 Peter 3 envisions not the literal obliteration of the cosmos, but rather its renovation after (radical) judgment.[45]

"Elements" as False Teaching in 2 Peter 3

So far we have explored the three most common proposals for the meaning of "elements" (*stoicheia*) in 2 Peter 3:10, 12. But besides the three typical interpretations, a fourth possibility might be relevant here. It is well known that *stoicheia* can mean something like "elementary teachings" in other parts of the New Testament. This is clearly the meaning in Hebrews 5:12, where the writer wonders whether readers need to learn the basics or rudiments (*stoicheia*) of the faith (translated as "basic elements" in the NRSV and "elementary truths" in the NIV).

Colossians 2:8 uses the term *stoicheia* specifically for false teaching, contrasting philosophy that is "according to human tradition" and according to *stoicheia* of the world with philosophy that is "according to Christ." A bit later, Colossians 2:20 affirms that those in Christ have died to the *stoicheia* of the world, which are then listed as a series of rules from which Christians have been set free (2:21). This suggests that the term refers to some form of teaching (the NASB has "elementary principles"). Even if the NRSV, ESV, and NET are right to translate *stoicheia* as "elemental spirits" (the NLT has "spiritual powers") in Colossians 2:8, 20, this simply associates the false teaching in

---

of the local referents of the Olivet discourse should not be generalized into his general eschatological position.

43. For Wolters's use of the term "meltdown," see his "Worldview and Textual Criticism," 409.

44. Adams, *Stars Will Fall*, 226 (emphasis in original). When Adams accuses Wolters of thinking that 2 Pet. 3 depicts "only the melting down of the heavens and the elements, not their destruction by fire" (ibid., 227), I have to admit that I am confused. Perhaps there is some fine distinction between the images of smelting by fire and dissolution by fire that does not annihilate; but at this point the disagreement seems to be semantic.

45. It seems that what Adams actually objects to is Wolters's use of the term "destruction" to mean annihilation, since that is not how Adams himself uses the term (he wants to retain the term "destruction" while dissenting from an annihilationist position).

question with the demonic, perhaps as the basis of the teaching.[46] Indeed, the term may be polyvalent in Colossians, as it is in Galatians 4, where *stoicheia* refers to the law in verse 3 and to false gods in verses 8–9.

Clifford T. Richards has recently argued that this fourth interpretation of *stoicheia* fits the context of 2 Peter very well, since the letter is especially concerned with false teaching (and mentions those who distort the teachings of the apostle Paul [3:15–16]). Richards thus suggests it is these very teachings (*stoicheia*), along with the false teachers who propound them, that will be destroyed at Christ's return.[47] And the destruction of false teachings, he declares, is not the same as the destruction of the cosmos.

Much of Richards's paper deals with the metaphorical character of judgment as fire, and the specifics of this discussion need not detain us here. Suffice it to say that his argument, when added to our previous analysis, suggests that the dissolution and melting of *stoicheia* in 2 Peter 3 makes sense on multiple levels, including judgment on demonic powers (thus purging the heavens of evil), the parting of the sky so the earth is exposed to God's judgment, and the destruction of false teaching (which may have its origin in the demonic). In no case, however, does the text mean to describe the annihilation of the cosmos.

Indeed, if we accept the possibility that *stoicheia* might also refer to false teachings, we may well wonder what specific teachings Peter thinks will be destroyed. It seems that the false teachers were distorting Paul's writings that touch on the subject of Christ's return. In the context of speaking about the new heaven and the new earth and exhorting his readers to live in accordance with this vision (2 Pet. 3:13–14), Peter says,

> So also our beloved brother Paul wrote to you according to the wisdom given him, speaking of this as he does in all his letters. There are some things in them hard to understand, which the ignorant and unstable twist to their own destruction, as they do the other scriptures. (2 Pet. 3:15b–16)

If "of this" in verse 16 (literally, "about these things") refers to Paul's own teaching about the coming of the Lord, and how we are to live in light of this expectation (the topic Peter has been discussing), this would mean that Peter understands his own teaching on the subject to be consistent with what Paul wrote. As we saw in the preceding chapter, Paul envisions the liberation of

46. Note that the NIV used to have "basic principles" for *stoicheia* in Col. 2:8, 20, but the 2011 revision has "elemental spiritual forces."

47. Clifford T. Richards, "A Strange Death: Cosmic Conflagration as Conceptual Metaphor in 2 Peter 3:6–13" (paper presented at the annual meeting of the Eastern Great Lakes Biblical Society, Erie, PA, April 4, 2013).

creation from its bondage to futility at Christ's return (Rom. 8). In that case, we have even more reason to think that 2 Peter 3 teaches the transformation and redemption of the world rather than the obliteration of the cosmos on the last day (as some claim). From Peter's point of view, the idea that the cosmos will be annihilated is thus a false teaching. And might we even infer that this very teaching will be destroyed when Christ returns? Or, we might say, "Left Behind" theology will finally be left behind!

The Cosmic Shakeup in Hebrews 12

We now turn to Hebrews 12:26–29, which seems to contrast the created order (heaven and earth) with the (uncreated) kingdom that we are waiting for.

The context of this passage is a series of three contrasts the author of Hebrews makes. First, there is a contrast between the Sinai theophany, characterized by a tangible shaking of the earth (12:18–21), and God's future shaking of not only earth, but also heaven—a truly universal, cosmic theophany (12:26), in which the manifestation of God's holiness will be much more intense than at Sinai. The contrast is between a specific historical, earthly event and a genuinely creation-wide event.

The second contrast drawn by the author of Hebrews is between the earthly mountain (Sinai) that could be touched (12:18), where God first made covenant with his people, and "Mount Zion," also called the "heavenly Jerusalem" (12:22), which is not accessible in the same way as Sinai. However, the "heavenly" character of this mountain does not mean that it is inaccessible—precisely the opposite. The paradox is that although the first mountain was tangible, no one but Moses could approach it. This helps explain why the author lists, along with the heavenly Zion/Jerusalem, the assembly of those "enrolled in heaven," God the judge of all, "the spirits of the righteous made perfect" (12:23), and Jesus the mediator of the new covenant (12:24). The point of this contrast is that while no one but Moses had access to Mount Sinai (ordinary Israelites had to stay back) and the covenant made there was unable to deal with sin (a point hammered home throughout Hebrews), all believers in Jesus have full access, through the new covenant, to Mount Zion (equivalent to citizenship in the heavenly Jerusalem), which is why they are said to be "enrolled in heaven" and have been "made perfect." This contrast of mountains (which is really a contrast of covenants) thus focuses on the greater privilege and blessings that come through Jesus.[48]

48. A similar distinction between the old covenant and the new covenant is drawn by Paul in 2 Cor. 3:8–18: whereas only Moses had access to God's presence at Sinai (and the glory

The third contrast that the author of Hebrews draws is between the admittedly terrible consequences of ignoring God's warning on earth that accompanied the Sinai theophany and the even more severe consequences for ignoring God's warning from heaven at the eschaton (12:25); with greater privilege comes stricter judgment. The overall point of the three contrasts is to emphasize that God's theophanic judgment at the eschaton will be universal, more intense than at Sinai, and totally unavoidable; therefore it should be taken with utmost seriousness.

The Epistle to the Hebrews finds Old Testament support for this future cosmic judgment in a prophetic oracle from Haggai 2:6 (reiterated in 2:21): "At that time [God's] voice shook the earth; but now he has promised, 'Yet once more I will shake not only the earth but also the heaven'" (Heb. 12:26). As we saw in chapter 6, the Haggai text promised judgment on the nations in the postexilic period, using the hyperbolic language of a cosmic shakeup, with the result that the wealth of nations would be used to refurbish the rebuilt temple.

As is typical of many Old Testament texts, what was originally a vivid metaphor for a local historical event becomes universalized in later Jewish and Christian interpretation. This is the case with Isaiah's vision of a renewed Jerusalem in the context of "a new heavens and a new earth" (Isa. 65:17). Originally promising healing for the communal life of God's people after the exile, this vision later was universalized to refer to genuine cosmic renewal in the eschatological future.

In the case of Haggai's prophecy, the author of Hebrews omits the original reference to God shaking the sea, the dry land, and the nations and reverses the order of earth and heaven found in the Haggai text; he even inserts "not only" and "but also" in order to emphasize the contrast of the coming eschatological judgment with the prior earthly shaking of Sinai. Then come the words that seem to be in tension with the redemption of creation:

> This phrase, "Yet once more," indicates the removal of what is shaken—that is, created things—so that what cannot be shaken may remain. Therefore, since we are receiving a kingdom that cannot be shaken, let us give thanks, by which we offer to God an acceptable worship with reverence and awe; for indeed our God is a consuming fire. (Heb. 12:27–29)

At first blush, we might think that the author is claiming that God's cosmic shakeup will obliterate the created order, which will be replaced by an unshakable "spiritual" kingdom. However, there are two important considerations

---

reflected in his face from that encounter eventually faded), believers in Christ have continuous access to God's glory.

here, the first lexical or linguistic, the second conceptual and canonical; whereas the first has to do with the meaning of the word translated as "removal," the second has to do with how this shift from the shaken to the unshaken is conceived elsewhere in Scripture.

Let us take the lexical issue first. The word translated as "removal" in Hebrews 12:27 is *metathesis*, a noun that can certainly mean "removal" but also can mean "change" or "transformation." The same noun is used in Hebrews 7:12, along with the related verb *metatithēmi*, to describe the changes that accompany the shift from the old covenant to the new one: "For when there is a change [*metatithēmi*] in the priesthood, there is necessarily a change [*metathesis*] in the law as well." Although this certainly could be interpreted as the end/disappearance/removal of the old to be replaced with something absolutely new, this is a shortsighted understanding of the logic of the Testaments, which sees the new covenant that Christ brings as the true fulfillment of what was only imperfectly accomplished in previous times.

Likewise, Hebrews 11:5 uses the noun *metathesis*, along with the verb *metatithēmi* (twice), to describe the taking up of Enoch before his death—his translation to a new mode of existence: "By faith Enoch was taken [*metatithēmi*] so that he did not experience death; and 'he was not found, because God had taken [*metatithēmi*] him.' For it was attested before he was taken away [*metathesis*] that 'he had pleased God.'" Again, while we could certainly speak of the end/disappearance/removal of Enoch (implied in the NRSV), it is better to understand the idea behind this "taking" as Enoch's transition to a new form of life.[49]

Related to the lexical issue is the concept underlying the terminology. Here it is helpful to turn to 1 Corinthians 15, where Paul articulates the relationship of the present corruptible, perishable, mortal human body (a body that can be "shaken," to use the terminology of Hebrews) to the future resurrection body, which will be incorruptible, imperishable, and immortal (one which is "unshakable"). Paul uses three metaphors to explain the relationship of the mortal body to the resurrection body.

First, he compares the mortal body to a seed, while the resurrection body is the plant (15:36–37). The one must die for the other to become a reality. But this is not a simple replacement. Paul is careful to stress the continuity of identity between the seed (mortal body) and the plant (resurrection body). In his terminology, the former is "sown" perishable and "raised" imperishable (15:42).

---

49. I will address the question of "where" Enoch was taken as part of my discussion of the intermediate state in the next chapter.

The second metaphor that Paul uses to describe the resurrection is that we will be "changed" (he notes that while those alive at Christ's return will not actually die, "we will all be changed" [15:51]). The verb here is *allassō*, used again in 15:52 to describe the transition from mortality to immortality. It may be significant that this is the same verb used in the Septuagint of Psalm 102:26 (quoted in Heb. 1:12) to describe God changing the heaven and earth like a garment, when they wear out. Instead of thinking that Psalm 102 points to the annihilation of the cosmos, we might reflect on the metaphor of changing clothes that the psalmist uses. Could Paul in 1 Corinthians 15 be thinking of a parallel between our putting off the mortality of our present bodies in order to get dressed up (if we might put it so) for the resurrection, on the one hand, and God putting off the perishable cosmos and replacing it with more permanent clothing (a new heaven and new earth), on the other?[50]

Although Paul's use of "changed" does not make this comparison of the body and the cosmos explicit, the third metaphor that he uses for the transition to the resurrection body pushes in this direction. Right after his second statement that "we will be changed" (15:52), Paul affirms that the perishable and the mortal will "put on" (*endyō*) imperishability and immortality, which he says is equivalent to death being swallowed up in victory (15:53–54). Beyond stating that it is death and not the body (or creation) that is swallowed up, this use of "put on" (*endyō*) is clearly language of investiture or clothing, presenting an important parallel to Pauline statements about putting off the corrupt life of the old humanity (Eph. 4:22; Col. 3:9) and putting on (*endyō*) the new humanity renewed in the image of God (Eph. 4:24; Col. 3:10). Thus we have an important conceptual parallel between three crucial transitions: from moral corruption to righteousness, from the mortal body to the resurrection body, and from the perishable creation to the new creation—all can be compared to changing clothes.[51]

Now, I do not want to force Hebrews to say the same thing that Paul says in 1 Corinthians 15; yet Paul's claim that "flesh and blood cannot inherit the kingdom of God, nor does the perishable inherit the imperishable" (1 Cor. 15:50) resonates very well with the statement in Hebrews that what can be shaken (the perishable creation) must be removed/changed so that the unshakable (the kingdom) can be received (Heb. 12:27–28). In neither case does

50. Note that Ps. 104:1–3 describes God as dwelling in the heavens like a tent and wearing the light of the sun like a garment.

51. Edward Adams makes a similar suggestion about the metaphor of changing clothes (*Stars Will Fall*, 197), qualifying his earlier forceful argument that Heb. 12 intends the physical dissolution, not simply the transformation, of the cosmos (ibid., 189–91). Indeed, he emphasizes that even this physical dissolution is not the same as the complete annihilation of creation (ibid., 190–91).

emphasizing the divine (uncreated) origin of God's kingdom have anything to do with transcending the created world; rather, the divine origin of the kingdom is a way of speaking of the new creation as a gift of pure grace. Beyond its divine origin, what both Paul and the author of Hebrews agree on is that the change/transformation of the old corruptible world results in a permanent, imperishable kingdom, in which believers will participate in newness of life as full citizens.

Indeed, it may be significant that while the Letter to the Hebrews studiously avoids any reference to the Jerusalem temple (perhaps as part of a rhetorical strategy to deny its validity), the Haggai 2 oracle of cosmic shaking originally culminated in the refurbishing of the rebuilt temple (v. 7). Thus, even if the author of Hebrews never intended it, a canonical reading of Hebrews 12 suggests that after the final, eschatological shaking of heaven and earth, the result is the renovation of the cosmic temple of heaven and earth, which is equivalent to God's unshakable or permanent kingdom. That Hebrews understands this kingdom to be permanent fits well with Isaiah 66, where YHWH affirms, "The new heavens and the new earth, which I will make, shall remain before me" (v. 22); and here we may remember Isaiah 66:1–2a, where God explicitly states that the cosmos (heaven and earth) is his "house" or temple.

While Hebrews 12 affirms that the present cosmos is indeed subject to decay and transience, just as our bodies are, the biblical hope is that the cosmos, just like the body, will be raised imperishable.[52]

The Passing Away of the Cosmos in Revelation 20–21 and the Olivet Discourse

Well, perhaps Hebrews 12 does not clearly portray the destruction of the cosmos. But what does Revelation 20 mean by the disappearance (or fleeing) of heaven and earth at the final judgment? "Then I saw a great white throne and the one who sat on it; the earth and the heaven fled from his presence, and no place was found for them" (v. 11).

It is sometimes thought that the disappearance of the heaven and earth in Revelation 20:11 is equivalent to the passing away of heaven and earth reported in 21:1, and both are taken to signify total cosmic destruction. Whether or not the two texts are equivalent, we should note that the report in Revelation 20 comes just one verse before the dead stand before God's throne (in heaven,

---

52. Even Edward Adams suggests there are "tantalizing indications" throughout the letter to the Hebrews that suggest the author envisions a renewed cosmos as the eschatological end state (ibid., 197–98). Adams, however, does not elaborate on this point.

which therefore has not been obliterated) and the sea gives up its dead (so the sea still exists). In the judgment scene of Revelation 20, we are therefore justified in taking the fleeing of heaven and earth as a vivid representation of the cosmic shaking that accompanies God's righteous presence.[53] Not even the physical cosmos can bear the awesome presence of the Holy One, who has come to judge the world.

Somewhat more problematic than Revelation 20:11 are the two explicit statements, in Revelation 21 and in the Olivet discourse, that heaven and earth will "pass away." Let us start with Jesus's words in the Olivet discourse.

At the conclusion of instructing his disciples about a series of signs that will precede the coming of the Son of Man, Jesus states, "Heaven and earth will pass away, but my words will not pass away" (Matt. 24:35; Mark 13:31; Luke 21:33). Is this simply a hypothetical statement, to the effect that even if heaven and earth were to "pass away" (*parerchomai*), Jesus's words (his predictions of the coming signs) are sure and trustworthy? We saw in chapter 6 that the impermanence of heaven and earth in Psalm 102 could be read as a hypothetical possibility, grounded in the ambiguity of the Hebrew verbs involved. But a similar reading is not supported by the Greek of Jesus's statement. He really does seem to be predicting the disappearance or passing of the cosmos. But passing in what sense?

Likewise, in Revelation 21 John the seer announces, "Then I saw a new heaven and a new earth; for the first heaven and the first earth had passed away" (v. 1). Although the verbs are slightly different (*parerchomai* in the Olivet discourse; *aperchomai* in Rev. 21), the prefixes *par-* and *ap-* do not indicate any discernable difference in meaning. Revelation 21 suggests that the world as we know it will be gone, to be superseded by a new cosmos. The question here is whether this is obliteration followed by replacement or a reference to some form of (admittedly radical) transformation.

Here we might recall the statement in 2 Peter 3:10 that "the heavens will pass away with a loud noise," where "pass away" is also *parerchomai*. The earlier discussion of 2 Peter 3 suggested that this verse had the purification of the heavens in view rather than their strict annihilation. But can we apply this interpretation also to Jesus's words in the Olivet discourse and to John's vision in Revelation 21?

To answer this question, let us turn to Paul's description of conversion as "new creation" in 2 Corinthians 5:17.[54] What follows is a literal translation:

53. Note the likewise vivid picture of the waters that cover the earth fleeing from God's thunder (pictured as a rebuke) in Ps. 104:6–7.

54. This is one of two places where Paul uses the term "new creation"; the other is Gal. 6:15 ("For neither circumcision nor uncircumcision is anything; but a new creation is everything!").

"If anyone is in Christ—new creation! The old things [*ta archaia*] have passed away; behold, new ones [*kaina*] have come!"[55] Here Paul uses the verb *parerchomai* for the ending of the old life, which is then replaced by a new life in Christ. Are we to believe that Paul thinks that the passing away of the old life is equivalent to the obliteration of the person, who is then replaced by a doppelgänger? All the Pauline writings, not to mention common sense, suggest that no matter how radical the shift required for conversion to Christ, this describes the transformation rather than obliteration of the person.

By analogy, then, the passing away of the present heaven and earth to make way for the new creation is also transformative and not a matter of destruction followed by replacement. This understanding of passing away as transformation and not as simple obliteration and replacement is supported by the pattern of Scripture, which assumes a parallel between the redemption of persons (including the body) and the redemption of the nonhuman world.[56]

Thus, we saw that 2 Peter 3 calls on believers to be found blameless at Christ's return, while affirming that after God's judgment the earth itself will be found. In 1 Corinthians 15 Paul addresses the change from the present corruptible body to the incorruptible resurrection body, while Hebrews 12 speaks of the transition from a cosmos that can be shaken to the unshakable kingdom that is coming. And Romans 8 speaks both of resurrection (the redemption of the body) and of the liberation of creation itself from its bondage to futility, so that it might share in the same glory that God's children will have.

The analogy between personal and cosmic renovation certainly suggests that radical purging is necessary. But in neither case is the picture one of replacement after annihilation. Whether it is the "new creation" of persons who are in Christ or "a new heaven and a new earth" at the end of Revelation (21:1), the point is that salvation consists in the rescue and transformation of the world that God so loves (John 3:16).

For thorough analysis of the concept and its background, see Moyer V. Hubbard, *New Creation in Paul's Letters and Thought* (Society for New Testament Studies Monograph Series 119; Cambridge: Cambridge University Press, 2002); T. Ryan Jackson, *New Creation in Paul's Letters: A Study of the Historical and Social Setting of a Pauline Concept* (Wissenschaftliche Untersuchungen zum Neuen Testament 2/272; Tübingen: Mohr Siebeck, 2010).

55. NRSV: "So if anyone is in Christ, there is a new creation: everything old has passed away; see, everything has become new!" Paul's language here draws on the theology of "new creation" in Second Temple Jewish literature, where the phrase typically refers to the cosmic renewal (see the studies by Hubbard and Jackson). In this text, however, the apostle applies it to personal transformation.

56. This parallel is grounded theologically in the inextricable linkage between humans and the earth, seen in the creation accounts of Genesis. It is especially prominent in the wordplay between "human" ('*ādām*) and "ground" ('*ădamâ*) throughout Gen. 2–3.

Will Everyone Be Saved?

Does this vision of cosmic redemption mean that everyone will be "saved"? While this is not the place for a full discussion of the (complex) topic of final judgment, perhaps something needs to be said in this chapter on "Cosmic Destruction at Christ's Return?"

Here it is important to emphasize the biblical priority of God's love for this world and all the people in it, and that he wants all to come to salvation. This is something that the Scriptures clearly communicate. Even in the context of addressing the final fiery judgment, 2 Peter 3:9 notes that the reason for the delay in the Lord's return is that he "is patient with you, not wanting any to perish, but all to come to repentance." This means that God certainly does not rejoice in judgment. And the suffering of God incarnate in Christ on the cross is a powerful indication that the love of God is far wider and deeper than we can comprehend. This leads me to think that we should not let our limited imagination determine what God can or will do.

Nevertheless, two factors suggest that not all persons will finally be saved. First, the Bible is quite clear about the fact of judgment. Not everyone automatically participates in salvation; entrance into the kingdom of God requires a radical and difficult reversal on the part of those whom God has gifted with freedom (the human creature); this reversal is so radical it can be compared to new birth (John 3:3, 7), an image from John's Gospel equivalent to repentance in the Synoptic Gospels (Matt. 4:17; Mark 1:15). Why is entrance into God's kingdom so difficult? Precisely because it means subordinating our will to that of the creator, submitting our life to God's rule.

Jesus's vivid images of judgment are troubling. He speaks of the weeping and gnashing of teeth in the outer darkness (Matt. 8:12; 22:13; 25:30; cf. Luke 13:28) or in the fiery furnace (Matt. 13:42, 50), and he uses the image of the fire of Gehenna (Matt. 5:22, 29, 30; 10:28; 18:9; Mark 9:43, 45, 47; Luke 12:5). However we parse the details of these images, they depict what is undeniably a terrible fate for those who reject God's rightful claim as ruler of creation.

While much is still mysterious about final judgment, perhaps we can find a clue in Jesus's teaching that the meek will inherit the earth (Matt. 5:5). Could this mean that final judgment is akin to cosmic disinheritance, permanent exile from God's good creation? This might mean that final judgment should be construed as annihilation of the person rather than the classical notion of eternal torment. However, the extreme imagery that Jesus uses should warn us that this is not something anyone would want to experience; we dare not tame his vivid warnings implicit in this imagery.

Beyond the explicit teaching of Scripture on the reality of final judgment, the very logic of holistic salvation suggests that universal salvation is highly unlikely. It is possible for those who hold to an otherworldly understanding of salvation to imagine all ethereal, disembodied "souls" united with God in the afterlife (whatever that might mean). Yet the realities of human sin and recalcitrance, combined with an understanding of holistic salvation, makes universalism in this sense practically impossible.

Since biblical salvation involves the actual transformation of real people, in their cultural and historical contexts, as they move from corruption toward righteousness, we would need to imagine all the people who have ever existed in the world changing both internally and externally, including the way they live concretely in the real world with their fellow human beings.[57] This transformation (beginning in this life, culminating in the eschaton) would need to apply to people such as dictators, terrorists, serial killers, child abusers, and rapists. How realistic is that?

The point is not that people who have committed heinous sins cannot come to repentance and salvation. None of us is inherently righteous, and salvation is only by grace. My point, however, is akin to a thought experiment. If salvation is not "pie in the sky when you die" but the concrete transformation of real persons (where their deeds begin to conform to their faith), then we would need to imagine a scenario in which everyone is actually transformed in their earthly context toward a life of righteousness. While not the "pie in the sky" that accompanies otherworldly salvation, this does seem to be "pie on the earth"—an unrealistic, unrealizable utopia.

Let me emphasize, however, that the grace of God is beyond human imagination (so my thought experiment might be flawed). I want to take seriously that the gates of the new Jerusalem are always open, according to Revelation 21:15 (cf. Isa. 60:11). Indeed, just before mentioning categories of people who are outside the gates (Rev. 22:15), the text affirms that those who "wash their robes" may enter (v. 14); and soon after that we find the invitation: "The Spirit and the bride say, 'Come.' And let everyone who hears say, 'Come.' And let everyone who is thirsty come. Let anyone who wishes take the water of life as a gift" (v. 17).

The call is absolutely universal. But you need to be thirsty; you need to want that water. And both the Bible and human experience suggest that some are not thirsty. Not all yearn for that water. I would like to think that universal salvation might be true—and surely God's mercy is beyond our

---

57. Inner change must be demonstrated by outward change. This is the point of being judged by our deeds or works (John 5:28–29; 2 Cor. 5:10; Rev. 22:11–12; cf. Rom. 8:13).

understanding—but a biblical understanding of holistic salvation suggests that this is wishful thinking.[58]

Eustace, Aslan, and the Biblical Vision of Radical Transformation

A powerful illustration of both the difficulty of genuine conversion and the comprehensive nature of biblical transformation is found in the story of Eustace Scrubb in C. S. Lewis's fantasy novel *The Voyage of the Dawn Treader*. On one of the islands at which the ship *Dawn Treader* has stopped, the boy Eustace (initially a most unlikable character) sees a dying dragon crawl out of a cave. Once he is convinced that the dragon is dead, he explores the cave, only to find that it is filled with the dragon's hoard of wonderful treasure, which he begins to appropriate for himself, all the time thinking of ways to keep it secret from the others on the ship. Eventually Eustace falls asleep on the treasure; when he wakes, he discovers that he himself has turned into a dragon, his outer appearance thus expressing his inner nature.[59]

Later in the story, after Eustace the dragon has become fully aware of his predicament and desperately wants to change, he encounters Aslan the lion (the Christ figure in the story), who takes him to a bubbling well and tells him to undress and bathe. After trying multiple times to "undress" by scratching off the dragon scales, only to find another layer beneath, Eustace finally submits to Aslan's claws, which painfully peel off the entire dragon skin, leaving him naked and vulnerable. Then, after bathing him, Aslan himself dresses Eustace in new clothes.[60]

This vivid picture of Eustace shedding his dragon skin evokes the biblical truth that radical transformation is necessary for salvation; indeed, such transformation is equivalent to salvation. As we have seen from as far back as the chapter on the exodus (chap. 4), salvation involves both rescue or deliverance and restoration to wholeness. Salvation is nothing less than the renewal of God's creational intent from the beginning.

And make no mistake, this world needs radical change. The Bible assumes that the proper functioning of creation (both human and nonhuman) has been disrupted by sin; in the case of humanity, this involves the will, conscience,

---

58. My thanks to Sylvia Keesmaat and J. Gerald Janzen for comments on my first draft of this material, which has helped clarify my thinking on some of these issues.

59. C. S. Lewis, *The Voyage of the Dawn Treader* (New York: MacMillan, 1952), chap. 6, "The Adventures of Eustace."

60. Ibid., chap. 7, "How the Adventure Ended."

desires, bodily life, and social relationships (including family, culture, art, education, political institutions, economic systems), none of which have unfolded or developed throughout history in accordance with God's norms for flourishing. The New Testament is ruthlessly honest about the struggle against evil, which culminated in the death of Jesus on a Roman instrument of torture and execution.

But the vision of the Scriptures is that a day is coming when bodies will be healed and human society will finally reflect God's ideas of mercy and justice. Jesus's teaching of the kingdom of God is predicated on the triumph of God's purposes over the powers of evil. Thus, in one of his parables, Jesus compares the kingdom of God to a woman who put some yeast into a large amount of dough; the result is that the entire dough was leavened (Matt. 13:33; Luke 13:20–21). The point is that although the kingdom of God may seem to be making only small inroads into the oppressive powers of evil, it will eventually transform the world, just as a little bit of yeast transforms the entire dough.

The comprehensive nature of the kingdom is also portrayed in Daniel's vision, where a huge idolatrous statue, symbolizing all the kingdoms of the world, is confronted by a stone, not made by human hands (that is, this is not any humanly constructed reality, but rather is the kingdom of God). Yet this seemingly small and insignificant stone strikes the statue and shatters it and then grows into an immense mountain that fills the entire earth (Dan. 2:31–36, 44–45). Scripture teaches that, like the yeast and the stone, God's kingdom, which is from heaven, will one day encompass the entire earthly creation. The growth of this kingdom is nothing less than God's redemptive purposes becoming manifest in history, until the earth is filled with the knowledge of God's glory as the waters cover the sea (Isa. 11:9; Hab. 2:14).

And Paul, living after the death/resurrection and victory of Jesus, understands this risen and ascended Messiah to be presently reigning as Lord of all; yet Paul anticipates a further stage in redemptive history when the Messiah, having subdued all powers that oppose God (including death, the final enemy), will hand the kingdom over to the Father (1 Cor. 15:24–26). Then, according to Revelation 11:15, the kingdom of this world will become the kingdom of God. And God, says Paul, will be all in all (15:28). Then the created order will once again respond in obedience and praise to its maker. In the end, the Bible envisions nothing less than the eschatological transformation of heaven and earth.

10

The Role of Heaven
in Biblical Eschatology

In the preceding chapter I addressed some of the New Testament texts that seem to contradict the Bible's emphasis on the redemption of creation, focusing on passages that seemed to depict the destruction of the cosmos.

The present chapter continues to examine problem texts, this time those that seem to hold out the promise of heaven hereafter. These texts are of three types. The first and most common sort of "heaven" text upholds heaven as an ideal in contrast to earth and seems to suggest that the Christian eschatological hope is for heaven when Christ returns. However, as we will see, the point of such texts is that heaven is meant to be manifested on earth in the present (ethics) and will be manifested on earth in the future (eschatology); in no case is heaven the final destination of the righteous.

Then there are a few texts that are used to support the idea of the "rapture" of the church. The church's rapture or removal from earth to heaven is, in dispensationalist theology, usually thought to be temporary, so that believers might escape the "tribulation"; however, in the popular Christian imagination this snatching of believers from earthly suffering is often treated as the beginning of a life of eternity in heaven. We will take a close look at the two primary "rapture" texts to see what they actually teach.

A third sort of text is often understood to promise heaven, not in the sense of a final destination, but as an interim or intermediate state between death and resurrection. It will be important to explore what the Bible actually teaches about this interim state and what its role might be in the overall Christian hope.

The Apocalyptic Pattern—Preparation in Heaven, Unveiling on Earth

A particularly helpful approach to understanding texts that seem to hold out a heavenly ideal (in contradistinction to life on earth) is to clarify an important pattern that frames New Testament eschatology. This is the apocalyptic pattern of preparation in heaven, followed by revelation or unveiling on earth. The designation "apocalyptic" is my own term for this pattern, since the word derives from the Greek *apokalypsis*, meaning "revelation," which is related to the verb *apokalyptō*, to "unveil" or "reveal."

Most students of the New Testament are aware of the fundamental eschatological contrast between the present age and the age to come. The New Testament anticipates that creation will be redeemed, but we do not presently see all things redeemed. Full redemption is a future hope, not yet a present reality. Instead, we live between the times—between the inauguration of the kingdom through Christ's life, death, resurrection, and ascension, on the one hand, and the consummation of the kingdom, which awaits Christ's return or parousia, on the other hand.[1]

The eschatological contrast can be stated in three main ways. The first contrast is found in the New Testament texts that distinguish the present corrupt age from the glorious age to come. The second contrast involves highlighting the difference between the corruption of earthly life with what believers presently have in heaven. In both cases the contrast is between sin and redemption, but the difference is that the first contrast looks ahead to the promised future, whereas the second contrast focuses on salvation in the present.

This means that a third eschatological contrast or tension is implied that combines elements of the other two. This is the contrast between the "already" of salvation, what we presently have (in heaven), and the "not yet," its future manifestation (on earth). Here the tension is not between sin and redemption, but rather between partial and complete redemption, with the partial (in heaven) being a guarantee of full salvation to come (on earth).

1. The Greek term *parousia* means "presence," but often it is translated "coming" in relation to Christ's return (Matt. 24:3, 27, 37, 39; 1 Cor. 15:23; 1 Thess. 2:19; 3:13; 4:15; 5:23; 2 Thess. 2:1, 8; James 5:8; 2 Pet. 1:16; 3:4, 12; 1 John 2:28).

The contrast between the "already" (partial) and the "not yet" (complete) is commonplace in discussions of New Testament eschatology, but what is not always fully grasped is the significance of the apocalyptic pattern in which this contrast is firmly embedded. This pattern brings together the contrasts of present and future and also of heaven and earth through the notion of preparation. The point is that the salvation presently being prepared in heaven is followed by its future unveiling on earth. The apocalyptic pattern of preparation and unveiling permeates the New Testament, and if properly understood, helps to clarify many biblical texts that on the surface seem to teach an otherworldly hope.

This apocalyptic pattern is clearly dependent on the temporal sequence of Christ's incarnation, ascension, and second coming, or parousia. In the incarnation Jesus comes from heaven to earth to accomplish his mission; the ascension is when he returns to heaven, enthroned at the right hand of the Father; and the parousia is Jesus's return to earth to bring all things to fulfillment.[2] We now live between Jesus's ascension and his second coming, the time of preparation (when Christ is in heaven). Of course, there is a certain sense in which the preparation predates the historical mission of Jesus, since God has anticipated and planned the outcome long ago, in ages past. Nevertheless, from the perspective of the current people of God awaiting the parousia, the present is the time of preparation.

The apocalyptic framework of preparation and unveiling is assumed in Acts 3: the apostle Peter says that God will "send the Messiah appointed for you, that is, Jesus, who must remain in heaven until the time of universal restoration that God announced long ago through his holy prophets" (3:20–21). Like Peter, we live in the time of preparation (after Jesus's ascension); the hoped-for restoration of all things is still future (awaiting Jesus's return).

Paul alludes to this apocalyptic framework when he speaks of an eschatological future that is beyond human expectation: "What no eye has seen, nor ear heard, nor the human heart conceived, what God has prepared for those who love him" (1 Cor. 2:9).[3] Then Paul goes on to say that the Spirit has revealed to us something of this future (2:10).

2. As the Apostles' Creed puts it, "He ascended into heaven and sits at the right hand of God the Father Almighty; from thence he shall come to judge the living and the dead."

3. Here Paul is citing the Old Testament: "From ages past no one has heard, no ear has perceived, no eye has seen any God besides you, who works for those who wait for him" (Isa. 64:4). This citation, which comes immediately after the prophet's plea for YHWH to come in a judgment theophany, presents a fascinating connection between the discussion of cosmic destruction in chap. 9 above and the theme of this chapter (10) on the role of heavenly preparation.

What exactly has the Spirit revealed? Here we may fruitfully turn to a whole series of New Testament texts that give us a glimpse of what God is preparing for those who love him (see table 10.1). It will be valuable to work our way though these texts one by one, noting variations in the pattern, especially the different terms for what is being prepared.[4]

Table 10.1. Preparation in Heaven (Present) for Revelation on Earth (Future)

New Testament Text	What	Verb	For Whom	Where	Future Expectation
1 Cor. 2:9		has prepared	for those who love him		
Matt. 25:34	kingdom	prepared	for you		to be inherited (at the judgment)
1 Pet. 1:3–5	inheritance, salvation	kept	for you	in heaven	to be revealed in the last time
Col. 1:5	hope	laid up	for you	in heaven	
2 Cor. 5:1–5	dwelling, house (= body)	prepared	for us	[heavenly]	to be clothed (with a resurrection body)
John 14:1–3	place, rooms	prepare	for you		Jesus will come again for the disciples
Phil. 3:20–21	citizenship		our	in heaven	coming of the Savior, who will transform our bodies (resurrection)
Heb. 11:13–16	homeland, country, city	prepared	for them	[heavenly]	
Rev. 21:1–2	holy city, new Jerusalem	prepared (and adorned)	for Christ	heaven	coming down out of heaven from God

Matthew 25:34

Let us start with Matthew 25:34, from Jesus's parable of the sheep and the goats, where the king commends the righteous, who have demonstrated

4. Given the diversity of details in this pattern, it is good to heed G. C. Berkouwer's warning about the difficulty of trying "to come up with a systematic harmonization" of "multiform" eschatological imagery in the New Testament. He suggests that when confronted by a diversity of seemingly incompatible images, we can still discern "what is intended in the passages" (*The Return of Christ*, trans. James Van Oosterom, ed. Marlin J. Van Elderen [Studies in Dogmatics; Grand Rapids: Eerdmans, 1972], 216–17).

compassion to those in need. Here God's preparation for the eschaton is said to predate the incarnation.

> Come, you that are blessed by my Father, inherit *the kingdom prepared for you* from the foundation of the world. (Matt. 25:34)

While both this text and 1 Corinthians 2:9 use the same verb "prepare" (*hetoimazō*), other verbs are used in different texts; likewise, the kingdom mentioned here is just one of many images used for the promised inheritance.

1 Peter 1:3–5

Two other images are used in 1 Peter 1:3–5, where the focus is on the permanent or imperishable nature of what has been promised.

> Blessed be the God and Father of our Lord Jesus Christ! By his great mercy he has given us a new birth into a living hope through the resurrection of Jesus Christ from the dead, and into *an inheritance* that is imperishable, undefiled, and unfading, *kept in heaven for you*, who are being protected by the power of God through faith for a *salvation ready to be revealed* in the last time. (1 Pet. 1:3–5)

Matthew's "kingdom" is here replaced with "inheritance" (which makes sense, since the righteous in Matt. 25:34 are to inherit the kingdom) and also with "salvation" (a comprehensive term equivalent to "kingdom"); another difference is that 1 Peter 1 uses "kept" (*tēreō*) instead of "prepared." Despite the variations, this text clearly fits the pattern of preparation in heaven and explicitly mentions that what is kept in heaven for us will be revealed or unveiled at the last day (v. 5).[5] This last point is crucial to remember when we look at texts that exhibit only part of the pattern.

Colossians 1:5

Although Colossians 1:5 does not mention the eschatological unveiling, it assumes the same pattern of preparation in heaven. Here we read the verse in wider context:

> 5. That this promised inheritance (which we have through the resurrection of Christ [1 Pet. 1:3]) is imperishable fits with Paul's description of the resurrection body in 1 Cor. 15:42, 50, 52, 54. And the language of 1 Cor. 15:50 ("flesh and blood cannot inherit the kingdom of God, nor does the perishable inherit the imperishable") connects the resurrection with Jesus's reference in Matt. 25:34 about inheriting the kingdom.

In our prayers for you we always thank God, the Father of our Lord Jesus Christ, for we have heard of your faith in Christ Jesus and of the love that you have for all the saints, because of *the hope laid up for you in heaven*. You have heard of this hope before in the word of the truth, the gospel that has come to you. (Col. 1:3–6)

Not only do we find the word "hope" where previously we saw "kingdom," "inheritance," "salvation," but also the verb is different: "laid up" (*apokeimai*, "stored up, reserved") instead of "prepared" or "kept." But the point is the same: the promised eschatological future (the redemption of heaven and earth) is secure, even in the present.

2 Corinthians 5:1–5

Then, in 2 Corinthians 5:1–5 we again have the English verb "prepared" (but from a different Greek verb, *katergazomai*). Speaking of the contrast between the present body and the resurrection body, Paul says,

> For we know that if the earthly tent we live in is destroyed, we have *a building from God, a house not made with hands, eternal in the heavens*. For in this tent we groan, longing to be clothed with *our heavenly dwelling*—if indeed, when we have taken it off we will not be found naked. For while we are still in this tent, we groan under our burden, because we wish not to be unclothed but to be further clothed, so that what is mortal may be swallowed up by life. *He who has prepared us for this very thing is God*, who has given us the Spirit as a guarantee. (2 Cor. 5:1–5)

Using the metaphor of the body as a dwelling or house, Paul says that he does not want to be "naked" or "unclothed" (that is, disembodied) in the eschaton, but rather to be clothed with a new, resurrection body, a building or dwelling prepared by God, hence "not made with hands" (v. 1). Paul's use of the phrase "not made with hands" for the resurrection body (pictured as a building) may depend on the words attributed to Jesus: "We heard him say, 'I will destroy this temple that is made with hands, and in three days I will build another, not made with hands'" (Mark 14:58).[6]

---

6. In his Areopagus sermon, Paul says, "The God who made the world and everything in it, he who is Lord of heaven and earth, does not live in shrines made by human hands" (Acts 17:24). And earlier in Acts, Stephen mentions that "the Most High does not dwell in houses made with human hands" (7:48) and then goes on to quote Isa. 66:1–2 about the contrast between the Jerusalem temple, which people build, and the cosmic temple of heaven and earth, built by God's own hand (7:49–50).

We will come back to 2 Corinthians 5, since it is a widely misunderstood text, but for now it is enough to note that here Paul assumes the apocalyptic pattern. The resurrection is future, but we already have, in some sense, the hoped-for building or dwelling "in the heavens," which is being made or prepared by God himself.

John 14:1–3

John 14:1–3 is another text that is often misunderstood, and it will be addressed in more detail later. But the point here is simply that Jesus's promise to his disciples in verses 2–3 fits the apocalyptic pattern.

> Do not let your hearts be troubled. Believe in God, believe also in me. In my Father's house there are many dwelling places. If it were not so, would I have told you that I go *to prepare a place for you*? And if I go and *prepare a place for you*, I will come again and will take you to myself, so that where I am, there you may be also. (John 14:1–3)

Jesus is going (presumably to heaven, though that is not stated) to "prepare" (*hetoimazō*) a "place" for his disciples, and here the same verb is employed as in 1 Corinthians 2:9 and Matthew 25:34. And he will "come again" so that we might be with him to enjoy what he has prepared. Clearly, Jesus's return will be the occasion for the unveiling of what has been prepared. But where will this take place?

Many Christians simply assume that a heavenly destiny is intended in John 14:3, but this is derived from an unbiblical worldview. The apocalyptic pattern I have been tracing suggests that the unveiling of what has been prepared will be on earth, since that is where Christ will be (though that is not stated here).

Philippians 3:20–21

Another widely misunderstood passage is Philippians 3:20–21. In contrast to those whose "end is destruction" (Phil. 3:19), Paul affirms,

> But *our citizenship is in heaven*, and it is from there that we are expecting a Savior, the Lord Jesus Christ. He will transform the body of our humiliation that it may be conformed to the body of his glory, by the power that also enables him to make all things subject to himself. (Phil. 3:20–21)

Although the text provides no verb like "prepare," "keep," "lay up" (even "is" has to be supplied for the translation "is in heaven"), the apocalyptic pattern of what we presently have in heaven (citizenship), followed by the parousia of Christ from heaven, is clear. "Citizenship" is parallel to the kingdom, inheritance, salvation, hope, building, house, dwelling, place, which will be revealed on the last day in our resurrection, described here as the transformation of the body of our humiliation. This transformation is grounded in the cosmic lordship of Christ, by which all things (*ta panta*) will be made subject to him.

Understanding the apocalyptic pattern that Philippians 3 draws on might help clear up the misunderstanding that many contemporary Christians have about heavenly citizenship. The text is talking not about going to heaven, but rather about the source of our confidence to live on earth in a manner different from (and in tension with) the present fallen world, until Christ's return.

Earlier in the chapter Paul has emphasized that he counts all present gain and status in this world as loss (Phil. 3:3–9), and that he seeks to share in Christ's sufferings in order to attain to Christ's likeness in the resurrection (3:10–11). He is thus seeking to live out his heavenly citizenship on earth, according to heaven's/God's values, until the day when earth is transformed to be like heaven.

It is worth noting that Philippi was a Roman colony and that many in the Philippian church would have been Roman citizens. In drawing on the analogy between Roman citizenship and citizenship in heaven, Paul not only was designating Jesus as the true "Savior" and "Lord" in contrast to Caesar (who was often described by these titles); he was also undoubtedly aware that Rome was crowded (indeed, overcrowded), and its citizens who were spread throughout the empire did not expect to settle in Rome one day. Instead, they expected to live out their citizenship wherever they were, as representatives of the empire. Likewise Christians, whose citizenship is in heaven, are expected to live as representatives of the kingdom of God on earth, manifesting Christ's rule, until the day when the true Lord returns from heaven (the mother city) to liberate them from their enemies and fully establish his rule in the colonies. Or, to put it in terms of the Lord's Prayer, the day when God's kingdom comes and God's will is done on earth as it is in heaven.[7]

---

7. Perhaps no one has brought the Roman imperial background to bear on Phil. 3:20 more helpfully for ordinary readers than N. T. Wright: "Paul's Gospel and Caesar's Empire," in *Paul and Politics: Ekklesia, Israel, Imperium, Interpretation; Essays in Honor of Krister Stendahl*, ed. Richard A. Horsley (Harrisburg, PA: Trinity Press International, 2000), 160–83 (esp. 173–74); *The Resurrection of the Son of God* (Christian Origins and the Question of God 3; Minneapolis: Fortress, 2003), 229–30; *Paul for Everyone: The Prison Letters; Ephesians, Philippians, Colossians, and Philemon* (Louisville: Westminster John Knox, 2004), 126–27.

Hebrews 11:13–16

Having addressed citizenship in heaven (Phil. 3:20–21) and the place that Jesus has prepared for us (John 14:1–3), we now consider what Hebrews 11 says about our true homeland. The text speaks of the faithful in Old Testament times, those who died before God's purposes for their salvation could be fulfilled.

> All of these died in faith without having received the promises, but from a distance they saw and greeted them. They confessed that they were strangers and foreigners on the earth, for people who speak in this way make it clear that they are seeking *a homeland*. If they had been thinking of the land that they had left behind, they would have had opportunity to return. But as it is, they desire *a better country*, that is, *a heavenly one*. Therefore God is not ashamed to be called their God; indeed, *he has prepared a city for them*. (Heb. 11:13–16)

Here the hoped-for homeland, country, and city are another way to picture the promised kingdom, inheritance, salvation, hope, building, house, dwelling, place, and citizenship mentioned in the previous texts. In none of these cases does the heavenly location of the items listed describe the destination of the faithful. Rather, this heavenly city (Heb. 11:16) is being "prepared" for us (or in this case, for "them," the Old Testament saints), and this "prepared" is the same verb (*hetoimazō*) as in 1 Corinthians 2:9; Matthew 25:34; and John 14:3. The implication, if we follow the apocalyptic pattern, is that we are not going "up" to the heavenly city; rather, the heavenly city is coming here, and it will be unveiled at the last day.[8] And this is exactly what we find in the book of Revelation.

Revelation 21:1–2

> Then I saw a new heaven and a new earth; for the first heaven and the first earth had passed away, and the sea was no more. And I saw *the holy city, the new Jerusalem, coming down out of heaven from God, prepared as a bride adorned for her husband*. (Rev. 21:1–2)

The descent of the holy city, the new Jerusalem, from heaven to earth is the centerpiece of John's vision of a new cosmos. This descent of the new Jerusalem from God was already promised in Revelation 3:12 (in the context of the letter to the church at Sardis). However, Revelation 21:2 not only mentions the

8. As Anthony Thiselton puts it, the city in Heb. 11 "lies not so much above . . . but ahead" (*Life after Death: A New Approach to the Last Things* [Grand Rapids: Eerdmans, 2001], 105).

city's descent from heaven, but also uses the same verb "prepared" (*hetoimazō*) that we have seen in previous texts, along with the verb "adorned" (a participle from *kosmeō*), which fits the image of a bride's (cosmetic) preparation for her wedding day.

John's vision in Revelation 21 of the new Jerusalem is important because it makes the apocalyptic pattern that we have discerned in many other New Testament texts more explicit than most. In some of the previous texts the reader often has to supply background information, such as where the apocalyptic unveiling will take place. Thus, when Jesus tells the disciples in John 14:3 that after preparing a place for them he will come and take them to be with him forever, many contemporary readers supply the place as (obviously) heaven. But that is based on an unbiblical set of assumptions, derived more from the history of theology than from the Bible itself. The fact that the city that God has prepared in heaven comes down to earth in Revelation 21 makes clear that the goal of heavenly preparation is an earthly future. We do not go to heaven; rather, what is prepared or stored in heaven is brought to us at Christ's return.

N. T. Wright nicely illustrates this point with his analogy of a parent telling a child in advance of Christmas that there is "a present kept safe in the cupboard for you." This does not mean that once Christmas comes, the child has to "go and live in the cupboard in order to enjoy the present there." Rather, the present will be brought from the cupboard to enrich the life of the child in the day-to-day world.[9]

The chart near the start of this chapter summarizes the apocalyptic pattern of preparation in heaven followed by unveiling on earth that we have seen in a variety of New Testament texts. Not every text includes all the details, but the pattern emerges from comparing the texts side by side (note the recurrence of "for you" in many of the texts). This pattern of preparation in heaven for unveiling on earth is consistent with the entire tenor of Scripture.

The Point of the Pattern

Although this apocalyptic pattern may seem strange to contemporary readers, it makes a very important set of theological (and thereby ethical) points.

First, the pattern of preparation in heaven for unveiling on earth emphasizes that salvation is not of our making, but rather is God's gift (note who is doing the preparing). In an important sense, we do not bring the eschatological

---

9. N. T. Wright, *New Heavens, New Earth: The Biblical Picture of the Christian Hope* (Cambridge: Grove Books, 1999), 7. This short volume is Wright's Drew Lecture on immortality given at Spurgeon's College (London) in 1993.

future (whether conceived as salvation, a kingdom, a city, an inheritance, etc.), though the church certainly is meant to embody this future in their communal earthly life, as a witness to the salvation or kingdom that God is bringing. So the apocalyptic pattern disabuses us of the temptation to self-righteousness or triumphalism. The coming new creation is an act of pure grace on God's part.

Second, the apocalyptic pattern emphasizes that until Christ returns, salvation is only partial; Christian hope thus involves waiting patiently for the unveiling on the last day. To be faithful in the interim, as we live toward the parousia, Christian discipleship will be cruciform, following the pattern of Christ's life, and will therefore often be characterized by suffering and sacrifice; this is because of the ethical tension between the promised kingdom of God and the powers of the present age. The cruciform pattern of the Christian life is very hard for contemporary Westerners to hear, since we (and I include myself here) typically want quick fixes, and we somehow think that our (presumed) faithfulness should make us immune to suffering. It turns out, on the contrary, that faithfulness to Christ and our love for others will often require a voluntary taking up of suffering on our part in order to live ethically in this fallen world.

But, third, the apocalyptic pattern assures us that even though we may not see the promised kingdom clearly in the world today—it is in many ways hidden or obscured by the continuing power of sin—God guarantees the final success of this kingdom. There will indeed be a final and complete unveiling of what is hidden, in which God's purposes for this world will come to fruition. The apocalyptic pattern thus encourages us to trust in, and seek to embody, the coming redemption of all things that God has promised, even when we are tempted to give up hope.

Beyond making these theological points (with ethical implications), the apocalyptic pattern is helpful also in clearing the ground of many potential objections to holistic eschatology that arise from misreading texts about "heaven." I have already addressed some of these texts while laying out the pattern; indeed, they contribute positively to the pattern. The point is that reading the New Testament through the lens of preparation in heaven for unveiling on earth disposes of much egregious interpretation of texts that supposedly support a heavenly future.

What about the Rapture?

Even if these texts do not teach a heavenly future, what about those texts that suggest Christians will be taken from the earth to heaven—the doctrine of the "rapture"?

Although the word "rapture" does not occur in any eschatological passages in the New Testament (at least in standard English translations), the idea of being "caught up" (which is what "rapture" means) is found in 1 Thessalonians 4:17 (where the Greek verb is *harpazō*).[10] Matthew 24:40–41 (// Luke 17:34–35) is a second text often appealed to in popular contemporary eschatology as support for the rapture, though the term there is "taken" (*paralambanō*), not "caught up." Let us examine each of these texts in turn.[11]

1 Thessalonians 4:13–18

First Thessalonians 4:13–18 is the classic "rapture" text. However, it does not intend to teach some esoteric doctrine about the second coming; that is not its point. Rather, Paul has a pastoral purpose in writing, which is why he concludes by saying, "Encourage one other with these words" (v. 18). Specifically, Paul is addressing the question of whether those who have died in the faith prior to the return of the Lord will be disadvantaged at Christ's return. He affirms that they will not be disadvantaged. Indeed, the dead in Christ will have precedence over the living, since they will be raised first. "*Then* we who are alive, who are left, will be caught up in the clouds together with them to meet the Lord in the air; and so we will be with the Lord forever" (v. 17). Paul is thus encouraging the church in Thessalonica, emphasizing that they need not worry about those from their midst who have passed away before the second coming.

Nevertheless, 1 Thessalonians 4:17 certainly seems, at first blush, to support the idea of living eternally in heaven, since having met the Lord in the air, "we will be with the Lord forever." It is intriguing, however, that this text (like John 14) does not actually say where we will be with the Lord forever.[12] This

---

10. The English word "rapture" is derived from the Latin verb *rapio*, which was used in the Vulgate to translate *harpazō* in 1 Thess. 4:17.

11. Historically, 1 Cor. 15:51–52 and John 14:1–3 have also been associated with the rapture, though they are not typically adduced as proof texts in most popular eschatologies today. While the 1 Cor. 15 text clearly describes the resurrection, locating it at Christ's second coming or parousia (and so need not be addressed at any length here), the John 14 text is often thought to teach a heavenly afterlife, and so I will address it later in the present chapter.

12. Note that "the air" (where believers are to meet Christ) is not exactly equivalent to "heaven" in contemporary Christian theology. Classical Greek authors often used the term *aēr* (which Paul uses here) to refer to the lower atmosphere (below the moon), characterized as dense and misty, in distinction from the *aithēr* (the pure upper region of the stars). While we cannot simply attribute this understanding of the air to Paul without further ado, the New Testament sometimes associates the air with the domain of Satan, who is called "the ruler of the power of the air" (Eph. 2:2), a phrase essentially synonymous with the Johannine expression "the ruler of this world" (John 12:31; 14:30). Note also the association of birds (which inhabit the air) with the evil one/Satan/the devil in different versions of the parable of the sower (Matt. 13:4, 19;

has to be supplied by the interpreter from the tenor of the rest of Scripture. As we have seen in chapter 8, Scripture suggests this will be on earth.

This conclusion is confirmed when we explore the meaning of two loaded terms that Paul uses, both of which have political overtones. First of all, Paul refers to the "coming [*parousia*] of the Lord" (1 Thess. 4:15). As is now recognized by New Testament scholars, *parousia* often refers to an official divine or imperial visit—the "coming" of a god or a king to a city, which clearly makes sense in our text.[13] In ancient times the *parousia* was a matter of great celebration, with much pomp and ceremony, thus Paul's reference to the public announcement of Christ's *parousia* by "the archangel's call" and "the sound of God's trumpet" (1 Thess. 4:16), and also the important issue of who would meet the Lord first.

Associated with the *parousia* is the idea of *apantēsis* ("meeting"), which Paul mentions in 1 Thessalonians 4:17.[14] As Gene Green has pointed out, "This was almost a technical term that described the custom of sending a delegation outside the city to receive a dignitary who was on the way to town."[15] This custom is seen in action at Jesus's triumphal entry into Jerusalem, when people "took branches of palm trees and went out to meet [*hypantēsis*] him," acclaiming him the "King of Israel" (John 12:13).[16] Paul himself experienced this sort of reception on his trip to Rome. "The believers from there, when they heard of us, came as far as the Forum of Appius and Three Taverns to meet [*apantēsis*] us" (Acts 28:15).

Mark 4:4, 15; Luke 8:5, 12). If any of these associations is relevant to 1 Thess. 4, Paul may be intending to say that redemption occurs on the devil's "turf," and he is powerless to impede it.

13. Néstor O. Míguez, *The Practice of Hope: Ideology and Interpretation in 1 Thessalonians*, trans. Aquíles Martínez (Paul in Critical Contexts; Minneapolis: Fortress, 2012), chap. 8, "The Political Analogy in Pauline Language," esp. 81–82 on *parousia*; Helmut Koester, "Imperial Ideology and Paul's Eschatology in 1 Thessalonians," in *Paul and Empire: Religion and Power in Roman Imperial Society*, ed. Richard A. Horsley (Harrisburg, PA: Trinity Press International, 1997), 158; Gene L. Green, *The Letters to the Thessalonians* (Pillar New Testament Commentary; Leicester: Apollos; Grand Rapids: Eerdmans, 2002), 223–25; Matthew Forrest Lowe, "Death Dismantled: Reading Christological and Soteriological Language in 1 Corinthians 15 in Light of Roman Imperial Ideology" (PhD diss., McMaster Divinity College, 2011).

14. The expression *eis apantēsin* or its variant *eis hypantēsin* (literally, "to a meeting" in the accusative case) is usually translated verbally, as an action ("to meet").

15. Green, *Thessalonians*, 226. Likewise, Erik Peterson notes that *apantēsis* refers to "a civic custom of antiquity whereby a public welcome was accorded by a city to important visitors"; thus Paul's point in 1 Thess. 4:13–18 is that Christians "will welcome Christ in the ἀήρ [*aēr*], acclaiming Him as κύριος [*kyrios*]" ("ἀπάντησις," *Theological Dictionary of the New Testament*, ed. Gerhard Kittel and Gerhard Friedrich, trans. Geoffrey W. Bromiley [Grand Rapids: Eerdmans, 1964], 1:380–81).

16. The two related nouns *hypantēsis* and *apantēsis* also occur in Jesus's parable of the wise and foolish virgins (or bridesmaids) in Matt. 25:1–13 (vv. 1, 6, respectively). The wise ones, who were prepared for the bridegroom's coming, "went out to meet him" (Matt. 25:6) and then escorted him to the wedding banquet.

It was customary for people to vie for pride of place in meeting the coming dignitary, hence Paul's assurance in 1 Thessalonians 4:15–16 that Christians who had already died would not be inconvenienced at this great event; rather, they would rise first (and thus be the first to meet the coming king). Since cemeteries were located outside city walls in the first century, often lining the main road leading to the city, Paul's readers could vividly imagine the scenario of the dead in Christ being raised as the king passed by, before those in the city went out to meet him as he approached the city gates.[17] This also makes sense of Paul's statement that "God will bring with him [Christ] those who have died" (1 Thess. 4:14); this suggests that those raised from the graves, who have met the returning Lord, will then enter the city with him.

The most important point in the foregoing scenario is that those who went out to meet the dignitary returned with him, escorting him in grand procession into their city.[18] In this case, this clearly means an escort to earth.[19]

Beyond the background custom of an imperial visit (represented by *parousia* and *apantēsis*) and the clear biblical teaching of the redemption of creation, there are further reasons to doubt that in 1 Thessalonians 4:13–18 Paul means to teach the rapture, as classically understood. First, the rapture is supposed to be a secret event, yet the coming of Christ in this text is announced with great fanfare, "with a cry of command, with the archangel's call and with the sound of God's trumpet" (v. 16). This is similar to the sound of the trumpet in 1 Corinthians 15:51–52, which describes the suddenness of Christ's coming, accompanied by the transformation of living believers and the resurrection of those who have died.

> Listen, I will tell you a mystery! We will not all die, but we will all be changed, in a moment, in the twinkling of an eye, at the last trumpet. For the trumpet will sound, and the dead will be raised imperishable, and we will be changed. (1 Cor. 15:51–52)

Furthermore, in its most popular form, the rapture is meant to remove living believers from earth so that the tribulation can begin (all dead believers are already in heaven). But in 1 Thessalonians 4 Paul speaks of both dead and

17. See also Koester, "Imperial Ideology," 160.
18. Green, *Thessalonians*, 228.
19. For more on the rapture and *apantēsis* in 1 Thess. 4, see Míguez, *Practice of Hope*, 142–44, "Excursus 1: On the Rapture"; also Robert H. Gundry, "The Hellenization of Dominical Tradition and Christianization of Jewish Tradition in the Eschatology of 1–2 Thessalonians," in *The Old Is Better: New Testament Essays in Support of Traditional Interpretations* (Wissenschaftliche Untersuchungen zum Neuen Testament 178; Tübingen: Mohr Siebeck, 2005).

living believers rising to meet Christ. The text is thus not about removal of believers from earth at all. Like 1 Corinthians 15, it addresses the resurrection of the dead and transformation of the living that will accompany Christ's decisive coming as Lord to judge the world and make all things new.[20]

Matthew 24:40–41

The other standard proof text for the rapture in popular eschatology is Matthew 24:40–41 (along with its parallel in Luke 17:34–35). In these texts Jesus explains what will happen when the Son of Man returns.[21]

According to Matthew 24:40–41, "Then two will be in the field; one will be taken and one will be left. Two women will be grinding meal together; one will be taken and one will be left." Luke 17:34–35 is similar: "I tell you, on that night there will be two in one bed; one will be taken and the other left. There will be two women grinding meal together; one will be taken and the other left." The common assumption of many biblical interpreters is that the one "taken" is the believer, going to heaven to be with the Lord. And this is identified with the "rapture" in 1 Thessalonians 4:17.

The problem is that we do not typically read these texts carefully enough. Let us pay close attention to the comparison Jesus makes in Matthew 24. He begins by describing what life was like in the time of Noah, when people did not expect the flood (vv. 37–39). Jesus's point in verse 39 is that just as the people of Noah's time "knew nothing until the flood came and swept them all away, so too will be the coming of the Son of Man."

Note carefully who is taken away, according to Jesus. The phrase "swept them all away" clearly describes judgment on the wicked; it was Noah and his family who were left on the earth after the flood. Thus, when Jesus introduces the eschatological equivalent to the days of Noah (in vv. 40–41), the analogy he draws between the two events makes it clear that the ones taken are the unrighteous: they are taken to judgment.

If we doubt this interpretation, we need only turn to Luke's version of this text, for he follows the narrative of one taken and one left (in 17:34–35) with a question from the disciples in verse 37.[22] "Where, Lord?" they ask. That is, where are they taken? Jesus replies, "Where the corpse is, there the vultures will gather." This is clearly a reference to judgment; the image is certainly not of

---

20. This also suggests that those who use 1 Cor. 15:51–52 as a supporting text to teach the rapture are on the wrong track.

21. Brian Walsh and I first addressed this putative "rapture" text in *The Transforming Vision: Shaping a Christian World View* (Downers Grove, IL: IVP Academic, 1984), 103–4.

22. Luke 17:36 is missing from the best Greek manuscripts.

"heaven."[23] We should not be surprised by this, for the same Jesus who taught about the last days in Matthew 24 proclaimed in the Beatitudes: "Blessed are the meek, for they will inherit the earth" (Matt. 5:5).[24]

Here we should observe that the two Greek verbs Jesus uses in Matthew 24:39–41 (*airō* and *paralambanō*), translated, respectively, as "swept away" and "taken" in the NRSV are rendered (respectively) as "taken away" and "taken" in the KJV and the NIV. This should have made Jesus's point even more obvious for readers of those translations. The fact that so many have misread who is taken and who is left, despite such clear verbal clues, is a powerful example of how our assumptions about what a text says can predetermine what we see in the text.

Although Matthew 24:40–41 is often used to support the rapture in popular eschatology (which is why I have addressed it here), it is significant that this text is not typically appealed to by dispensationalist theologians and Bible scholars (even though the rapture is a distinctively dispensationalist doctrine).[25] Even Hal Lindsey's bestseller, *The Late, Great Planet Earth*, which resolutely emphasizes the rapture, never appeals to the verses about being "taken" in Matthew 24 or Luke 17. These verses are also notably absent from the discussion in both the first and second editions of *Three Views of the Rapture* (1984, 1996) published by Zondervan in its Counterpoints series; indeed, when the introduction to the second edition lists texts that either explicitly or implicitly teach the rapture, Matthew 24:36–42 is not on the list.[26]

Although early dispensationalists such as John Nelson Darby and William E. Blackstone cited this text in arguing for the rapture,[27] as early as 1925 dispensationalists had begun to back off from using it as part of their argument.[28] And by the mid-twentieth century the majority of dispensationalists

---

23. The image that Jesus alludes to is the valley of Ben-Hinnom (*gê' ben-hinnōm* or Gehenna), southwest of Jerusalem, which had become the city dump in the Second Temple period, used for incinerating garbage, dead animals, and executed criminals. In the Old Testament the valley of Ben-Hinnom is associated with idolatry and child sacrifice (by burning) to Baal or Molech.

24. See the cartoon in chap. 3 above, where one character says that the Bible predicts the destruction of the earth; to which another character replies, "Do the meek know this?"

25. For more on dispensationalism and the rapture, see the appendix to this book.

26. Craig Blaising, Alan Hultberg, and Douglas Moo, *Three Views of the Rapture: Pretribulation, Prewrath, or Posttribulation* (Counterpoints: Bible and Theology; Grand Rapids: Zondervan, 2010), 11–12, from the introduction, written by Hultberg.

27. J. N. Darby, *Collected Writings* (Oak Park, IL: Bible Truth Publishers, 1882), 2:290–300; 11:118–67; 24:219–32; 30:166–67, 286–301; William E. Blackstone, *Jesus Is Coming* (New York: Revell, 1908), 63–66, 135.

28. Arno C. Gaebelein, *The Olivet Discourse* (Greenville, SC: The Gospel Hour, 1925), 77–108.

had come to the conclusion that Matthew 24:36–42 did not address the rapture at all, conceding instead that it referred to events after the tribulation.[29] Thus, dispensationalist John F. Walvoord critiques those who use this text to support the rapture, emphatically stating, "Those taken away were taken away in judgment."[30]

The fact that a rapture interpretation of Matthew 24:40–41 (// Luke 17:34–35) persists in the North American evangelical tradition indicates how far this tradition has departed from the classic tenets of dispensationalism. I, for one, agree with those contemporary dispensationalists who affirm that Matthew 24 does not teach the rapture.[31] And if neither 1 Thessalonians 4 nor Matthew 24 teaches the rapture, we have no good reason to think that this idea is any part of biblical eschatology.

Will We Go to Heaven (Temporarily) When We Die?

But what about texts that seem to promise heaven immediately at death? Do the righteous go to heaven when they die? This is an important question for many Christians. Although speculation about end-times prophecies and events—such as the antichrist, the tribulation, the millennium—gained in popularity throughout the twentieth century, not all Christians throughout history (or even in recent times) have been enamored of such speculation. Instead, it has been more typical for those looking to the future to focus on what happens at death (often called "personal eschatology"). For many Christians throughout

29. See Stanley Toussaint, "Are the Church and the Rapture in Matthew 24?," in *The Return: Understanding Christ's Second Coming and the End Times*, ed. Thomas Ice and Timothy J. Demy (Grand Rapids: Kregel, 1999), 121–36. For his summary account of this shift within dispensationalism, I am indebted to R. Todd Mangum, "High Hopes for 21st-Century Dispensationalism: A Response to 'Hope and Dispensationalism: An Historical Overview and Assessment' (by Gary L. Nebeker)" (paper presented to the Dispensational Study Group of the Evangelical Theological Society, Nashville, TN, November 2000, 13–14n21).

30. John F. Walvoord, *The Blessed Hope and the Tribulation: A Historical and Biblical Study of Posttribulationalism* (Grand Rapids: Zondervan, 1976), 89.

31. For the popularity of the rapture interpretation of Matt. 24:40–41 // Luke 17:34–35, we need to turn to Larry Norman's famous 1969 song, "I Wish We'd All Been Ready," released on what is usually regarded as the first Christian rock album (*Upon This Rock* [Capitol Records, 1969]). After evoking the great tribulation in the first verse of the song, the second verse is a poetic restatement of Luke 17:34: "A man and wife asleep in bed, / She hears a noise and turns her head, he's gone; / I wish we'd all been ready. / Two men walking up a hill, / One disappears and one's left standing still; / I wish we'd all been ready." According to Norman, the song "talked about something I had never heard preached from a pulpit as I grew up" (a comment he made in 1969: http://everything2.com/title/Larry+Norman). The chorus ("There's no time to change your mind, / The Son has come and you've been left behind") arguably generated the title of the Left Behind series of books and movies.

the ages, postmortem blessedness in heaven has been the most important part of the Christian hope.

Yet we have seen that the general thrust of biblical eschatology is that at Christ's return God will raise the faithful to new life (resurrection) and redeem the cosmos, resulting in a new creation. What, then, are we to do with biblical texts that seem to hold out the hope for heaven immediately at death? How do such texts fit into the overall biblical hope of a new heaven and earth?

One approach is to admit that such texts refer not to the final state but rather to a temporary period of blessedness between death and resurrection, often described as the interim or intermediate state.[32] Let us take a look at the most obvious of such texts to see how they might fit into the biblical hope of a new creation.

John 14:1–3

Perhaps the most commonly cited text that seems to point to the promise of heaven hereafter is John 14:1–3:

> Do not let your hearts be troubled. Believe in God, believe also in me. In my Father's house there are many dwelling places. If it were not so, would I have told you that I go to prepare a place for you? And if I go and prepare a place for you, I will come again and will take you to myself, so that where I am, there you may be also. (John 14:1–3)

We have already examined these verses as part of the apocalyptic pattern of preparation in heaven for revelation on earth. When read as part of this pattern, Jesus's words of comfort to his disciples do not mean that he is going to take them to heaven, but only that this is where the preparations are being made for the last day; biblical expectation suggests that Jesus will be with us in the renewed creation.

But might Jesus be implying that in the interim time (between death and resurrection) his disciples would be with him in heaven? The only support for this possibility is that the term "dwelling places" (*monai*; singular *monē*) in John 14:2 could refer to temporary resting places (such as rooms in an inn); so this could conceivably mean that while preparing the final cosmic redemption, Jesus is also preparing an interim stopping place after death for his disciples.[33]

---

32. Since the intermediate state is typically referred to as "life after death," N. T. Wright is famous for speaking of the resurrection and renewed creation as "life *after* life after death" (*Surprised by Hope: Rethinking Heaven, the Resurrection, and the Mission of the Church* [San Francisco: HarperOne, 2008], 148, 151, 169, 197–98, 231).

33. Evidence for this meaning of *monē* is based on extrabiblical Greek, and it is sometimes linked to an Aramaic word that can "refer to a night-stop or resting place for a traveler on a

Yet the evidence for this meaning of *monē* is far from certain, especially given that later in the same chapter Jesus uses this same term for what does not seem temporary: his dwelling with the disciples through the Spirit. In John 14:23 Jesus promises those who obey him that both he and the Father will come to them "and make our home [*monē*] with them."[34] Beyond the expected permanence of this dwelling, we might note Jesus promising that he will come to the disciples rather than the disciples going to him.

Indeed, we might even suggest that Jesus's use of the phrase "my Father's house" in John 14:2 is not a decisive reference to heaven at all (although many interpreters take it as a reference to the heavenly sanctuary). This phrase could just as easily refer to the entire cosmos, since heaven and earth are together described as God's "house" or temple in Isaiah 66:1.[35] In other words, against the backdrop of the wider biblical worldview, John 14:1–3 could simply mean that Jesus is preparing (in heaven) the final redemption of the cosmos as a fitting place for God to dwell, in which there will be plenty of room for all his disciples.

2 Corinthians 5:6–9

But if John 14:1–3 does not unambiguously teach the intermediate state, what about 2 Corinthians 5:6–9? More than any other, this New Testament text seems clearly to indicate a blessed hope in heaven immediately after death.

Indeed, the literary context of these verses in 2 Corinthians seems to support an otherworldly orientation. In an extended discussion stretching from 4:8 to 5:10, Paul appears to contrast bodily life in the present with a heavenly, eternal future. At the end of chapter 4 he speaks of our outer nature wasting away, while our inner nature is being renewed (v. 16), and he contrasts what

---

journey" (Raymond E. Brown, *The Gospel according to John: Introduction, Translation, and Notes* [Anchor Bible 29–29A; Garden City, NY: Doubleday, 1966–70], 2:618n2). However, while *monē* can be used to refer to a temporary dwelling, it certainly is not limited to this meaning.

34. Furthermore, this noun is cognate to the verb *menō* ("dwell, abide, remain"), which is often used in the Gospel of John for the (enduring) relationship of Jesus to the Father and of both to the disciples (14:10, 17; 15:4–10). Just like the noun, the verb can be used to refer to a temporary or permanent dwelling.

35. Given the centrality of this concept in biblical theology (see the discussion in chap. 8 above), it is perplexing that J. Ramsey Michaels comments (in connection with John 1) that "it is hard to see how 'the world' (v. 10) can be viewed as 'home' to the Word"; it is "not his 'home' in the sense of either place of origin or permanent dwelling" (*The Gospel of John* [New International Commentary on the New Testament; Grand Rapids: Eerdmans, 2010], 66). Clearly, Jesus's origin as the Word is from heaven (not from this world [John 8:23]), but he has indeed come to make this world his permanent dwelling.

is seen and transitory with what is unseen and eternal (v. 18). It makes perfect sense, then, that in chapter 5 Paul would say,

> So we are always confident; even though we know that while we are at home in the body we are away from the Lord—for we walk by faith, not by sight. Yes, we do have confidence, and we would rather be away from the body and at home with the Lord. So whether we are at home or away, we make it our aim to please him. (2 Cor. 5:6–9)

On the surface, these verses seem to emphasize a heavenly future. Does Paul not say plainly that he would prefer to be "at home with the Lord" (presumably in heaven) than in his present body (on earth)? Does this not clearly teach the hope of heaven that begins immediately at death (when we are separated from our bodies)?

Not necessarily. By now we should be just a bit suspicious of our habituated approach to such texts, given the biblical teaching of God's plan to redeem creation.

The first thing we should note is how Paul has already stated in 5:1–2 that his actual hope is for the heavenly dwelling that God has prepared (the resurrection body), and in 5:3–4 he affirms that he does not want to be "naked" or "unclothed" (disembodied). And yet Paul says that he prefers to be away from the (present) body and at home with the Lord (5:8). Could Paul have contradictory hopes? Does Paul long for the resurrection while shunning a disembodied state and at the same time prefer a disembodied state to his present life? Perhaps he has a hierarchy: the resurrected body, then a disembodied state in heaven, then the present earthly body. Many read the text this way.

However, we do not need such an artificial solution to this seeming contradiction. Rather, we need to pay attention to Paul's key statement near the end of chapter 4 about the basis of his hope even amid tribulations and suffering (vv. 8–12). The reason why Paul says he can live faithfully in the midst of suffering is this: "We know that the one who raised the Lord Jesus will raise us also with Jesus, and will bring us with you into his presence" (v. 14). There is no separation here of resurrection and being with Christ. Not only does Paul look forward to the resurrection but he also conceives of being in a resurrected (embodied) state in the Lord's presence.

This means that when Paul comes to speak of being "at home with the Lord" in 5:8, there is no reason to separate this from his hope of resurrection (except that we are habituated to reading the text this way). Paul is not speaking of being with Christ immediately at death; rather, he is looking to the second coming, at which time we will be raised and be with Christ in the new creation.

A plain reading of 5:6–9 in the context of 5:1–2 and 4:14 thus suggests that being at home with the Lord is nothing other than Paul's expectation that the Lord will dwell with redeemed humanity in a new creation. Thus it is not at all clear that 2 Corinthians 5 actually teaches an interim (disembodied) state as any part of the Christian hope.

Philippians 1:23

We can make a similar point about Philippians 1:23, where Paul links death to being "with Christ" (hence, "dying is gain" [1:21]). In context (vv. 21–24), Paul refers to his dilemma of remaining for ministry with the church at Philippi or going to be with Christ.

> For to me, living is Christ and dying is gain. If I am to live in the flesh, that means fruitful labor for me; and I do not know which I prefer. I am hard pressed between the two: my desire is to depart and be with Christ, for that is far better; but to remain in the flesh is more necessary for you. (Phil. 1:21–24)

While interpreters often take Paul as expressing a preference for death ("my desire is to depart and be with Christ" [v. 23]), since it would usher him into the immediate presence of Christ, the text does not actually say that it would be immediate. Yes, he wants to be "with Christ," but he does not elaborate on where or exactly when this will be. Once again, the rest of Scripture would lead us to expect that Paul is thinking of the eschaton. There is no clear teaching here of any interim state in heaven.

And if an interim state is not clearly taught in these three texts (John 14:1–3; 2 Cor. 5:6–9; Phil. 1:23), we should be very careful in trying to derive such teaching from less clear texts, such as Luke 16:19–31 and Revelation 6:9–10.

Luke 16:19–31

The reference to Lazarus in the bosom of Abraham in Luke 16:19–31 is a vivid, imaginative picture used in a parable by Jesus to make a particular point about the finality of judgment (and the delusions of wealth). Or are we to believe that he meant to teach that those in Hades (awaiting final judgment) can actually see (across a distance) the righteous in close proximity to Abraham (hence "in his bosom" [KJV])? While Jesus may indeed be drawing on traditional Jewish understandings of the afterlife,[36] his point has to do with the

36. Several possible parallels about the afterlife could be considered. The picture of the wicked and the righteous in separate compartments of Hades reflects both *1 Enoch* and the *Apocalypse*

finality of death and the futility of thinking that someone coming back from the dead could lead to the repentance of the living.[37] As one scholar puts it, "In this parable, Jesus no more provides information about the intermediate state than, in other parables, does he provide instruction on correct agricultural practices (Luke 15:4–6) or investing tips (Luke 16:1–13)."[38] We simply cannot base belief in an intermediate state on this parable, especially in the absence of clear teaching elsewhere in the New Testament.[39]

Revelation 6:9–10

Likewise, the reference to the "souls" of the martyrs under the altar in Revelation 6:9–10 is of little help, since these righteous dead are clearly not at peace (as in the traditional picture of heaven), but rather are crying out, "How long?" on behalf of those suffering on earth. Indeed, the Old Testament emphasis on the connection between life and blood (the life [nepeš] is in the blood, according to Lev. 17:11) might lead to an interpretation of the souls in Revelation 6 as not much different from the blood of slain Abel crying out from the ground (Gen. 4:10).[40] Even John Cooper, whose book Body, Soul,

---

of Zephaniah. In 1 Enoch 22 (about 160 BC) the author describes four hollow sections in Sheol that are separated from each other, two for the wicked and two for the righteous. Likewise, the Apocalypse of Zephaniah (a Jewish text with Christian additions, dated between 100 BC and 70 AD) portrays the souls of the wicked suffering in fiery Hades (chap. 6), with the place of the righteous separated from this by a river, which Zephaniah crosses in a boat (8:1; 9:1–2); on the other side are Abraham, Isaac, and Jacob, along with Enoch, Elijah, and David (9:4).

The term "Abraham's bosom" could be connected to the notion that Abraham, Isaac, and Jacob would receive those Jews martyred for their faith (4 Macc. 13:17). In the long recension of the Testament of Abraham 20:14 (a first- or second-century AD Jewish work with Christian additions), God tells Michael and the other angels to take Abraham (at his death) to the place of the righteous, with "Isaac and Jacob in his bosom" (the ungrammatical and clumsy feel of the entire sentence, along with the issue of Abraham going to join his sons who are already in his bosom, suggests that this is an addition; indeed, it is followed by a reference to the Christian Trinity). Later rabbinic works, such as Qiddušin 72b in the Babylonian Talmud and Lamentations Rabbah 1.85, also mention the "bosom of Abraham." And Hippolytus of Rome (a third-century Christian) distinguishes between two sections of Hades, one for the wicked, the other for the righteous who are awaiting resurrection, and calls the latter "Abraham's bosom" (Against Plato, On the Cause of the Universe, chap. 1); note that even in the third century, this is pictured as a section of Hades and not heaven.

37. Part of Jesus's point is that if the living do not attend to the Scriptures (Moses and the prophets), then even a resurrection from the dead will not open their eyes (v. 31).

38. Tony Wright, "Death, the Dead and the Underworld in Biblical Theology, Part 2," Churchman 122 (2008): 114.

39. Not to mention that the righteous in the parable are not in heaven but rather in a compartment of Hades.

40. The Hebrew word for "life" (nepeš) is often translated by the Greek psychē (also in the Septuagint of Lev. 17:11), and the plural of this term (psychas) is used in Rev. 6:9 for those who cry out; the word for the "blood" of Abel is also plural in Gen. 4:10.

and Life Everlasting is a concerted defense of a "dualistic" understanding of the person (including an intermediate state of disembodied existence), admits that Revelation 6 cannot be used to support his position, given the imaginative nature of apocalyptic symbolism.[41]

Luke 23:39–43

But surely Luke 23:39–43 teaches an intermediate state in the account of Jesus's interaction with the criminal (traditionally, the "thief") on the cross. When the criminal pleads, "Jesus, remember me when you come into your kingdom" (v. 42), Jesus answers, "Truly I tell you, today you will be with me in Paradise" (v. 43).

To understand this text properly, we first need to address the common assumption of many readers that the "kingdom" in verse 42 is the same as "paradise" in verse 43, and that both refer to the afterlife. However, the "kingdom" that Jesus will come into is nothing other than his messianic rule over the world, which will be established at his return; the term does not refer to the life after death at all.[42]

Perhaps, then, Jesus is telling the criminal that he does not need to wait for the eschaton; he already has access to paradise "today," in the sense that he will go directly to heaven at death. Of course, this hinges on the question of whether "today" goes grammatically with "I tell you" or "you will be with me in Paradise" (the Greek can be taken either way). Assuming that Jesus is affirming an immediate place with him in paradise, there are still two complicating issues for taking this as reference to a disembodied existence between death and resurrection.

First of all, as we saw in the discussion of the new Jerusalem (in chap. 8), the Greek word *paradeisos* ("paradise") is how the Septuagint translates the Hebrew word for "garden" (*gan*), as in the garden of Eden account in Genesis 2–3. According to the end of Genesis 3, humanity was expelled from the garden and denied access to the tree of life, and the way was guarded by cherubim and a flaming sword (vv. 23–24).

Various Second Temple Jewish traditions thus developed about the inaccessibility of paradise and the tree of life (some of these texts are contemporaneous with the New Testament, some earlier, some later). These traditions centered on the idea that God took the garden/paradise up into heaven or removed it to the top of a high mountain (in the sky/heaven) or at the ends of the earth,

---

41. John W. Cooper, *Body, Soul, and Life Everlasting: Biblical Anthropology and the Monism-Dualism Debate* (2nd ed.; Grand Rapids: Eerdmans, 2000), 117.

42. For a fuller discussion of Jesus's understanding of the kingdom of God, see chap. 11.

in order to guarantee its continued inaccessibility—until the last day, when it would be revealed upon the earth.[43] Speculation also arose as to whether Enoch, whom God "took" (Gen. 5:24), and Elijah, who was taken upward in a fiery chariot (2 Kings 2:11), thereby entered paradise. Speculation about Enoch and Elijah seems to have assumed that they entered paradise in bodily form (since they had not died), which makes sense of the fact that this term (paradise) refers to the primal earthly state of blessedness. Yet other Second Temple speculation about paradise (under the influence of Platonism) thinks that the souls or spirits of the righteous dead are there, awaiting resurrection.[44]

This is clearly not the place for an extended discussion of Second Temple Jewish speculation on this question, and it is enough to recognize that the core idea of "paradise" is the earthly blessedness that the human race lost and that is being prepared by God for the righteous, to be enjoyed in the eschaton on a renewed earth.[45] This means that we can easily add paradise to the list of items that the New Testament says are prepared by God for eschatological unveiling. It is part of the apocalyptic pattern. And this fits the book of Revelation, where Jesus promises the church at Ephesus, "To everyone who

43. In 4 Ezra 4:7–8 paradise seems to be located in the heavens (above the firmament), while in 2 Enoch 8–9 Enoch is taken up into the "third heaven," from which he looks down at paradise (a fruitful garden, with the tree of life), which is distinguished from the earth, although its roots go down to the earth. Paradise seems to be located between the third heaven (identified with incorruptibility) and the earth (identified with corruptibility). The Apocalypse of Moses (a Greek work, also known in a longer Latin version called The Life of Adam and Eve) distinguishes between two paradises, the original "paradise on the earth" (38:5) and the "paradise in the third heaven" (40:2). The former is the paradise from which Adam was expelled (1:1; 28:1–4; 29:2, 7; 42:6); the latter is the promised inheritance of "the holy people," which they will enjoy at the resurrection, "at the end of times," along with the tree of life (13:2–3; 28:4). When Paul is forced to "boast" to the Corinthians, he speaks (in the third person) of an ineffable experience that he had in "Paradise" (2 Cor. 12:4), which he assumes was in "the third heaven" (12:2).

44. The Apocalypse of Moses has Adam's body buried in the original earthly paradise (38:1–5), while his soul is taken up into the paradise in the third heaven until the day of judgment (37:4–5). In the Testament of Abraham, Abraham is carried up by a chariot of cherubim on a cloud into the sky (chap. 10), to "the first gate of heaven" to see the judgment that happens to souls after death, where he sees the narrow gate leading to life "and they that enter through it go into Paradise" (chap. 11). Later we are told that a soul saved at the judgment is taken by an angel, who "carried it up into Paradise" (chap. 14). When Paul recounts his unusual experience of paradise, he twice says he is unsure about whether it was in the body or out of the body (2 Cor. 12:2–3).

45. While 2 Enoch 9:1 describes paradise as the "place . . . prepared for the righteous," for their "eternal inheritance," 2 Baruch 4 speaks in similar terms of both paradise and a city to come (equivalent to the new Jerusalem in Rev. 21). The latter text (2 Baruch) says that the true city (surpassing present Jerusalem) was "prepared beforehand," at the time when God decided to make paradise, and it was shown to Adam before he sinned (4:3); then both city and paradise were removed from Adam when he sinned (4:3); but both city and paradise are "preserved" with God until the last day (4:6).

conquers, I will give permission to eat from the tree of life that is in the paradise of God" (2:7); and then in chapters 21–22 there is a vision of the new Jerusalem, intertwined with elements of paradise/the garden (including the tree of life), "coming down out of heaven from God."[46]

Although there might be an argument for understanding the temporary location of paradise in heaven, as part of what God is preparing for the saints, paradise is not simply equivalent to heaven. More to the point, paradise is not (in either Jewish literature or the New Testament) an immaterial realm or place, which is the way that heaven is typically conceived in contemporary Christian theology. Even Origen, the church father with the clearest commitment to Platonism, understands the "paradise" promised to the saints as "some place situated on the earth."[47]

But beyond the issue of the concrete, earthly character of paradise, there is still the complicated question of what it might mean that the criminal would be there with Jesus "today" (Luke 23:42). Jesus's assurance that they would both be in paradise immediately at death (which is what "today" seems to mean) confuses matters considerably. It is difficult to harmonize with the New Testament's own reckoning that Jesus was not raised until the third day and did not ascend to heaven for some time after that (Luke 24:50–53; Acts 1:9–11; see also Mark 16:19).[48] Given this complication, Luke 23:42 might actually be used to support the notion of "soul sleep," the idea that there is no consciousness of the intermediate state, but that one moves subjectively from death to resurrection. This might make sense of Paul's seeming expectation (in 2 Cor. 5:5–6 and Phil. 1:23) of the immediate presence of Christ at death even while conceiving this presence as happening at the eschaton, in a resurrected body. Perhaps Oscar Cullmann is right about the interim state: "We wait, and *the*

---

46. An ancient epitaph on the gravestone of a Christian named "Leontius" (possibly from the fifth century) aptly portrays the concreteness of paradise:

O God, give him rest with the devout and the just
in the place where green things grow
and refreshment is and water,
the delightful garden
where pain and grief and sighing
are unknown.
Holy, holy, holy Lord God, Sabaoth;
heaven and earth are full of your holy glory.

This prayer is from *Early Christian Prayers*, ed. A. Hamman, trans. Walter Mitchell (Chicago: Henry Regnery; London: Longmans, Green, 1961), 84.

47. This is why he is constrained to portray the afterlife in terms of a journey from paradise to heaven; it is unthinkable for him that earth could be the final destiny for those who are truly spiritual. See Origen, *On First Principles* 2.11.6–7.

48. Mark 16:9–20 is generally regarded as not original to Mark's Gospel.

dead wait. Of course, the rhythm of time may be different for them than for
the living; and in this way the interim-time may be shortened for them."[49] Or
as F. F. Bruce puts it, "The tension created by the postulated interval between
death and resurrection might be relieved today if it were suggested that in the
consciousness of the departed believer there is no interval between dissolution
and investiture, however long an interval might be measured by the calendar
of earth-bound human history."[50]

When I began research on the intermediate state, I was ready to concede
that there might be some sporadic evidence in the New Testament that pointed
to such a state, even though it was clear from Scripture that this was not the
emphasis of Christian hope. I was prepared to concur with C. S. Lewis's classic
statement: "The earliest Christian documents give a casual and unemphatic
assent to the belief that the supernatural part of a man survives the death of
the natural organism. But they are very little interested in the matter. What
they are intensely interested in is the restoration or 'resurrection' of the whole
composite creature by a miraculous divine act."[51]

Lewis is correct about where the focus of New Testament interest lies, but
I now think he may have conceded too much in his comment about "casual
and unemphatic assent" to personal survival at death.[52] Having studied the
relevant texts, I am surprised at how little evidence there actually is for an
interim state in the New Testament, certainly less than I had expected.[53] In the
end, however, it does not matter. Authentic Christian hope does not depend
on an intermediate state; nor do Christians need the Platonic notion of an immortal soul in order to guarantee personal continuity between present earthly
existence and future resurrection life. The God who brought the universe into
being is the guarantor of the eschatological future. In the memorable words of
2 Timothy 1:12 (which became the refrain of a famous 1883 hymn by Daniel W.

49. Oscar Cullmann, *Immortality of the Soul or Resurrection of the Dead? The Witness of
the New Testament* (London: Epworth, 1958), 57 (emphasis in original).

50. F. F. Bruce, *Paul, Apostle of the Heart Set Free* (Grand Rapids: Eerdmans, 1977), 312n40.

51. C. S. Lewis, *Miracles: A Preliminary Study* (London: Fontana, 1960 [1947]), 33.

52. And this is even apart from Lewis's use of the quite unbiblical categories of "supernatural"
and "natural" (categories that developed in medieval philosophy and theology); such categories
are inappropriate because there is nothing "supernatural" (transcending the natural) about any
part of being human. We are simply creatures, dependent on the grace and power of God for
existence and flourishing.

53. An implication of my discussion here is that N. T. Wright (a scholar for whom I have
the utmost regard) may also have conceded too much in his claim that Second Temple Judaism
and the New Testament typically assume an intermediate state. Nevertheless, Wright correctly
warns that concern with "life after death" (the intermediate state) can be "a serious distraction"
both from the biblical concern with resurrection and new creation ("life *after* life after death")
and from "life *before* death" (*Surprised by Hope*, 197–98).

Whittle): "I know whom I have believed, and am persuaded that he is able to keep that which I have committed unto him against that day" (KJV). We place our hope in the God of Jesus Christ, the Lord of the universe, who is able to raise the dead and who has promised to renew heaven and earth.

Whatever we think about the intermediate state (and I acknowledge that belief in such a state is dear to many Christians), it is clear from Scripture that heaven is not the final destination of the redeemed. This is the upshot of those biblical texts that explicitly promise a new creation, and it is confirmed by an examination of supposed counterexamples to a holistic vision of redemption. A close reading of texts that seem to promise heaven hereafter reveals that they simply do not teach an otherworldly destiny for redeemed humanity. Rather, these "problem" texts fit remarkably well with the dominant tenor of Scripture, which portrays the redemption of the entire created order and human redemption as the restoration of bodily life on earth—that is, the renewal of God's creational intent from the beginning.

Not only is the term "heaven" never used in Scripture for the eternal destiny of the redeemed, but also continued use of "heaven" to name the Christian eschatological hope may well divert our attention from the legitimate expectation for the present transformation of our earthly life to conform to God's purposes. Indeed, to focus our expectation on an otherworldly salvation has the potential to dissipate our resistance to societal evil and the dedication needed to work for the redemptive transformation of this world. Therefore, for reasons exegetical, theological, and ethical, I have come to repent of using the term "heaven" to describe the future God has in store for the faithful. It is my hope that readers of this book would, after thoughtful consideration, join me in this repentance.

Part 5

The Ethics
of the Kingdom

11

The Good News at Nazareth

I n this book I have been laying the foundation for a biblical eschatology that clarifies God's consistent intentions for redeeming this world he loves. To that end, chapter 1 addressed the problem of otherworldly expectation, while chapters 2 and 3 explored the human calling in God's world and sketched an overview of the core plot of the biblical story, from creation to eschaton. Chapters 4 through 6 then focused on relevant elements of Old Testament theology to illustrate the scriptural vision of holistic, earthly flourishing. Chapters 7 through 10 then turned to the New Testament to examine eschatology proper, clarifying the inner logic of resurrection hope and displaying God's intent to redeem the created order, including humanity and the earth.

It is now time to ask, "So what?" What are some of the ethical implications of this holistic vision of a new creation? Although some reflections on living out holistic eschatology have been touched on at various points along the way, it is time to address the ethics of holistic eschatology more intentionally.

But how do we approach this massive subject? It is impossible to answer this question comprehensively in a short space, since the implications of holistic eschatology are legion, impacting every aspect of human life. One way to focus the question, however, is to examine Jesus's teaching at Nazareth, at the start of his public ministry (Luke 4:16–30), as a case study in the ethics of the kingdom. Not only does this episode contain a programmatic statement of Jesus's mission at the start of the Gospel of Luke, clarifying some of the core ethical implications of salvation, but also it introduces us to the powerful biblical concept of the kingdom God.[1] In this chapter and the next, we will look at the two sides of Jesus's proclamation at Nazareth: first the good news of the kingdom, then the radical challenge that the kingdom brings.

The Kingdom of God Is at Hand

In the Synoptic Gospels (Matthew, Mark, Luke) Jesus begins his public ministry by announcing the good news that God's kingdom is near. Having remained out of the public eye for thirty years, this Galilean carpenter leaves his home in Nazareth and travels to the Jordan River to be baptized by a fiery Jewish preacher, John, who likewise has been proclaiming the kingdom and gathering converts.[2] As Jesus comes up out of the water, a voice from heaven announces that he is God's beloved "Son" (a standard messianic term in the first century).[3] Jesus is then led by God's Spirit into the Judean wilderness for forty days of fasting and testing. During this time he is confronted by the devil and successfully resists a series of temptations about the nature of the kingdom and his role in it as God's Son. Jesus then returns to Galilee in the power of God's Spirit, with a riveting message: "The time is fulfilled, and the kingdom of God is at hand; repent and believe in the gospel" (Mark 1:15).

What did Jesus mean by the "kingdom of God"? And how does this help us understand the topic of this book—holistic eschatology? To begin with, we need to be clear what Jesus did not mean. As Walter Rauschenbusch colorfully puts it, the Christian faith "was born of revolutionary lineage. Its cradle was rocked by the storm wind of popular hopes. What was it that brought the multitudes to the Jordan to hear John and that thrilled the throngs that followed Jesus about in Galilee? Was it the desire to go to heaven one by one when they died?"[4] That would be, Rauschenbusch rightly acknowledges, a

1. This passage from Luke's Gospel was also what first clarified for me the holistic vision of Scripture and sparked my interest in an alternative to otherworldly eschatology. I wrote two papers on Luke 4 during my final year as an undergraduate student in Jamaica, one for a Greek exegesis course and one for a philosophy course that addressed a Christian worldview.

2. Although it is traditional to refer to Jesus as a carpenter, the actual term used in the Gospels is *tektōn* (Mark 6:3; cf. Matt. 13:55), which could refer to any sort of artisan or builder, including a stonemason (though carpenter is not thereby excluded).

3. References to God's "son" do not always have a messianic meaning in the Old Testament. The term is applied to Israel (Exod. 4:22; Hosea 11:1), angelic beings (Job 38:7), and the Davidic king (2 Sam. 7:14; Pss. 2:6–12; 89:25–27); this last use is the basis of the term taking on a messianic meaning (see, for example, 1QSamuel 2.11–12 in the Dead Sea Scrolls).

4. Walter Rauschenbusch, *Christianizing the Social Order* (New York: Macmillan, 1912), 48–49.

fundamental misinterpretation, forcing the New Testament to conform to later, unbiblical eschatological ideas. It would also ignore Jesus's own context.

So what did Jesus mean?

The Ancient Jewish Background of the Kingdom of God

Jesus did not invent the idea of the kingdom of God out of thin air; rather, he drew upon a long and ancient tradition stretching far back into the Old Testament. It is true that God is only rarely called "king" or said to "rule" in the Pentateuch (Genesis through Deuteronomy) and the Former Prophets (Joshua through Kings). Nevertheless, the underlying idea of God as ruler and judge of Israel, indeed of all creation, is a basic background assumption of the entire Old Testament.[5] This idea shows up especially in the pervasive understanding of God as lawgiver, to whom both Israel and all creation owe obedience. Whether in the Torah given through the covenant that God establishes with Israel or in the analogous language of God's "decrees," "laws," and "statutes" by which God established heaven and earth, an implicitly royal picture of Israel's God is evoked, as the divine sovereign to whom the whole creation owes allegiance.[6]

Royal language for God, however, is both explicit and common in the poetry of Psalms and the prophetic books, which not only call God "king" but also envision him as enthroned in heaven (and in a secondary sense also in Zion, in the Jerusalem temple), from where he rules or judges Israel, the nations, and indeed the entire earth. Thus Psalm 22:28 affirms that "dominion belongs to the LORD, / and he rules over the nations." Likewise, Psalm 103:19 claims, "The LORD has established his throne in the heavens, / and his kingdom rules over all." This claim is sometimes even tied to the stability of the created order, as in Psalm 96:10a: "Say among the nations, 'The LORD is king! / The world is firmly established; it shall never be moved.'"

While God is typically viewed as the present ruler of the cosmos, a distinctive theme in the Psalms and the Prophets is the expectation of God's future coming to vanquish evil and establish a reign of righteousness and justice. In

5. The background assumption becomes explicit in only six references to God as king or as ruling in the Pentateuch and Former Prophets. Three of those references are found in poetic sections of the Pentateuch (Exod. 15:18; Num. 23:21; Deut. 33:5) and speak of God's rule prior to the monarchy in Israel (Exod. 15:18 may well be contrasting God's rule with the oppression of Pharaoh in Egypt). The three nonpoetic references, all in the Former Prophets (Judg. 8:23; 1 Sam. 8:7; 12:2), explicitly contrast God's rule with that of human rulers.

6. On the royal picture of God as cosmic lawgiver, see J. Richard Middleton, *The Liberating Image: The* Imago Dei *in Genesis 1* (Grand Rapids: Brazos, 2005), chap. 2, esp. 65–74.

many cases this message targets the ending of the sixth-century Babylonian exile and the return of God's people to their homeland. A classic example is Isaiah 52:7, a text that Jesus may well have drawn on for his own "good news" announcement of God's coming kingdom:

> How beautiful upon the mountains
>> are the feet of the messenger who announces peace,
> who brings good news,
>> who announces salvation,
>> who says to Zion, "Your God reigns."

But the Old Testament also anticipates a future coming of God that is not specifically tied to the end of Babylonian exile. Based on the growing sense that human life is presently under the sway of corruption and injustice, Psalm 96 lyrically affirms that a time will come when the earth shall once more be conformed to the creator's will.

> Let the heavens be glad, and let the earth rejoice;
>> let the sea roar, and all that fills it;
>> let the field exult, and everything in it.
> Then shall all the trees of the forest sing for joy
>> before the LORD; for he is coming,
>> for he is coming to judge the earth.
> He will judge the world with righteousness,
>> and the peoples with his truth.
>> Psalm 96:10b–13

The motif of God's coming reign defeating evil and establishing righteousness becomes a central theme in apocalyptic literature such as the book of Daniel, which envisions the establishment of God's universal and everlasting kingdom, as dominion is taken from the unjust rulers of this world and given to God's holy people (7:13–14, 27). This future expectation of God's coming kingdom proliferates in Jewish apocalyptic literature outside the Bible. It is found, for example, in the *War Scroll* from Qumran (one of the Dead Sea Scrolls), which anticipates a cataclysmic battle when God's people will defeat the enemies of righteousness. *Testament of Moses* 10:1 envisions the coming victory of God this way: "Then his kingdom will appear throughout his whole creation. Then the devil will have an end. Yea, sorrow will be led away with him."[7]

7. Translation from J. Priest, "Testament of Moses," in *Apocalyptic Literature and Testaments*, vol. 1 of *The Old Testament Pseudepigrapha*, ed. James H. Charlesworth (New York:

In the two centuries immediately preceding Jesus, many ancient Jewish writings look not only for the coming of God's kingdom but also for some sort of messianic deliverer and ruler (a king or priest or even a prophet; some envisioned multiple messiahs) who would restore Israel, subdue God's enemies, and establish God's righteous reign from Zion over the land of Israel, or indeed over the entire world. There were, however, differing views both of the coming kingdom and of the nature of the messianic ruler (varying from a human political leader to a preexistent angelic or quasi-divine figure), and certainly not all Jews gave equal prominence to messianic ideas.[8] Nevertheless, the coming of God's reign in history to rectify a world out of whack with his original intent and to fulfill his promises to Israel had, by the time of Jesus, become a central expectation in much Jewish life.

What Does Jesus Mean by the "Kingdom of God"?

This expectation forms the most important conceptual background to Jesus's proclamation of the kingdom. Indeed, Jesus is only one among a number of Jewish messianic figures of the first century who claimed to inaugurate God's kingdom.[9] Given this background of expectation, we can almost sense the electricity in the air when Jesus begins his own ministry with a public announcement in Galilee (his home province) that the kingdom of God has "come near" or is "close at hand" (Matt. 4:17; Mark 1:15). But Jesus does not simply initiate his ministry with this opening declaration. The kingdom of God is the defining theological theme of his entire ministry, permeating his teaching from beginning to end. This theme is so prominent that it is mentioned over one hundred times in the Synoptic Gospels (50 times in Matthew, 15 times in Mark, 39 times in Luke).[10]

Doubleday, 1983), 931. This document (translated from a sixth-century Latin manuscript, but thought to be based on a first-century AD Greek text) has also been called the *Assumption of Moses*.

8. On the variety of messianic ideas in Second Temple Judaism, see the succinct summary in Michael F. Bird, *Are You the One Who Is to Come? The Historical Jesus and the Messianic Question* (Grand Rapids: Baker Academic, 2009), chap. 2, "Messianic Expectations in Second Temple Judaism." This chapter contains copious references to primary and secondary source materials for anyone who wishes to follow up on the topic.

9. Michael Bird (ibid., 47–52) notes that whereas Jesus was the only person explicitly designated as Messiah/Christ/Anointed in the first century (and Simon ben Kosiba in the second century), there were other implicitly messianic historical figures in the first century, including Judas the Galilean, Simon the servant of Herod, Athronges the shepherd, Menaham, and Simon bar Giora.

10. This counts versions of the phrase "kingdom of God," such as "kingdom of heaven" (Matthew's favored term), "my kingdom," "his kingdom," "the kingdom," and "my father's

In John, however, the kingdom motif surfaces only five times, twice near the beginning of the Gospel, in Jesus's conversation with Nicodemus, and three times near the end, in his trial before Pilate. The conversation with Nicodemus is the famous passage in which we find the phrase "born again" (or possibly "born from above"). Anyone who wants to see or enter the kingdom of God, says Jesus to this pious teacher of the law, must undergo new birth (John 3:3, 5). Because human life has been corrupted by sin, an infusion of new life from above is needed to radically transform our priorities and allegiances, to align us with God's coming reign. This new life, which in the Synoptic Gospels is the life of the kingdom (or life lived under the reign of God), is typically called "eternal life" in John's Gospel. Although the future is not excluded, "eternal life" in John's Gospel refers not primarily to some postmortem reality (after temporal life is over), but rather to a new quality of life in the here and now (this is why it is called abundant life in John 10:10). "Eternal life" is basically John's preferred way of referring to the kingdom of God, which itself is both future and present in the Synoptics. Thus, in John's Gospel new birth functions in a manner similar to repentance and faith in the Synoptics; it is required to infuse new life and thus reorient us toward God's kingdom purposes.

The trouble is that many contemporary Christians understand eternal life primarily as a reference to life after death (often connected to the idea of dwelling in heaven forever) and then use this unbiblical concept to interpret the kingdom of God. But this puts matters precisely the wrong way around. The strategic place in John 3 where the kingdom of God is linked to the new birth suggests that it functions as a transition from the persistent emphasis on the kingdom in the three preceding Gospels, and toward John's distinctive terminology. This means that before we can faithfully interpret John's basic theological categories, we must first understand what the Synoptic Gospels mean by the "kingdom of God."

But apart from unbiblical preconceptions of what "eternal life" means, two other impediments stand in our way. Two long-standing misunderstandings of the kingdom that have plagued the history of the Christian church must be addressed. Both are rooted in an unbiblical sacred/secular dualism or two-level worldview. In this worldview a supernatural, "spiritual" reality is contrasted with the natural, ordinary, mundane world of our experience, and the assumption is that God's rule is manifest primarily, or exclusively, in the former. This worldview underlies both misunderstandings of the kingdom.

---

kingdom." The figure for Mark is sometimes given as fifteen, which perhaps reflects the ambiguity of the reference in Mark 11:10.

The first misunderstanding views the kingdom as basically equivalent to the church; this interpretation was made popular by Augustine (esp. in *The City of God*), but it is found in differing versions among Christians through the ages. According to this view, while Satan or the evil one or the powers of corruption dominate the wider world, including the social and political spheres, God's rule is thought to be manifest in the people of God, either in their interior spirituality or in their communal life or in the institution of the church (this last is Augustine's view). Thus, if the Bible says that the kingdom of God was spreading throughout the country, this might be taken to mean that the church was experiencing growth.

One biblical text often cited for the interior version of this misreading is Luke 17:21b, traditionally translated as "the kingdom of God is within you" (KJV, NIV 1984).[11] However, given the range of meanings of the Greek preposition *entos*, along with the actual context of this saying in Jesus's teaching and ministry, it is much more likely that Jesus meant that the kingdom was already "among" or "in the midst of" his hearers than that it was within them (many translations reflect this more likely meaning [as in NASB, NRSV, NIV 2011]).

The other persistent misunderstanding is that the kingdom is equivalent to heaven (as opposed to earth). The same basic dualism of two hierarchical or opposing realms—one belonging to God, the other intrinsically evil or inferior—tends to underlie this interpretation. A biblical text often cited in support is John 18:36, the only other place in John's Gospel besides chapter 3 that mentions the kingdom. Here Jesus tells Pilate, at his trial, "My kingdom is not from this world. If my kingdom were from this world, my followers would be fighting to keep me from being handed over to the Jews. But as it is, my kingdom is not from here."[12] A careful reading, however, suggests that Jesus is not identifying his kingdom with heaven; rather, he is locating the origin of his power. This is sometimes obscured by translations, such as the KJV, that say his kingdom is not "of" this world, which might be taken to mean it does not concern this world.[13] The point, however, is that Jesus's kingdom (like the eternal life that he brings) is *from* God, who reigns from heaven, but it is *for* the earth. This understanding is reflected in the Lord's Prayer, where Jesus

---

11. See, for example, Thomas à Kempis, *The Imitation of Christ*, book 2, section 1, where the quotation of this text is followed by this exhortation to the reader: "Learn indifference to all that lies outside you and devote yourself to the life within, and you will see the kingdom of God coming in you" (*The Imitation of Christ*, trans. Betty I. Knott [London: Collins, 1963], 83).

12. The NRSV (given above) has the most literal rendering of John 18:36.

13. Similar misleading translations are found in the NIV, NASB, NAB, NLT, and NJB. Some of these translations go significantly beyond the Greek in the last phrase, which is literally "my kingdom is not from here," to say "my kingdom is not an earthly kingdom" (NLT) or "my kingdom is not of this realm" (NASB). Translation is always interpretation.

teaches his disciples to pray (Matt. 6:10): "Your kingdom come. Your will be done, on earth as it is in heaven." That is, while earth is, indeed, presently out of harmony with heaven, the coming of the kingdom is meant precisely to conform earth to heaven.

This misidentification of the kingdom with heaven receives further impetus from Matthew's propensity to use the expression "kingdom of heaven" rather than "kingdom of God." Many Christians approach the phrase "kingdom of heaven" guided by an unbiblical dualism that associates earth intrinsically with evil or inferiority, such that God's reign could not extend to earth. They therefore commonly take the phrase "kingdom of heaven" to mean "the kingdom which *is* heaven."[14] "Kingdom" and "heaven" are thus treated as simple equivalents. But this misreads Matthew's intent.[15]

The partial truth of the misreading is that since earth is presently in the grip of sin, no earthly kingdom fully conforms to God's will. Indeed, during the present age God's kingdom is in tension with all earthly kingdoms. But heaven and earth are not intrinsically antithetical; although presently out of whack, they will be in harmony once again when God's heavenly kingdom (in the sense that its origin is not from earth, but from heaven, the seat of God's rule) is finally extended to earth.

The point is that "heaven" in the phrase "kingdom of heaven" is a metonym, a figure of speech in which one thing stands for another. A contemporary analogy is the pronouncement: "This morning the White House issued a statement on the economy." Everyone knows that the building did not speak; the message comes from the president. "White House" in this pronouncement functions just like "heaven" in the phrase "kingdom of heaven." It substitutes the location of the person referred to for the person per se.

But why does Matthew engage in this substitution? Why does he prefer "kingdom of heaven" to "kingdom of God"? In the past, the explanation given was the supposed reticence among Jews in the ancient world to pronounce the name of God. The argument has been that Matthew therefore substituted "heaven" for "God" in the phrase "kingdom of God" as a form of reverential circumlocution (to piously avoid saying the word "God"). However, as Jonathan Pennington has decisively shown, the evidence for any reticence in ancient Jewish writings to avoid either the word "God" (or even the name

---

14. Matthew contains almost half of the references to the kingdom in the Synoptic Gospels, which may account for the persistence of this misreading.

15. Another misreading is the classical dispensational distinction between the kingdom of heaven (taken as a reference to the millennium) and the kingdom of God (taken as a reference to a "spiritual" reality). This distinction is no longer operative in so-called progressive dispensationalism.

"YHWH") is quite ambiguous.[16] Plus, Matthew shows no general avoidance of the word "God."[17] Instead, Matthew's use of "kingdom of heaven" draws on the notion of God's universal kingdom, articulated especially in Daniel 2–7, which typically associates God with heaven as a way to assert divine sovereignty over all creation and thus to distinguish God's form of rule from all despotic (and partial) earthly kingdoms.[18]

So let us be clear: "kingdom of heaven" in the Gospel of Matthew refers to the same reality as "kingdom of God" in Mark and Luke.[19] The issue, then, is what Mark and Luke mean by this freighted term.

The Nazareth Manifesto

To answer this question, it is heuristic to turn to Jesus's Nazareth manifesto in Luke 4:16–30, the sermon that he preaches at the start of his public ministry, in which he programmatically lays out his mission. Why is this particular sermon so important? The answer lies in its narrative placement, where it occurs in the order of events recorded in Luke. Along with the other Synoptic Gospels, Luke recounts Jesus's baptism by John (Matt. 3:13–17; Mark 1:9–11; Luke 3:21–22), followed by his temptation in the wilderness (Matt. 4:1–11; Mark 1:12–13; Luke 4:1–13). Then all three Synoptics have Jesus returning to Galilee (Matt. 4:12–16; Mark 1:14–15; Luke 4:14–15). In Matthew and Mark, Jesus announces the coming of the kingdom in a short, succinct statement (Matt. 4:17; Mark 1:15); but Luke has an extended account of a synagogue message that Jesus delivers in Nazareth (Luke 4:16–30), yet without including any explicit mention of the kingdom.

In Luke's account, when Jesus moves on from Nazareth, he goes to Capernaum, another town in Galilee. And when he is about to leave Galilee to continue his mission in Judea, he informs his listeners, "I must proclaim the good news of the kingdom of God to the other cities also; for I was sent for

16. The reverential circumlocution argument is decisively debunked in Jonathan T. Pennington, *Heaven and Earth in the Gospel of Matthew* (Supplements to Novum Testamentum 126; Leiden: Brill, 2007; reprint, Grand Rapids: Baker Academic, 2009), chap. 1, "Challenging the Circumlocution Assumption."

17. Matthew actually uses the word "God" fifty-one times, four of which are in the phrase "kingdom of God" (12:28; 19:24; 21:31, 43).

18. This is the gist of Pennington's persuasive argument concerning the significance of Matthew's "heaven" terminology as part of his discourse concerning God's transcendence and universal rule. Chapter 12 of his insightful book (ibid.) specifically addresses the "kingdom of heaven" in Matthew, affirming that it is from heaven for the earth.

19. Technically, we could say it has the same denotation or referent. It does, however, have different connotations, or other layers of meaning, as Pennington shows.

this purpose" (Luke 4:43). The implication is that this is precisely what Jesus has, in fact, been doing in Nazareth and Capernaum, even though the term "kingdom of God" did not appear in Luke 4 prior to verse 43.

This means that Jesus's sermon in Nazareth is meant to be an example of his preaching about the kingdom of God. Indeed, it is a paradigmatic example, a model that can help us understand concretely what the kingdom means. Attending carefully to the episode at Nazareth (both the initial message that Jesus delivers and what he says in the aftermath) will help us gain greater clarity about Jesus's understanding of the kingdom of God.

There are two main aspects of Jesus's message at Nazareth in Luke 4:16–30, and they generate two separate responses from his audience. First of all, Jesus reads a prophetic text from Isaiah and claims that it is being fulfilled in his ministry (vv. 16–21). This receives a positive response from the audience (v. 22). Jesus then proceeds to alienate his hearers with narratives about two prophets from the book of Kings (vv. 23–27). This so infuriates his audience that they attempt to kill him (vv. 28–30).

Contemporary readers, however, have a tendency to conflate the two sections of the story. It is amazing how often preachers (and even commentators) read the second response to Jesus (vv. 28–30) as if it directly follows the initial claim that he makes from Isaiah (vv. 16–21). But it is crucial to differentiate the two episodes of the story, because only if we understand what Jesus's audience initially liked about his message can we begin to grasp the nature of the kingdom of God and in what sense it could be "good news." The remainder of this chapter focuses on the first episode of the story (the good news), while the next chapter will address the second episode (the challenge of the kingdom).

In Luke 4 we learn that after his testing in the wilderness, Jesus begins teaching in the synagogues of Galilee, to much acclaim (vv. 14–15). He arrives in Nazareth, his hometown, and attends the synagogue on the Sabbath day, as was his custom (v. 16). When he stands to read the Scripture, he is handed the scroll of Isaiah. He opens the Isaiah scroll to what we know as chapter 61 and reads the following words:

> The Spirit of the Lord is upon me,
>   because he has anointed me to bring good news to the poor.
> He has sent me to proclaim release to the captives
>   and recovery of sight to the blind,
>   to let the oppressed go free,
> to proclaim the year of the Lord's favor.
>
> Luke 4:18–19

At that point (having read only Isa. 61:1 and the first line of 61:2) Jesus rolls up the scroll, hands it back to the synagogue attendant, and sits down. Luke says, "The eyes of all in the synagogue were fixed on him. Then he began to say to them, 'Today this scripture has been fulfilled in your hearing'" (vv. 20–21).

The crucial question for us here is this: What is Jesus talking about? Specifically, what does he mean by "good news to the poor," "release to the captives," "recovery of sight to the blind," and "to let the oppressed go free"? In what way do these actions signify "the year of the Lord's favor"? And how do they clarify the nature of the kingdom of God, which is being fulfilled in Jesus's ministry?

It has been the tendency of Christian interpreters through the ages (right up to the mid- to late twentieth century) to assume that this text in Luke 4:18–19 is referring primarily, if not exclusively, to so-called spiritual matters. There has been general, widespread agreement among generations of past interpreters about the referents of the terms Jesus uses. "The poor"? That means the poor in spirit. "Captives"? That means those in bondage to sin. "The blind"? That would be the spiritually blind (okay, maybe this could be taken literally). "The oppressed"? Those oppressed by the devil or by their own wretched sinful state.

This customary way of interpreting the text is indebted to an unbiblical dualism that separates this good world that God made into artificial categories of sacred and secular, holy and profane, spiritual and material, personal and social. Until recently, many commentaries on Luke 4:16–30 downplayed the idea that God in Christ was actually concerned about real flesh-and-blood poor people, or captives, or those oppressed by societal injustice (this would put salvation into direct contact with the secular, profane, material, social realm).

This bifurcated view of reality has prevented the church, and still prevents many readers today, from hearing the good news of the first episode during the events at Nazareth. It prevents us from grasping how amazingly *good* the news is that Jesus brings. By our otherworldly dualism, which devalues the concrete, fleshly, embodied world that God made, we limit the scope of God's redemptive activity in Christ and so conceive of salvation as snatching sinners out of this world so that they might inhabit another realm, "heaven"—giving that term a theological weight and interpretation completely out of alignment with its biblical significance. The numerous Bible studies on Luke 4:16–30 that I have led over the years in both church and campus ministry settings confirm that this dualism is an ongoing problem for Christians; it prevents many who read this text from taking Jesus's claims with the full force with which they were intended.

The Isaiah Background to Luke 4:16–30

If we track Jesus's quotation from Isaiah 61:1–2a, we begin to find an important antidote to an otherworldly misreading of Luke 4:18–19. In its original historical context, Isaiah 61 proclaims "good news" for sixth- or fifth-century Jews who had been impoverished and oppressed by Babylonian exile.[20] After returning to the promised land after the disruption of exile, the returnees were mired in factionalism, with their society still in ruins and their hopes for the fulfillment of God's ancient promises of blessing for his people hanging by a thread. In this context an unnamed prophet in the tradition of Isaiah of Jerusalem proclaims to them God's commitment to what we might call "urban renewal," the healing and restoration of the social order.

The Isaiah text that Jesus read was, of course, written in Hebrew, whereas Luke, writing in Greek, quotes the Greek translation of this passage in the Septuagint (see table 11.1). But whether Hebrew or Greek, Isaiah 61 proclaims the same basic message. Now, it is true that there is one line in the Hebrew text of Isaiah 61:1 that is somewhat different in the Septuagint.[21] The last phrase of Isaiah 61:1, which the NRSV translates as "release to the prisoners," is literally in Hebrew "an opening for the prisoners." This reference to opening prison doors (which allows the light in) is taken by the Septuagint of Isaiah 61:1 to refer to the opening of eyes, which results in the phrase "recovery of sight to the blind"; this is what Luke 4:18 quotes.[22]

Also, one line from Isaiah 61:1 is missing from Luke's quotation. It is the line about binding up (Hebrew) or healing (Septuagint) the brokenhearted. This line may have been missing from the version of the Septuagint that Luke used; we do not know. But the omission does not seem to be significant for Jesus's message in Luke 4:16–30. Despite the variations, Jesus clearly is drawing on an ancient prophetic text (Isa. 61) that promised an end to the bondage

20. The dating of the oracles in Isa. 56–66 (which scholars sometimes refer to as Third Isaiah) is subject to dispute. The oracles seem to address the situation of the people after they have returned from exile in Babylon, either near the end of the sixth century or toward the start of the fifth century (Jews began returning to the land in 538 BC, and the mission of Nehemiah is usually put at 445 BC).

21. The Hebrew text that Jesus read consisted of consonants only; vowel points were added only later, in medieval times (seventh through tenth centuries) by Jewish scholars known as the Masoretes. The standard Hebrew text of the Old Testament that we use today, known as the Masoretic Text (MT), is dated about AD 1000. Among the Dead Sea Scrolls, however, two ancient texts of Isaiah have been discovered, one containing the entire book (the *Great Isaiah Scroll*), dating from about 100 BC. This text is similar to what Jesus would have read in the synagogue.

22. The Septuagint translators may have been influenced by Isa. 42:7, which lists what the servant of the Lord will accomplish, including opening blind eyes and bringing prisoners out from the dungeon; this verse even mentions releasing "from the prison those who sit in darkness."

Table 11.1. Comparison of Isaiah 61:1–2 with Luke 4:18–19

MT Isaiah 61:1–2 (NRSV)	LXX Isaiah 61:1–2 (author's translation)	Luke 4:18–19 (NRSV)
[1]The spirit of the Lord GOD is upon me,	[1]The Spirit of the Lord is upon me,	[18]The Spirit of the Lord is upon me,
because the LORD has anointed me;	because he has anointed me;	because he has anointed me
to bring good news to the oppressed,	to bring good news to the poor	to bring good news to the poor.
he has sent me*	he has sent me;	He has sent me
to bind up the brokenhearted,	to heal the brokenhearted,	- - - - - - - - - - - - - - - - -
to proclaim liberty to the captives,	to proclaim release to the captives,	to proclaim release to the captives
and release to the prisoners;	and recovery of sight to the blind;	and recovery of sight to the blind,
[to let the oppressed go free (Isa. 58:6)]	[to let the oppressed go free (Isa. 58:6)]	to let the oppressed go free,
[2]To proclaim the year of the LORD's favor,	[2]To declare the year of the Lord's favor,	[19]to proclaim the year of the Lord's favor.
and the day of vengeance of our God;	and the day of recompense;	- - - - - - - - - - - - - - - -
to comfort all who mourn;	to comfort all who mourn;	- - - - - - - - - - - - - - - -

*The NRSV has "he has sent me to bring good news to the oppressed," but I have reversed the order of these two lines to correspond to the order of the Hebrew text.

or captivity of God's people, understood as their fragmented and oppressive social situation in the early postexilic period (though the Septuagint could be including also physical healing as part of the package of restoration).

The concrete, this-worldly nature of the salvation proclaimed in Luke 4:18–19 is made even clearer by the fact that Jesus (or Luke) adds one line not found in Isaiah 61. The last line of Luke 4:18 ("to let the oppressed go free") has no equivalent in Isaiah 61; it is actually an interpolation from Isaiah 58:6, the phrase being almost identical in both Luke 4 and the Septuagint of Isaiah 58.[23] Here the reference is clearly to social justice, even economic justice. Isaiah 58 (the context in which this phrase occurs) is a prophetic oracle critiquing those who piously pray and fast (vv. 2–3a) while at the same time oppressing their hired workers (v. 3b) and engaging in strife with each other (vv. 4, 9b). It is in the context of the breakdown of Israel's social norms that Isaiah 58 comes as

23. The only difference is that whereas the Septuagint of Isa. 58:6 has the imperative of the verb *apostellō* (for sending or letting go), Luke 4:18 has the infinitive.

a clarion call for postexilic Jews to extend their zeal for religious rituals into the realm of social justice. Fasting is fine; but, says God,

> Is not this the fast that I choose:
> to loose the bonds of injustice,
>   to undo the thongs of the yoke,
>   *to let the oppressed go free*
>   and to break every yoke?
>   Isaiah 58:6

The text goes on to call God's people to take care of the hungry and oppressed (v. 10) and promises them that if they fulfill God's requirements for justice with their neighbors, the social order will be healed:

> Your ancient ruins shall be rebuilt;
>   you shall raise up the foundations of many generations;
> you shall be called the repairer of the breach,
>   the restorer of streets to live in.
>   Isaiah 58:12

Notice how similar these lines are to what is said in Isaiah 61 just two verses after the section that Jesus quotes:

> They shall build up the ancient ruins,
>   they shall raise up the former devastations;
> they shall repair the ruined cities,
>   the devastations of many generations.
>   Isaiah 61:4

It makes sense that Jesus (or Luke) connected Isaiah 61 and Isaiah 58; both have to do with social renewal in postexilic Judah. So the insertion of Isaiah 58:6 at the end of Isaiah 61:1 further affirms the this-worldly nature of the kingdom that Jesus was proclaiming.

The Jubilee Background to Isaiah 61

This understanding of the kingdom becomes even more solidified when we consider that Isaiah 61 is drawing on the theology of the Jubilee year and the Sabbath year (from Lev. 25), that time when debts were to be canceled and slaves set free. The primary indicator for this interpretation is the important phrase "proclaim liberty" (or "proclaim release") in Isaiah 61:1. This phrase

(the verb *qārā'* with the noun *děrôr*) is how Leviticus 25:10 signals the Sabbath/
Jubilee year. The phrase occurs also in Jeremiah 34:8, 15, 17, in a narrative
about King Zedekiah's attempt to partially implement the Sabbath year in
sixth-century Judah just prior to the exile (this is the only reference in the
Old Testament to anyone actually practicing the Sabbath/Jubilee ideal).[24]

Here a bit of clarification of the relationship of the Sabbath and Jubilee
years is in order, since this will help us understand Isaiah 61 and Jesus's use
of that text. Whereas the Sabbath year enshrines a special practice every seventh year in ancient Israel, the Jubilee is to happen after seven sets of Sabbath
years—that is, after forty-nine years. The fiftieth year is the Jubilee year, which
essentially puts two Sabbath years back to back—the forty-ninth and the
fiftieth. The Jubilee is basically a special Sabbath year.

The instructions for the Jubilee year occur only in Leviticus 25, a text that
begins by discussing the Sabbath year (vv. 1–7) and then moves on to the Jubilee (starting at v. 8). Three other Old Testament texts address the meaning of
the Sabbath year; these are Deuteronomy 15 and a couple of brief references
in Exodus 21:1–11 and 23:10–11. Basically, what we know about the Sabbath
year or the Jubilee can be pieced together from these Old Testament texts.

The Jubilee consists of three sets of ethical practices, three interrelated components that God's people were to embody at seven-year intervals, and then
again in the fiftieth year. First, there is to be liberty for the inhabitants of the
land. That is, any Israelite sold into debt slavery as a result of poverty was to be
set free in the seventh year (Deut. 15:1–6) and in the fiftieth, Jubilee year (Lev.
25:10, 35–43).[25] Second, the land is to have rest; that is, it is to lie fallow. It must
not be plowed or sown either in the Sabbath year (Exod. 23:10–11; Lev. 25:1–7)
or in the Jubilee year (Lev. 25:11–12, 18–22); further, the poor are allowed to
share in whatever the fields or vineyards produce in the Sabbath year, and what
they leave the wild animals may eat (Exod. 23:11). The third practice, associated
specifically with Jubilee but not with the Sabbath year, is that the land is to
return to its original owners, to those who sold their ancestral inheritance due
to poverty or indebtedness. People uprooted by debt receive back their homes
and land, a place to live and work in peace and security (Lev. 25:10, 13, 23–28).

---

24. In fact, Jer. 34:14 suggests that it had not been practiced before this event, which can be
dated to just before the fall of Jerusalem (perhaps in 588 BC).

25. "Proclaim Liberty throughout all the land unto all the inhabitants thereof" (KJV) is
inscribed on the iconic Liberty Bell, with an attribution to Lev. 25:10. The bell was forged in
1751 to commemorate the fiftieth year (the Jubilee) of the charter of Pennsylvania and was
famously rung in 1774 to announce the First Continental Congress, which convened to discuss
the American colonists' desire for socioeconomic and political freedom from England. In 1837
the bell was formally given the name "Liberty Bell" and adopted (quite appropriately) by the
American Anti-Slavery Society as a symbol for the abolitionist movement.

These three practices together embody an ideal of a periodic breaking of the cycle of poverty and bondage in ancient Israel. They constitute a communal practice, an ethic of redemptive living. But as important as these practices are ethically, it is just as important to understand their underlying religious or theological significance. For each of these three Jubilee practices is rooted squarely in the Old Testament narrative of redemption.

Take, for example, liberty for slaves. Why are debt slaves to be released in the seventh year? "For they are my servants, whom I brought out of the land of Egypt; they shall not be sold as slaves are sold. You shall not rule over them with harshness [as Pharaoh did], but shall fear your God" (Lev. 25:42–43). The setting free of debt slaves in the Sabbath and Jubilee years is rooted explicitly in the exodus, when God heard the cry of his suffering people and intervened to liberate them from bondage in Egypt. And the people of God, on a regular basis, are to go against their corrupt desires to exploit each other, and intentionally they are to embody the memory of their own liberation, in the practice of Jubilee.

Likewise, letting the land lie fallow is rooted in the Old Testament story of God's people, though less explicitly. It is rooted in the next stage of the narrative, after the exodus, the wandering in the wilderness. When Jeremiah tells the story of the exodus and wilderness wandering, he describes the wilderness as a land "not sown" (Jer. 2:2). The wilderness represented a time in Israel's history when they could produce no food for themselves, when they had no control over their survival and had to depend on God alone to provide manna and sometimes quail (Exod. 16:11–36; Ps. 105:40). For forty years in the wilderness, Israel had been taught by intensive experience that human beings are not autonomous, that they do not sustain themselves. God is the sustainer, the provider of all good gifts, indeed of life itself.

Life was different in the promised land, however; it involved sowing, planting, and reaping crops. The pervasive temptation was to believe that the fruitfulness of the land was due to one's own efforts, that God was unnecessary (see the warnings against this notion in Deut. 8:10–18). Therefore, letting the land lie fallow in the Sabbath year was a recapitulation of the wilderness experience, when God's people were thrown into utter dependence on God's provision. They had to trust that whatever crops were planted in the sixth year would suffice for the seventh also. That was risky enough. But the Jubilee was an even more radical practice; it required trusting that God would see to it that the crops planted in the forty-eighth year would suffice not just for that year, but for two more (Lev. 25:18–22).[26] And trust in God's provision was to spill over into providing for others in need (Exod. 23:11).

---

26. What Lev. 25:21 refers to as the "sixth year" is the forty-eighth year of the Jubilee cycle (the sixth year of the seventh Sabbath year cycle); so the "eighth year" in verse 22 is the Jubilee year.

The third practice of Jubilee, the redemption of the land, where it reverts to its original owners, is also rooted in the Old Testament founding narrative, in the gift of the promised land. Leviticus 25:23 explains the basis for this third practice: "The land shall not be sold in perpetuity, for the land is mine; with me you are but aliens and tenants." This is the theology of the ancestral inheritance (*naḥălâ*) that Naboth appealed to when King Ahab tried to purchase his vineyard (1 Kings 21:1–4). Even the king could not force an Israelite farmer to give up his ancestral allotment of land. The same principle that allowed Naboth to refuse the king meant that if anyone did sell land due to extreme economic privation, it would return to the family in the Jubilee year. So the return to their ancestral land by those disinherited or displaced by poverty or debt embodies a commitment to God's lordship and ownership of the land—a land that none is free to manipulate for their benefit, at others' expense.

Sabbath and Jubilee thus constitute a set of ethical social practices rooted in crucial moments of Israel's story of redemption (the exodus, the wilderness, the gift of land) that reveal God's gracious intentions toward his people, specifically his purposes to enact justice on their behalf. God's people are called to embody in their lives, in their communal relationships, this very redemptive grace and commitment to justice that they have experienced from God.

But Israel in the late sixth and early fifth centuries, having returned to the land after the exile, was not embodying God's purposes for a just and righteous communal life. In this context Isaiah 61 takes the language of bondage or captivity found in Leviticus 25 (which is debt bondage, forced servitude due to poverty) and applies it metaphorically to the plight of the postexilic people living in their own land. Isaiah's point is that Israel's form of corrupt social life is equivalent to living in bondage.

An earlier text in Isaiah had applied the metaphor of debt slavery to the exile itself. Isaiah 40 proclaimed double comfort to the Judeans who were returning to the land ("Comfort, O comfort my people, says your God" [v. 1]) and announced to Jerusalem (the city standing for the people) "that she has served her term, / that her penalty is paid, / that she has received from the LORD's hand / double for all her sins" (v. 2). While exile as a term of service involving alienation from one's ancestral land draws on the general concept of debt slavery, the notion of double penalty for Israel's sin goes back specifically to Jeremiah 16:18, where exile as double penalty is first stated and is the consequence of Israel defiling the land through idolatry.

Interestingly, the idea of a double penalty matched by double restoration surfaces again in Isaiah 61, just a few verses after the section that Jesus quotes at Nazareth.

> Because their shame was double,
>   and dishonor was proclaimed as their lot,
> therefore they shall possess [in their land] a double portion;
>   everlasting joy shall be theirs.
>
>   Isaiah 61:7

The NRSV strangely omits the phrase "in their land," which is unambiguously present in the Hebrew and appears in the standard English translations (this may simply have been an oversight by the NRSV translators). The text clearly refers to land return after exile.[27] Isaiah 61 thus affirms that the entire community, like the individual Israelite in Leviticus 25, will return to their inheritance after a time of debt servitude. And since the alienation or servitude was so severe, the restoration will be wondrous indeed.

By the time of Isaiah 61, however, Israel was already in the land; yet exile and servitude were, in a certain sense, still continuing. Isaiah 61 thus uses bondage or captivity as a metaphor not for exile, but rather for the state of postexilic Israel's fractured social life, and proclaims an era of liberty or release analogous to the Jubilee.[28] Isaiah 61 proclaims "good news" to the broken and dispirited people that the "year of YHWH's favor" is at hand, a new epoch of grace toward Israel in which God's ancient promises of salvation and restoration are being fulfilled.

The Comprehensive Scope of the Gospel

With this background to Jesus's sermon at Nazareth—reaching back though Isaiah 61 (and Isa. 58) to Leviticus 25—the meaning of his proclamation comes into clearer focus. The texts that Jesus cites at Nazareth are rich with allusion and promise of concrete, this-worldly deliverance and restoration.

This is confirmed if we read on in Luke's Gospel, especially in chapter 7. For here Jesus himself interprets the meaning of his manifesto. In Luke 7:18–23

27. While some translations (KJV, NIV 1984, NIV 2011, NASB, NLT, ESV) render the first half of Isa. 61:7 such that only the restoration, and not the shame, is double (a legitimate translation possibility because the Hebrew is ambiguous), the second half of the verse clearly mentions a double portion of land (and translations are generally agreed on this). Besides the NRSV, other translations that mention double shame include the NAB, NJPS, and HCSB.

28. This postexilic use of the metaphor of bondage is also seen in Ezra 9:7–9; Neh. 9:36–37; and in various extracanonical Jewish texts such as Judith 8:22–23; Additions to Esther 14:8; 2 Macc. 1:27; Josephus, *Jewish War* 5.395–96; idem, *Jewish Antiquities* 18.4. Alternately, we could say that Isa. 61 uses exile as a metaphor for Israel's continuing alienation while in their own land. For an extended analysis of this motif, see Bradley C. Gregory, "The Postexilic Exile in Third Isaiah: Isaiah 61:1–3 in Light of Second Temple Hermeneutics," *Journal of Biblical Literature* 126 (2007): 475–96.

John the Baptist, who is in prison at the command of Herod (3:19–20), sends his disciples to Jesus, asking, "Are you the one who is to come [the Messiah we have been expecting], or are we to wait for another?" (7:19). In the next chapter I will address the basis for John's question (that is, why he asks it), but Jesus's response is helpful here in clarifying the nature of the kingdom that he is bringing. When John's disciples relay to Jesus the question of whether he is really the Messiah (7:20), Luke delays Jesus's answer by noting that at that very time Jesus healed many of diseases and evil spirits and gave sight to many who were blind (7:21). Then he reports that Jesus answered John's disciples, "Go and tell John what you have seen and heard: the blind receive their sight, the lame walk, the lepers are cleansed, the deaf hear, the dead are raised, the poor have good news brought to them" (7:22 [cf. Matt. 11:5]).

Notice that the signs of the messianic kingdom, both in Luke's narrative summary of what Jesus was doing (7:21) and in Jesus's own list of his activities (7:22), are concrete, this-worldly acts of healing and restoration. The Messiah's mission is to proclaim in word and deed that God is at work restoring this fractured world—breaking the grip of evil, healing diseased bodies, bringing life out of death. Beyond that general observation, we should also note that the first and last items on Jesus's list (regarding the blind and the poor) come explicitly from the Nazareth manifesto. That is, Jesus is beginning to fulfill precisely what he promised to do in Luke 4:16–30.

It is fascinating that one of the texts from the Dead Sea Scrolls, known as the *Messianic Apocalypse* (4Q521), dates from the century before Jesus and has a similar list of what will happen when the Messiah comes.[29] Although the text is fragmentary, we can piece together some lines quite well. The coming of God's anointed will be signaled by God "freeing prisoners, giving sight to the blind, straightening out the twisted,"[30] and he "will heal the badly wounded and will make the dead live; he will proclaim good news to the poor."[31] A number of these very items show up in Luke 7:22, suggesting

29. This text has also been called *On Resurrection*, since the raising of the dead is one of the signs of the messianic kingdom. See James D. Tabor and Michael O. Wise, "4Q521 'On Resurrection' and the Synoptic Gospel Tradition: A Preliminary Study," *Journal for the Study of the Pseudepigrapha* 10 (1992): 149–62.

30. *Messianic Apocalypse* (4Q521), fragment 2, column 2, line 8; translation from Florentino García Martínez and Eibert J. C. Tigchelaar, *The Dead Sea Scrolls Study Edition* (Leiden: Brill; Grand Rapids: Eerdmans, 1999), 2:1045. This line is almost a verbatim quotation from Ps. 146:7–8. The appropriateness of using Ps. 146 to describe the kingdom of God is evident from its last verse, which proclaims that "YHWH will reign forever" (v. 10).

31. *Messianic Apocalypse* (4Q521), fragment 2, column 2, line 12 (trans. ibid.). Tabor and Wise ("4Q521 'On Resurrection'") assume that the text states that the Messiah himself will accomplish these signs; but it is possible that God, not the Messiah, is the intended subject of the verbs of healing and restoration. However we resolve this question, the text certainly claims that

that Jesus's holistic notion of the kingdom was in line with at least some Jewish expectation in the Second Temple period. It is further interesting that the *Messianic Apocalypse* claims that heaven and earth will "listen to" (or obey) the Messiah, and "all that is in them" will follow the instructions of his saints.[32] These saints are described as those who seek the Lord and who hope in their hearts; they are characterized as the pious, the righteous, the poor, and the faithful.[33] It is these poor/pious ones who receive the good news of the kingdom. Indeed, the text declares that they will be honored or glorified on the throne of an eternal kingdom.[34]

This is not to say that Jesus (or Luke) is explicitly citing the *Messianic Apocalypse*. Rather, these ideas were simply part of the messianic expectation of the time. So when Jesus raises someone from the dead (Luke 7:11–15), it is a powerful sign that something new and decisive is happening. And Luke reports the people's response: "Fear seized all of them; and they glorified God, saying, 'A great prophet has risen among us!' and 'God has looked favorably on his people!'" (Luke 7:16).

To put it differently, "the year of the Lord's favor" has begun (Luke 4:19; Isa. 61:2). God's Jubilee reign of grace, anticipated in Isaiah 61, is finally coming; indeed, it is "fulfilled in your hearing" (Luke 4:21). This is nothing less than "the age to come" (*ha'ôlām habbā'*) of Jewish expectation, a new epoch in history, no longer limited to every fiftieth year or seventh year, in which God is at work healing the world, making things right once again.[35] It is the age of the kingdom of God, inaugurated by Jesus, in which God is restoring broken, fallen, needy human beings and reversing evil (every form of bondage, poverty, and blindness) so that the world (the *kosmos*, which God so loved, says John 3:16) might again manifest God's true purposes from the beginning—purposes for shalom and blessing.

It therefore becomes clear that we cannot with impunity "spiritualize" Jesus's message to make it only internal, about people's inner attitudes or

---

when God's anointed appears, these will be the signs of the messianic age. See Lidija Novakovic, "4Q521: The Works of the Messiah or the Signs of the Messianic Time?," in *Qumran Studies: New Approaches, New Questions*, ed. Michael Thomas Davis and Brent A. Strawn (Grand Rapids: Eerdmans, 2007), 208–31.

32. *Messianic Apocalypse* (4Q521), fragment 2, column 2, lines 1–2 (trans. García Martínez and Tigchelaar, *Dead Sea Scrolls*, 2:1045). It is possible these lines are an echo of Ps. 146:6, which mentions "heaven and earth, the sea, and all that is in them." The likelihood of this is based on the fact that line 8 is clearly taken from this psalm.

33. *Messianic Apocalypse* (4Q521), fragment 2, column 2, lines 3–6.

34. *Messianic Apocalypse* (4Q521), fragment 2, column 2, line 7.

35. In Isa. 56:1 this is called "working righteousness" (*'āśû ṣĕdāqâ*). In later Judaism this cosmic mending would come to be called *tikkûn 'ôlām*. This is what New Testament scholar N. T. Wright likes to call God "putting things to rights."

states of being. Rather, Jesus is addressing the entire complex situation of his hearers, which includes both their inner bondage (which is why he called people to repent) and their oppressive external situation. So when Jesus claims that he has come to announce "good news to the poor" (Luke 4:18), or when he says in the Sermon on the Plain, "Blessed are you who are poor, for yours is the kingdom of God" (Luke 6:20), we need to take seriously that he literally meant to include those who were economically impoverished and politically marginalized in first-century Israel.

Jesus's statements are not meant to suggest that poverty is a good thing or that the poor are "happy" (as the Beatitudes are often mistranslated), but they do indicate that among the poor were those faithful to the traditions of Israel, who trusted not in their own resources (indeed, they had none), but rather in God's gracious promise of deliverance, rooted in the exodus, when YHWH had first acted to redeem his people from Egyptian bondage. These were the *ʿănāwîm* (the "oppressed," "afflicted," "needy") of Isaiah 61:1 and the *Messianic Apocalypse* (fragment 2, column 2, line 6), a term that the Septuagint of Isaiah 61:1 translates as "poor" (*ptōchoi*). And they waited, with patient humility and expectant hope, for a new redemptive act of God that would complete what God himself had started so many years before when he heard the cries of Hebrew slaves groaning in their oppression in Egypt. For all those in Jesus's own day who existed in oppressive circumstances, crying out in faith for redemption, his message is good news indeed.

It certainly was recognized as such by Jesus's audience in Nazareth. His hearers understood themselves as the poor to whom the good news of the kingdom was addressed. If all first-century Jews could justifiably understand themselves as the *ʿănāwîm* of old, those awaiting a second exodus, a new liberation from oppression, then rural Galileans like those in Nazareth were doubly justified in seeing themselves so, for they were among the poorest of the poor in Israel. So when Jesus proclaims his agenda, his manifesto, this is wonderful news in Nazareth. The people respond out of a deep sense of their own need: God cares even for us! We are going to participate in God's promised redemption! No wonder, as Luke reports, "All spoke well of him and were amazed at the gracious words that came from his mouth" (4:22).

But the message of Jesus was good news not just for his original hearers; it is good news for us today as well. Jesus's proclamation of the kingdom at Nazareth can help us unlearn dualistic habits of mind that shackle our reading of the gospel and limit the scope of God's salvation. But it does more than change our understanding, important as that is.

The message of the kingdom that Jesus brings is good news most fundamentally because we, no less than his original hearers, desperately need the healing and redemption that he came to bring, a redemption that touches all we do. For we are, in multiple ways, caught up in the brokenness of the world, complicit in sin not just at the individual level but also as part and parcel of the fallen social order, which is out of whack with God's purposes, living in a creation that is groaning for redemption. And we yearn for healing. The good news is that the coming of God's kingdom impacts the entirety of our lives—our bodies, our work, our families, all our social relationships, even our relationship to the earth itself. The good news of the kingdom is nothing less than the healing (literally, the establishing) of the world (*tikkûn ʿōlām*), in which we are all invited to participate.

12

The Challenge of the Kingdom

In the preceding chapter I argued that Jesus's proclamation of the kingdom of God in his sermon at Nazareth was good news because it addressed his hearers' full-bodied, concrete earthly needs. But the episode at Nazareth did not end on a positive note, with the praise of his audience. It is the burden of this chapter to explore how Jesus went on to complicate this good news, so that it would not be understood superficially and self-righteously. Rather, the good news of the kingdom can be grasped only through a radical challenge that requires a fundamental reorientation of life.

Jesus concluded the first phase of his message in the Nazareth synagogue by claiming that the Isaiah 61 text that he had read was being fulfilled in his own person and mission. For this, he received glowing praise from his audience. "All spoke well of him and were amazed at the gracious words that came from his mouth. They said, 'Is not this Joseph's son?'" (Luke 4:22).

We should note that the reference to Joseph is not, in this context, meant to be derogatory.[1] Jesus is being recognized positively as one of the Nazareth community, who has gone out into the wider world and has come back to help his own people. He is accepted as an insider, whose message connects deeply with his townspeople's yearning for the kingdom of God.

---

1. This is, admittedly, different from the negative tone of the comment in Matt. 13:53–57 // Mark 6:1–4. Luke's account is the only one that divides the response that Jesus receives from his townspeople into two stages (the first positive, the second negative). John 6:42 also has a negative comment from the crowds about Jesus being Joseph's son, set in a different context (in Capernaum, not Nazareth).

But precisely at this point Jesus begins to thwart their expectations. They say, in essence, "Good sermon, pastor," and then he goes out of his way to antagonize them. Jesus is clearly not satisfied with the praise of his hearers. So he puts words into their mouths that initially make no sense: "Doubtless you will quote to me this proverb, 'Doctor, cure yourself!' And you will say, 'Do here also in your hometown the things that we have heard you did at Capernaum'" (Luke 4:23). We can imagine Jesus's audience protesting loudly, "No, we're not asking for any miracles. We actually believe you!"

Yet Jesus seems intent on alienating them. "Truly I tell you," he says, "no prophet is accepted in the prophet's hometown" (Luke 4:24). "But *we* accept you," they might interject. "We actually like your message!" Nevertheless, Jesus proceeds to make his abrasive prophetic point:

> But the truth is, there were many widows in Israel in the time of Elijah, when the heaven was shut up three years and six months, and there was a severe famine over all the land; yet Elijah was sent to none of them except to a widow at Zarephath in Sidon. There were also many lepers in Israel in the time of the prophet Elisha, and none of them was cleansed except Naaman the Syrian. (Luke 4:25–27)

The emphatic nature of Jesus's comments at the start of verses 23, 24, and 25 is startling: "Doubtless . . . Truly I tell you . . . But the truth is . . ." He seems to be trying to hammer his point home.

But what is his point?

Broadening the Scope of the Kingdom

Jesus here focuses on the outsider status of the two recipients of divine grace in the narrative in 1 Kings 17:1–24 and 2 Kings 5:1–19. While these Old Testament texts clearly regard these two as outsiders, neither text goes as far as Jesus does in emphasizing the contrast with Israelites in need. There were many Israelite widows and lepers, he explains, who desperately needed help from God. However, Elijah and Elisha were sent to none of them, but rather to a Sidonian widow and a Syrian leper. According to Jesus, the God of Israel acted not on behalf of his own people, but instead on behalf of two gentiles in need—in one case to provide a food supply for a poor woman during famine and then to raise her son from the dead, and in the other to heal a powerful military leader.[2]

2. Technically, the widow's food supply was meant to be shared with Elijah (1 Kings 17:9–16), but this is not something that Jesus mentions.

By these examples, Jesus clearly intends to have his listeners understand that the kingdom of God breaks down the opposition between Jew and gentile that had been hardening among many first-century Jews into an unbridgeable gulf. And since his two examples involve a poor woman and a powerful man, Jesus effectively dismantles the male/female hierarchy and the distinction between rich and poor or privileged and marginal. All people, of whatever ethnicity, gender, or social status, can be recipients of God's grace. God plays no favorites. Indeed, since Naaman, after initially resisting Elisha's instructions for healing due to his sense of pride, finally humbles himself to obey the prophet (2 Kings 5:9–15), he qualifies as one of the *'ănāwîm*, the poor or needy who receive good news of God's favor.[3] Jesus thereby makes the radical statement that this receptive attitude, and not ethnicity (or gender or social status), is the sole criterion for receiving God's salvation and healing. This attitude is equivalent to the repentance and faith required for the new birth that allows one to enter the kingdom of God.

Here Jesus goes beyond the idea that the kingdom is open to various categories of Israelite outcasts, such as tax collectors, prostitutes, and "sinners" (Matt. 21:31–32; Luke 5:29–31; 7:34–39). His point in appealing to the Elijah and Elisha narratives is that the kingdom is open to total outsiders—at least, to those whom his hearers take to be outsiders. Yet from the perspective of the narrative sweep of Israel's own Scripture, they are not outsiders at all. The Sidonian widow and the Syrian leper are, like all gentiles, human beings made in God's image (Gen. 1:26–28), members of the same human family of which Israel is a part.[4] The original human family certainly has diversified over time into many nations, with differing cultures and languages (Gen. 10), but all of them derive from the same ancestors, according to Israel's own canonical narrative.

Yet the distinction between Jew and gentile is, in one sense, legitimate; it is traceable back to God's election of Israel from out of all the nations of the world to be his special people, with a priestly mission to bring blessing to all the nations or families of the earth (Gen. 12:1–3; Exod. 19:3–6). However, the

---

3. For an excellent study of this episode in 2 Kings, see Frank Anthony Spina, *The Faith of the Outsider: Exclusion and Inclusion in the Biblical Story* (Grand Rapids: Eerdmans, 2005), 72–93 (especially the contrast between Naaman the outsider and Elisha's Israelite servant).

4. Our creation in the image of God is not just a fact (a gift we are born into); it is also a normative calling (as we saw in chap. 2). Jesus himself teaches that the basis for loving our enemies is the imitation of God. He explains that the result of loving our enemies is "that you may be children of your Father in heaven; for he makes his sun rise on the evil and on the good, and sends rain on the righteous and on the unrighteous" (Matt. 5:45), or (in Luke's version) that "you will be children of the Most High; for he is kind to the ungrateful and the wicked. Be merciful, just as your Father is merciful" (Luke 6:35–36).

legitimate distinction between Israel and the other nations had evolved over time into something of a contrast, even to the point where one's identity as a Jew might be defined over against those who are not Jews.

Whereas in the beginning Israel was simply one (admittedly unique) nation among the other nations, the term "nations" (= gentiles) came to be reserved for non-Israelites. This parallels the split between clergy and laity in the history of Christianity. Although originally those with a pastoral leadership role were simply one group among the people (*laos*) of God, the term "people" (= laity) came to be reserved for those who were not clergy. In both cases this terminology serves to distance one group (with a distinctive mission) from the larger group of which they were originally members. Election for ministry or service becomes transformed into an elite or even oppositional sense of identity, which ends up subverting the original purpose of the distinction (which was about function, not status).

One crucial factor that contributed to this sense of contrast with, and even hostility toward, outsiders in the case of some first-century Jews was the very real oppression that Israel endured from a whole succession of foreign nations, beginning with the bondage that they experienced in Egypt. If we combine the special privilege of being God's elect with the perpetual attacks from various surrounding nations in the time of the judges, the trauma of conquest by Assyria and then Babylon, followed by postexilic life under Persian rule, then oppression by the empires of Greece and Rome (with only a brief respite under the Maccabees)—we can easily understand how Israel's sense of privilege through election evolved over time into an "insider versus outsider" mentality that could be vitriolic in its condemnation of non-Israelites (see, for example, Psalm 137 concerning Babylon and Edom, or the book of Nahum concerning Assyria).[5]

Although there is no vitriol toward outsiders in the instructions for Sabbath and Jubilee years in the Old Testament (which form part of the background for Luke 4:16–30, as we saw in the preceding chapter), there are clear limits to the applicability of these instructions, given Israel's "insider versus outsider" schema. Thus Deuteronomy 15 makes it clear that only Hebrew slaves are set free in the Sabbath year (v. 12); and the land, by definition, can be returned only to Israelites. Leviticus 25 even distinguishes how an Israelite can legitimately treat a Hebrew slave versus a slave from another nation (vv. 44–46). And in

---

5. In *Yet I Loved Jacob: Reclaiming the Biblical Concept of Election* (Nashville: Abingdon, 2007), Joel S. Kaminsky argues that Israel's Scriptures distinguished between three groups: the elect (Israel), the anti-elect (certain specific nations singled out for destruction, such as the Canaanites and Amalekites), and the nonelect (all the other nations and peoples). In practice, however, such fine distinctions are not always preserved in popular consciousness.

general the texts apply the Jubilee/Sabbath principle of debt release to "your neighbor" (Lev. 25:14, 15; Deut. 15:7, 9) or "your kin" (Lev. 25:25, 35)—that is, to a fellow Israelite.

What Jesus is doing, therefore, in his appeal to the prophetic narratives concerning Elijah and Elisha is significantly broadening the scope of the Sabbath/Jubilee principle.[6] We therefore misunderstand the significance of his quoting from Isaiah 61, and the force of his appeal through that text to the ideal of Jubilee, if we ignore the import of these two prophetic narratives. They constitute the lens through which he is reading (or rereading) Isaiah 61. These two prophetic narratives are the key to interpreting the Nazareth manifesto. This is something that Jesus's audience at Nazareth needed to grasp.

The Challenge of the Son of God

Jesus's hearers at Nazareth understood quite well the point that the kingdom of God involves the comprehensive transformation of this world, that no dimension of earthly life is in principle excluded—neither bodily health nor social and economic realities. This point may be challenging for us today who read Luke 4:16–30 in the wake of two thousand years of "spiritualizing" the text; but it was unproblematic for Jesus's original audience, steeped in the Old Testament's understanding of holistic salvation. So Jesus does not need to make much of this point: he simply takes it for granted.

What Jesus's hearers had problems with was the other sense in which God's kingdom is comprehensive. They could not countenance, especially given the current oppression that they were experiencing under Roman rule, the possibility that God's kingdom is meant to encompass all people on equal footing, that no one is in principle excluded, not even those they counted as enemies. They did not function, as many Christians do today, with a worldview that divides the sacred from the secular, a dualism of two realms (one higher, one lower). Their problem was what we might call a sociological dualism, an us/them dichotomy of two intractable, antagonistic groups.

This "insider versus outsider" mentality on the part of his audience might explain why Jesus stops his quotation from Isaiah 61 after the first line of verse 2. The verse continues with "and the day of vengeance of our God." Jesus omits that phrase not because he is soft on judgment: he often pronounced

6. Jesus widens the related notion of loving your neighbor (from Lev. 19:18) by drawing on the idea of loving the alien (in Lev. 19:34) in the parable of the good Samaritan (Luke 10:25–37). For an excellent analysis of the parable, see David I. Smith, *Learning from the Stranger: Christian Faith and Cultural Diversity* (Grand Rapids: Eerdmans, 2009), chap. 4, "On Loving Foreigners."

judgment on his hearers (for example, Luke 10:13–15; 11:29–32). The problem is that Isaiah 61 goes on to speak of the subservience of the nations to Israel in the last days (vv. 6–7). In a simple reversal of roles, Israel is pictured as no longer in bondage to others; rather, it will be the other way around. And while the text does not explicitly say that this reversal is what is meant by God's vengeance in verse 2, it could be easily implied. Isaiah 61 suggests that while good news is for Israel, judgment (vengeance) is for everyone else. But this is antithetical to Jesus's message, since it would simply entrench his audience in the very "us against them" framework that he wants to challenge.

So beyond stopping his quotation from Isaiah 61 short, in mid-verse, Jesus objects to his hearers' facile applauding of his message and goes on to appeal to the Elijah and Elisha narratives, highlighting the fact that the ministry of these prophets was to outsiders, to those beyond the limits of the covenant community. In fact, you could say that he rubs this fact in his hearers' faces. And Jesus does this just as they respond positively to his message and express amazement at his "gracious words" (Luke 4:22).

Part of their positive response was to ask rhetorically, "Isn't this Joseph's son?" Yet for Luke it isn't a rhetorical question.

It is no coincidence that the genealogy of Jesus (just one chapter earlier in Luke's Gospel) begins by recounting, "He was the son [as was thought] of Joseph" (3:23). And throughout the temptation narrative, which directly precedes the Nazareth manifesto, we find this recurring challenge from the devil, which prefaces two of the temptations: "If you are the Son of God" (4:3, 9). And before that, at Jesus's baptism, the voice from heaven says, "You are my Son, the Beloved; with you I am well pleased" (3:22).

So, far from Jesus being simply Joseph's son—the homeboy, one of the club, one of our kind of people, whose message simply confirms us in our present assumptions—he is the son of none other than *God*. And the Son of God challenges his hearers (then and now) well beyond their comfort zones.

The Son of God challenges us to take seriously the holistic, comprehensive nature of the kingdom in two ways. First, he challenges us not to limit the scope of salvation to the "soul" (or the inner person) or to life in "heaven" hereafter. Rather we, especially contemporary readers, need to grasp the biblical vision that salvation pertains to God restoring the full functioning of human beings (bodies and all) in their real historical, sociocultural context; indeed, it will ultimately involve the restoration of the entire created order (though that is not made explicit in Luke 4:16–30). But, second, Jesus challenges us not to limit the scope of this holistic salvation simply to "us" or to "our kind" of people.

Indeed, there is an intrinsic connection between the two parts of Jesus's message at Nazareth. The holistic renewal of the social order involves people living out just and merciful relationships with one another, at multiple levels. Given the enmity that exists between individuals and social groups (both in the world of Jesus's day and in our day), the restoration of healthy social functioning must therefore involve concrete reconciliation between people; otherwise, it is nothing more than a pipe dream. Furthermore, this renewal and restoration cannot be limited simply to Jews—or to whites or blacks, or Americans, or the middle class, or Christians; God's will is for the renewal and restoration of the entire human family in accordance with his purposes in creation.

But this social renewal will not happen automatically, from the outside. It requires our intentional participation in God's plan of reconciliation. This means that it is impossible to genuinely embrace the good news of the kingdom (which is meant to restore the human community to wholeness) unless we are open to the salvation of others different from ourselves.[7] Our restoration to wholeness depends on theirs.[8] And this applies even to people (or groups of people) whom we view, for all kinds of legitimate historical reasons, with suspicion or even hostility.

The integral connection between the two dimensions of Jesus's message at Nazareth is confirmed if we turn again to Luke 7, to the answer that Jesus gives John's disciples when they relay John's question about whether Jesus is the Messiah: "Go and tell John what you have seen and heard: the blind receive their sight, the lame walk, the lepers are cleansed, the deaf hear, the dead are raised, the poor have good news brought to them" (v. 22). We have already seen that Jesus's reply illustrates the holistic, this-worldly nature of the salvation he brings. And we noted (in the preceding chapter) that two items on this list—"the blind receive sight" and "the poor have the good news brought to them"—are explicit citations from the Isaiah 61 text that Jesus read at Nazareth. What we also need to realize is that two other items on the list are also from the Nazareth incident, but from the second episode at Nazareth, in which Jesus alienates his audience. The phrases "the lepers are cleansed" and "the dead are raised" allude to the Elijah and Elisha stories, in which Elisha heals Naaman of leprosy and Elijah restores the widow's son to life. Luke 7 thus confirms that both the Isaiah 61 quote and the prophetic

---

7. I am using the term "salvation" here in its holistic biblical sense, and not reducing it to justification by faith (important as that is). The salvation of others thus includes their familial, economic, social, and even medical wholeness (with profound implications for issues such as immigration reform and health care).

8. Note the words of Jeremiah to the exiles living in Babylon, the very nation that had oppressed them: "But seek the welfare of the city where I have sent you into exile, and pray to the LORD on its behalf, for in its welfare you will find your welfare" (29:7).

narratives from Kings are integral to Jesus's message and ministry, as signs of the coming messianic age.

Table 12.1. The Nazareth Manifesto and Luke 7:22 Compared

	The Nazareth Manifesto (what was promised)	Luke 7:22 (what was fulfilled)
Luke 4:18-19	Preach good news to the poor	✔
	Freedom for prisoners	(missing)
	Recovery of sight for the blind	✔
	Release the oppressed	(missing)
Luke 4:25-27	(excess)	Lame walk
	The Elisha story (4:27)	Lepers healed
	(excess)	Deaf hear
	The Elijah story (4:25-26)	Dead are raised

But there are also two items on the list in Luke 7 that are mentioned in neither episode at Nazareth. "The lame walk" and "the deaf hear" are possible allusions to Isaiah 35:3–6, the text that inspired Charles Wesley's celebratory hymn "O for a Thousand Tongues to Sing!" The appearance of these two items on Jesus's list in Luke 7:22 represents what we might call an "excess" of the salvation that the Messiah brings—beyond what is explicitly promised. The point is that if the kingdom is indeed holistic, pertaining to all of life, then it is impossible to capture the full range of what is involved in one summary statement (whether in Luke 4 or elsewhere). Even the list that Jesus gives in Luke 7:22 is illustrative, not exhaustive. There are more dimensions of holistic salvation than are dreamed of in our theology!

The Stumbling Block—for John and for Us

However, we should also notice that there is a significant omission in Luke 7:22. Since this verse gives concrete examples of the fulfillment of Jesus's mission articulated in Luke 4:16–30, the fact that he leaves out the references to "release for captives" and "freedom for the oppressed" is startling. Why does Jesus omit these important lines? The answer lies in the basis for John's question: "Are you the one who is to come, or are we to wait for another?" (Luke 7:19). John is asking frankly, "Are you the Messiah we have been expecting?" The reason he asks is fairly obvious, once we think about it. After all, John has heard reports of Jesus's Nazareth manifesto, his claims of what he has come to accomplish. Yet Jesus's announcement that he will set free the oppressed/the captives—which is central to Luke 4:16–30—has not been fulfilled in the case of John. Having been imprisoned by Herod, the plain fact is that John has not been released from prison by the coming of Jesus.[9] So John has legitimate doubts.[10]

That is precisely why Jesus ends his response to John's disciples with this challenge: "And blessed is anyone who takes no offense at me" (Luke 7:23). That "anyone" is, in the first instance, John himself. John is being personally warned about a possible stumbling block to his expectations of the kingdom. Jesus implies that he cannot guarantee that John will immediately participate in the liberative benefits of God's Jubilee reign. Indeed, it turns out that John will die in prison (Matt. 14:3–11; Mark 6:17–29); in his case there will be a delay of the kingdom's benefits, until the resurrection. Can John live with Jubilee being for others—for the time being—while he remains in prison?

Yet John was not wrong to expect release. He had the proper biblical expectation that (to paraphrase the Lord's Prayer) when the kingdom of God comes, the will of God will be done on earth as it is in heaven. The coming of the kingdom meant (and means) nothing less than the restoration of our earthly life to the fullness of God's original intentions for blessing, shalom, and justice in the earth (and that certainly includes the liberation of those unjustly imprisoned). What John did not understand was that the kingdom does not come all at once. John was in danger of stumbling over Jesus on this point. He expected too much, too quickly.

Historically, however, many Christians have had the opposite problem. We have not expected enough. And what we have expected, we have often delayed until "heaven" and the return of Christ. We have not really believed that God cares about this world of real people in their actual historical situations, which often are characterized by oppression and suffering. Our understanding of salvation has been characterized by an unbiblical otherworldliness. So our expectations of the future have often not reflected the full-orbed good news that Jesus proclaimed at Nazareth.

In other words, John is not the only one in danger of stumbling over Jesus. Given the message that Jesus proclaimed at Nazareth, contemporary Christians might find themselves asking John's question ("Are you the coming one?"), but for a different reason. This holistic vision of the kingdom of God (which was received as good news by Jesus's audience at Nazareth) might be disorienting

9. Whereas bondage or imprisonment in Isa. 61 was a metaphor, it has a quite literal application to John. But setting the oppressed free would also apply to John even if we take the reference to imprisonment as metaphorical.

10. It is as if John is asking (as the character Ray Kinsella does, in a memorable moment in the film *Field of Dreams*), "What's in it for me?"

for us because it challenges our preconceptions. It seems too earthly or worldly. This does not look like the kingdom that we have been expecting. Indeed, the kingdom of God, as presented in the previous chapter, might sound too much like the "social gospel"—a term that is anathema in many so-called conservative sectors of the church today, especially among Christians raised on the idea of Jesus as "personal savior," where this is contrasted with the supposedly liberal notion of the salvation of the social order.

However, if we find this holistic teaching challenging, perhaps it is time to rise to the challenge that the Son of God brings. For, though it may indeed be disorienting for us, the Bible is quite clear that salvation involves the restoration of human life (in its bodily and social aspects) to what it was meant to be. Perhaps it is time to go back to the Bible and "conserve" its teaching of holistic salvation rather than "liberally" departing from it (as so many in the church have done).

But this vision of holistic salvation is only initially disorienting. It is ultimately good news—even great news! For if we are honest about it, the kingdom of God is exactly what we need, since it addresses both our present brokenness and our deepest yearnings for restoration and renewal. We know that brokenness pervades church and society, at individual and communal levels; this includes failed marriages, drug addiction, sexual promiscuity, domestic violence, racism, poverty, disease, war, genocide, greed, and despair. And we yearn and hope desperately for God's healing and shalom. If only we would dismantle our ingrained bifurcated habits of mind and life (our division of reality into sacred and secular, into spiritual and earthly), then we could begin to open our hearts to the power of God's holistic salvation; for the good news is that God wants to heal all our brokenness, both internal and external, whether personal or social.[11]

Worldview Shifts—Signs of Hope and Danger

And thankfully, many Christians are learning. The worldview of many in the church is slowly being transformed in a more holistic direction. With new ears

---

11. The fact that John died in prison should warn us of the difference between a biblical understanding of the kingdom and the triumphalistic assumptions of much that goes under the name of the "health-and-wealth gospel" or the "prosperity gospel." Jesus himself endured rejection and death before resurrection, thus paralleling Israel's experience of bondage in Egypt before deliverance and their exile in Babylon before return to the land. Paul himself says that we must suffer with Christ in order to attain to the resurrection (Phil. 3:10–11). Indeed, all creation is groaning in its bondage, awaiting liberation (Rom. 8:18–25). In other words, while resurrection, healing, and holistic restoration constitute the appropriate Christian hope—and there is substantial healing and restoration possible in the present—"hope" means that we trust in what is coming but is not yet with us in its fullness. We live between the times, after the inauguration of the kingdom but before its final consummation.

we are even beginning to hear the first episode of the story in Luke 4:16–30. Many Christians are beginning to grasp the biblical truth that redemption is holistic, that no dimension of earthly life (and that includes the social order) is in principle excluded from God's transformative purposes.

But this shift in our worldview comes with some confusion and even danger. The trouble is that the evolving "Christian" worldview, as embodied in the North American church today (but not only there), often continues to be dualistic; but it is a dualism of a different, more pernicious kind. We are in danger of replacing the old two-realm dualism with a new version of the "in-group versus out-group" framework that plagued Jesus's audience at Nazareth. Having cast out the old demons of otherworldliness, we have not always, in humility, sought to replace them with a truly biblical ethos. Instead, in our ambition to make a difference in *this* world, we may have allowed wandering spirits of the age—unclean spirits—to inhabit our imaginations (see Matt. 12:43–46 // Luke 11:24–26).

The point is that the transition from otherworldly salvation to a holistic understanding of the kingdom of God is impossible without personal transformation. The shift to a truly biblical understanding of salvation cannot be limited to head knowledge without moral responsibility. To put it another way, we cannot separate eschatology from ethics.

If we omit the ethical challenge of the kingdom, our newly found this-worldliness will simply confirm our selfish consumerist/materialistic, upwardly mobile, late-modern lifestyle; that is, our affirmation of the world (our holistic vision of salvation) will be construed to benefit us (whoever we are), while we ignore the needs of the wider world, especially the concrete needs of people who are different from our favored in-group. The tragedy is that many upwardly mobile North American Christians today often hoard and guard their religious identity and economic privilege, with little concern for the poor or for immigrants, or those of other nations, cultures, or religions. This problem is, of course, not limited to North Americans or even specifically to Christians. But, given the primary audience of this book, and the extraordinary religious and economic privilege of those living in North America, we need to take this challenge seriously.[12]

We need to take seriously the fact that the kingdom of God is not coterminous with the church or with any nation or any set of cultural ideals; rather, it refers to God's restorative rule over the entire earth. The very point of holistic salvation, according to Jesus in Luke 4:16–30, is that all people have

---

12. As the old song goes, "It's me, it's me, O Lord, / standin' in the need of prayer. / Not my brother nor my sister, but it's me, O Lord, / standin' in the need of prayer."

a share in the fullness of the blessing that God has promised and that surely is coming. Since the church is called to mediate the blessings of this rule to others, this means that Christians must take up the very challenge the devil threw at Jesus in the temptation account: "If you are the Son of God . . ." Just as Jesus had to deal with the temptation to use the kingdom of God for his own benefit, or as a means to his own ends, so Christians today need to engage in self-examination concerning our motivations and way of life. For it is by how we live for others that we will show ourselves to be God's children. Only then will we hear God identify us as "my son/daughter, my beloved, in whom I am well pleased."

But as dangerous as the shift from an otherworldly sacred/secular framework to a more holistic understanding of salvation might be if not accompanied by humility and personal transformation, there is equal danger for those still mired in a two-realm worldview. Admittedly, few contemporary Christians are still trapped in a radical sort of dualism, denigrating this world as purely evil and hoping for escape to heaven. On the contrary, many Christians are beginning to embrace a fuller affirmation of earthly life than older generations in the church would have been comfortable with. Nevertheless, there are still many Christians who retain a semblance of the old sacred/secular split.

Table 12.2. The Dangers of Combining Two Types of Dualism

"Sacred" (spiritual ideals)	Equality of all people (in principle)	
"Secular" (real world of society, economics, politics)	"Us" (America, men, middle class, white, citizens, developed nations, Western nations)	"Them" (other nations, women, poor, nonwhite, immigrants/ foreigners, developing nations, non-Western nations)

What we have in many sectors of the church is the insidious temptation to combine an otherworldly two-realm worldview with the "us versus them" sociological dualism in a most pernicious way. The hybrid worldview allows us piously to affirm the ideal of the equality of all people in the sight of God (as a "spiritual" truth), while continuing with our entrenched and self-serving "us versus them" framework in the "real" world of politics and economics, in matters of the social order and the nation-state (and even in the family, in relationships between males and females). In the realm of the "sacred," we are quite willing to declare the equality of all people and to share the gospel (understood in a minimalist sense, as the way to "heaven"); but in the "secular" realm of realpolitik on earth, we horde our wealth and cling to our (national, class, economic) privilege. Granted, perhaps we might give away some of our wealth as charitable giving or tithing, but this requires no substantial change in our way of life, in our this-worldly (well-nigh idolatrous) commitments to success, material progress, and national identity.

But I submit that if we fail to open ourselves to the second part of Jesus's message at Nazareth, we will not really hear the first part either, at least not as he intended it. That is, our this-worldliness will be mere consumerism and selfishness, disconnected from a this-worldly passion for justice and love shown toward those in need, no matter who they are. In other words, we need the very same conversion or transformation that Jesus's audience at Nazareth needed if we are to become priestly mediators of blessing in this world, ministers of reconciliation of the *full* gospel.

Beyond an "Us versus Them" Hermeneutic

The reconciliation of real people to God, reconciliation affecting their embodied social contexts, is central to the kingdom of God. But this is not just nice theology; it is not meant to be "pie in the sky." Such reconciliation must involve real-life change on the part of the reconciled, and that change includes reconciliation between people. The New Testament makes clear that the coming of the kingdom through Christ breaks down the wall of separation between Jew and gentile (Eph. 2:14–16). Indeed, in the first century the kingdom of God required changed relationships at the practical level even in the hierarchical, elite Greco-Roman household, including the relationships between husbands and wives, parents and children, masters and slaves (Eph. 5:21–6:9).[13]

It is sometimes disturbing to contemporary (more "progressive") readers that the household code in Ephesians does not explicitly advocate the eradication of hierarchical institutions (especially slavery). Nevertheless Ephesians 5 enjoins a radical redefinition of roles, predicated on everyone in the church submitting themselves to everyone else (5:21) and modeling their lives on Christ's love (5:1–2).[14] So radical was this redefinition that in

13. Many New Testament scholars have come to recognize that Eph. 5 is not addressing families in general, but only a certain form of wealthy, elite family in which one man (the *pater-familias*) was simultaneously husband, father, and slave master of an extended household (the *familia*); it was this form of rigid, hierarchical family system that most needed transformation in the first century. The free men of such households usually ate meals together, apart from women, children, and slaves; so it turns out that one of the most central challenges to this family hierarchy was the communal meal that accompanied the Lord's Supper in the early church, where all ate together (see 1 Cor. 11:17–33). For a short, lucid account of how Eph. 5 critiques the Greco-Roman elite *familia*, see Gordon D. Fee, "The Cultural Context of Ephesians 5:18–6:9," *Priscilla Papers* 16 (2002): 3–8.

14. The paradox is that the very same injunctions given to husbands ("love") and to wives ("submit") are also given to the entire church (Eph. 5:1–2, 21). In other words, a careful reading

practice it led to changed family relationships and ultimately to the eradication of the institution of slavery.[15] Through Christ, the historical divisions that have arisen between human beings are overcome. As Paul puts it elsewhere, "There is no longer Jew or Greek, there is no longer slave or free, there is no longer male and female; for all of you are one in Christ Jesus" (Gal. 3:28).[16] But this is not just a "heavenly" or "spiritual" truth; it must be lived out concretely on earth.

So the challenge that Jesus puts to us, as he did to his original audience at Nazareth, is whether we are willing to serve as priestly ministers of reconciliation between the God of creation and the rest of the human family; this inevitably will involve changed relationships between actual human beings. Our willingness to take up this challenge is a sign of our openness to the gospel of the kingdom.[17]

Apparently Jesus's audience was not up to the challenge. They understood full well the point he was making about the ministry of Elijah and Elisha to those outside the covenant, but all it did was raise their hackles. Luke reports that when Jesus highlighted the outsider status of these two gentiles, the people in the synagogue "were filled with rage. They got up, drove him out of the town, and led him to the brow of the hill on which their town was built, so that they might hurl him off the cliff. But he passed through the midst of them and went on his way" (Luke 4:28–30).

The tragedy is that the very people who were called (through Abraham) to be a blessing to all the families of the earth had come to position themselves

---

of Eph. 5 suggests that husbands are also to submit to their wives and that wives are also to love their husbands. This is simply an implication of the general injunctions to love and submission in 5:1–2, 21. But the apostle is careful not to explicitly say this, as it might be too radical to be heard in a first-century context. Yet if we think about it, there can be no practical difference between love and submission if Christ is the model. So Eph. 5 plants the seeds of the unraveling of hierarchy and oppression in the family.

15. See also the household code in Col. 3:18–4:1 and the specific unraveling of slavery in the Epistle to Philemon (which is placed in the context of the church at Colossae). For a radical reading of Colossians, see Brian J. Walsh and Sylvia C. Keesmaat, *Colossians Remixed: Subverting the Empire* (Downers Grove, IL: IVP Academic, 2004), esp. 202–12 for their illuminating and imaginative retelling of Philemon's story.

16. Note the different language that Paul uses in Gal. 3:28 (accurately reflected in the NRSV) for the male-female relationship in contrast to the other two sets of relationships mentioned. Whereas he intends the abolition the ethnic distinction between Jew and Greek and the eradication of the institution of slavery (reflected by the use of the word "or" in both of these cases), he intends only a changed relationship between "male and female," not the abolition of the distinction (signaled by his retention of the word "and" in what is likely a quotation from Gen. 1:27).

17. Jesus rebuked his disciples for wanting to call down fire from heaven to destroy a village of Samaritans who did not welcome him (Luke 9:52–55).

antagonistically toward outsiders. Many in Israel (though certainly not all Israelites) had come to exalt their own privileged nearness to God and to despise, if not outright oppose, persons from those very nations to whom they were called to bring blessing. Instead of inviting gentiles into a relationship with the only true God of creation and history, they excluded them as, in effect, perpetually under God's curse.

Now, Christians reading this story have every right to get upset with the response of Jesus's hearers. We rightfully want to support our Lord, the one who came to effect salvation even for gentiles (which includes most of us).[18] Contrary to his hearers, Jesus understood the Scriptures aright, that the election of Israel was not strictly for their own sake, but rather for the sake of the wider world, the *kosmos*, says John 3:16, that God so loved.

But although Christians are understandably upset at the violent reaction of Jesus's hearers to his message at Nazareth, ultimately that response on our part is too tame and, more importantly, too self-serving. It does not take the radicalness of the gospel seriously enough. Indeed, at its worst it can lead (as it has historically) to a violent anti-Semitism on the part of the church, such that it sponsors persecution of "Christ killers" in the name of Christ. But this would mean reproducing the very same attitude toward outsiders that Jesus's audience was guilty of. By reading the text as a critique of "them" in opposition to "us," we reveal that we share the same impediment to hearing Jesus's message that his hearers at Nazareth had.[19]

I do not want for a minute to excuse the response of Jesus's hearers, but I would suggest that for us really to grasp the radical force of Jesus's message in this second part of the Nazareth account, we need to get beyond reading Luke 4:16–30 (and the rest of Scripture) with a truimphalist "us versus them" hermeneutic that always places Jesus on our side (as if we are the good guys) and thus seals us off hermetically from the challenge of the text. Rather, we need a hermeneutic of immersion and habitation, so that we might indwell the text and hear Jesus calling our own church practices and lives into question in the radical light of the gospel. Otherwise we will

18. I am, by the way, of Jewish heritage, born of a Jewish mother.

19. James Sanders calls this approach to Scripture "constitutive hermeneutics" (where the text brings us only comfort, rooted in a domesticated understanding of God), in contrast to genuine "prophetic hermeneutics" (which is able to call us into question, rooted in God's genuine transcendence). See James A. Sanders, *Canon and Community: A Guide to Canonical Criticism* (Philadelphia: Fortress, 1984), 53, 70; "Hermeneutics," in *Interpreter's Dictionary of the Bible, Supplementary Volume*, ed. Keith R. Crim, Victor P. Furnish, and Lloyd R. Bailey (Nashville: Abingdon, 1976), 402–7; "Hermeneutics in True and False Prophecy," in *Canon and Authority: Essays in Old Testament Religion and Theology*, ed. Burke O. Long and George W. Coats (Philadelphia: Fortress, 1977), 21–41. .

not be able to receive the good news of Luke 4:16–30 except in a superficial, facile, self-serving way.[20]

So we need to ask how we would respond if Jesus had given examples of God's love not to gentiles (that is too easy), but rather to groups of people that we in the church denigrate and oppose (perhaps, as did first-century Israel, for understandable reasons). Who these people would be depends, of course, on where in the church we locate ourselves—whether in its more liberal or conservative wings. Although I am unsure whether the terms "liberal" and "conservative" have value anymore (if they ever were helpful),[21] the question for us (however we identify ourselves) is what our response would be if Jesus had held up as examples of people on equal footing with ourselves, not gentiles, but instead members of whatever group most offends our ethical and religious sensibilities. If we were honest, who would we say are furthest from the kingdom of God? Who, as we see it, are our enemies or the enemies of God? Whom would we simply prefer not to associate with? Unless we address such difficult questions for ourselves, we are not ready for the holistic gospel of salvation that Jesus brings in Luke 4:16–30.

I believe that Clarence Jordan's famous Cotton Patch Version of the New Testament helps us think about the significance of Jesus's message for the contemporary world. Jordan, whose interracial Koinonia Farm in Georgia helped shape the perspective of both Jimmy Carter and Millard Fuller in their

20. The danger of adopting an "us versus them" oppositional worldview is particularly evident among some branches of consistent preterist eschatology (which, on the Internet at least, is the most vocal alternative to dispensationalist rapture theology). Adherents to a consistent preterist approach to eschatology have rightly renounced an otherworldly view of the future; however, they also claim (as I do not) that all biblical prophecies are already fulfilled, and we are now in the new heavens and new earth, working toward the implementation of God's kingdom in this world. Apart from the question of whether this approach is exegetically justified or adequately grasps the theological disjunction between this age and the age to come, the ethical problem is that especially those branches of consistent preterism associated with the movement known as theonomy or Christian reconstruction often combine their understanding of the kingdom of God with visions of American cultural and economic superiority (baptizing one nation and its capitalist economy as "Christian") and seek to "conquer" the world in Christ's name, even praying for the destruction of enemies of the faith by name in worship. See David Chilton, *Paradise Restored: A Biblical Theology of Dominion* (Tyler, TX: Reconstruction Press, 1985), 216–19.

21. I have been called "more liberal than the liberals and more conservative than the conservatives"—a phrase coined by a former student of mine (Lyle Freeman) as he introduced me to his local church, where I was leading a weekend teaching retreat. I think that this adequately breaks down the distinction. The important question is not whether a person aligns with the artificial package of causes usually associated with "conservative" or "liberal" Christianity, but whether one is faithful to Scripture and to the Lord of Scripture. Thankfully, there are such people in every theological camp.

early years, contextualized the Gospels in terms of the issues of racism in the American South of the 1960s. In his translation of Luke, called *Jesus' Doings*, Jordan imagined Tiberius as United States president, Pilate as governor of Georgia, Herod as governor of Alabama, Philip as governor of Mississippi, and Lysanias as governor of Arkansas, "while Annas and Caiphas were co-presidents of the Southern Baptist Convention" (Luke 3:1–2).[22] He then has John the Baptist saying to the crowds,

> You sons of snakes, who put the heat on you to run from the fury about to break over your heads? You must give some *proof* that you've had a *change of heart*. And don't start patting one another on the back with that "we-good-white-people" stuff, because I'm telling you that if God wants to, he can make white-folks out of this pile of rocks. Already the axe is lying at the taproot of the trees, and every tree that doesn't perform some worthwhile function is chopped down and burned up. (Luke 3:7–9)

Then, after Jesus preaches in his home church in Valdosta (the equivalent of the synagogue in Nazareth) to great positive acclaim, Jordan has him say to his audience,

> Surely some of you will cite to me the old proverb, "Doctor, take your own medicine. Let us see you do right here in your home town all the things we heard you did in Columbus." Well, to tell the truth, no prophet is welcome in his own home town. And I'm telling you straight, there were a lot of *white* widows in Georgia during the time of Elijah, when the skies were locked up for three years and six months, and there was a great drought everywhere, but Elijah didn't stay with any of *them*. Instead, he stayed with a *Negro* woman over in Terrell County. And there were a lot of sick *white* people during the time of the great preacher Elisha, but he didn't heal any of *them*—only Naaman the African. (Luke 4:24–27)

My point is not that we should get all worked up on behalf of various social issues. After all, the so-called Tea Party movement in America today is very worked up about issues of immigration and health care, and most fundamentally about the intrusive role of government. But so far, members of this movement are basically upset at the perceived loss of their own privilege; they are not angered by the injustice shown to others, especially not others who are different from them. This sort of self-righteous anger has nothing to do

22. Originally published as Clarence Jordan, *The Cotton Patch Version of Luke and Acts: Jesus' Doings and the Happenings* (New York: Association Press, 1969); reissued as *Clarence Jordan's Cotton Patch Gospel: Luke and Acts* (Macon, GA: Smyth & Helwys, 2004).

with the kingdom Jesus proclaimed, except perhaps that it is an impediment to entering this kingdom.[23]

The impulse behind the Tea Party movement is the very opposite of the motivations of the abolitionists, like William Wilberforce in eighteenth-century England, who tirelessly opposed the West African slave trade on the basis of Christian principles. Indeed, the self-interest of many conservative Christians in America today is in direct contradiction to the impetus that drove the nineteenth-century evangelist Charles Grandison Finney, who, while president of Oberlin College—along with other faculty members—broke the recently enacted fugitive slave law and harbored escaped slaves in defiant acts of civil disobedience, rooted in the gospel of Jesus Christ.[24]

Perhaps the issue of racism is not quite as explicit in the church today as it used to be (though it may simply be more hidden, under the surface), so let us bring the message of Luke 4:16–30 closer to home. Suppose Jesus said to an American congregation in a state bordering Mexico, "There were many middle-class American citizens living in California who lost their homes due to the housing crisis and the stock market crash, but God was pleased to provide an illegal Mexican worker in Santa Fe with housing and health care for his family." Or let us imagine that Jesus said, "There were many retired evangelical Christian missionaries dying of cancer and heart disease in Wheaton, Illinois, but God healed none of them and instead healed a gay man with AIDS in San Francisco." What response would statements like these receive in a typical conservative church in America on a Sunday morning? Indeed, what response does that evoke from us reading this right now? The point is that our response to such claims of God's working outside our normal comfort zones will determine whether we truly hear the gospel of the kingdom that Jesus proclaimed at Nazareth.

I do not seek to pontificate about what particular issues Christians should support or oppose today in the so-called culture wars. In fact, I want to do precisely the opposite. We need to extricate ourselves from these wars, which are predicated on an oppositional dualism of "us versus them" (or "in-group versus out-group"), since this dualism is antithetical to the gospel of the

23. The difference between advocating on behalf of others (even if it means self-sacrifice) and the self-righteous protection of privilege is particularly evident in recent political movements throughout the world. On biblical grounds, we should be willing to declare that any movement founded on protecting one's own privilege is fundamentally un-Christian in its motivations and program.

24. For the fascinating story of Finney and Oberlin College, see Donald W. Dayton, *Discovering an Evangelical Heritage* (Peabody, MA: Hendrickson, 1976), chap. 2, "Reform in the Life and Thought of Evangelist Charles G. Finney"; and chap. 5, "Civil Disobedience and the Oberlin-Wellington Rescue Case."

kingdom. The Christian gospel understands the true antithesis between good and evil (between the kingdom of God and the powers of destruction) to run not between groups, but rather through every human heart. Therefore, as an antidote to unthinking involvement in the culture wars, Christians need to have their imaginations grasped by the radically holistic vision of redemption that the Bible teaches, and to engage their world, at individual and communal levels, with daily acts of courage and love on behalf of those in need, even if—especially if—they are different from us.

There is a sense, therefore, in which this chapter is meant to serve as a warning to the reader, especially any reader positively attracted to the holistic vision of redemption that the rest of this book sketches. Yes, this holistic vision is a powerful antidote to our narrow, constricted understandings of salvation. And it is certainly good news for us. But we dare not simply appropriate this holistic vision in a selfish manner, construing the kingdom purely for our benefit—on pain of being unfaithful to the gospel of Jesus Christ.

The Hope of the Kingdom

Although I am utterly serious about the temptation and seduction of an "us versus them" oppositional identity among Christians today, I do not believe that it is a fait accompli. It is a pervasive temptation and possibility, but thankfully not yet a ubiquitous fact. And I have faith in the broad community of faith that nurtured me in love and compassion all these years. To paraphrase the writer of Hebrews, I believe better things of the church.[25]

Many sectors of the church today have proved to be faithful inheritors of the Pentecost experience of the early Jesus movement, when people from "all nations under heaven" heard and responded to the gospel in their native languages. What happened that day, explained Peter (Acts 2:17–18), was a fulfillment of the prophetic vision of Joel, which proclaimed equal access to God's Spirit by male and female, young and old, slave and free (Joel 2:28–29).[26]

25. "Even though we speak in this way, beloved, we are confident of better things in your case, things that belong to salvation" (Heb. 6:9).

26. Although this democratizing vision was applied on the day of Pentecost to Jews of every nation and language, it was not until the Jerusalem Council, recorded in Acts 15, that the early church came to grips with the truly universal implications of the gospel, precipitated by some of the Jewish believers demanding that gentiles become Jews in order to partake of the benefits of salvation in Jesus. After some deliberation, which involved both listening to testimony about what God was already doing among the gentiles (vv. 4, 7–12) and reflection on Scripture (vv. 15–18), the council made it clear that gentiles were accepted members of God's people in their own right (vv. 19–20). The analogy for today might be for the North American church to

The church that I have come to know (spread over many denominations and local assemblies in different countries) embodies a significant foretaste of the vision of Revelation 7:9–10. Here John sees "a great multitude that no one could count, from every nation, from all tribes and peoples and languages, standing before the throne and before the Lamb, robed in white, with palm branches in their hands. They cried out in a loud voice, saying, 'Salvation belongs to our God who is seated on the throne, and to the Lamb!'"

This vision is itself a fulfillment of Revelation 5, which anticipates the gathering of God's saints from "every tribe and language and people and nation" made into a new humanity, redeemed by Christ for the priestly task of reigning on this earth (5:9–10). Not only is this a multiethnic group of worshipers, but their earthly reign manifests the "salvation" for which they praise God. It is this doubly comprehensive and holistic vision of God's kingdom (the redeemed from every culture reigning on earth) that should guide us as we read the entirety of Scripture and live our lives in the expectation of Christ's return. The overall thrust of the biblical canon (from creation to eschaton) unveils for us—if we have eyes to see—a vision of the kingdom of God that is both applicable to every dimension of earthly life and open to the entire human family. Let us not reduce the gospel of the kingdom to anything less.

---

recognize that people from other nations and cultures can come to faithful submission to the gospel of Christ without the accretions of Western culture (or even Western theology).

Appendix

Whatever Happened to the New Earth?

Att this point the reader might be sensing a significant tension between the Bible's holistic vision of the redemption of earthly creation and the way that many, if not most, Christians think about the future of the earth. How did it come about that so many in the church today seem unaware of God's intent to redeem this world? How did the idea of an otherworldly destiny in heaven displace the biblical teaching of the renewal of the earth and end up dominating Christian eschatology? It is the task of this appendix to briefly explore the history of eschatology in order to understand how the redemption of creation has largely disappeared from the popular theology of the church. Thankfully, the eclipse of holistic eschatology in the history of the church is not the whole story. There has been a partial recovery of the biblical vision of the renewal of the earth in recent times, which this chapter will also address.[1]

The impetus in Christian eschatology to envision future hope as transcending earthly existence has always stood in some tension with the pervasive biblical emphasis on the redemption of the world. Thus, many Christian theologians who have shared (often unconsciously) the general Platonic vision of the afterlife have nevertheless, laudably, tried to honor the biblical

---

1. This appendix does not attempt anything like a complete account of the history of holistic eschatology. Due to space limitations (not to mention my present expertise), this account is somewhat impressionistic, meant to suggest only the main currents in the eclipse and recovery of the idea of a redeemed earth. A fuller account of the history of holistic eschatology awaits a separate book.

this-worldly emphasis in their eschatology. They have typically done this in two main ways. The first way this biblical emphasis shows up is through the prominent New Testament doctrine of the resurrection of the body; the second is through the idea of the millennium, the thousand-year rule of Christ on the earth, found in Revelation 20:1–5. Only rarely prior to the twentieth century do we find Christian theologians explicitly addressing the eschatological renewal of the earth.

Holistic Eschatology in the First Centuries

Almost every Christian writer in the first few centuries of the church affirms the resurrection of the body, some even defending the notion against gnosticism, which often outdid Platonism in its suspicion of materiality. A famous exception is Origen of Alexandria (185–254), who, it turns out, had been significantly influenced by the Platonic vision.

In his famous work *On First Principles*,[2] Origen affirms that since only God is strictly bodiless, we will indeed have bodies at the resurrection; yet he claims that the resurrection body will not be in "the grosser and more solid condition of the body" that is characteristic of "lower beings," but instead will shine with "the splendour of 'celestial bodies'" fit for "more perfect and blessed beings."[3] Indeed, he is adamant that the resurrection body will be "a spiritual body, which can dwell in the heavens."[4]

At a different point in *On First Principles*, Origen proposes three possibilities of what the final state of human blessedness might be (all of which show an aversion to physicality). These include "a bodiless existence" (immortality of the soul), an "ethereal" (nonphysical) body, and an existence in the highest realm of "the true heaven," beyond even the "fixed" heavenly sphere of the

2. Quotations of this work are from Origen, *On First Principles*, trans. G. W. Butterworth (reprint, Gloucester, MA: Peter Smith, 1973). Although Origen wrote his *Peri archōn* in Greek, only a few fragments remain. Instead, most of what we know of this work comes from Latin translations or summaries by others. In Rufinus's Latin translation (titled *De principiis*) we have the most "orthodox" version of Origen's thought; but Jerome's citations portray a more heterodox Origen, which fits well with criticisms of Origen found in other early writers and with some of the extant Greek fragments. Butterworth's translation is based on a critical text that supplements Rufinus with the Greek fragments and with Jerome. On this issue, see Butterworth's introduction; see also Brian E. Daley, *The Hope of the Early Church: A Handbook of Patristic Eschatology* (reprint, Peabody, MA: Hendrickson, 2003), 54. A readily available though less reliable translation (based simply on Rufinus's Latin) is by Frederick Crombie, in *Ante-Nicene Fathers*, vol. 4, ed. Alexander Roberts, James Donaldson, and A. Cleveland Coxe (Buffalo, NY: Christian Literature Publishing, 1885), http://www.newadvent.org/fathers/.

3. Origen, *On First Principles* 2.2.2 (Butterworth, 81–82).

4. Ibid., 2.10.3 (Butterworth, 141).

planets.[5] It is not clear how this third option is on a par with the other two since it describes not the state of the body of the blessed, but rather the realm in which they will dwell.[6]

Furthermore, in an attempt to reconcile this third option with Matthew 5:5 ("Blessed are the meek, for they will inherit the earth"), Origen suggests that while some "may be found worthy of a dwelling place in the earth," the truly obedient and wise "may be said to gain the kingdom of that heaven or heavens," and he concludes that "there seems to be opened a road for the progress of the saints from that earth to those heavens, so that they would appear not so much to remain permanently in that earth as to dwell there in the hope of passing on, when they have made the requisite progress, to the inheritance of the 'kingdom of heaven.'"[7]

Later in *On First Principles*, Origen expands this notion of upward progress in the afterlife, suggesting that while the saints may begin in "paradise," which is "some place situated on the earth," they may "ascend" through increasing knowledge and wisdom to "the region of the air," passing through the planetary realm (the visible heavens), until they arrive at the "invisible" heavens (where the mind feasts eternally on "the contemplation and understanding of God").[8]

But Origen was something of an aberration; the importance of the resurrection (including its physicality) was rarely questioned as a component of eschatological hope in the early centuries of the church. Yet if Origen's interpretation of an immaterial resurrection body was widely rejected, his view of the ideal location of this body in "heaven" came to be standard fare.

More debatable than the resurrection was the millennium, the thousand-year kingdom of righteousness and peace to be established by Christ on earth, prior to the final judgment and redemption of the world—an idea found in only

5. Ibid., 2.3.7 (Butterworth, 93). Origen suggests the second option of a resurrection body composed not of earthly matter but of "ether" in other places as well, such as in *On First Principles* 1.6.4 (Butterworth, 58).

6. Jerome's version of the third option is slightly different from Rufinus's (quoted above), and it has Origen suggesting both that the "fixed" sphere of the heavens "shall be dissolved into nothing," and that the heaven that "will serve as a dwelling-place for the saints" is two levels up from this sphere (quoted in Butterworth, 92–93n7).

7. Origen, *On First Principles* 2.3.7 (Butterworth, 93–94). It is significant that even Origen had to grapple with the clear teaching of the New Testament of an earthly final state (something that many contemporary Christians simply ignore).

8. Ibid., 2.11.6–7 (Butterworth, 152–54). Not only did Origen tend toward interpreting the resurrection body in immaterial or quasi-immaterial terms, but he also believed in the preexistence and prenatal fall of the soul, with embodiment on earth as punishment for this fall (*On First Principles* 1.8.1; this section is not found in Rufinus's Latin, but is taken from an extant Greek fragment [Butterworth, 67–68]). It makes sense that if earthly embodiment were regarded as punishment for sin, this would logically incline one toward a final state that is disembodied.

one place in the Bible, at the start of Revelation 20.[9] While several Christian writers of the second and third centuries affirm the millennium and grant it an important role in their eschatology, it is rejected with great scorn both by Origen (in the third century) as a Jewish and overly literal interpretation of Scripture[10] and by Eusebius (in the fourth century) in his renowned *Ecclesiastical History* as "materialistic."[11] Whereas Origen's Platonism led him to critique the earthly, physicalistic elements of the millennial hope, since the kingdom of God is progressively established within the believer's soul, Eusebius based his rejection of the millennium on his reinterpretation of the kingdom, seeing it not as an eschatological future cosmic event but rather as the church's providential growth in the Roman Empire that was occurring under Constantine.[12]

Admittedly, the logic of the millennium is difficult to understand. Why, prior to the beginning of the final eschatological state (the new heaven and new earth in Rev. 21–22), does there need to be a temporary redeemed creation? Why have a "first resurrection" just of the righteous martyrs, and then after the thousand years a general resurrection and judgment? Some recent literary and exegetical work on Revelation has plausibly suggested that the book intends the millennium not as a temporal period *prior* to the final state, but rather as the first thousand years *of* this state—a probationary period, if you will, in the redeemed creation before the final judgment, for those still alive at Christ's return who have not yet acknowledged his kingship.[13] One wishes, however, that the author of the book of Revelation had made this somewhat clearer. It would have saved the early church (and later interpreters) a lot of trouble.

The problem is that when a dominant Platonic background of otherworldly aspiration is combined with belief in a temporary earthly millennium, all the biblical promises and descriptions of the redemption of the cosmos (and there are many) tend to be squeezed into this thousand-year rule of Christ, which leaves the final state to be reinterpreted as "heaven."

9. The idea of a temporary messianic kingdom is also found in some Jewish apocalyptic literature, such as *2 Baruch* 29:2–30:1.

10. Origen, *On First Principles* 2.11.2 (Butterworth, 142); see also Origen, *Commentarium series in evangelium Matthaei* 17.35.

11. Eusebius, *Ecclesiastical History* 7.24–25.

12. Granted that some of the overreaction to the idea of the millennium derives from the extravagant, even sensual way it was described by Cerinthus and others (see Eusebius, *Ecclesiastical History* 3.28). Such writers may have been picking up on descriptions of the kingdom of God in late Jewish apocalyptic texts such as *2 Baruch* 29:5–8.

13. This is part of the complex argument in J. Webb Mealy, *After the Thousand Years: Resurrection and Judgment in Revelation 20* (JSOTSup 70; Sheffield: JSOT Press, 1992); for Mealy's summary, see 239, 241, 244. See also Gerhard A. Krodel, *Revelation* (Augsburg Commentary on the New Testament; Minneapolis: Augsburg, 1989), 327, 330.

Thus some millenarians or chiliasts (words derived from the Latin and Greek, respectively, for "one thousand") interpret the millennium of Revelation 20 as the fulfillment of all Old Testament prophecies of the flourishing of nature and the just social order that God will bring.[14] They also view the millennium as equivalent to the many New Testament anticipations of the restoration or renewal of all things, including the liberation of creation from its bondage to decay (described in Rom. 8),[15] though these clearly have reference to the eternal state.[16] In fact, due to the Platonic assumption that the final destiny of the righteous must be supramundane, some of the early millenarians do not even distinguish between the millennium in Revelation 20:1–5 and the new heaven and new earth in Revelation 21, identifying both with the thousand-year reign of Christ on earth and distinguishing both from final eschatological salvation[17]—an interpretation that appears also among historians of the millennium (so pervasive is the Platonic assumption).[18]

Among second-, third-, and early fourth-century Christian writers who clearly affirm a temporary earthly millennium, one has to read carefully to discern if they take the final state to be earthly and concrete or rather to be transcendent and acosmic. In many cases it is simply difficult to tell.

The second-century *Epistle of Barnabas*, for example, anticipates a millennial age or Sabbath coming after six "days" of world history (a day being equivalent to a thousand years).[19] But when the author goes on to claim that this Sabbath/seventh day will be followed by an "eighth day, that is, a beginning of another world,"[20] it is unclear whether this is meant to refer to a permanently renovated cosmos or to heaven. The designation "eighth day" might suggest

---

14. Both Justin Martyr (*Dialogue with Trypho* 81) and Irenaeus (*Against Heresies* 5.35.2) cite the new heaven and new earth of Isa. 65 as evidence of the millennium.

15. Irenaeus (*Against Heresies* 5.32.1) quotes Rom. 8:19–21 as evidence of the millennium.

16. The only debatable text sometimes cited by millenarians is 1 Cor. 15:24–28, since it suggests a two-stage kingdom. However, nowhere else in Paul's writings does he suggest anything like a millennium in the sequence of events at Christ's return. The two stages of the kingdom in 1 Cor. 15:24–28 most likely refer to the distinction between Christ's present rule (the "already" of the kingdom) and the final state, which begins after evil is eradicated from the world (the "not yet" of the kingdom).

17. Irenaeus (*Against Heresies* 5.35.2) distinguishes the first four verses of Rev. 21 from verse 5, treating the former as referring to the millennium and the latter to the eternal state.

18. This confusion clouds Brian Daley's otherwise illuminating analysis of patristic eschatology in *The Hope of the Early Church*. The opposite confusion is found in the work of A. H. Armstrong (see at notes 50–51 below), who tends to view patristic references to the millennium as describing the climactic renovation of the cosmos.

19. This pseudepigraphical work, usually dated to the early second century, is the first Christian work to utilize the classic schema of six thousand years of world history, followed by the Sabbath.

20. *Epistle of Barnabas* 15.8. Quotations of this work are from Alexander Roberts and James Donaldson, in *Ante-Nicene Fathers*, vol. 1, ed. Alexander Roberts, James Donaldson, and A. Cleveland Coxe (Buffalo, NY: Christian Literature Publishing, 1885), http://www.newadvent.org/fathers/.

another stage in world history (as opposed to a world beyond history), but we cannot be sure, since the *Epistle of Barnabas* is simply not forthcoming about the nature of the final state. Nevertheless, the text displays a positive, this-worldly hope in its anticipation of the day "when we ourselves, having received the promise, wickedness no longer existing, and all things having been made new by the Lord, shall be able to work righteousness."[21]

Justin's *Dialogue with Trypho* (also second century) is likewise ambiguous. Justin first affirms a literal, earthly reign of Christ for "a thousand years in Jerusalem, which will then be built, adorned, and enlarged,"[22] declaring that this will be followed by the "general" or "eternal" resurrection.[23] Later in the *Dialogue with Trypho*, he compares Joshua and Jesus (as type and antitype), claiming that just as Joshua distributed the land to Israel, so Jesus "will distribute a good land to each one, though not in the same manner."[24] For whereas "the former gave them a temporary inheritance, . . . the latter, after the holy resurrection, shall give us the eternal possession."[25] The words "after the holy resurrection" and "eternal possession" suggest that the "good land" that Jesus distributes is a reference to the final state (and not the millennium), especially when Justin goes on to say that through Jesus "the Father will renew both the heaven and the earth."[26] Yet the fact that he can cite Isaiah's prophecy of the new heaven and new earth as evidence for the (temporary) millennium is confusing.[27] Does the new heaven and new earth refer both to the millennium and to the eternal state? Or does he mean it to refer literally to the millennium, with the good land/eternal possession functioning as a metaphor for heaven? Later, when Justin says that "there shall be a future possession for all the saints in this same land," hence "they shall be with him in that land, and inherit everlasting and incorruptible good,"[28] we find interpreters disagreeing on whether this refers to the millennium or the final state.[29]

---

21. *Epistle of Barnabas* 15.7. The placement of this statement in the argument of chap. 15 makes it likely, though not certain, to be a reference to the millennium/Sabbath rather than to the eighth day.

22. Justin, *Dialogue with Trypho* 80. Quotations of this work are from Marcus Dods and George Reith, in *Ante-Nicene Fathers*, vol. 1, ed. Alexander Roberts, James Donaldson, and A. Cleveland Coxe (Buffalo, NY: Christian Literature Publishing, 1885), http://www.newadvent.org/fathers/.

23. Ibid., 81.

24. Ibid., 113.

25. Ibid.

26. Ibid.

27. Ibid., 81.

28. Ibid., 139.

29. Justin claims that those "who say there is no resurrection of the dead, and that their souls, when they die, are taken to heaven" are not true Christians (*Dial.* 80); this suggests where he ultimately comes down on this question.

An equally complex case is Irenaeus (ca. 130–202). On the one hand, Irenaeus views the millennium as a preparatory time for the redeemed to become acclimatized, in the familiar setting of earth, to the ultimate goal of participating in the divine nature.[30] This suggests that we will somehow ultimately transcend earthly existence. Yet Irenaeus clearly refers to the final state as the new heaven and the new earth, and he seems to understand this as a real, physical, renovated cosmos.[31] Nevertheless, the impulse to transcend earthly existence shows up in his view of the differing levels of reward that the redeemed will experience in this new world. While the most worthy go straight to heaven, others go to paradise ("presumably a place between heaven and earth"),[32] while still others will "possess the splendor of the city" (the new Jerusalem, which has come down out of heaven to earth, according to Rev. 21).[33] But this "gradation and arrangement of those who are saved" is not a fixed hierarchy, since the redeemed will have the opportunity to "advance" and "ascend" in the new creation (seemingly with heaven as the ultimate destination).[34] Complex though Irenaeus's scheme may be, he does not simply dismiss the redemption of the earth, as many current Christians do.

The case of Methodius (third century) initially seems to be less ambiguous. In the *Symposium* (known also as the *Banquet of the Ten Virgins*), Methodius interprets the Old Testament Feast of Tabernacles as allegorically representing the millennium. Just as the Israelites left Egypt, then celebrated the Feast of Tabernacles, then journeyed to the land of promise, so after departing "the Egypt of this life," Methodius says, he will "celebrate with Christ the millennium of rest, which is called the seventh day, even the true Sabbath"[35] (equivalent to the Feast of Tabernacles), following which he "shall pass . . . to greater and better things, ascending into the very house of God above the heavens."[36]

---

30. Irenaeus, *Against Heresies* 5.32.1; 5.35.2. Quotations of this work are from Alexander Roberts and William Rambaut, in *Ante-Nicene Fathers*, vol. 1, ed. Alexander Roberts, James Donaldson, and A. Cleveland Coxe (Buffalo, NY: Christian Literature Publishing, 1885), http://www.newadvent.org/fathers/.

31. Irenaeus, *Against Heresies* 5.35.2; 5.36.1.

32. Daley, *Hope of the Early Church*, 31. The idea of paradise as midway between heaven and earth may draw on Jewish extrabiblical writings that understand paradise (which is how the Septuagint refers to the garden of Eden) as taken up to heaven (or concealed on a high mountain) after the sin of Adam and Eve, when paradise became off-limits to humanity (see *4 Ezra* 4:7–8 on paradise kept from humans in heaven; and *2 Baruch* 4:1–6 on both paradise and the heavenly Jerusalem kept from humans, yet the latter revealed to Moses on Mount Sinai). It was thought that paradise would descend from heaven to earth at the eschaton to be the centerpiece of the new creation (see Rev. 21–22).

33. Irenaeus, *Against Heresies* 5.36.1–2.

34. Ibid., 5.36.2. In this, he anticipates Origen's later schema of progress from earth to heaven.

35. Methodius, *Symposium* 9.5.

36. Ibid.

But just when we find Methodius clearly teaching a final heavenly destiny for the redeemed, elsewhere he seems to say the opposite. In his *Discourse on the Resurrection*, Methodius upbraids those who think that the cosmos will be destroyed (as opposed to being renewed through purification), explaining that this viewpoint would disparage God because it assumes that God chose the lesser of two options in creating the world, which he will then remedy by the more perfect option of destroying it at the eschaton.[37] On the contrary, says Methodius, "God did not establish the universe in vain, or to no purpose but destruction, as those weak-minded men say, but to exist, and be inhabited, and continue. Wherefore the earth and the heaven must exist again after the conflagration and shaking of all things."[38] Admitting that Scripture uses the hyperbolic language of destruction to describe radical change, Methodius explains, "We may expect that the creation will pass away, *as if it were* to perish in the burning, in order that it may be renewed, not however that it will be destroyed."[39] And he insightfully links the redemption of the cosmos to the resurrection of the body, stating that "it is silly to discuss in what way of life our bodies will then exist, if there is no longer air, nor earth, nor anything else."[40]

But how does emphasis on the purification of the cosmos square with Methodius's claim that after the millennium the redeemed go to heaven? Perhaps in a redeemed cosmos the saints will be able to pass from earth to heaven at will. At any rate, we have not yet arrived at the later position that heaven, and definitely not earth, is the final destination of the righteous. Indeed, in the *Epistle of Barnabas*, Justin, Irenaeus, and Methodius we find a significant affirmation of this-worldly redemption, even if we cannot conclusively decide that all of them taught the permanent renewal of the cosmos.

Although it is difficult to find unambiguous statements of final cosmic redemption in the early Christian fathers, the idea of a temporary earthly millennium shows up in a number of writers. An earthly millennium is clearly taught by Papias, Justin, Irenaeus, and the *Epistle of Barnabas* (all second century), Tertullian (late second/early third century), Hippolytus, Methodius (both third century), Commodianus (third century, or possibly fifth),[41] and

---

37. Methodius, *Discourse on the Resurrection* 1.8. Quotations of this work are from William R. Clark, in *Ante-Nicene Fathers*, vol. 6, ed. Alexander Roberts, James Donaldson, and A. Cleveland Coxe (Buffalo, NY: Christian Literature Publishing, 1886), http://www.newadvent.org/fathers/.

38. Ibid.

39. Ibid., 1.9, emphasis added.

40. Ibid.

41. See the discussion in Daley, *Hope of the Early Church*, 162–64.

Lactantius (early fourth century).[42] The fact that other early Christian writers do not explicitly mention the millennium does not constitute evidence that they were opposed to the idea, since if we had only Justin's two *Apologies* (and not his *Dialogue with Trypho*), we would never have known he was a millenarian. The same is true of Irenaeus, who mentions the millennium only in book 5 of *Against Heresies*, and not in books 1–4.[43]

The very persistence of the millennial idea during the first few centuries of the church, despite derogatory comments by its detractors regarding its "Jewish" or "materialistic" nature, testifies to the ongoing power of the biblical vision of this-worldly redemption, even among those who had begun to assimilate a Platonic vision of the afterlife. By the fifth century, however, both millenarianism and the idea of a permanent renovation of the cosmos (with the exception of the resurrection body) had effectively disappeared from Christian eschatology.

The Augustinian Synthesis

The main blow to the vision of a renewed cosmos came from the magisterial synthesis by Augustine (354–430) in the fourth and fifth centuries. By interpreting the millennium as equivalent to the entire history of the church, Augustine not only extended the vision of Eusebius, but he also, significantly, assimilated a Neoplatonic framework for theology, first through the preaching of Bishop Ambrose of Milan (who linked Plotinian philosophy to the Logos teaching of the Gospel of John) and then through his reading of Plotinus's *Enneads* in Marius Victorinus's Latin translation.[44]

42. There is disagreement over which early Christian writers clearly teach an earthly millennium, with the ones I have listed being the least debatable. For the millennial views of these writers, see Justin, *Dialogue with Trypho* 80–81 (and possibly 139); Irenaeus, *Against Heresies* 5.32–35; *Epistle of Barnabas* 15; Tertullian, *Against Marcion* 3.25; *The Shows* 30; Hippolytus, *On the Antichrist* 5; Commodianus, *Instructiones* 1.44.1–15; 2.38.12–16; Methodius, *Symposium* 9.5; Lactantius, *Divine Institutes* 7. Papias's opinions on the millennium are known only through fragments quoted in Irenaeus.

43. Donald Fairbairn (drawing on the works of Art Marmorstein and A. J. Visser) advances a very reasonable explanation for the silence about the millennium in the works of many early Christian writers. He suggests that the church fathers do not typically mention the millennium in works addressed to pagan audiences, both because they typically avoid doctrinal controversies in apologetic works and because reference to an earthly messianic kingdom might be taken by the Roman authorities as a political challenge. See Donald Fairbairn, "Contemporary Millennial/Tribulational Debates: Whose Side Was the Early Church On?," in *A Case for Historic Premillennialism: An Alternative to the "Left Behind" Eschatology*, ed. Craig L. Blomberg and Sung Wook Chung (Grand Rapids: Baker Academic, 2009), 109–10.

44. For a brief analysis of Platonism and Neoplatonism, see chap. 1 above.

When it came to the question of the reign of God on earth, Augustine's *City of God* stands as a monumental articulation.[45] Like Eusebius, he disassociated himself from the millennial views of a future reign of Christ on earth and claimed that "the Church even now is the kingdom of Christ, and the kingdom of heaven."[46] Unlike Eusebius, however, who over a century earlier had interpreted God's reign as embodied in the progressive triumph and spread of the church after Constantine's edict (which halted persecution of Christians and restored their property),[47] Augustine's more turbulent historical context could not allow him such optimism.[48] He viewed the church as engaged in a pilgrimage through this world, with which it was in significant conflict throughout history, and which clearly was not its homeland.

But it was not just the times in which he lived that fueled Augustine's more pessimistic, otherworldly outlook. We also need to account for his Neoplatonic framework, which is pervasive in his writings. It is especially prominent in his famous notion of the two exclusive loves—love of the eternal versus love of the temporal—and in his consistent devaluing of the body vis-à-vis the soul. In Augustine's thinking the motif of allegiance to God versus apostasy and disobedience (a central and legitimate biblical motif) is superimposed on (and continually struggles with) the Neoplatonic value framework of two realms, one transcendent and higher, the other earthly and lower.[49] And while the biblical notion of original created goodness certainly tempers his articulations somewhat in the direction of Plato's *Timaeus*, rather than the radical dualism of the *Phaedo*, there is simply no redemption of the cosmos in Augustine's eschatology.[50]

Admittedly, Augustine's understanding of the reign of Christ with the saints unfolding throughout the history of the church (a view that in the twentieth century came to be called "amillennialism") might suggest a positive valuation of historical reality.[51] Yet this affirmation of the historical process stands

45. Augustine's approach to the kingdom of God was influenced by Tyconius's allegorical/typological approach to biblical interpretation (Tyconius, *Book of Rules*), especially as applied to the book of Revelation (Tyconius, *Commentary on the Apocalypse*).

46. Augustine, *City of God* 20.9. Quotation from St. Augustine, *Concerning the City of God against the Pagans*, trans. Henry Bettenson (London: Penguin, 2003), 915.

47. The Edict of Milan in AD 313 introduced tolerance for all religions, including Christianity.

48. Augustine's *City of God* (begun in AD 413) is often regarded as a theological response to the decline and fall of Rome, especially its pillaging by Alaric in AD 410.

49. For a positive appreciation of Augustine's motif of love of or desire for God, when extricated from his two-realm dualism, see James K. A. Smith, *Desiring the Kingdom: Worship, Worldview, and Cultural Formation* (Cultural Liturgies 1; Grand Rapids: Baker Academic, 2009).

50. For the contrast between Plato's *Timaeus* and *Phaedo*, see the discussion in chap. 1 above.

51. The term "amillennialism" came into use sometime in the early or middle twentieth century to designate what had previously been referred to as a particular form of postmillennialism: the view that the entirety of church history (and not just its final thousand years)

in significant discontinuity with his view that the ultimate goal of earthly history is a heavenly realm beyond history. Final redemption, for Augustine, was fundamentally acosmic and atemporal.

I believe that A. H. Armstrong, a famous historian of Neoplatonism, was on to something important when he stated in his 1966 Villanova lecture,

> It does seem to me that St. Augustine and, to a great extent, the other Christian thinkers of his age, missed the chance of carrying out a much deeper and more dynamic transformation of Platonism than they in fact effected . . . and that, in one respect, their thought about the material universe shows a certain regression in comparison with that of pagan Platonism, or at least fails to make the necessary Christian advance.[52]

Armstrong, who counts himself a Christian Neoplatonist, continues,

> I think that in the [necessary] rejection of the cosmic religion [of paganism] something important was in danger of being completely lost, and an opportunity was, in the 4th and 5th centuries, missed. *What was in danger of being lost was the sense of the holiness, the religious relevance of the cosmos as a whole, and with it, inevitably, the sense of the holiness of ordinary human life and bodily activities.*[53]

Once this opportunity had been missed, and a holistic vision of the world lost, it took a very long time for the redemption of the cosmos to reappear in the history of eschatology.

From Augustine to the Reformation

Indeed, the redemption of the cosmos entirely fades from view in the Middle Ages. As Caroline Walker Bynum explains in her historical account of the resurrection of the body,

> The bodily resurrection hoped for by Jews and Christians in the centuries just before and after the beginning of the Common Era was supposed to occur in a

---

was equivalent to the millennium in Rev. 20. For an attempt to discover the origin of the term "amillennialism," see Richard B. Gaffin Jr., "Theonomy and Eschatology: Some Reflections on Postmillennialism," in *Theonomy: A Reformed Critique*, ed. William S. Barker and W. Robert Godfrey (Grand Rapids: Zondervan, 1990), 197–224 (see especially the beginning of the article).

52. A. Hilary Armstrong, *St. Augustine and Christian Platonism* (Villanova, PA: Villanova University Press, 1967), 13. The regression that Armstrong mentions alludes to the fact that Plato thought that the physical cosmos was eternal (so it would never be destroyed).

53. Ibid., 16, emphasis added.

reconstituted universe—a "new heaven and new earth." . . . Such hopes had not disappeared by the fifth century, but few any longer expected the millennial age to come soon and eschatological yearning was increasingly focused on heaven, to which soul might go while the bones still reposed underground.[54]

Notice that hope for the permanent restoration of all things is here reduced to the notion of a temporary millennium. But even that is no longer a significant hope. Instead, there is a shift of expectation from earth to heaven, accompanying a shift from the resurrection of the body to the immortality of the soul. Walker Bynum explains the shift this way: "Early Christians expected the body to rise in a restored earthly paradise, whose arrival was imminent. Most late medieval Christians thought resurrection and the coming of the kingdom waited afar off in another space and time"—a euphemistic way to refer to an immaterial realm.[55]

This is true even for Thomas Aquinas, whose commitment to an Aristotelian view of the soul as the form or unity of the body inclined him to emphasize the importance of bodily resurrection as central to the Christian hope.[56] Aquinas even argues for the eschatological renewal of the world rather than its destruction.[57] Yet before we celebrate this bold move, we should note that Aquinas understands this renewed world, in which the resurrected saints will spend eternity, as an atemporal reality (time will cease)[58] and a world without animals or plants (indeed humans, though bodily, will have transcended their animal nature).[59]

Hope for a literal earthly millennium did surface from time to time after Augustine, particularly in late medieval reform movements (many inspired by Joachim of Fiore, a twelfth-century Cistercian monk) and among Anabaptists

54. Caroline Walker Bynum, *The Resurrection of the Body in Western Christianity, 200–1336* (New York: Columbia University Press, 1995), 13.

55. Ibid., 14.

56. For Thomas Aquinas's account of the resurrection of the body, see *Summa theologiae,* vol. 5, part 3, supplement after second section, question 77: "Of the Time and Manner of the Resurrection" (questions 75–85 address various aspects of the resurrection). For Aquinas's view of the person as a composite of soul and body, see *Summa contra Gentiles* III.52.5; for his critique of Plato's view of the soul as the essential person, see *Summa contra Gentiles* II.57.

57. Aquinas, *Summa Theologiae,* vol. 5, part 3, supplement after second section, question 91, article 1: "Whether the World Will Be Renewed."

58. Aquinas, *Summa Theologiae,* vol. 5, part 3, supplement after second section, question 91, article 2: "Whether the Movement of the Heavenly Bodies Will Cease."

59. Aquinas, *Summa Theologiae,* vol. 5, part 3, supplement after second section, question 91, article 5: "Whether the Animals and Plants Will Remain." For a contemporary version of Aristotle's view of the final state, see Peter Kreeft, *Everything You Wanted to Know about Heaven—But Never Dreamed of Asking!* (San Francisco: Ignatius, 1990). According to Kreeft, heaven is an objectively real yet immaterial "place" where the righteous will dwell in a resurrection body that will be "spiritual" in the sense of being composed of immaterial substance.

in the sixteenth century (the so-called Radical Reformation).[60] In these cases hope in the millennium was linked to protest against an unjust and corrupt status quo. The hoped-for millennial kingdom functioned as an earthly ideal, alternative to political injustice and economic corruption in society and church.[61] But, by and large, the theology of both the Middle Ages and the magisterial Reformation was amillennial, along the lines inaugurated by Augustine.[62]

The idea of the new earth, however, begins to make an inconsistent appearance in the writings of Martin Luther (1483–1546) and John Calvin (1509–1564).[63] While Luther can speak of being "raised up as new beings on that Day" when "there will be new heavens and a new earth, in which righteousness will dwell,"[64] he does not consciously reflect on the significance of cosmic restoration, but rather focuses on the eschatological redemption of people and typically refers to the final state as "heaven."[65]

The idea of a renovated cosmos shows up from time to time in Calvin's commentaries on relevant biblical texts (where he tries to do justice to what the particular passage actually says), such as his comment on 2 Peter 3:10 that "heaven and earth will be cleansed by fire so that they may be fit for the kingdom of Christ,"[66] and on Romans 8:21 that "God will restore the

60. For a fascinating study that compares the eschatology of Joachim and Aquinas, see Jürgen Moltmann, "Christian Hope: Messianic or Transcendent? A Theological Discussion with Joachim of Fiore and Thomas Aquinas," trans. M. D. Meeks, *Horizons* 12 (1985): 328–48.

61. See Norman Cohn, *The Pursuit of the Millennium: Revolutionary Millenarians and Mystical Anarchists of the Middle Ages* (rev. ed.; Oxford: Oxford University Press, 1961); Walter Klaassen, *Living at the End of the Ages: Apocalyptic Expectation in the Radical Reformation* (Lanham, MD: University Press of America, 1992).

62. By the time of the Reformation the millennium had been so marginalized that the forty-first of the original Anglican Articles framed by Thomas Cranmer in 1553 described it as a "fable of Jewish dotage" (though this is omitted from the 1563 revision under Elizabeth I). Likewise, article 17 of the Augsburg Confession condemned Anabaptists and others "who now scatter Jewish opinions that, before the resurrection of the dead, the godly shall occupy the kingdom of the world, the wicked being everywhere suppressed." See Philip Schaff, *History of the Christian Church*, vol. 2, *Ante-Nicene Christianity, AD 100–325* (Edinburgh: T&T Clark, 1884), 619n4.

63. For an analysis of this inconsistency in the case of Calvin, see J. H. van Wyk, "John Calvin on the Kingdom of God and Eschatology," *In die Skriflig* 35 (2001): 191–205.

64. Martin Luther, *Lectures on Galatians*. See *Luther's Works: American Edition*, vol. 26, *Lectures on Galatians: Chapters 1–4* (1535), ed. Jaroslav Pelikan and Walter A. Hansen (St. Louis: Concordia, 1963), 235.

65. Indeed, a 1989 doctoral dissertation on Luther's eschatology does not even raise the question of whether Luther's view of the final state is earthly or heavenly (rather, the work is dominated by Luther's problematics of the relationship of present justification and final reconciliation to God). See Jane E. Strohl, "Luther's Eschatology: The Last Times and the Last Things" (PhD diss., University of Chicago, 1989).

66. John Calvin, *Calvin's New Testament Commentaries*, vol. 12, *Hebrews and 1 & 2 Peter*, trans. William B. Johnston, ed. David W. Torrance and Thomas F. Torrance (Grand Rapids: Eerdmans, 1994), 365.

present fallen world to perfect condition at the same time as the human race."[67] However, such salutary exegetical comments stand in tension with Calvin's exposition of doctrine in the *Institutes of the Christian Religion*, where he typically distinguishes between the spiritual, heavenly kingdom of Christ (in which the church has its citizenship) and the earthly, temporal kingdom of God (of which civil society is a part).[68] Acknowledging that Scripture might seem to promise an eternal earthly kingdom, Calvin explains that "the prophets, because they could not find words to express that spiritual blessedness in its own nature, merely sketched it in physical terms."[69] And although Calvin does not denigrate Christian participation in civil society (it is a legitimate and honorable activity), he has no place in his theology for the redemption of the social order or the physical cosmos, but rather portrays the church as on a pilgrimage or journey to its true (heavenly) homeland.[70]

Holistic Eschatology in the Modern Period

The closest we come to any widespread sense of the redemption of this present world after the Reformation is the postmillennialism of the Great Revivals of the eighteenth and nineteenth centuries. This modern interpretation of the millennium, which developed most fully in America, expected the ameliora-tion of social conditions on earth leading up to a period of a thousand years of perfection, at the end of which Christ would return.[71] This vision is found in the works of Jonathan Edwards, John Wesley, George Whitefield, and

67. John Calvin, *Calvin's New Testament Commentaries*, vol. 8, *Romans and Thessalonians*, trans. Ross MacKenzie, ed. David W. Torrance and Thomas F. Torrance (Grand Rapids: Eerd-mans, 1995), 174. Even Susan E. Schreiner's beautiful study, *The Theater of His Glory: Nature and the Natural Order in the Thought of John Calvin* (Grand Rapids: Baker Academic, 1991), limits the idea of the renovation or renewal of creation to Calvin's commentaries (see 97–99, with notes on 151–52, 156).

68. For Calvin's clearest statements on the two kingdoms, see *Institutes* 3.19.5; 4.20.1; *Com-mentary on Romans* 13.1. See also David VanDrunen, "The Two Kingdoms: A Reassessment of the Transformationist Calvin," *Calvin Theological Journal* 40 (2005): 248–66.

69. Calvin, *Institutes* 3.25.10. This helps explain his reference to heaven as "a restoration of the world" (3.25.11); it is a restoration not of the physical state of the world, but rather of its true (spiritual) blessedness. At other points Calvin dismisses the idea of a physical kingdom as "Jewish vanity" (4.20.1) and calls the idea of a literal earthly millennium a "fiction" that is "too childish" to bother refuting (3.25.5). Quotations from this work are from John Calvin, *Institutes of the Christian Religion*, vol. 2, ed. John T. McNeill, trans. Ford Lewis Battles (Library of Christian Classics 21; Philadelphia: Westminster, 1960).

70. See Calvin, *Institutes* 2.16.14; 3.2.4; 3.7.3; 3.10.1; 3.25.11–12; 4.20.2.

71. Although postmillennialism is generally associated with a form of American Calvin-ism, its systemization into a viable eschatological option is usually attributed to Daniel Whitby (1638–1726), an English clergyman of Arminian persuasion in the Church of England.

Charles Finney (among many others); it had the salutary function of providing a theological impetus for addressing the social ills of the broader culture, though most postmillennialists expected the transformation of society to result primarily from the conversion of individuals rather than through any attempt to change social policy.[72] Indeed, it was this postmillennial vision, in tandem with an emphasis on the Great Commission of Matthew 28, that motivated William Carey at the end of the eighteenth century to launch the modern missionary movement, in the expectation of the gradual Christianization of the world.[73]

The period of earthly perfection expected by postmillennialists was, however, only temporary, to be followed by the return of Christ, who would usher in the final state, which usually was understood in immaterial fashion. Although language of "a new heaven and a new earth" certainly was used by postmillennialists such as Edwards (in the eighteenth century) and Finney (in the nineteenth century), this was more a picturesque way to speak of an acosmic final state than anything to be taken literally. Edwards, for example, claims the new heavens and earth will not be the present physical creation "renewed and purified" but rather something entirely different and "vastly and immensely more glorious."[74] Indeed, he states that he cannot imagine the "eternal state" being "upon this individual globe of the earth, which is manifestly a fleeting thing, as the whole solar system, and must necessarily come to an end."[75]

One important exception among postmillennialists on the final state is John Wesley (1703–1791), who toward the end of his life (during his last decade) came more and more to appreciate the value of the earthly creation and its role in God's redemptive plan.[76] Although Wesley often referred (as did most of his contemporaries) to the final state of blessedness as "heaven," he also

---

72. The relationship of eschatology and social vision is addressed in Woodrow W. Whidden, "Eschatology, Soteriology, and Social Activism in Four Mid-Nineteenth Century Holiness Methodists," *Wesleyan Theological Journal* 29, nos. 1 and 2 (Spring–Fall, 1994): 92–110.

73. Carey laid out his motivations in *An Enquiry into the Obligations of Christians to Use Means for the Conversion of the Heathens* (Leicester: Ann Ireland, 1792). This postmillennial vision is found in H. Ernest Nichol's 1896 hymn "We've a Story to Tell to the Nations," which begins with the words "We've a story to tell to the nations, / That shall turn their hearts to the right," and affirms in the refrain, "For the darkness shall turn to dawning, / And the dawning to noonday bright; / And Christ's great kingdom shall come on earth, / The kingdom of love and light."

74. Jonathan Edwards, "Notes on the Apocalypse," in *The Works of Jonathan Edwards*, vol. 5, *Apocalyptic Writings*, ed. Stephen Stein (New Haven: Yale University Press, 1977), 158, 140 (for his convoluted attempts to explain the new heavens and new earth, see notes 41, 62).

75. Ibid., 142.

76. Wesley was so interested in the natural world that he compiled (from the works of others) *A Compendium of Natural Philosophy, Being a Survey of the Wisdom of God in Creation*, ed. Robert Mudie (3 vols.; London: Thomas Tegg & Sons, 1836).

speaks of "the new earth"[77] and explains in his notes on Romans 8:21, "The creation itself shall be delivered—Destruction is not deliverance: therefore whatsoever is destroyed, or ceases to be, is not delivered at all. Will, then, any part of the creation be destroyed?"[78] And in some of his later sermons, such as "The Great Deliverance" (on Rom. 8:19–22) and "The New Creation" (on Rev. 21:5), we find Wesley's explicit and sustained focus on the ultimate redemption of the entire cosmos (including the "brute creation").[79] It is this emphasis on creation in the later Wesley that leads Louís Wesley de Souza and Howard Snyder to argue that the so-called Wesleyan Quadrilateral (first articulated by Albert C. Outler)[80]—concerning the contribution of reason, church tradition, and personal experience to the interpretation of Scripture—needs to be supplemented by Wesley's emphasis on the wisdom of God embedded in the created order.[81]

After Wesley, at least two significant movements of the nineteenth century, which continue in various incarnations even today, envisioned the final state as earthly. They stand as exceptions to the typical Christian expectation of a heavenly destiny for the righteous during this period. First, we have the case of the Seventh-day Adventist Church, which developed under the inspiration of Ellen G. White (1827–1915) out of the Sabbatarian Adventist movement.[82] Founded in 1863, and originally regarded as a heterodox sect by mainstream Christians, by the late 1950s and early 1960s evangelical leaders were convinced that at least some streams of the Seventh-day Adventist Church (who distanced themselves from some of White's more extreme teachings) were within the pale of orthodox Christianity. Central to White's vision of the climax of history was a renewed and restored earth (indeed, a renewed cosmos), cleansed

77. In his sermon "The New Creation" (see below).

78. John Wesley, *Explanatory Notes upon the New Testament* (New York: Carlton & Porter, 1754), http://wesley.nnu.edu/john_wesley/notes/index.htm.

79. John Wesley, "The General Deliverance," sermon 60 (on Rom. 8:19–22); "The New Creation," sermon 64 (on Rev. 21:5), in *The Sermons of John Wesley* (1872 ed.), ed. Thomas Jackson, http://wesley.nnu.edu/john-wesley/the-sermons-of-john-wesley-1872-edition/.

80. See Outler's essays in *The Wesleyan Theological Heritage: Essays of Albert C. Outler*, ed. Thomas C. Oden and Leicester R. Longden (Grand Rapids: Zondervan, 1991), 21–37, 39–54, 97–110, 111–24.

81. Louís Wesley de Souza, "The Wisdom of God in Creation: Mission and the Wesleyan Pentalateral," in *Global Good News: Mission in a New Context*, ed. Howard A. Snyder (Nashville: Abingdon, 2001), 138–52; see also Howard A. Snyder, "The Babylonian Captivity of Wesleyan Theology," *Wesleyan Theological Journal* 39 (2004): 7–34. Snyder suggests that this emphasis on creation is needed to address worldview dualism in some contemporary Wesleyan theology (his critique is equally applicable to other theological traditions).

82. White was originally a member of the Millerites, a premillennialist group following William Miller (1782–1849), whose precise yet failed predictions of the second coming of Christ led to great disillusionment among his followers.

of all evil, a teaching still prominent in Adventist faith. White's final words in *The Great Controversy* are worth quoting:

> The entire universe is clean. One pulse of harmony and gladness beats through the vast creation. From Him who created all, flow life and light and gladness, throughout the realms of illimitable space. From the minutest atom to the greatest world, all things, animate and inanimate, in their unshadowed beauty and perfect joy, declare that God is love. [83]

It is significant that Seventh-day Adventists attempted from the start to work out implications of the redemption of the earth for holistic living (including matters of holistic health) and more recently have begun to address the integration of faith and learning as part of their ethical calling.[84]

Also envisioning an earthly final state were many of the early nineteenth-century founders of the Stone-Campbell movement, also known as Restorationists. This movement led ultimately to the founding of denominations such as the Churches of Christ and the Christian Church (also known as Disciples). It is intriguing that many of the movement's founders, such as David Lipscomb and James Harding, taught (and some present-day members still teach) a permanent eschatological redemption of heaven and earth.[85]

But these movements that envisioned cosmic redemption were exceptions to the rule. The dominant approach to eschatology in most branches of modern Christendom was otherworldly. Even the social gospel movement at the end of the nineteenth century and the start of the twentieth, which focused resolutely on the improvement of human life in its social and economic dimensions, had no categories with which to conceive of an earthly, embodied afterlife. Thus Walter Rauschenbusch (1861–1918), who came to be the foremost spokesperson for this movement in the early twentieth century, promulgated in his many writings a powerful ethical vision of a this-worldly kingdom consisting in restored social relations on earth, yet

---

83. Ellen G. White, *The Great Controversy* (Mountain View, CA: Pacific Press, 1911), 678, the conclusion of chap. 42, "The Controversy Ended."

84. The prime mover behind the faith-learning initiative has been Humberto M. Rasi, who in 1987 founded an Institute for Christian College Teaching (now known as the Institute for Christian Teaching) to help Seventh-day Adventist college professors (and high school teachers) develop a holistic Christian worldview that would impact their teaching and research. See http://circle.adventist.org/files/CD2008/CD1/ict/ifl_definition.html. I gave a series of Christian worldview lectures for this institute in its early years.

85. See John Mark Hicks and Bobby Valentine, *Kingdom Come: Embracing the Spiritual Legacy of David Lipscomb and James Harding* (Abilene, TX: Leafwood, 2006); Al Maxey, "Paradise Regained," *Reflections* 310 (August 6, 2007); "Questions from Abroad," *Reflections* 311 (August 10, 2007): http://www.zianet.com/maxey/reflx311.htm.

linked this vision (inconsistently) to an immaterial and disembodied view of the afterlife.[86]

This survey so far largely confirms the judgment of historian Richard Tarnas concerning the state of nineteenth-century eschatology (with only slight adjustment required): "The early Christian belief that the Fall and Redemption pertained not just to man but to the entire cosmos, a doctrine already fading after the Reformation, now disappeared altogether: the process of salvation, if it had any meaning at all, pertained solely to the personal relation between God and man."[87] We have seen that there were exceptions to this in the nineteenth century. Nevertheless, Tarnas is largely correct in his assessment.[88]

The Impact of the Rapture Doctrine

Perhaps the most important development in eschatology during the nineteenth century, which served to further marginalize the idea of the redemption of the cosmos, was the interpretive framework known as dispensationalism, deriving from the teaching of the Irish clergyman John Nelson Darby (1800–1882) of the Plymouth Brethren. From its beginning in the 1830s, dispensationalism sharply distinguished between God's covenants with Israel and the church and ended up dividing history into (typically) seven distinct "dispensations" or epochs in which God related to humanity in differing ways. Although dispensationalists expected the coming of Christ to usher in a literal earthly millennium prior to the final state, this form of premillennialism did not have the same ethical function to challenge the status quo as in late medieval and Anabaptist visions of the millennium. Instead, this more recent belief in the millennium typically was combined with a jigsaw-puzzle approach to prophecy (sometimes called "newspaper exegesis") and a deep pessimism about the present world, which

86. The one place where Rauschenbusch explicitly addressed the nature of the afterlife is chap. 18 of his last book, *A Theology for the Social Gospel* (New York: Macmillan, 1917), 208–39. Although he resolutely tried to rethink the nature of the afterlife in continuity with his kingdom vision, this took the form of speculating on the social nature of life in "heaven" and the possibility of moral development there. He did not, however, even consider the possibility that the restoration of the earth could be part of the Christian hope.

87. Richard Tarnas, *The Passion of the Western Mind: Understanding the Ideas That Have Shaped Our World View* (New York: Ballantine, 1991), 306–7.

88. A similar judgment is quoted by G. C. Berkouwer from Adolf Köberle, *Der Herr über alles: Beiträge zum Universalismus der christlichen Botschaft* (Hamburg: Furche-Verlag, 1957), 103: "This cosmic aspect of redemption was increasingly lost to Western Christendom since the Age of Enlightenment, and to this day we have been unable to restore it to its strength and clarity." See G. C. Berkouwer, *The Return of Christ* (Studies in Dogmatics; Grand Rapids: Eerdmans, 1972), 211n1.

was expected to become worse and worse until Christ returned. And when the temporary millennium was complete, classical dispensationalists either reverted to a vision of heaven as an immaterial final state or affirmed the idea of a replacement heaven and earth after the annihilation of the present cosmos (citing 2 Pet. 3:10 and Rev. 21) without any awareness of possible implications for holistic living in the present.[89]

The reason for this lack of awareness was the prominent dispensational doctrine of the "secret rapture" popularized by Darby (beginning around 1840), according to which believers would exit earth for heaven just before the "great tribulation."[90] Whereas Darby popularized the rapture idea via Bible prophecy conferences in Canada, the United States, and Britain, where much of the impetus was to figure out the prophetic timetable, Dwight L. Moody (1837–1889) latched on to this doctrine for a different reason. Moody used the rapture to undergird his revivalist preaching, especially his evangelistic calls to conversion. Although Moody did not have a clearly worked-out eschatology and tended to avoid eschatological controversies, the rapture fit very well with his persistent emphasis on being ready to meet God at any time. Beyond that, it served to buttress Moody's somewhat negative view of the present world and his counteremphasis on an otherworldly heaven as the Christian hope.[91] Thus Moody famously stated in an 1877 sermon, "I look on this world as a wrecked vessel. God has given me a life-boat, and said to me, 'Moody, save all you can.'"[92] Many revivalist preachers in the nineteenth century after Moody also utilized the rapture to ground the urgency of their evangelistic preaching. And the growing popularity of this doctrine was a major factor contributing to the otherworldly, escapist attitude of the burgeoning evangelical Christian movement at the end of the nineteenth century.

89. It is possible to trace roughly three stages in the history of dispensationalism, which may be distinguished as "classical," "revised," and "progressive" dispensationalism. See Craig A. Blaising, "Premillennialism," in *Three Views of the Millennium and Beyond*, ed. Darrell L. Bock (Counterpoints: Exploring Theology; Grand Rapids: Zondervan, 1999), 160–81.

90. There is great debate among supporters of the doctrine of the rapture concerning when this doctrine first appears in the history of Christian thought. Although there may indeed be examples of people who propounded this idea in the centuries before Darby, it clearly did not become widely propagated until the mid- to late nineteenth century, and it was not until the twentieth century that it became the eschatological doctrine of choice in evangelical and fundamentalist churches.

91. It is telling that a famous collection of Moody's sermons is titled *Heaven: Where It Is, Its Inhabitants, and How to Get There* (New York: Revell, 1887). Although the idea of the resurrection of the body appears in some of these sermons, in many others he speaks of the afterlife as populated by spirits or souls of the righteous.

92. Dwight L. Moody, "That Gospel Sermon on the Blessed Hope," sermon 16, in *New Sermons, Addresses and Prayers* (St. Louis: N. D. Thompson, 1877), http://www.gutenberg.org/files/27316/27316-h/27316-h.htm.

In the early twentieth century the rapture idea gained significant impetus through the immense popularity of the Scofield Reference Bible. First published by Oxford University Press in 1909 (revised in 1917), this edition of the King James Version with study notes by Cyrus I. Scofield (1843–1921) gave near canonical status to dispensational interpretations of Bible prophecy in the "last days," so much so that dispensationalism has become the preferred eschatological framework of North American evangelicals and fundamentalists.

After the impact of Scofield and the early dispensationalists, the rapture doctrine gained even greater exposure later in the twentieth century through the prolific writings of Hal Lindsey, beginning with his 1970 runaway bestseller *The Late Great Planet Earth*,[93] and this exposure has only intensified through the Left Behind series of books and movies.[94] While *The Late Great Planet Earth* acknowledges that the New Testament envisions the final state as "the new heaven and the new earth," less than two pages are devoted to this topic.[95] Further, one searches the book in vain for any sense that the renewed creation could be a significant prod to ethical action.[96] It turns out that the re-creation of the cosmos is not, for Lindsey, its redemption, but rather is a brand-new creation following the destruction of the present created order. Tellingly, *The Late Great Planet Earth* ends by connecting the coming of Christ not with the redemption of creation, but with the church saying "Good-bye."[97]

Despite the original dispensationalist context of the rapture doctrine, many current believers in the rapture are somewhat hazy about the details of the various dispensations; and they are often confused regarding what seem like wild speculations about which contemporary events fulfill which biblical

---

93. Hal Lindsey, with C. C. Carlson, *The Late Great Planet Earth* (Grand Rapids: Zondervan, 1970). When I purchased my copy of this book in 1975, it was in its forty-fifth printing and had already sold nearly 4.5 million copies. The book ended up selling over 35 million copies and has been translated into many languages.

94. The series began with Tim F. LaHaye and Jerry B. Jenkins, *Left Behind: A Novel of the Earth's Last Days* (Wheaton: Tyndale House, 1995).

95. The discussion of the new heaven and new earth is found at the end of chap. 13, "The Main Event" (167–68).

96. The new heaven and new earth in the typical dispensationalist scheme is simply one more piece of the prophetic puzzle, figured out in quasi-scientific fashion; it typically does not serve to ground any significant theological or ethical reflection.

97. Chapter 11, on the rapture, is called "The Ultimate Trip," and the book's fourteenth and final chapter, "Polishing the Crystal Ball," is focused not on the new creation but rather on the tribulation, the coming judgment, and especially the rapture. The picture is not significantly changed in Lindsey's later book *The Rapture: Truth or Consequences* (New York: Bantam, 1983), which ends with the author's heartfelt prayer that the book would help the reader "have a sure hope of the Lord's 'any moment' return to take you to His Father's House" (176)—that is, heaven.

prophecies, such as are found in dispensationalist publications and on dispensationalist websites and radio and television shows.[98] This is because most evangelicals today are "dispensationalist by osmosis,"[99] having absorbed one central piece of the dispensationalist picture (the rapture) rather than being convinced of the entire dispensationalist schema.

This resolute focus on the church's imminent exit to heaven has the effect of inclining believers in the rapture to treat the future (and thus the present) of the earth as unimportant.[100] This lack of concern for our earthly future in the early part of the twentieth century was clearly tied to an otherworldly heavenly-mindedness, but as the century progressed, it has resulted in the free reign of consumerism and greed among North American evangelicals, since there is little theological ground in a rapture-oriented eschatology for ecological or social responsibility.[101]

The Time Is Ripe

Despite the centrality of the rapture doctrine in popular evangelical eschatology, a significant change is in the air. Perhaps the most important indicator of this change is seen among so-called progressive dispensationalists, who are trying to take seriously the biblical emphasis on earthly hope and the negative ethical implications of rapture theology. Thus R. Todd Mangum, who has impeccable dispensationalist credentials (a doctorate from Dallas Theological Seminary and a recipient of the John F. Walvoord Award for outstanding work in eschatology)[102] admits that "little good has come of dispensationalists' emphasis on a pre-tribulational rapture up to now; there is promise for

98. This speculative approach to the fulfillment of biblical prophecy in the contemporary world requires such "prophecies" to be read completely apart from their original literary or historical context. The process of interpretation then becomes overly subjective.

99. Thanks to my student Steven Eames for this phrase.

100. Randy L. Maddox reports on sociological studies of Christian faith and the environment that show a correlation between dispensational eschatology and lack of interest in ecological stewardship ("Anticipating the New Creation: Wesleyan Foundations for Holistic Mission," *Asbury Journal* 62 [2007]: 49–66, esp. 66nn70–71).

101. For an analysis of the loss of social vision among evangelicals after the Second Great Awakening, tied to the shift from postmillennialism to premillennialism, including the prominence of the rapture doctrine, see Donald W. Dayton, *Discovering an Evangelical Heritage* (Peabody, MA: Hendrickson, 1976), chap. 10, "Whatever Happened to Evangelicalism?"; idem, *The Theological Roots of Pentecostalism* (Peabody, MA: Hendrickson, 1991), chap. 6, "The Rise of Premillennialism."

102. R. Todd Mangum received the award for his dissertation, published as *The Dispensational-Covenantal Rift: The Fissuring of Evangelical Theology from 1936 to 1944* (Studies in Evangelical History and Thought; Bletchley, UK: Paternoster, 2007).

even less good to come of such emphasis in the future."[103] He suggests that dispensationalists adopt a posture of "rapture agnosticism," both because of the doctrine's negative ethical effects and because it is not clearly taught in Scripture.[104] Mangum proposes instead an "inaugurated kingdom ethic," which is more in line with the teaching of Jesus and the New Testament.[105]

Other progressive dispensationalists, such as Darrell Bock and Craig Blaising, emphasize the this-worldly nature of the kingdom. In an extended study Bock, a New Testament scholar, examines the biblical basis for the inaugurated kingdom of God in the midst of history, while also affirming the kingdom's culmination in "the cosmos as a whole."[106] Blaising's work as a systematic theologian is important for his clear distinction between what he calls a "spiritual vision model" of eschatological escape to heaven and a more biblical "new creation model," which "expects the earth and the cosmic order to be renewed and made everlasting through the same creating power that grants immortal and resurrection life to the saints."[107]

The approach of progressive dispensationalists such as Mangum, Bock, and Blaising has significant affinities with the eschatology of New Testament scholar George Eldon Ladd, whose writings in the 1960s and 1970s (while teaching at Fuller Theological Seminary) articulated a consistent theology of the redemption of the created order. Ladd considered himself a "historic premillennialist" (that is, he affirmed a literal millennium but dissented from the dispensationalist framework and its arcane speculations about contemporary prophetic fulfillment) and was tireless in explaining that the direction

103. R. Todd Mangum, "High Hopes for 21st-Century Dispensationalism: A Response to 'Hope and Dispensationalism: An Historical Overview and Assessment' (by Gary L. Nebeker)" (paper presented to the Dispensational Study Group of the Evangelical Theological Society, Nashville, TN, November 2000), 9.

104. Ibid., 15.

105. Ibid., 6.

106. Darrell L. Bock, "The Kingdom of God in New Testament Theology," in *Looking into the Future: Evangelical Studies in Eschatology*, ed. David W. Baker (Evangelical Theological Society Studies; Grand Rapids: Baker Academic, 2001), 48. Bock articulates how his progressive dispensational stance differs both from covenant theology (54–55) and from earlier dispensationalism (58n53).

107. Blaising, "Premillennialism," 163. Blaising has also traced developments within the dispensationalist movement in a two-part article, "Developing Dispensationalism, Part 1: Doctrinal Development in Orthodoxy," *Bibliotheca sacra* 145 (1988): 133–40; "Developing Dispensationalism, Part 2: Development of Dispensationalism by Contemporary Dispensationalists," *Bibliotheca sacra* 145 (1988): 254–80. In a later essay Blaising categorizes the development of dispensationalism into three stages—classical, revised, progressive—with each stage evidencing greater propensity to validate an eternal future state for all believers (along with other distinctions) ("The Extent and Varieties of Dispensationalism," in Craig A. Blaising and Darrell L. Bock, *Progressive Dispensationalism* [Wheaton: BridgePoint, 1993], 9–56).

of salvation in the Bible was from heaven to earth, not the other way around. In Ladd's words, "Thus the final redemption is not flight from this world to another world; it may be described as the descent of the other world—God's world—resulting in a transformation of this world."[108] Specifically, for Ladd, the final state is not "the gathering of the souls of the righteous in heaven, but the gathering of a redeemed people on a redeemed earth in perfected fellowship with God."[109]

A significant movement toward holistic eschatology is also seen in the Reformed theological tradition, which traces its roots back to Augustine and Calvin and typically is amillennial. Some Reformed theologians and biblical scholars have clearly moved beyond traditional amillennialism in that they explicitly affirm a this-worldly final state. Thus A. A. Hodge in the nineteenth century wrote in his *Outlines of Theology*, "God will revolutionize our portion of the physical universe," and "this world will be reconstituted, and gloriously adapted to be the permanent residence of Christ and his church."[110]

More recently, Anthony Hoekema's classic 1979 work, *The Bible and the Future*, concludes with a lucid chapter titled "The New Earth," in which he speaks of "the new earth which God will bring into existence after Christ comes again—a new earth which will last, not just for a thousand years, but forever."[111] And Calvin Schoonhoven's 1982 article "Heaven, New" in *The International Standard Bible Encyclopedia* explicitly states that the distinctive biblical hope is characterized by "the redemption of the created order."[112] Even more recently, Vern Poythress wants to be known as an "earthy amillennialist" because of his emphasis on the culmination of salvation as the "renewal of this earth."[113]

---

108. George Eldon Ladd, *The Pattern of New Testament Truth* (Grand Rapids: Eerdmans, 1968), 37. See also Ladd, *The Presence of the Future: The Eschatology of Biblical Realism* (Grand Rapids: Eerdmans, 1974), which is a revision of his earlier *Jesus and the Kingdom* (New York: Harper & Row, 1964).

109. Ladd, *Pattern of New Testament Truth*, 14. See also Ladd, *A Commentary on the Revelation of John* (Grand Rapids: Eerdmans, 1972), 275; idem, *A Theology of the New Testament*, ed. Donald A. Hagner (rev. ed.; Grand Rapids: Eerdmans, 1993 [1974]), 681–83.

110. A. A. Hodge, *Outlines of Theology: Revised and Enlarged* (rev. ed.; New York: Hodder & Stoughton, 1878), 577–78 (from chap. 40, answers to questions 1, 3).

111. Anthony A. Hoekema, *The Bible and the Future* (Grand Rapids: Eerdmans, 1979), 276.

112. Calvin R. Schoonhoven, "Heavens, New," in *The International Standard Bible Encyclopedia*, vol. 2, ed. Geoffrey W. Bromiley et al. (Grand Rapids: Eerdmans, 1982), 656. See also Schoonhoven, *The Wrath of Heaven* (Grand Rapids: Eerdmans, 1966).

113. Vern S. Poythress, "Currents within Amillennialism," *Presbyterion* 26 (2000): 21–25, http://www.frame-poythress.org/poythress_articles/2000Currents.htm. Others working generally in the Reformed theological tradition who espouse earthly redemption include Wesley Granberg-Michaelson, *A Worldly Spirituality: The Call to Redeem Life on Earth* (San Francisco: Harper & Row, 1984); Michael E. Wittmer, *Heaven Is a Place on Earth: Why Everything You Do Matters to God* (Grand Rapids: Zondervan, 2004).

One important strand of the (historically amillennial) Reformed tradition traces it roots back to Dutch theologian and statesman Abraham Kuyper (1837–1920), who gained prominence in North America for his 1898 Stone Lectures at Princeton Theological Seminary, in which he introduced the English-speaking church to the idea of a Christian worldview (which he called a "life-system" or a "world-and-life view").[114] In these lectures Kuyper described the holistic impact the Christian faith ought to have in all spheres of life.[115] Whereas Kuyper was very much an activist—starting a Christian university, newspaper, and political party—his associate Herman Bavinck (1854–1921) was a professional theologian. In his *Reformed Dogmatics* (published in Dutch in 1895–1901), Bavinck articulated a coherent vision of the redemption of creation.[116] According to Bavinck, "God's honor consists precisely in the fact that he redeems and renews the same humanity, the same world, the same heaven, and the same earth that have been corrupted and polluted by sin."[117] A more recent Dutch theologian who has fully understood the biblical logic of the redemption of the earth is G. C. Berkouwer. In an illuminating chapter called "The New Earth," Berkouwer observes how easily Christians simply (but wrongly) assume that heaven is their final destination[118] and warns, "When the expectation of a new earth is denied or relativized, the meaning of life *on this earth* breaks down."[119]

This Kuyperian or Neocalvinian tradition (as it is sometimes known) gave birth to various associations and groups in the United States and Canada in the mid-twentieth century (including the Institute for Christian Studies in Toronto) that have been tireless in promulgating a holistic stance of Christian involvement in earthly life.[120] Those influenced by this tradition typically have grounded their sense of calling to cultural, intellectual, and political

---

114. Published by Eerdmans, originally in 1931 under the title *Calvinism*, more recently in different editions as Abraham Kuyper, *Lectures on Calvinism*.

115. On the legacy of Abraham Kuyper, see Peter S. Heslam, *Creating a Christian Worldview: Abraham Kuyper's Lectures on Calvinism* (Grand Rapids: Eerdmans, 1998); Richard J. Mouw, *Abraham Kuyper: A Short and Personal Introduction* (Grand Rapids: Eerdmans, 2011).

116. Herman Bavinck, *Reformed Dogmatics*, vol. 4, *Holy Spirit, Church, and New Creation*, ed. John Bolt, trans. John Vriend (Grand Rapids: Baker Academic, 2008); published in English initially as a stand-alone volume, *The Last Things: Hope for This World and the Next*, ed. John Bolt, trans. John Vriend (Grand Rapids: Baker Books, 1996).

117. Bavinck, *Reformed Dogmatics*, 4:717; *Last Things*, 137. See Bavinck's entire analysis in *Reformed Dogmatics*, 4:715–30, chap. 18, "The Renewal of Creation"; *Last Things*, 155–69, chap. 7, "The Renewal of Creation."

118. Berkouwer, *Return of Christ*, 213–14.

119. Ibid., 227 (emphasis in original). Berkouwer's chap. 7, "The New Earth" (211–34), is an excellent analysis of the exegetical, theological, and ethical importance of the redemption of the earth.

120. On the Institute for Christian Studies, see Robert E. VanderVennen, *A University for the People: A History of the Institute for Christian Studies* (Sioux Center, IA: Dordt College Press, 2008).

engagement in two aspects of biblical teaching: the cultural mandate (the human calling to be stewards of creation) and an eschatological vision of cosmic redemption. Contemporary writers grounded in or shaped by this tradition and who explicitly promote a final redeemed earthly state include Brian Walsh, Sylvia Keesmaat, Al Wolters, Steven Bouma-Prediger, Cornelius Plantinga Jr., Paul Marshall, Michael Goheen, and Craig Bartholomew.[121]

The Kuyperian tradition is also the source of the holistic approach to culture promoted by Francis Schaeffer, the American missionary who founded L'Abri in Switzerland in the 1960s as an informal study center for Christian reflection on culture. Schaeffer was influenced by Hans Rookmaaker of the Free University in Amsterdam, who himself had been nurtured in the Kuyperian tradition. Not only did Schaeffer come to affirm the hope of a renewed cosmos as central to his eschatology (declaring that Christ's death "will redeem all nature . . . at the time when we are raised from the dead"),[122] but this same hope continues to be taught by Schaeffer's intellectual heirs, some of whom are associated with L'Abri study centers in different parts of the world.[123] A book by two of Schaeffer's early associates is aptly titled *Being Human: The Nature of Spiritual Experience*, which illustrates well this holistic vision.[124] And Wim Rietkerk, associated with Dutch L'Abri, has written *Millennium Fever and the Future of This Earth*, an expansion of his earlier work *The Future Great Planet Earth*, both of which clearly espouse the redemption of creation as God's ultimate purpose.[125]

121. The following is a sampling of works by these authors: Brian J. Walsh and J. Richard Middleton, *The Transforming Vision: Shaping a Christian World View* (Downers Grove, IL: IVP Academic, 1984); Brian J. Walsh and Sylvia C. Keesmaat, *Colossians Remixed: Subverting the Empire* (Downers Grove, IL: IVP Academic, 2004); Sylvia C. Keesmaat, *Paul and His Story: (Re)Interpreting the Exodus Tradition* (Journal for the Study of the New Testament: Supplement Series 181; Sheffield: Sheffield Academic Press, 1999); Al Wolters, *Creation Regained: Biblical Basics for a Reformational Worldview* (Grand Rapids: Eerdmans, 1985; 2nd ed., 2005); Steven Bouma-Prediger, *For the Beauty of the Earth: A Christian Vision of Creation Care* (Grand Rapids: Baker Academic, 2001; 2nd ed., 2010); Cornelius Plantinga Jr., *Engaging God's World: A Christian Vision of Faith, Learning and Living* (Grand Rapids: Eerdmans, 2002); Paul Marshall, with Lela Gilbert, *Heaven Is Not My Home: Learning to Live in God's Creation* (Nashville: Thomas Nelson, 1999); Craig G. Bartholomew and Michael W. Goheen, *The Drama of Scripture: Finding Our Place in the Biblical Story* (Grand Rapids: Baker Academic, 2004); Michael W. Goheen and Craig G. Bartholomew, *Living at the Crossroads: An Introduction to Christian Worldview* (Grand Rapids: Baker Academic, 2008).

122. Francis Schaeffer, *Pollution and the Death of Man: The Christian View of Ecology* (Wheaton: Tyndale House, 1970), 66.

123. For example, Wim Rietkerk, Jerram Barrs, and Udo Middlemann regularly give talks on the subject of the redemption of the cosmos and its implications for ethics.

124. Ranald Macauly and Jerram Barrs, *Being Human: The Nature of Spiritual Experience* (Downers Grove, IL: InterVarsity, 1978).

125. Wim Rietkerk, *The Future Great Planet Earth* (Landour-Mussoorie, India: Nivedit Good Books, 1989); idem, *Millennium Fever and the Future of This Earth: Between False Expectations*

In contrast to the typical amillennialism of the Reformed tradition, one recent stream of this tradition has advocated a version of postmillennialism. Beginning in the early to mid-twentieth century, the Christian reconstructionist movement (also known as Christian theonomy) taught a triumphalist version of the millennial hope in which this world (especially America) would become Christianized, with society run according to Mosaic law from the Old Testament (some reconstructionists even advocated Mosaic sanctions, such as stoning children for disobedience to parents [see Deut. 21:18–21]).[126] The triumphalism of this vision comes to the fore in the call for Christians to "take over" the culture for Christ.[127] Whereas early reconstructionists generally distinguished their vision of the postmillennial kingdom from the final state (which also would be earthly), one offshoot of the reconstructionist movement has morphed into a position known as consistent or full preterism.[128]

Preterist interpretation, which is standard in Old Testament scholarship, interprets prophetic literature as addressing the prophet's own situation with a message about God's historical intervention for judgment and salvation. A preterist approach to New Testament eschatology results in taking the prophecies of Jesus in the Olivet discourse (Matt. 24; Mark 13) or John's predictions in the book of Revelation as primarily addressing events and issues of their own day. This is the position of many (if not most) New Testament scholars, though in addition most would claim that Jesus and John also looked ahead to a final cosmic fulfillment at the second coming.

Consistent preterists, however, claim that all prophecy has been fulfilled (the second coming has already happened), so that we are already in the new heaven and the new earth.[129] All that remains is the gradual and progressive coming of God's kingdom over time, which will result in the eventual conquest

126. The two foundational texts of Christian reconstruction are Rousas John Rushdoony, *Institutes of Biblical Law: A Chalcedon Study* (Nutley, NJ: Craig, 1973); Greg L. Banhsen, *Theonomy in Christian Ethics* (Nutley, NJ: Craig, 1977). For a helpful summary of the movement, see Rodney Clapp, *The Reconstructionists* (2nd ed.; Downers Grove, IL: InterVarsity, 1990).

127. See Gary North, *The Dominion Covenant: Genesis* (Tyler, TX: Institute for Christian Economics, 1982), especially the final chapter on the Great Commission (interpreted as a commission to conquer the world for Christ). It was the reconstructionist vision that shifted televangelist Pat Robertson (host of the *700 Club*) from his previous escapist rapture theology and motivated him to run in the 1988 United States presidential race.

128. The complexities of the different reconstructionist and preterist movements are analyzed in Sam Frost, "A Brief History of Covenant Eschatology," *Living Presence Journal* 14, no. 2 (summer 2004), http://www.preteristarchive.com/StudyArchive/f/frost-samuel.html.

129. One of the most sustained arguments for this position is in a nineteenth-century work, James Stuart Russell, *The Parousia: A Critical Inquiry into the New Testament Doctrine of Our Lord's Second Coming* (London: Dalby, Isbister, 1878 [and later editions]). This book significantly

of personal and societal evil.[130] I need to be clear that this is not the position that I am advocating in this book.

The redemption of the cosmos is also an important theological motif among many in the Wesleyan theological tradition.[131] Thus theologian Howard Snyder, picking up on the mature Wesley's vision of the new creation, proposed a holistic, this-worldly "kingdom consciousness" in his 1977 book *The Community of the King*, and more recently he made the redemption of creation central in his 2007 essay "Salvation Means Creation Healed," which was expanded into a coauthored book with the same title.[132] Similar holistic theological moves may be found, backed by a wealth of exegetical detail, in the work of Wesleyan New Testament scholars Joel Green and Andy Johnson.[133]

But this resurgent awareness of the Bible's vision of the redemption of the cosmos cannot be limited to the Reformed or Wesleyan traditions. Thus, the Baptist theologian Russell D. Moore emphasizes, "The point of the gospel is not that we would go to heaven when we die. Instead, it is that heaven will come down, transforming and renewing the earth and the entire universe."[134]

Many contemporary biblical scholars of varying theological stripes are beginning to make it clear that the Bible teaches a renewed earth rather than a heaven hereafter. Some, such as T. Desmond Alexander and Greg Beale, give

---

influenced many consistent preterists of the twentieth century, and reprint editions have been made available from Baker Books and the International Preterist Association.

130. The postmillennialism of consistent preterism and the rapture theology of popular dispensationalism are not only the two most polarized eschatological positions, but also the shrillest voices in eschatology today (if the Internet is any evidence).

131. See Maddox, "Anticipating the New Creation"; Theodore Runyon, *The New Creation: John Wesley's Theology Today* (Nashville: Abingdon, 1998).

132. Howard A. Snyder, *The Community of the King* (Downers Grove, IL: InterVarsity, 1977), esp. chap. 1 ("Kingdom Consciousness"); idem, "Salvation Means Creation Healed: Creation, Cross, Kingdom, and Mission," *Asbury Journal* 62 (2007): 9–47; Howard A. Snyder with Joel Scandrett, *Salvation Means Creation Healed: The Ecology of Sin and Grace; Overcoming the Divorce between Earth and Heaven* (Eugene, OR: Cascade, 2011). See also Maddox, "Anticipating the New Creation"; Runyon, *New Creation*.

133. Joel B. Green, *Salvation* (Understanding Biblical Themes; St. Louis: Chalice, 2003); idem, *Why Salvation?* (Reframing New Testament Theology; Nashville: Abingdon, 2014); Andy Johnson, "Turning the World Upside Down in 1 Corinthians 15: Apocalyptic Epistemology, the Resurrected Body, and the New Creation," *Evangelical Quarterly* 75 (2003): 291–309; idem, "The 'New Creation,' the Crucified and Risen Christ, and the Temple: A Pauline Audience for Mark," *Journal of Theological Interpretation* 1 (2007): 171–91; Phil Hamner and Andy Johnson, "Holy Mission: The 'Entire Sanctification' of the Triune God's Creation," *Didache* 5 (2005): 1–8, http://media.premierstudios.com/nazarene/docs/didache_5_1_holy_mission.pdf. I identify my own location as the Wesleyan theological tradition, though I have been significantly impacted along the way by the Neocalvinian/Kuyperian tradition; indeed, on the point of holistic salvation, the two traditions converge.

134. Russell D. Moore, "Personal and Cosmic Eschatology," in *A Theology for the Church*, ed. Daniel L. Akin (Nashville: B&H, 2007), 913.

this theme a prominent place in their writings.[135] In the case of others—such as Robert Mounce, Alan Johnson, and Douglas Moo (just to name a few)—one needs to know where to look for their comments on the subject, typically in biblical commentaries or essays on particular biblical texts.[136] Careful search can also find an articulation of holistic redemption among biblical scholars of earlier generations, such as Kenneth Wuest (who taught at Moody Bible Institute), writing in the early twentieth century; or Adam Clarke (the British Methodist scholar), writing in the early nineteenth century.[137]

In recent years, however, perhaps no biblical scholar has given the New Testament teaching of the redemption of creation such wide exposure as N. T. Wright.[138] Particularly in *Surprised by Hope*, his hugely popular work on eschatology, and in his more scholarly study *The Resurrection of the Son of God*, Wright has been a superb teacher of the worldwide church on this theme, helpfully emphasizing the ethical and even political implications of the biblical vision of God's kingdom coming on earth, as it is in heaven.[139] As

135. T. Desmond Alexander, *From Eden to the New Jerusalem: An Introduction to Biblical Theology* (Grand Rapids: Kregel, 2009); G. K. Beale, *The Temple and the Church's Mission: A Biblical Theology of the Dwelling Place of God* (New Studies in Biblical Theology 17; Downers Grove, IL: IVP Academic, 2004); idem, *A New Testament Biblical Theology: The Unfolding of the Old Testament in the New* (Grand Rapids: Baker Academic, 2011); idem, *The Book of Revelation* (New International Greek Testament Commentary; Grand Rapids: Eerdmans, 1998).

136. Robert H. Mounce, *The Book of Revelation* (rev. ed., New International Commentary on the New Testament; Grand Rapids: Eerdmans, 1998), 384, 385, 401; Alan F. Johnson, "Revelation," in *The Expositor's Bible Commentary*, vol. 12 (Grand Rapids: Zondervan, 1981), 592; Douglas J. Moo, "Creation and New Creation," *Bulletin for Biblical Research* 20 (2010): 39–60; idem, "Nature in the New Creation: New Testament Eschatology and the Environment," *Journal of the Evangelical Theological Society* 49 (2006): 449–88.

137. Kenneth Wuest, *Romans in the Greek New Testament for the English Reader* (Grand Rapids: Eerdmans, 1955), 137–38; reprinted as part of *Wuest's Word Studies from the Greek New Testament for the English Reader*, vol. 1 (Grand Rapids: Eerdmans, 1973); Adam Clarke, *The New Testament of Our Lord and Saviour Jesus Christ* (Philadelphia: Thomas, Cowperthwait, 1844), 457 (this is a one-volume edition of the three New Testament volumes of Clarke's commentary on both Testaments, originally published 1820–26; Clarke's commentary has been published in many different editions).

138. N. T. Wright even promoted this vision on the *Colbert Report* (June 19, 2008), in an interview with Stephen Colbert (on Wright's book *Surprised by Hope*, see next note), http://thecolbertreport.cc.com/videos/m7daav/bishop-n-t—wright.

139. N. T. Wright, *Surprised by Hope: Rethinking Heaven, the Resurrection, and the Mission of the Church* (San Francisco: HarperOne, 2008); idem, *The Resurrection of the Son of God* (Christian Origins and the Question of God 3; Minneapolis: Fortress, 2003). Also relevant is Wright's lesser-known 1993 Drew Lecture on Immortality at Spurgeon's College, London, published as *New Heavens, New Earth: The Biblical Picture of Christian Hope* (Grove Biblical Booklets 11; Cambridge: Grove Books, 1999). A slightly updated version of this 24-page booklet was published as "New Heavens, New Earth," in *Called to One Hope: Perspectives on Life to Come; Drew Lectures on Immortality Delivered at Spurgeon's College*, ed. John Colwell (Carlisle: Paternoster, 2000), 31–51.

Wright puts it in *How God Became King*, orthodox Christian doctrine affirms "God's rescue of the created order itself, rather than the rescue of saved souls *from* the created order."[140]

Many have misread Wright as a full or consistent preterist, generalizing from his interpretation of the teaching of Jesus in the Olivet discourse (which he connects to the fall of Jerusalem in AD 70) or his characterization of Jewish apocalyptic (as metaphorical description of historical events).[141] Yet as early as 1999 Wright attempted to explain that he was not denying a future cosmic coming of Christ: "Let me say this as clearly as I can (since I have often been misunderstood on this point)."[142] Although Wright certainly thinks that Jesus's teachings focused on immediate future judgment, culminating in the destruction of Jerusalem, he acknowledges that Jesus also anticipated a final cosmic redemption (for example, his mention in Matt. 19:28 of the coming regeneration or renewal of all things). Indeed, Wright clearly affirms, "The belief that the creator God will at the last recreate the whole cosmos and that Jesus will be at the center of that new world is firmly and deeply rooted in the New Testament."[143]

But the idea of the redemption of the earth has not remained the province of biblical scholars and professional theologians. As Tim Keller (pastor of Redeemer Presbyterian Church in New York City) puts it, "The Bible teaches that the future is not an immaterial 'paradise' but a new heaven and a new earth. In Revelation 21, we do not see human beings being taken out of this world into heaven, but rather heaven coming down and cleansing, renewing, and perfecting

140. N. T. Wright, *How God Became King: The Forgotten Story of the Gospels* (San Francisco: HarperOne, 2012), 17 (this is one of Wright's best-written books). Wright's earliest articulation of a holistic vision of culture and salvation is found in *New Tasks for a Renewed Church* (London: Hodder & Stoughton, 1992), written as a series of Lenten meditations for the parish of Newcastle-upon-Tyne.

141. For Wright's views on apocalyptic, see *The New Testament and the People of God* (Christian Origins and the Question of God 1; Minneapolis: Fortress, 1992), 280–86.

142. Wright, *The Challenge of Jesus: Rediscovering Who Jesus Was and Is* (Downers Grove, IL: InterVarsity, 1999), 117.

143. Ibid. For Wright's account of how (beginning in 1983) he came to shift from a dualistic worldview to the holistic vision he is now famous for, see his autobiographical essay "My Pilgrimage in Theology," *Themelios* 18 (1993): 35 (available online: http://www.ntwrightpage.com /Wright_My_Pilgrimage.htm). Although not explicitly noted in the autobiographical essay, one of the prods to this shift from dualism to a holistic worldview was a series of conversations that Wright had at McGill with Brian Walsh during the time Walsh and I were writing *The Transforming Vision*; it is gratifying to think that the early work Brian Walsh and I did on holistic salvation might have made some small contribution to the development of Wright's holistic eschatological vision (for more on this, see: http://jrichardmiddleton.wordpress.com/2014/04/23 /the-tom-wright-connection-part-4/).

this material world."[144] Holistic eschatology is found in other popular works such as John Eldredge's *The Journey of Desire* and Randy Alcorn's *Heaven* (though Alcorn's continued use of the term "heaven" for the new creation tends to confuse matters somewhat).[145] And this is just the tip of the iceberg.[146]

One particularly telling sign of the times is that the Lausanne Committee for World Evangelization (which traces its heritage back to Billy Graham in the 1970s) published an Occasional Paper in 2005 that leans toward holistic eschatology. In the midst of discussing the relationship of Christian spirituality to world evangelization, the authors declare, "Popular Christian eschatology has a destructive and negative view of creation, whereas a biblical view . . . is for an eschatology that rids creation of sin and evil and seeks a holistic creation."[147] When an organization associated with Billy Graham (who has historically sounded like D. L. Moody, with his lifeboat theology) produces a document that affirms the redemption of this world, it is clear that we are in the midst of a paradigm shift.[148]

There is, of course, no guarantee that this shift will be complete in our lifetime. However, given the consistent biblical vision of God's intent to redeem creation and the church's checkered history on this point, I believe that the time is ripe for contemporary Christians to engage in serious reflection on the shape of our eschatology. This eschatology must be grounded firmly in the entire biblical story, beginning with God's original intent for earthly flourishing and culminating in God's redemptive purpose of restoring earthly life to what it was meant to be—a purpose accomplished through Christ. We especially need to grapple with the robust ethical implications of this biblical eschatology, exploring how a holistic vision of the future can motivate and ground compassionate yet bold redemptive living in God's world.

144. Timothy Keller, *The Reason for God: Belief in an Age of Skepticism* (New York: Riverhead Books, 2008), 32.

145. John Eldredge, *The Journey of Desire: Searching for the Life We've Only Dreamed Of* (Nashville: Thomas Nelson, 2000), chap. 7, "The Great Restoration"; and chap. 9, "The Adventure Begins"; Randy Alcorn, *Heaven* (Wheaton: Tyndale House, 2004).

146. A strange combination of rapture and new-earth eschatology is found in John W. Schoenheit, *The Christian's Hope: The Anchor of the Soul—What the Bible Really Says about Death, Judgment, Rewards, Heaven, and the Future Life on a Restored Earth* (Indianapolis: Christian Educational Services, 2001).

147. Philip Johnson et al., "Religious and Non-Religious Spirituality in the Western World ('New Age')" (Lausanne Occasional Paper 45; Sydney, Australia: Lausanne Committee for World Evangelization and Morling Theological College, 2005): 27; this is a 70-page document produced by Issue Group 16 for the 2004 Forum for World Evangelization, Pattaya, Thailand, http://www.lausanne.org/documents/2004forum/LOP45_IG16.pdf.

148. The Lausanne Committee for World Evangelization grew out of the 1974 International Congress on World Evangelization, held in Lausanne, Switzerland, which was organized at the impetus of Billy Graham (see http://www.lausanne.org/about.html).

Subject Index

Abel, 93
Abraham, 61–62, 89, 231–32
Adam, 42n9, 166
Adams, Edward, 191, 196–98, 203n51, 204n52
Adventists, Seventh-Day, 298–99
afterlife, the, 23–27, 31–34, 132–39, 227–37. *See also* resurrection
agent, 58–59, 84–85
agriculture, 41–42, 101–2, 255–56
air, rapture and, 222n12
all things, 24, 157–58, 163. *See also* creation
amillennialism, 292–93
Anabaptists, 294–95
ancestors, sleeping with, 134n6
angels, 117, 184–87. *See also* hosts, heavenly
anger, God's, 83n11, 112
animals, 42–43, 106
apocalypse
  creation and, 168–75
  the kingdom and, 244, 259–60
  pattern of, 211–21, 234–35
  resurrection and, 136–39, 143, 152–53
Aristotle, 32
Aslan, 209
astral realm, 32–33
Augustine of Hippo, 291–93

Babel, Tower of, 54–55, 93
baptism, Jesus's, 189, 242
Baptist, John the, 259, 270–71

Bavinck, Herman, 306
Ben-Hinnom, 226n23
Berkouwer, G. C., 306
Bezalel, 47–48
Bible and the Future, The (Hoekema), 305
Blaising, Craig, 304
blessings, wholeness and, 96–98
blind, the, 82, 252
Bock, Darrell, 304
body, the, 31–32, 155–56, 159, 284–85, 293–94
born again, 246
bosom of Abraham, 231–32
brachy, meaning of, 149
breath, God's, 47–49
building, creation and, 46–48

Cain, 93
Calvin, John, 295–96
Carey, William, 297
caught up. *See* rapture, the
change, resurrection and, 203
chaos, creation and, 50–51, 169
Chaoskampf, 50
Chosen One, the, 142–43
church, the, 167–68, 247
citizenship, heavenly, 218
City of God (Augustine), 292
clergy, the, 266
clothes, metaphor of, 203
Codex Siniaticus, 162

Codex Vaticanus, 162
combat, creation by, 50
complication, narrative. *See* impediment,
 narrative
comprehensive, salvation as, 156–63
confession of trust, 119
consistent preterism, 308–9
constitutive hermeneutics, 277n19
construction, creation and, 46–48
consumerism, 273–75
consummation, eschatological, 38n3
contrast, eschatological, 212–14
Cotton Patch Version, 278–79
covenant, Israel as, 92
creation
 God's presence and, 163–65, 168–72
 intention for, 39–52, 59–61, 100–102
 renewal of, 24–27, 155–56, 159–60, 205–6
 salvation and, 72–73, 84–87, 92–93
 violence and, 52–55
 wisdom and, 99–100, 101–2
cross, the, 221, 233–35
Crouch, Andy, 173
cry for help, 80–81. *See also* need, human
cube, Jerusalem as, 170–71
Cullmann, Oscar, 155–56
cult statues, 43, 48–49
culture, 23–24, 41–55, 172–75. *See also*
 creation
curses, wholeness and, 96–98
curtain, temple, 189

Darby, John Nelson, 300–301
darkening, judgment and, 115–17, 121, 182
David, 66
De anima (Aristotle), 32n29
death, 25–27, 53n34, 132–39, 227–37
debt, the kingdom and, 255–58
Decalogue, the, 97–98. *See also* Torah, the
destruction, eschatological, 180–82
devil, the, 185–87
Dialogue with Trypho, 288
disappearance, judgment as, 204–6
disclosed, earth as, 161–62, 190, 193–95
Discourse on the Resurrection (Methodius),
 290
dispensationalism, 211, 226–27, 248n15,
 300–305

dominion, God's, 50–52. *See also* kingdom,
 God's
double restoration, 257–58
dragon, the, 186–87
dualism, 31–32, 246–48, 251, 267–70, 272–81
dwelling, presence as, 167, 169–70, 228–29

earth, the. *See* creation
earthly flourishing. *See* salvation
earthquake, 112–14, 183–84, 200–204
Eden, garden of. *See* garden, the
Edwards, Jonathan, 297
election, Israel's, 265–66
elements, the, 189–91, 198–200
Elijah, 112n4, 234, 264–65, 276
Elisha, 264–65, 276
Enoch, 93, 202, 234
1 Enoch, 142–43
entanglement, narrative. *See* impediment,
 narrative
Enuma Elish, 50
Epistle of Barnabas, 287–88
Erasmus, 161–62
eternal life, 246
ethics, eschatology and, 23–24. *See also*
 kingdom, God's; obedience; purpose,
 human
ethnocentrism, 52, 278–80
Eusebius, 286
exile, 105–7, 124–25, 257–58
exodus, the, 25, 79–91, 255–56

Fairbairn, Donald, 291n43
faith, injustice and, 104–5
fall, the, 53n32
false teaching, 198–200
family, the kingdom and, 275–76
Feast of the Tabernacles, 289
female-male. *See* gender
finding, judgment as, 161–62, 190, 193–95
Finney, Charles Grandison, 280
fire, 112–13, 121–24, 191–98
first resurrection, 153, 286
fleeing, judgment as, 204–6
flood, the, 54, 93, 195–96
flourishing, earthly. *See* salvation
folly, wisdom and, 99
forgiveness, 106

Forms, the, 32n29. *See also* ideal, Platonic
found, earth as, 161–62, 190, 193–95
foundry, metallurgic, 194
Fujiura, Makoto, 173
full preterism, 308–9

garden, the, 41–42, 164, 171–73, 233–35. *See
  also* land, promised
Gehenna, 226n23
gender, 52, 276n16
gentiles, the. *See* nations, the
Gideon, 65
glory, God's. *See* presence, God's
God, image of. *See imago Dei*
golden calf, the, 89
Gomorrah, 192–94
good news, the. *See* kingdom, God's
Graham, Billy, 312
Great Commission, the, 68–69. *See also*
  nations, the
Great Revivals, 296–98
ground, the, 42, 86–87. *See also* agriculture;
  creation; garden, the; land, promised

Hades. *See* Sheol
health-and-wealth gospel, 272n11
heaven
  the afterlife and, 23, 31–34, 225–37
  the kingdom and, 71–73, 81–82, 212–21,
    248–49
  resurrection and, 27–31, 150–52, 221–25
heavens, the, 72, 114–21, 182–89, 191–93
help, cry for, 80–81. *See also* need, human
hierarchy, social, 275–76
Hoekema, Anthony, 305
holistic, salvation as, 156–63
hosts, heavenly, 117, 184–87, 192–93
house, God's, 229
household codes, 275–76
humankind, 39–50, 59–61, 139–54, 160,
  172–75
husbandry, animal, 42–43
husbands, 275n14
hymns, 27–31

ideal, Platonic, 31–32
idolatry, 89
imagery, biblical, 120–21

imago Dei
  humans as, 43–54, 165, 265
  Jesus as, 166–68
  resurrection and, 141, 148
imitatio Christi, 141
impediment, narrative, 38, 59, 80, 82–83
inaugurated eschatology, 71, 212–14, 221
incarnation, the, 167
injustice, 103–5
insider vs. outsider, 267–70, 272–81
interim state, heaven as, 228–37
Irenaeus, 289
Israel, 61–71, 79–92, 165–66, 264–70, 276–78

James, book of, 104–5
Jerusalem, 90, 124–25, 168–75, 200, 219–20
Jesus
  the exodus and, 82–83, 85, 88
  God's presence and, 166–68, 189, 228–29
  as God's Son, 67–68, 242, 268–70
  the kingdom and, 146–53, 245–46, 249–51,
    258–70
  Satan and, 186
  Torah and, 103, 105
Joachim of Fiore, 294–95
Job, 96n2
John the Baptist, 259, 270–71
Jordan, Clarence, 278–79
Joseph, 263, 268
Jubilee, the, 254–58, 266–70
judges, Israelite, 64–65
judgment
  angels and, 184–87, 192–93
  creation and, 164n16, 181–84, 200–206
  disclosure as, 161–62, 190, 193–95
  the rapture and, 222–25
  salvation and, 83, 109–28, 207–10
justice, 103–5
justification, 79
Justin Martyr, 288
Juza, Ryan, 192–93

Keller, Tim, 311–12
kingdom, God's
  the church and, 247
  heaven and, 26–27, 233, 247–49
  Jesus and, 242, 245–46, 249–51, 263–72
  in the Old Testament, 243–45, 252–58

scope of, 210, 258–62, 264–67, 275–82
    worldview and, 246–48, 272–81
kings, 43–45, 65–66
Koinonia Farm, 278–79
Kuyper, Abraham, 306–7

L'Abri, 307
Ladd, George Eldon, 304–5
laity, the, 266
Lamb, the, 70, 152, 172
Lamech, 53
laments, 119
land, promised, 86–87, 89–90, 105, 107,
    255–57. *See also* creation; garden, the;
    ground, the
Late Great Planet Earth, The (Lindsey), 302
Lausanne Committee, 312
law, the. *See* Torah, the
Lazarus, 231–32
leadership, the prophets and, 106–7
Lewis, C. S., 127, 236
Liberty Bell, the, 255n25
life, earthly. *See* salvation
life, tree of, 171–72, 233–35
lightning, theophany and, 111–14, 121
Lindsey, Hal, 302
Little Isaianic Apocalypse, 136–38
Little Red Riding Hood, 58–59
loosing, narrative, 38
love, creation and, 52
Lucifer, 185–87
Luther, Martin, 295

Magnificat, the, 140–41
Magnum, R. Todd, 303–4
male-female. *See* gender
Marduk, 50
marginalized, the. *See* need, human
Marley, Bob, 29–30
marriage, 275n14
Masoretes, the, 252n21
materialism, 273–75
mediation, presence and, 49
meeting, rapture as, 223–24
Messiah, the, 245, 259–60. *See also* kingdom,
    God's
Messianic Apocalypse, 143, 259–60
metallurgy, 122–24, 194

Methodius, 289–90
millennialism, 153, 285–95, 296–98, 300–303,
    308–9
mind, Platonic, 31–32, 232–33
Miriam, 84n14
mis pî, 48–49
Moody, Dwight L., 301
Moore, Russell D., 309
Moses
    as agent, 63–64, 84
    the land and, 89–90
    song of, 82–83, 84n14, 86, 89
    Torah and, 101
mountain, paradise as, 171–72
mouth, opening of the, 48–49
music, church, 27–31

Naaman, 265
name, God's, 25n7
narrative, biblical, 38–39, 57–73
nationalism, creation and, 52
nations, the
    the kingdom and, 264–70, 276–78, 281–82
    the prophets and, 106, 118
    salvation and, 68–71, 173–74
Nazareth, sermon in, 249–51, 261, 263–70,
    276–80
need, human, 80–83, 88, 255–56, 261,
    273. *See also* help, cry for
Neocalvinian tradition, 306–7
Neoplatonism, 33
new birth, 246
new creation, 205–6. *See also* creation
newspaper exegesis, 300
New Testament, 77–78
nihonga, 173
Noah, 54, 93
nose, long of, 83n11
Nous, the, 33

obedience, 87–88, 96–98, 103
Old Testament, 77–78
Olivet discourse, 180, 182–87, 193, 204–6
On First Principles (Origen), 284–85
Origen, 284–86

Parables, Book of the, 142–43
paradise, 171–72, 233–35. *See also* garden, the

parousia, the, 212–13, 223
passing away, judgment as, 205–6
paterfamilias, 275n13
Paul, the apostle, 145, 146, 148
Pentecost, 281–82
personal eschatology, 227–37
Phaedo (Plato), 31
Philippi, colony of, 218
pit pî, 48–49
Platonism, 31–34, 292–93
plot, biblical, 38–39, 57–73
Plotinus, 33
poor, the, 255–56, 261, 273. *See also* need, human
postmillennialism, 296–98, 308–9
power, God's, 50–52. *See also* kingdom, God's
Poythress, Vern, 305
premillennialism, 304–5
preparation, apocalyptic, 212–21
presence, God's, 46–49, 89–90, 107, 164–68
preterist eschatology, 278n20, 308–9
priests, 44–45
Primeval History, the, 92–93
Prince Caspian (Lewis), 127
prism, *imago Dei* as, 49
privilege, protection of, 273–75, 279–80
progressive dispensationalism, 303–5. *See also* dispensationalism
prophetic hermeneutics, 277n19
prophets, 66–67, 103–7, 250–58
prosperity gospel, 272n11
Psalm 18, 90–91
purpose, human, 39–50, 59–61, 69–71, 174–75

racism, 52, 278–80
Radical Reformation, 294–95
rapture, the, 221–27, 300–304
Rasi, Humberto M., 299n84
Rastafarianism, 29–30
Rauschenbusch, Walter, 299–300
receiver, 58–59
reconciliation, 268–70, 275–81. *See also* salvation
reconstructionist movement, 308–9
redemption. *See* salvation

refining, judgment as, 122–24, 194
Reformation, the, 295–96
Reformed Dogmatics (Bavinck), 306
Reformed tradition, 305–9
Rehoboam, 66
reign, spiritual, 150–52. *See also* rule, human
relationship, 22, 89, 91
removal, judgment as, 202–4
renewal. *See* salvation
resolution, narrative, 38
responsive, God as, 81–82. *See also* need, human
restoration. *See* salvation
Restorationism, 299
resurrection
    bodily, 155–56, 159, 202–4, 284–85, 293–94
    hope of, 25–31, 131–32, 136–39, 222–25, 229–31
    human rule and, 139–45, 150–54
resuscitation, resurrection and, 137n15
revelation. *See* apocalypse
reversal, great, 140–47
Revivals, Great, 296–98
Richards, Clifford T., 199
righteousness, 106–7
rising, resurrection as, 141
river, God's presence as, 171–72
Rome, citizenship and, 218
rule, human, 139–54, 175. *See also* kingdom, God's

Sabbath year, 254–58, 266–70
Sadducees, the, 154
salvation
    characteristics of, 79, 163
    creation and, 24–27, 38, 155–56, 163–75
    the exodus and, 78–91
    judgment and, 118–20, 121–28, 207–10
    scope of, 156–63, 268–70
    worship and, 27–31
Samson, 65
Samuel, 65
sanctification, 87–88
Satan, 185–87
Schaeffer, Francis, 307
Schoonhoven, Calvin, 305
Scofield, Cyrus I., 302

scroll, sky as, 188–89
Scrubb, Eustace, 209
sea, the, 169
secret rapture, 301
seed, resurrection and, 202
sender, 58–59
Seventh-Day Adventists, 298–99
sexism, 52. *See also* gender
shaking, judgment as, 112–14, 183–84,
    200–204
shalom, 52
Shekinah, 48, 167. *See also* presence, God's
Shema, the, 97
Sheol, 132–36, 231–32
Sidonian widow, 264–65
silence, theophany and, 112n4
sin, 52–55, 79, 106, 160
Sinai, theophany at, 110–14, 200–201
Siniaticus, Codex, 162
sky, the. *See* heavens, the
slavery, 255–58, 275–76
sleep, death as, 133n5, 235–36
slow to anger, God as, 83n11
smelting, 122–24, 194
Snyder, Howard, 309
social gospel movement, 299–300
sociological dualism, 267–70, 272–81
Sodom, 192–94
Solomon, 66
Son, God's, 242, 268–70
Song of the Sea, 82–83, 84n14, 86, 89
songs, resurrection and, 27–31
Songs, Servant. *See* Suffering Servant, the
son of man, 139–40, 147. *See also*
    humankind
soul, Platonic, 31–32, 232–33
soul sleep, 235–36
Spirit, the, 47–49
standing up, resurrection as, 141
stars, 32–33, 117, 141, 184–87
statues, cult, 43, 48–49
still small voice, 112n4
Stoicism, 191, 196–98
Stone-Campbell movement, 299
storm, theophany and, 111–14, 121, 164n16
Suffering Servant, the, 85, 92, 147
swallowing, death and, 137
Symposium (Methodius), 289

tabernacle, the, 47–48, 89, 166–67. *See also*
    temple, creation as
Tabernacles, Feast of, 289
taken, death as, 136, 222–25
Tarshish, 124–25
task, narrative, 58–59
teaching, false, 198–200
Tea Party, 279–80
temple, creation as, 46–49, 163–65,
    168–72. *See also* tabernacle, the
temporary, heaven as, 228–37
Ten Commandments, the, 97–98. *See also*
    Torah, the
tension, narrative. *See* impediment, narrative
Tetragrammaton. *See* YHWH
textual criticism, 161–62
theonomy, Christian, 308–9
theophany, judgment and, 110–21, 164n16,
    181–82, 200–204
third heaven, 234n43
Thomas Aquinas, 294
thunder, theophany and, 111–14
thunderstorms, 111–14, 121, 164n16
Tiamat, 50
Timaeus (Plato), 31–32
Tischendorf, Constantin von, 162
Torah, the, 87–88, 96–98, 100–105, 243
Tosh, Peter, 30
Tower of Babel, 54–55, 93
Tozer, A. W., 29–30
transcendence, 81–82. *See also* heaven
transformation, salvation and, 202–10
translation, biblical, 161–62
transubstantiation, 48–49
tree of life, 171–72, 233–35
triumphalism, 272n11, 308–9
tying, narrative. *See* impediment, narrative

universal, salvation as, 157, 207–9
unveiling. *See* apocalypse
us vs. them, 267–70, 272–81

value, dualism and, 32n30
Vaticanus, Codex, 162
violence, creation and, 52–55
visit, rapture as, 223–24
Voyage of the Dawn Treader, The (Lewis),
    209

Wailers, the, 29–30
warrior, YHWH as, 82–83
Watchers, Book of the, 142
water of life, 171–72
well-being. *See* salvation
Wesley, John, 297–98, 309
White, Ellen G., 298–99
wholeness. *See* salvation
widow, Sidonian, 264–65
Wilberforce, William, 280
wisdom, 46–47, 96, 98–102

wives, 275n14
Wolters, Al, 194–95, 198
worldview, 21n1, 246–48, 251, 272–81, 306–7
worship, 27–31, 39–41, 104
wrath, God's, 83n11, 112
Wright, N. T., 196–97, 310–11

YHWH, 25n7, 81–91, 97–98

Zacchaeus, 88
Zion, Mount, 200

Scripture Index

Old Testament

Genesis

1 40n7, 49, 50–51, 105
1–2 40
1–11 53, 54–55
1:1 72
1:2 47, 48, 50, 115
1:3 115
1:4 51, 85n19
1:5 51
1:6–10 84
1:8 51
1:10 51
1:11–12 85n19
1:12 51
1:18 51, 85n19
1:20–21 85n19
1:21 51
1:22 51, 53
1:24–25 85n19
1:24–28 86
1:25 51
1:26–27 43, 45, 46
1:26–28 25, 26, 39, 43, 51,
    54, 59, 84, 86, 141, 154,
    164, 265
1:27 276n16
1:27–28 52

1:28 51, 53, 54, 80, 92, 93,
    165
1:29–30 51, 86
1:31 25, 51, 103n12
2 41–42, 48–49, 105
2:3 53
2:5 41
2:6 41
2:7 42, 42n9, 62
2:7–8 41
2:8 171n32, 173
2:9 171
2:10 171
2:11–12 173
2:15 25, 39, 42, 59, 86, 154,
    164, 171n32
2:15–17 164
2:16 41, 171n32
2:17 53, 53n34
2:19–20 51
3 52–53, 61
3:1 171n32
3:2 171n32
3:3 171n32
3:6 53
3:8 164n16, 171n32
3:8–19 164
3:10 171n32
3:14 53

3:16 53
3:16–17 53n33, 54n36
3:17 53, 97n3, 160, 170
3:17–19 53
3:19 26, 139
3:23 97n3, 171n32
3:23–24 53, 171, 233
3:24 171n32
4 45, 53
4–11 61
4:1 42n9
4:1–2 92
4:2 93
4:8 53
4:10 232
4:11 53
4:15 93
4:17 45, 53
4:17–22 92
4:17–5:32 92
4:19 53
4:20 45
4:20–22 53
4:21 45
4:22 45
4:23–24 53
4:25 92
4:26 92
5:1–2 54

5:1–3 46
5:1–5 93
5:3 54
5:3–32 54
5:24 93, 136, 234
5:29 53
6 54
6:1–4 186n8
6:5 54
6:6 54, 54n36
6:9 93
6:11 54, 160, 165
6:11–12 54
6:11–13 61
6:13 54
6:18–7:5 93
7:4 195n35
8:18–19 54
8:21 54, 61
8:22 54, 93
9:1 54, 93
9:6 46, 54, 93
9:7 54, 93
9:9–17 93
9:11–12 54
9:13 54
9:15–17 54
9:20 54
9:21 54
9:22–27 54
10 52, 92
10:5 54
10:18 54
10:20 54
10:31 54
10:32 54
11:1–9 54, 61, 93
11:10–32 92
12:1–3 61, 265
12:3 45, 61, 165
14:18–20 44n17
17:5 61n9
17:7–8 89, 174
18:17–18 61n10
18:18 165
18:19 62n11
18:22–33 193
18:26–32 193

19 192
19:12–13 193n27
19:14 193n27
19:24 192, 195n35
22:17–18 61n10
22:18 165
26:4 165
26:4–5 61n10
28:14 61n10, 165
37:35 134
41:38–39 47n21
47:30 133n5

Exodus

1:7 80
1:8–14 62
1:10–11 80
1:12 80
1:13–14 80
1:16 80
1:20 80
1:22 80
2:23 80, 81
2:23–24 159
2:24 80
3:1–4:18 63
3:6 91
3:7–10 80
3:8 79, 81, 84, 86, 91
3:10 84
4:22 242n3
5:15–16 82
6:1 83
6:1–13 63
6:5–6 80
6:6 79, 90, 159
6:7 89, 91, 174
6:8 90
7:3–4 83
7:5 91
7:17 91
8:10 91
8:19 83
8:22 91
9:3 83
9:14 91, 92
9:16 92

9:29 91, 92
10:2 91
10:7 91
13:21–22 113
14:4 91
14:13 84
14:14 83
14:16 84
14:18 91
14:30 80
15:1 84n14
15:1–2 86
15:1–18 84n14, 109
15:2 80
15:3 82
15:6 85
15:7 83
15:8 83, 83n11, 90
15:10 85
15:11 83, 85
15:13 89, 159
15:13–17 86
15:15 80
15:17 89
15:18 83, 243n5
15:20–21 84n14
15:21 84n14
16:11–36 256
18:13–26 101
18:15–16 101
19 69, 70
19:3–6 62, 265
19:4–5 87
19:4–6 64
19:5 92
19:5–6 69
19:6 45, 64n15, 92, 165
19:9 110
19:10 110
19:12–13 110
19:16 110
19:16–20 109
19:18 110
19:21 110
19:22 110
19:23 110
19:24 110
20:1–17 87

20:2 87
20:2–3 97
20:4–6 97
20:7–17 98
20:23 97
21:1–11 255
21:1–23:19 87, 98
22:1 88
22:21–24 88
22:25–27 88
23:9 88
23:10–11 255
23:11 255, 256
24:7 87
25–40 166
29:45–46 89, 107
31 47
31:2–5 47
31:3 47n21
32–34 166
32:11–14 89
33:14–16 89
34:6 83n11
35 47
35:30–35 47
35:31 47n21
40:34–35 48, 166
40:36–38 166
40:38 166

Leviticus

17:11 232
18:24–28 97
19:18 103, 267n6
19:33–34 88
19:34 88, 267n6
20:22 97
25:1–7 255
25:8 255
25:10 255
25:11–12 255
25:13 255
25:14 267
25:15 267
25:18–22 255, 256
25:21–22 256n26
25:23 257

25:23–28 255
25:25 267
25:25–38 88
25:35 267
25:35–43 255
25:39–43 88
25:42–43 256
25:44–46 266
25:54–55 88
26:3–13 97
26:11–12 89, 107
26:14–39 97

Numbers

10:11–13 63
14:14 166
14:20 166
14:21 166
14:22–23 166
23:21 243n5
24:17 141

Deuteronomy

4:6 102
6:2 98
6:4 97
6:5 97, 98, 103
6:20–25 86
8:10–18 256
10:17–19 88
15:1–6 255
15:7 267
15:9 267
15:12 266
17:18–20 66
21:18–21 308
24:17–18 88
26:5–10 86
28:1–14 97
28:5 97
28:6 97
28:15–19 97
28:20–68 97
30:15–20 97
30:19 98
31:16 133n5
33:5 243n5

Joshua

24:1–14 86

Judges

2:16 65
2:18 81
5:4–5 112
5:5 189
5:20 117
6:11–23 65
8:23 243n5
11:34 84n14
17:6 65
18:1 65
19:1 65
21:25 65

1 Samuel

2:7–9 140
2:8 141
2:12 243n5
8:4–5 45, 65
8:6 65
8:7 65, 243n5
8:9–18 65
8:20 65
8:22 65
9:15–16 65
10:10 65n17
10:11–14 65n17
10:15 65n17
10:16 65n17
18:6–7 84n14

2 Samuel

7 66n19
7:12 133n5
7:14 242n3
20:24 66n20
22 90n24

1 Kings

2:10 133n5, 134n6
5:13–18 66
5:14 66n20

6:20 171
8:10–11 166n18
8:27 170
11:3–8 66
12:1–20 66
17:1–2 66
17:1–24 264
17:7–24 136
17:9–16 264n2
19:9–13 112n4
21:1–4 257

2 Kings

2:11 234
4:32–37 136
5:1–19 264
5:9–15 265
8:15 66
13:21 136

1 Chronicles

21:1 187n10
29:11 137n12

2 Chronicles

7:1–3 166n18
14:1 133n5

Ezra

9:7–9 258n28

Nehemiah

9:6–31 86
9:36–37 258n28

Job

1–2 187n10
1:1 96n2
1:8 96n2
2:3 96n2
3:13–15 133
3:17–19 133
28:25–27 99
28:28 96n2, 98

38:4–7 47
38:7 117, 242n3

Psalms

2:4 81
2:6–12 242n3
6:5 133
8 40, 42–43, 85n18, 149n36
8:4–6 148
8:4–8 26, 141, 154
8:5 43
8:5–8 25, 39, 42, 59
11:4 81, 170
14:2 170
18 90–91
18:1–19 90
18:3–6 134
18:4–5 90
18:6 90
18:7 114n5
18:7–14 90
18:11–14 113
18:15 90
18:16–18 90
18:19 91
18:69 134
19:1–6 100
19:7–13 100
22 81
22:8 243
29 111, 164n16
29:6 127
29:9 127
30:7 134
30:9 133
33:6 40n7
33:6–9 100
33:9 40n7
36:6 93
39 81
46:2–3 120
46:6 114n6
49:7–10 136
49:11–14 136
49:15 136
72 66
73:1–14 135

73:16 135
73:17–20 135
73:22 135
73:23–24 135
73:24 136
73:26 135
73:27 135
78 86
88 81
88:3–6 134
88:4–5 133
88:10–12 133
89:25–27 242n3
89:48 133
96 40n7, 83, 127–28
96:10 126, 243
96:10–13 109, 244
96:11–13 126–27
97:1 122
97:2–5 113, 114, 122
97:6 122
97:8–12 122
98 83, 127n19
98:7–9 109
102:24 119
102:25–26 181
102:25–27 119
102:26 119, 203
102:28 119
103:19 243
104 40, 42, 51
104:1–3 81, 203n50
104:5 126
104:6–7 205n53
104:10–30 51
104:13 126
104:14–15 42
104:16 125
104:21–22 42
104:23 42
104:29 134, 139
104:31 126
104:32 126
104:33 114n6
104:35 42n11, 114n6, 126
105 86
105:25–27 120
105:40 256

106 86
111:10 98
115:4–8 49
115:16 72
115:17 133
116:3 134
116:8 134
119:89–96 100
119:91 100
136 86
139:7–8 133n4
143:7 134
146:6 260n32
146:7–8 259n30
146:10 259n30
147:7–9 40n7, 51
147:15–18 101
147:19–20 101
148 40–41, 48
148:5–6 40n7, 100
148:8 40n7, 100

Proverbs

1:7 98
1:12 137n11
1:20–33 99
2:1–8 98
2:20–22 98
3:13–18 98
3:19–20 46–47, 99
4:18 141n19
7:1–27 99
8:1–36 99
8:22–26 99
8:22–31 99
8:27–31 99
8:30 99n7
8:31 47
8:32–36 99
9:1–12 99
9:10 98
9:13–18 99
14:27 98
16:6 98
19:23 98
21:28 137n12
22:17 96n1

22:17–24:22 96n1
24:3–4 47

Ecclesiastes

9:4–6 133
9:10 133

Song of Songs

8:6 153

Isaiah

1 191
1:10–20 104
1:19 103
1:20 103
1:22 123
1:25–27 123
1:31 123
2:1–4 125
2:2–4 106
2:4 125
2:7 125
2:12–16 124
2:20 125
5:14 137n11
6:1 170
7:14 166, 183
11:1–5 106
11:6–9 106
11:9 107, 168, 210
11:10–12 105
11:16 105
13:1–22 192
13:6 192
13:9–10 115–16
13:10 192
13:13 115, 192
13:17 192
13:19 192
14 185–86, 187n10
14:2–21 185
14:4–11 185
14:9–11 133
14:12–14 185
19:23–25 106
24 121

24:1–13 121
24:14–16 122
24:17–20 121
24:19–20 117
24:21 117, 185
24:21–23 121
24:23 117, 122
25:6 136, 174
25:6–8 25
25:7 174
25:7–8 136
25:8 137, 174
26:13–18 137
26:14 137
26:17–18 137–38
26:18 141
26:19 138
28:24–25 101
28:26 102
28:27–28 101
28:29 102
29:6 112
30:20–21 106
30:30 112
32:1 106
34 184–86
34:1–17 192
34:2 118n11
34:4 117, 118, 184, 187, 188, 192
34:5 118, 192
34:5–10 192
34:9–10 192
34:12 184
35:1–2 106
35:3–6 270
35:5–6 105
35:6–7 106
35:8–10 105
35:10 105
38:18 133
40:1–2 257
40:22 81
42:1–7 85
42:6 92
42:7 92, 252n22
44:28 85
45:1 85

45:13 85
49:6 92
50:3 184
51:5 118
51:6 118
52:7 244
52:13 147n31
52:13–53:12 85, 147n31
53:4–6 85
53:10–11 147n31
53:10–12 85
54:10 120, 188
55:1 171
55:12–13 105, 106
56:1 260n35
57:15 141
58:1–14 104
58:2–3 253
58:4 253
58:6 253–54
58:6–14 103
58:9 253
58:12 254
59:20–21 106
60:1–2 105
60:3 106
60:4 105
60:5 125
60:5–16 106
60:6 125
60:9 124, 125
60:11 125, 173, 208
60:13 124
60:17 125
60:18–22 105
61:1 261
61:1–2 251–58
61:1–4 105
61:2 251, 260, 267, 268
61:4 254
61:5–6 106
61:6–7 268
61:7 105, 258
61:9 105, 106
61:11 106
62:4–7 105
62:12 105

63:15 81
64:1 189
64:1–3 188
64:4 213n3
65:17 24, 106, 109, 201
65:18–24 105
65:19 105
65:25 106
66:1 170, 229
66:1–2 48, 72, 81, 141, 204,
    216n6
66:22 24, 204

Jeremiah

2:2 256
2:6–7 86
3:15 107
3:17 106
4 121
4:23–24 115
4:24 188n12
4:28 115
7:1–15 104
7:3 103
7:5–7 103
7:8–9 103
7:14–15 103
8:7 40n7, 100
10:12 99
22:15–16 104
22:29 127n22
23:5–6 107
29:7 269n8
30:9 107
31:4–6 105
31:11–14 105
31:31–34 106
31:33 89
32:17–23 86
32:37 105
32:37–41 90, 107
32:40 106
34:8 255
34:14 255n24
34:15 255
34:17 255
50:20 106

Ezekiel

11:19 106
28:1–19 171
28:13 171
28:14 171
32 121
32:7 117n9
32:7–8 116
34:23–24 107
34:25 106
34:25–31 90, 105, 107
34:26–29 106
34:27 105
34:28 106
34:30 89
36:8–11 105, 106
36:26 106
36:33–36 105
36:34–35 106
37 25, 138
37:5–6 105
37:11–14 105
37:12 105
37:14 105
37:22–25 107
37:23 106
37:24–28 90, 107
37:27 89
38:19–20 114n5
40–44 170
41:4 171
43:7 170
47:1–12 106, 171
47:7 172
47:12 172

Daniel

2:31–36 210
2:44–45 210
4:13 186n8
7:2–8 139
7:2–27 139
7:11–12 139
7:13 139, 140n16
7:13–14 139, 244
7:17 139
7:19–21 139

7:22 140
7:23–26 139
7:26 139
7:27 140, 244
12 140, 141
12:1 139
12:2–3 26, 139

Hosea

3:5 107
11:1 242n3

Joel

2 121
2:23–24 106
2:28–29 106, 281
2:28–32 116n8
2:30–31 116
2:31 184
2:32 82
3:15–16 115
3:18 106

Amos

5:4–7 104
5:10–12 103
5:11–12 104
5:14–15 103, 104
5:16–17 103
5:20 117n9
5:21–24 104
5:26–27 103
8:9 117n9
9:5 114n6
9:6 81
9:7 92
9:11–12 107
9:13 106
9:14 105
9:15 105

Micah

1:3–4 83, 114
4:1–3 125n17
4:1–4 106

5:2–4 107
6:1–8 104

Nahum

1:5–6 114n5

Habakkuk

2:14 107, 168, 210
3:6 114
3:10–11 116

Zephaniah

1:15 117n9
3:11–18 105
3:19–20 105

Haggai

2:6 181
2:6–7 122
2:7 122, 204
2:21 201
2:21–22 122
2:26 201

Zechariah

2:11 106, 107
3 191
3:1–2 187n10
8:1–5 105
8:7–8 90, 105, 107
8:11–15 105
8:12 106
8:20–23 106
9:9–10 107
10:9 107
13:1 122
13:9 122–23
14:3–5 113n5
14:4 180n1
14:8 106
14:9 107

Malachi

3 191
3:1 123n15

3:2–3 123, 194
4:1 124, 194
4:2 124

Apocrypha

Additions to Esther

14:8 258n28

Judith

8:22–23 258n28

2 Maccabees

1:27 258n28
7:6 142
7:9 142
7:11 142
7:14 142
7:17 142
7:19 142
7:20 142
7:23 142
7:29 142
7:31 142
7:34–35 142
7:36 142
12:45 133n5

4 Maccabees

13:17 232n36

Sirach

24:1–12 167n20

Wisdom of Solomon

1:13–15 144
3:1 143
3:1–9 26
3:2–3 143
3:4 143, 144
3:5 143
3:7–8 143
3:11 143
5:14 143
5:15–16 144

New Testament

Matthew

1:22–23 166
1:23 183
3:13–17 249
3:16 189
4:1–11 249
4:12–16 249
4:17 207, 245, 249
5:5 26, 72, 207, 226, 285
5:22 207
5:29 207
5:30 207
5:43–48 52
5:45 265n4
6:10 72, 168, 248
7:21–29 105
8:12 207
8:17 85n20
9:35 68
9:37 68
10:1–16 68
10:2 68
10:5–8 68
10:6 68
10:15 193n28
10:28 207
11:5 259
12:28 249n17
12:40 132
12:43–46 273
13:4 222n12
13:19 222n12
13:33 210
13:42 207
13:43 141
13:50 207
13:53–57 263n1
13:55 242n2
14:3–11 271
15:24 68
16:15–16 67
16:21 132
17:9 132
17:22–23 132
18:9 207

18:20 167
19:6 188n13
19:24 249n17
19:27 146
19:27–30 26
19:28 24, 146, 311
19:29–30 146
20:19 132
21:31 249n17
21:31–32 265
21:43 249n17
22:13 207
22:23–33 154
22:37 103n12
22:40 103
23:23 104
24 308
24:1–3 182
24:3 180n1, 182n2, 212n1
24:4–8 182
24:9–14 182
24:15–26 182
24:21 182
24:27 212n1
24:29 180, 182, 187
24:29–30 182
24:35 180, 205
24:36–42 226–27
24:37 212n1
24:37–39 225
24:37–41 42n11
24:39 212n1, 225
24:39–41 226
24:40–41 222, 225–27
24:43 193
24:46 193
25:1 223n16
25:1–13 223n16
25:6 223n16
25:23 147n33
25:30 207
25:31–46 105
25:34 214–15, 217, 219
27:51 189
27:52 133n5
28 131
28:18–20 68, 70

Mark

1:9–11 249
1:10 189
1:12–13 249
1:14–15 249
1:15 207, 242, 245, 249
4:4 223n12
4:15 223n12
5:41 141
6:1–4 263n1
6:3 242n2
6:17–29 271
8:31 132
9:9 132
9:31 132
9:43 207
9:45 207
9:47 207
10:9 188n13
10:34 132
10:46–52 82
11:10 246n10
12:18–27 154
12:24–27 132
12:30 103n12
13 308
13:1–4 182
13:3 180n1
13:5–8 182
13:9–13 182
13:14–23 182
13:24 182, 187
13:24–25 180
13:24–26 182–83
13:26 140n16
13:31 180, 205
14:58 216
14:62 140n16
15:38 189
16 131
16:9–20 235n48
16:19 235

Luke

1:52 140
3:1–2 279
3:7–9 279

3:19–20 259
3:21 189
3:21–22 249
3:22 268
3:23 268
4:1–13 249
4:3 268
4:9 268
4:14–15 249, 250
4:16 250
4:16–21 250
4:16–30 249–54, 259, 266, 267, 268, 270–71, 273–74, 277–78, 280
4:18 26, 252, 253, 261
4:18–19 250–54, 270
4:19 260
4:20–21 251
4:21 260
4:22 250, 261, 263, 268
4:23 264
4:23–27 250
4:24 264
4:24–27 279
4:25–27 264, 270
4:28–30 250, 276
4:43 249n17
5:29–31 265
6:20 261
6:27–35 52
6:35–36 265n4
7:11–15 260
7:16 260
7:18–23 258–59
7:19 259, 270
7:20 259
7:21 259
7:22 259–60, 269, 270
7:23 271
7:34–39 265
8:5 223n12
8:12 223n12
9:22 132
9:52–55 276n17
10:12 193n28
10:13–15 268
10:17 186
10:18 186

10:27 103n12
10:35–37 267n6
11:5–13 81
11:14 186
11:20 186
11:21–22 186
11:24–26 273
11:29–32 268
12:5 207
12:39 193
12:43 193
13:20–21 210
13:28 207
14:11 140n18
14:14 132, 140n18
15:4–6 232
16:1–13 232
16:10 147n33
16:19–31 231–32
16:31 232n37
17:21 247
17:22–37 195n34
17:34 227n31
17:34–35 222, 225
17:36 225n22
17:37 225
18:1–8 81
18:33 132
18:35–43 82
19:8 88
19:9 88
21:5–7 182
21:8–11 182
21:11 182n3
21:12–19 182
21:20–24 182
21:25 182, 187
21:25–26 180, 183n4
21:25–27 182
21:33 180, 205
22:24 146
22:25–27 146
22:28–29 146
22:28–30 146
22:37 85n20
22:58 149n38
23:39–43 233–35
23:42 233, 235

23:43 233
23:45 189
24 131
24:50–53 235

John

1:1–18 167n20
1:10 229n35
1:12 150
1:14 67, 149–50, 167, 169
1:14–18 147
1:18 67, 149–50
2:19–22 132
3:3 207, 246
3:5 246
3:7 207
3:14 147n31
3:16 206, 276n17
5:27 148n34
5:28–29 139n15, 208n57
6:7 149n38
6:42 263n1
8:23 229n35
8:28 147n31
10:10 246
10:17–18 132
11:11 133n5
12:13 223
12:31 222n12
12:32–34 147n31
12:38 85n20
14:1–3 214, 217, 219, 222n11, 228–29, 231
14:2 228–29
14:3 217, 219, 220
14:9 67, 167
14:10 229n34
14:17 229n34
14:23 229
14:30 222n12
15:4–10 229n34
18:36 247
20–21 131

Acts

1:1–9 131
1:3 132

1:9–11 235
1:22 132
2:16–21 116n8
2:17 184n6
2:17–18 281
2:21 82
2:24 132
2:32 132
3:15 132
3:17–21 163
3:19–21 157
3:20–21 213
3:21 24, 157, 163
3:25–26 67
5:34 149n38
7:48 216n6
7:49–50 216n6
7:60 133n5
8:32–34 85n20
10:39–41 132
15 101n10
15:4 281n26
15:7–12 281n26
15:15–18 281n26
15:19–20 281n26
17:24 216n6
17:24–29 148
17:30 148
17:31 148
23:6–10 154
24:15 139n15
27:58 149n38
28:15 223

Romans

1:2–4 132
4:13 150
4:23–25 132
5:12–19 67, 166
5:17 150
6:4–5 132
7:4 132
8 200
8:11 132
8:13 208n57
8:17 146
8:18–25 272n11

8:19–22 27, 298
8:19–23 81, 159–60, 163
8:21 83, 159, 163, 295, 298
8:22 160
8:23 159–60, 163
8:29 149
8:34 132
10:9 132
10:13 82
11:15 138
11:17–24 69
12:1–2 40

1 Corinthians

2:9 213, 214, 215, 217, 219
2:10 213
3:10 196
3:10–15 195–96
3:11 196
3:12 196
3:13 196
3:14 196
3:15 196
3:16–17 168
6:1–6 145
6:2–3 145
6:14 132
6:19 168
7:39 133n5
11:17–33 275n13
11:30 133n5
12:12–27 168
15 132, 139n15
15:6 133n5
15:12 132n1
15:18 133n5
15:20 26, 133n5
15:20–23 150
15:23 212n1
15:24–26 210
15:24–28 26, 83, 287n16
15:26 26, 168
15:28 168, 210
15:35 132n1
15:36–37 202
15:42 202, 215n5
15:49 69

15:50 203, 215n5
15:51 133n5, 203
15:51–52 222n11, 224, 225n20
15:52 203, 215n5
15:52–54 144–45
15:53–54 203
15:54 26, 137, 145n28, 152n42, 215n5
15:58 132n1, 154

2 Corinthians

1:9 132
3:8–18 200n48
3:18 69, 168
4:4–6 67, 166
4:8–12 230
4:8–5:10 229
4:14 132, 230, 231
4:16 229
4:18 230
5:1–2 230, 231
5:1–5 214, 216–17
5:3–4 230
5:5–6 235
5:6–8 231
5:6–9 229–31
5:8 230
5:10 104, 208n57
5:15 132
5:17 205–6
5:18 85
6:16 89, 168
12:2 234n43
12:2–3 234n44
12:4 234n43

Galatians

1:1 132
3:28 276, 276n16
4:3 199
4:8–9 199
6:15 205n54

Ephesians

1:3 151
1:7–10 163

1:9–10 157–58
1:10 24, 163
1:20 132
1:20–22 151
2:2 222n12
2:4–6 151
2:8–9 104
2:10 104
2:11–22 69
2:14–16 275
2:15 69, 168
2:21 168
2:22 168
3:5–9 151
3:10 151
4:7–16 69n24
4:10 168
4:13 69
4:22 69n23, 203
4:22–24 69, 69n24
4:24 69n23, 168, 168n24, 203
5:1 69n24
5:1–2 275
5:21 275
5:21–6:9 275
6:10–18 151
6:12 151

Philippians

1:6 154
1:21 231
1:21–24 231
1:23 231, 235
2:5 141
2:5–8 146
2:5–11 69, 146
2:6–8 67, 141
2:9–11 141
2:10–11 147
2:12 88
2:15 141
3:3–9 218
3:10–11 132, 146, 218, 272n11
3:19 217
3:20–21 214, 217–18, 219
3:21 132

Colossians

1:3–6 216
1:5 214, 215–16
1:13 83
1:15 67, 166
1:15–20 158
1:16 158
1:16–20 163
1:17 158–59
1:18 69
1:19 166–67
1:19–20 158–59
1:20 24, 158–59, 163
2:8 198, 199n46
2:20 198, 199n46
2:21 198
3:1–4 152
3:5–17 69n24
3:9 69n23, 203
3:9–10 69, 168
3:10 69n23, 203
3:18–4:1 276n15

1 Thessalonians

1:10 132
2:19 212n1
3:13 212n1
4:13–15 133n5
4:13–18 222–25
4:14 132, 224
4:15 212n1, 223
4:15–16 224
4:16 132, 223, 224
4:17 222, 223, 225
4:18 222
5:23 212n1

2 Thessalonians

2:1 212n1

2 Timothy

1:12 236
2:8 132, 150n39
2:11 132
2:11–12 150

2:12 69
2:18 132

Hebrews

1:1–2:4 148
1:3 67, 166
1:12 203
2 149n36
2:5 148
2:5–9 148–49
2:6–8 148
2:7 149
2:9 149
2:10 150
2:11–14 149
2:14–17 149
2:15 149
2:16 150
2:17 149
5:12 198
6:2 132
6:9 281n25
7:12 202
8:10 89
11:5 202
11:13–16 214, 218
11:16 219
11:35 132
12:18 200
12:18–21 200
12:22 200
12:23 200
12:24 200
12:25 201
12:26 200, 201
12:26–27 197n42
12:26–28 180
12:26–29 200–204
12:27 202
12:27–28 203
12:27–29 201
13:20 132

James

1:27 105
2:14–26 105
5:8 212n1

1 Peter

1:3 132, 215n5
1:3–5 214, 215
1:5 215
1:7 194
1:21 132
2:9 70
2:22–25 85n20

2 Peter

1:16 212n1
2:6–9 193n27
3 189–200
3:3–4 193n27
3:4 133n5, 212n1
3:5–13 197n42
3:6 195
3:7 195
3:9 193n27, 207
3:10 161–62, 163, 180, 190,
    192, 193, 194, 198, 205,
    295, 301
3:10–12 190
3:10–13 160–63
3:11 190
3:12 180, 190, 198, 212n1
3:13 24, 87, 161, 163, 175,
    195
3:13–14 199
3:14 193, 194
3:15–16 199
3:16 199

·1 John

2:28 212n1
3:2 69

Jude

14–15 142

Revelation

1:18 137n13
2:7 235

2:10 152
2:26–28 152
3:11 152
3:12 219
3:21 152
5:6 70, 132
5:9 152
5:9–10 70, 174, 282
5:10 152, 175
6 182–89
6:9–10 231, 232–33
6:12–13 188
6:12–14 180, 183–84
6:13 184
6:14 188, 189
6:15 184
7:9 174
7:9–10 282
8:19–21 287n15
9:1 186
11:15 27, 175, 210
12:4 186
12:7–8 186
12:9–10 186
12:10 186
12:12 187n9
12:13 187n9
12:17 187n9
13:1 169
18:11–18 169
18:17–18 169
19:7 173n36
19:7–8 173n36
20:1 186
20:1–3 187
20:1–5 284, 287
20:4 153
20:5 153
20:5–6 132, 139n15
20:6 153
20:10 187
20:11 180, 204, 205
20:11–13 153n43
20:11–15 139n15
20:13–14 137, 153

20:14–15 153n43
21 301, 311–12
21:1 24, 87, 163, 169, 181,
    204, 205, 206
21:1–2 153, 214, 219–20
21:1–5 287n17
21:1–22:5 90
21:2 172, 173, 219
21:3 90, 153, 169, 170, 174
21:4 26, 137, 174
21:5 170, 298
21:6 171
21:7 152
21:8 171n31
21:10 172
21:11 172
21:15 208
21:16 170
21:18 173
21:18–21 173
21:21 173
21:22 172
21:22–23 59n6
21:23 172
21:24 173, 174
21:25 171
21:26 106, 173
21:27 171n31
22:1 170, 171
22:1–5 153
22:2 171, 172
22:3 59n6, 170
22:3–4 153
22:5 69, 153, 175
22:11–12 208n57
22:14 171, 208
22:15 208
22:17 171, 208